Politeness in Europe

MULTILINGUAL MATTERS SERIES
Series Editor: Professor John Edwards,
St. Francis Xavier University, Antigonish, Nova Scotia, Canada

Other Books in the Series
Beyond Boundaries: Language and Identity in Contemporary Europe
Paul Gubbins and Mike Holt (eds)
Bilingualism: Beyond Basic Principles
Jean-Marc Dewaele, Alex Housen and Li Wei (eds)
Can Threatened Languages be Saved?
Joshua Fishman (ed.)
A Dynamic Model of Multilingualism
Philip Herdina and Ulrike Jessner
English in Africa: After the Cold War
Alamin M. Mazrui
Identity, Insecurity and Image: France and Language
Dennis Ager
Ideology and Image: Britain and Language
Dennis Ager
Jewish Sociolinguistics: Towards a Synthesis
John Myhill
Language and Society in a Changing Italy
Arturo Tosi
Linguistic Minorities in Central and Eastern Europe
Christina Bratt Paulston and Donald Peckham (eds)
Maintaining a Minority Language
John Gibbons and Elizabeth Ramirez
Motivation in Language Planning and Language Policy
Dennis Ager
Multilingualism in Spain
M. Teresa Turell (ed.)
Quebec's Aboriginal Languages
Jacques Maurais (ed.)
The Other Languages of Europe
Guus Extra and Durk Gorter (eds)
Where East Looks West: Success in English in Goa and on the Konkan Coast
Dennis Kurzon

Other Books of Interest
Language, Culture and Communication in Contemporary Europe
Charlotte Hoffman (ed.)
Language, Discourse and Borders in the Yugoslav Successor States
Birgitta Busch and Helen Kelly-Holmes (eds
Medium or Message? Language and Faith in Ethnic Churches
Anya Woods
Negotiating of Identities in Multilingual Contexts
Aneta Pavlenko and Adrian Blackledge (eds)
Understanding Deaf Culture: In Search of Deafhood
Paddy Ladd

Please contact us for the latest book information:
Multilingual Matters, Frankfurt Lodge, Clevedon Hall,
Victoria Road, Clevedon, BS21 7HH, England
http://www.multilingual-matters.com

MULTILINGUAL MATTERS 127
Series Editor: John Edwards

Politeness in Europe

Edited by
Leo Hickey and Miranda Stewart

MULTILINGUAL MATTERS LTD
Clevedon • Buffalo • Toronto

Library of Congress Cataloging in Publication Data
Politeness in Europe/Edited by Leo Hickey and Miranda Stewart.
Multilingual Matters: 127)
Includes bibliographical references and index.
1. Sociolinguistics–Europe. 2. Etiquette–Europe. I. Hickey, Leo. II. Stewart, Miranda.
III. Series.
P40.5.E752E856 2004
306.44'094--dc22 2003024120

British Library Cataloguing in Publication Data
A catalogue entry for this book is available from the British Library.

ISBN 1-85359-738-4 (hbk)
ISBN 1-85359-737-6 (pbk)

Multilingual Matters Ltd
UK: Frankfurt Lodge, Clevedon Hall, Victoria Road, Clevedon BS21 7HH.
USA: UTP, 2250 Military Road, Tonawanda, NY 14150, USA.
Canada: UTP, 5201 Dufferin Street, North York, Ontario M3H 5T8, Canada.

Typeset by Patrick Armstrong Book Production Services.
Printed and bound in Great Britain by the Cromwell Press Ltd.

Contents

Eastern Europe

Southern Europe

Notes on the Contributors

Eleni Antonopoulou is Associate Professor in the Faculty of English Studies, University of Athens. Her main interests are semantics, pragmatics (especially humour and politeness theories), cognitive linguistics and translation. Among her publications is *From the Philosophy of Language to the Philosophy of Linguistics* (Athens, Parousia Monographs 42, 1997).

Maria Helena Araújo Carreira is Professor and Head of the Département d'Etudes des Pays de Langue Portugaise at Université Paris 8, France. Her main interests are general and Portuguese linguistics, semantics, pragmatics, text and discourse and comparison between languages (Portuguese/French). Among her publications is *Semântica e Discurso. Estudos de Linguística portuguesa e comparada (português-francês).* Porto: Porto Editora, 2001.

Lóránt Bencze is Professor of Linguistics at Apor Vilmos Catholic College, Zsámbék, Hungary. His interests include biblical studies, iconic grammar, discourse analysis and text linguistics, Hungarian Literature and Linguistics. He has published on the Church as communication and on the iconography of the frescoes at the Benedictine Abbey at Pannonhalma.

Bernard de Clerck works in the Department of English Linguistics at the University of Ghent as a PhD student funded by the Fund for Scientific Research, working on a corpus-based analysis of the pragmatic uses of the imperative in British English. He has also studied politeness in Spanish native/non-native discourse.

Emmanuelle Danblon works at the Université Libre de Bruxelles as a researcher in the *Text Linguistics and Cognitive Pragmatics Laboratory*. Her research field is argumentation, rhetoric and pragmatics, applied to the emergence of modern criticism and persuasion phenomena.

Elin Fredsted is Professor and Head of the Institute of Danish Language and Literature at the University of Flensburg, Germany. Her main interests are language contact, bilingualism and cross-cultural pragmatics, having written on Danish and German syntax, semantics and pragmatics, politeness, language convergence and other language contact phenomena and on bi- and multi-lingualism in the Danish–German border region.

Thorstein Fretheim is Professor of general linguistics at the University of Trondheim (now the Norwegian University of Science and Technology). His interests include pragmatic theory, the semantics/pragmatics interface, pragmatic particles and connectives in Norwegian, applications of relevance theory and studies of the contributions of (especially Norwegian) intonation to the pragmatic interpretation of utterances.

Silvia Irene Haumann has published on German as a Foreign Language ('Gespräche unter Österreichern', 'Discourse Analyis' and 'Speech Acts' (in Michael Byram (ed.) *Language Teaching and Learning*, [London: Routledge 2000]).

Gudrun Held is Associate Professor in the Department of Romance Languages, University of Salzburg. Apart from linguistics and history of the Romance languages, her interests centre on pragmatics, communication or interaction theory and media languages. She has written on linguistic politeness in French and Italian.

Leo Hickey has been Professor of Spanish at the University of Salford, where he is now a Research Professor. His publications deal mainly with Spanish linguistics, stylistics and pragmatics, including translation theory and practice. He has edited *The Pragmatics of Translation* (Clevedon: Multilingual Matters, 1998).

Juliane House is Professor of Applied Linguistics at the University of Hamburg and a member of the German Science Foundation's research centre on multilingualism. Her publications include *A Model for Translation Quality Assessment: A Model Revisited* (1997) and *Concepts and Methods of Translation Criticism: A Linguistic Perspective* (2000).

Romuald Huszcza is Professor of General Linguistics and Baltic Studies at Warsaw University. He also lectures on Japanese and Korean linguistics in the Department of Japanese and Korean Studies and at Jagiellonian University in Cracow. His research areas are honorifics in Polish and East Asian languages, functional sentence perspective, polysystemism and co-systemism in East Asian languages. His main publications include a volume on Japanese grammar.

Cornelia Ilie is Professor of English Linguistics at Örebro University, Sweden. Her interests include interdisciplinary approaches within pragmatics, institutional discourse analysis, argumentation and rhetoric. Her publications on parliamentary discourse explore the participants' rhetorical appeals, metadiscursive argumentation and insults as cognitive forms of confrontation

Jeffrey L. Kallen is a Senior Lecturer in Linguistics at Trinity College Dublin. His interests include the English language in Ireland (Hiberno-English), a field in which he publishes regularly. He has also published on language and ethnicity, bilingualism, dialectology, discourse analysis, semiotics, phonology and language acquisition.

Leelo Keevallik, is a PhD student at the Department of Finno-Ugric Languages at Uppsala University and the Department of Estonian Languages at Tartu University, where she also teaches. Her interests include variation in Estonian, especially variable rules and the dependence of a morphological variable (past participle ending *–nud*) on the formality of the situation and on linguistic context. She has written on Estonian address forms.

Catherine Kerbrat-Orecchioni is a Professor at Lumière University, Lyon, and holds the 'Linguistics of Interaction' Chair at the Institut Universitaire de France. Her main interests are pragmatics, discourse analysis and interaction. She is the author of several books including *Les Interactions verbales* (3 vols) (Paris: Armand Colin,1990, 1992, 1994).

Ursula Koch has research interests in pragmalinguistics, particularly discourse analysis, and ancient languages.

Johannes Kramer is Professor of Romance Linguistics at the University of Trier, Germany. He has published on politeness in Luxemburg.

Giuseppe Manno is a Lecturer in French Linguistics at the University of Zurich. His research interests are sociolinguistics, pragmatics and regional French. He is currently working on a contrastive study of politeness in a corpus of French directive written texts.

Jiří Nekvapil teaches sociolinguistics, conversation analysis and pragmatics in the Department of General Linguistics at Charles University, Prague. His interests are in language interaction and he is the author of the intercultural training module *Sprechen über Personen: Soziale Kategorisierung im tschechisch-deutschen Kontakt* (CD-ROM + video). His current research focuses on language biographies of Czech Germans, language management and ethnomethodologically-informed analysis of media discourse.

J.V. Neustupný teaches applied linguistics and intercultural communication at Obirin University, Tokyo, having previously been Chair of the Department of Japanese Studies at Monash University, Melbourne. His interests are in sociolinguistics and the linguistics of language problems: from theory to intercultural communication and language teaching. His publications include *Post-Structural Approaches to Language* (University of Tokyo Press, 1978).

Jean-Pierre van Noppen has been active at the Université Libre de Bruxelles as a grammarian, lexicographer and bibliographer in addition to teaching English linguistics. His current interests are in non-literary (pragma)stylistics and critical linguistics. His publications include *Transforming Words*, a critical analysis of 18th-century Methodist discourse.

Rob le Pair has been at the University of Nijmegen since 1985. His main interests are in Spanish in business contexts, pragmatics from a contrastive Dutch–Spanish perspective and intercultural communication. His recent publications have been on interlanguage pragmatics, especially the use of politeness strategies by learners of Spanish as a part of their communicative competence.

Maria Sifianou is Professor of Linguistics at the Faculty of English Studies, University of Athens. Her publications include *Politeness Phenomena in England and Greece* (Oxford University Press, 1992) and *Discourse Analysis* (Leader Books, 2001) and her co-edition of *Linguistic Politeness across Boundaries: The Case of Greek and Turkish* (Benjamins, 2001). Her main interests include politeness phenomena and discourse analysis from an intercultural perspective.

Karl Sornig works in the Linguistics Department of the University of Graz, Austria. His main interests are in semantics, sociolinguistics and pragmalinguistics. He has published on a variety of topics, including linguistic elements in magic, linguistic variation, the linguistics of political exploitation and language teaching.

Miranda Stewart is Senior Lecturer in the University of Strathclyde, Glasgow, where she is Head of Spanish and Latin American Studies. Her interests include interactional pragmatics with work on pronominal usage in French and Spanish, the negotiation of face in dialogue interpreting, and politeness in the provision of academic feedback in Spanish and English. She has published *The Spanish Language Today* (London: Routledge, 1999).

Marina Terkourafi's interests span the areas of post-Gricean pragmatics, sociolinguistics and cognitive linguistics. As A.G. Leventis Postdoctoral Research Fellow at the British School in Athens and a Visiting Fellow in the Department of Linguistics, University of Cambridge, she is currently researching the interactional bases for grammatical systems, using evidence from Greek.

Valma Laura Yli-Vakkuri is Professor Emerita at the University of Turku. Her main interests are syntax, especially the syntactic resources of Finnish used for coding affective meanings in speech and contact between the languages spoken around the Baltic Sea. She has published in the SCLOMB Project (1991–98, Syntax Archives, University of Turku).

Introduction

LEO HICKEY AND MIRANDA STEWART

Politeness is an area of interactional pragmatics which has experienced an explosion of interest over the past quarter of a century and in which empirical studies have proliferated, examining – individually and cross-culturally – languages and language varieties from around the world. The present volume aims to give a broad picture of politeness across 22 of the countries of Europe and to engage with some of the theoretical debates at the heart of politeness studies. While the contributors here generally draw on mainstream theories of politeness, essentially those formulated in the English-speaking world, in order to provide an empirical snapshot of issues of politeness in their respective societies, their work draws also on alternative formulations and refinements to politeness theory and tests these on a range of related and unrelated languages. A number of the chapters clearly engage with critical debates in the field and use data from their respective linguacultures to advance and refine current theoretical frameworks, others use local data to provide evidence of how politeness may be done in a particular cultural context. Our contributors' work not only takes a fresh look at the means which different individuals within different societies use to project their identity and achieve their interactional goals, it also brings together an outstanding range of bibliographic references, significant numbers of which have not been published in English. This, in itself, provides a fascinating account of the state of the art in Europe today.

Issues such as the degree to which a given society favours positive or negative politeness, tolerates 'small-talk' and phatic exchange, requires routinised formulas, conventional usage of formal and informal pronouns of address, honorifics and personal reference in general, preferences for conventional or non-conventional politeness and, in some societies, the very choice of a particular language itself are amongst the debates which emerge from the wide variety of perspectives in the volume. Nor does the volume confine itself to politeness models which merely focus on language: the role of silence (see Kallen) and of paralinguistic features (such as eye movement, eye contact and gestures) (see Fredsted) are two resources available to speakers to do politeness which are frequently neglected in purely pragmalinguistic accounts. Fredsted, for example, finds that Danes use more non-verbal strategies than their relatively verbose German counterparts.

Another clear issue is the degree to which a society's expectations of its members in terms of face-work can change over time. This comes into particularly sharp focus in some of the countries of Eastern Europe where there are competing paradigms and it is mirrored in the changes charted in the use of personal pronouns of address across a wide range of the languages included here. Huszcza shows that in Poland there are moves away from traditional 'titlemania' towards a grammaticalised system of honorifics. Bencze explains how differences in norms between members of traditional, as opposed to modern, cultural paradigms in Hungary lead to cross-cultural miscommunication within that society. Nekvapil and Neustupný show that speakers are aware of recent changes in norms in the Czech Republic and use avoidance as a means of negotiating face. Sifianou and Antonopoulou point to the fact that technological advance has created new domains of interaction governed by different rules which are worth exploring: they cite the example of the colloquial and multimodal forms of discourse to be found on the Internet and the emergent 'netiquette'.

It emerges, though hardly surprisingly, from these chapters that language is not necessarily co-terminous with culture and a number of the chapters address issues such as the differences between rural and urban norms (see, for example, Haumann *et al.*, Van Noppen *et al.*) or the effects on politeness strategies of speaker variables such as age, class, gender, ethnic group and nationality. Domain also plays its part: Terkourafi demonstrates that the use of the diminutive in Cypriot Greek is increasingly confined to the home and to informal situations as a solidarity marker.

Consequently, the chapters which make up this volume could be grouped in a number of different ways. For, while there may be certain general pragmatic tendencies shared between different language groupings – say, the Romance, the Nordic, the Slavonic, the Hellenic or the Germanic – other factors, such as nationality, also have a role to play. Furthermore, within the same country there may co-exist different, often conflicting, language communities. Hence, in this volume, we have opted to present the chapters in broad geographical groupings, aware at the same time that the similarities, say, between Finnish (Northern Europe) and Estonian (Eastern Europe) may be far greater than, say, between Estonian and Polish which here are both grouped under Eastern Europe and that in certain countries (e.g. Switzerland and Belgium) both Romance and Germanic languages are spoken side by side. Indeed, Manno, referring to the case of Switzerland, suggests that it is nationality rather than language which is the more important factor in determining politeness behaviour. Kramer argues that while the expressions used in Luxemburg may be no different linguistically from those of the three languages spoken in that country, they may be used in pragmatically different ways. Furthermore, the majority of the chapters use a broadly comparative approach to shed light on the specificities of the data they use: this may be between varieties of the same language (e.g. Cypriot and mainland Greek), broadly cognate languages (e.g. Portuguese and French) or unrelated languages such as Dutch and Spanish.

While even before 1978 politeness had already emerged as an area of linguistic interest (see, for example, Lakoff's ground-breaking work of 1973), it was Penelope Brown and Stephen C. Levinson's pioneering formulation of politeness theory (1978), republished as a monograph in 1987 with an extensive new introduction, which laid the current bases for this field. From this seminal work and others based more or less directly on its findings, it has become clear that people do not speak to one another just to convey information or even merely to do things (to one another) but also to establish and maintain interpersonal relationships within a particular sociocultural context.

Both Brown and Levinson's 'face-saving' and Leech's 'conversational maxim' views of politeness derive from Gricean pragmatics (Grice, 1975). They owe much to speech act theory (e.g. Searle, 1969) and are primarily concerned with linguistic realisation. While hugely influential, they have nevertheless attracted wide criticism, some of which can be directly attributed to the very choice of the term 'politeness' to refer to their views on this dimension of interactional pragmatics. As Grundy (2000: 164) notes: 'Much of our thinking about politeness is bedevilled by the fact that "politeness" is a folk term.' In other words, the concept of politeness belongs to two traditions: one primarily concerned with conventional courtesy, etiquette or good manners, the other more interactionally pragmatic or face-saving, as developed in Brown and Levinson's model. This model does not necessarily view language in terms of a polite/impolite cline but rather in terms of the extent to which speakers strategically deviate from Gricean maxims in order to save their own face and/or that of others. More recently, the 'common-sense' form of politeness has come to be known as 'first-order politeness', with politeness, in its technical sense, being referred to as 'second-order politeness' (see, for example, Ehlich, 1992). Richard Watts (1992) makes a useful distinction between individual strategic politeness (which he terms 'politeness') and a form of behaviour 'which is conventionally appropriate to the ongoing social activity' (p. 92). The ability to be conventionally appropriate he terms 'politic behaviour'.

A number of chapters in this volume make distinctions of this nature. Held teases out the historical evolution of first-order politeness in Italy in order to focus subsequently on individual strategic politeness, also within a historical frame. She finds a gulf emerging between written politeness ('still trapped in formalities and formal routines unconsciously reflecting centuries-old scales and social hierarchies and their regulative impact') and spoken discourse favouring informality and individuality. Ilie, in the case of Sweden, focuses on the interface between language-based politeness rules, institution-based politeness strategies and culture-based communication principles. She finds that where, in this case, members of the Swedish parliament have a choice in the terms they use for self or other reference, a shift away from the unmarked, or institutionally-favoured, term can involve different discursive, as well as institutional and interpersonal, relationship patterns. For example, they occasionally use, instead of the unmarked third-person singular form, the second-person plural pronoun *ni* (you) 'as an addressee-targeted face-threatening act, reinforcing the competitive and/or conflictual relationship between the interlocutors'.

House strongly favours a 'first-order politeness first' approach which focuses on what individuals actually 'do' to indicate that they belong to a particular group. She finds that 'German subjects tend to interact in ways that are more direct, explicit and verbose, more self-referenced and content-oriented; they are also less prone to resort to verbal routines than English speakers'. She, like Terkourafi, adopts a sociocognitive rather than a purely social approach and espouses a Sperberian (1996) view of culture as a collective, supra-individual, phenomenon, similar to a number of recent approaches to politeness which have sought to cast it within a Relevance-Theoretic perspective (e.g. Escandell Vidal, 1998).

One of Brown and Levinson's (1987: 253) stated hopes is that their 'model of the universals in linguistic politeness' can be used 'to characterise the cross-cultural differences in ethos, the general tone of social interaction in different societies'. One implication of this is that some cultures may be characterised, crudely speaking, as negative politeness cultures and others as positive politeness cultures (p. 245). However suggestive this view may be, it is in issues such as these that the Brown and Levinson model proves difficult to operationalise. Spencer-Oatey (e.g. 2002) finds that their approach is particularly susceptible to ethnocentrism and argues for a framework based on universal sociopragmatic interactional principles which enable researchers to explore the importance that people attach to them in different contexts and different languages and cultures. The anthropological distinction between emic and etic perspectives (Pike, 1990, 1967, 1954 in Eelen, 2001: 76–8), essentially the difference between the cultural insider's and outsider's viewpoints, casts some light on the difficulties inherent in designing reliable cross-cultural research. Le Pair, contrasting directness in requests in Dutch and Spanish, argues that it is necessary to know considerably more about the perception and situational appropriateness of (in)directness in each society before these societies' politeness strategies can properly be compared. Perhaps the most influential early study which attempted to grapple with some of these issues was Shoshana Blum-Kulka and Elite Olshtain's (Blum-Kulka & Olshtain, 1984) project Cross-Cultural Speech Act Research Project (CCSARP), which was a cross-cultural investigation of the realisation strategies used in order to effect the speech acts of requests and apologies in a range of languages: Australian English, American English, British English, Canadian French, Danish, German, Hebrew and Russian. However, such projects are fraught with difficulty and, in this volume, Hickey, for example, shows the problems inherent in taking an Anglo-centric model of politeness and simply applying it to another culture or nation such as that of Spain.

Bayraktaroğlu and Sifianou (2001) rightly point out that English 'has hitherto been the playground of theory-makers'. Yet it has frequently been researchers from cultures outside the Anglo-American tradition who have questioned the bases of these theories. For example, Matsumoto (1988) and Ide (1989) are unhappy with the central notion of 'face' as defined by Brown and Levinson. Ide advances the twin notions of 'Volition' and 'Discernment': a speaker, in the first case, is able to exercise free will in linguistic choice but, in the second, is constrained to use the forms which social convention dictate. Eelen (2001: 19) contrasts Ide with Watts in that the latter 'associates politeness with volition only, while Discernment is associated with politic behaviour'. Researchers such as Fukushima (2000: 61) have rejected these criticisms as merely deriving from sociolinguistic features of Japanese and Chinese and not being pragmatically significant. However, theory-making has not entirely been the preserve of the English-speaking world and the 1980s and 1990s also saw pioneering projects such as those by Schulze (1985) and Held (1995), published in German, and the widely influential work of Kerbrat-Orecchioni (1992) in French.

This leads us to another criticism of Brown and Levinson's model, implicit in the approach of, say, House, which is that it provides little guidance on the definition of the three sociological variables on which it relies. Power, distance and the weight of an imposition differ from culture to culture and yet there is little clarification on how they are calculated, even before attempting cross-cultural comparisons of the linguistic or other means used in different cultures for implementing such strategies. Consequently, some researchers have attempted to refine these variables.

For example, Baxter (1984) introduces a 'liking factor' as influencing linguistic strategy, Holtgraves (1986) posits 'reciprocal liking', Brown and Gilman (1989: 192) demonstrate that politeness and liking (rather than reciprocity) are proportionate and Kerbrat-Orecchioni (1992: 36) proposes, in addition to power and distance, a variable relating to the degree to which the relationship between the interlocutors is conflictive or consensual. She develops her approach in this volume and, like House, stresses the importance of the cultural context in which the doing of politeness is embedded and the value systems which enable speakers and hearers both to do and interpret politeness. For example, within French culture, interruptions, far from disrupting local conversational management systems and threatening the face of the participants, very often 'help speed up the tempo of a conversation, they can brighten up an exchange and make it sparkle, give it warmth, spontaneity, and a sense that everyone is fully involved'.

This reconceptualisation of the relationship between interlocutors coincides with attempts, following Goffman's (1971: 66) 'supportive moves', to reclassify certain acts (e.g. thanks, apologies and compliments) as 'face-supporting' (Edmondson, 1981; Holmes, 1986, 1988) or 'face-boosting' (Bayraktaroğlu, 1991) or 'face-enhancing' and 'face-flattering' (Kerbrat-Orecchioni, 1997: 14 and this volume). Brown and Levinson did, of course, point out the need to classify such acts in terms of the weightiness attached to them in different cultures. In this sense, acts (for example, compliments) are essentially equivocal and cannot be seen as univocally either face-threatening or face-enhancing in themselves: their interpretation is dependent on extra-linguistic factors. There have also been criticisms of their approach as being 'rather paranoid' or as seeing communication as being 'fundamentally dangerous and antagonistic behaviour' (Kasper, 1990: 194). In this volume, Stewart looks at non-conventional indirectness and some of the culturally determined skills required for identifying and recovering implicatures, concluding that certain British cultures are relatively tolerant of the use of off-record strategies and may indeed indulge in a degree of 'paranoia' in decoding them. Van Noppen *et al.* re-examine Brown and Levinson's computation of the Face-Threatening Act in the light of the use of routinised requests in service encounters preceded by *alstublieft/s'il vous plaît* if you please. As these politeness markers correspond to no perceivable threat to face, they conclude that face management acts of this nature function as a condition for the interaction to continue but not as a goal to be pursued in its own right.

A more thoroughgoing critique, not just of Brown and Levinson, but of the whole area of politeness studies has been launched by Gino Eelen (2001) who argues for 'the incorporation of individual variability and social change' into current conceptualisations of politeness in social life (p.257). In addition to the work of Lakoff, Leech and Brown and Levinson, he evaluates the contributions to politeness theory made by Ide (e.g. 1989), Blum-Kulka (e.g. 1992), Gu (e.g. 1990), Fraser and Nolen (e.g. 1981), Arndt and Janney (e.g. 1985) and Watts (e.g. 1989) and concludes that '[c]urrent theories of politeness manifest a triple conceptual bias: towards the polite side of the polite–impolite distinction, towards the speaker in the interactional dyad and towards the production of behaviour rather than its evaluation' (Eelen, 2001: 119). However, it may be more true to say that the majority of empirical studies of politeness have neglected these aspects rather than that the theories are all incapable of accommodating them. For example, Culpeper (1996) has created a framework parallel to that of Brown and Levinson to investigate impoliteness in contexts such as military training and altercations between car-owners and traffic wardens. However, if Brown and Levinson's frame as a model is taken to account for face-saving, from which politeness or impoliteness may be a by-product, then impoliteness may be accounted for within the model. That the evaluation rather than the production of behaviour has been of less interest to linguists may be due in large part to the fact that the analyst does not have access to the intentions or interpretations of speakers and hearers even assuming that these are conscious and unitary. However, there is an increasing awareness by analysts of the need to analyse linguistic behaviour in context and an interlocutor's intervention in an on-going speech event provides some evidence, albeit indirect, of the interpretation they have drawn of the previous speaker's contribution.

Indeed, there are areas covered by current theories which have been largely neglected by empirical research. In this connection, Chen (2001) has noted that the bulk of politeness studies are concerned with attempts by the speaker to save the face of the hearer. He has attempted to build a model of self-politeness within Brown and Levinson's theory whereby speakers rely on a range of strategies to protect their own face in conversation. Others (e.g. Stewart) have called on Bell's (1984) theory of audience design to take into account, not only speakers and hearers, but also other participants in the communicative event, such as auditors and overhearers.

As noted earlier, over the 1980s and 1990s there has been an explosion of empirical studies of politeness investigating languages and varieties of language from all five continents and theoretical refinements to the state of the art. Three of the principal English-language journals in this field, *Pragmatics* (volume 9, no. 1, March 1999), *The Journal of Pragmatics* (volume 14, 1990 and volume 21, 1994) and *Multilingua* (volume 7, no. 4, 1989 and volume 12, no. 1, 1993), have produced special issues devoted to politeness, as well as covering the area extensively in their regular volumes. *Applied Linguistics* is another of many journals which also devote considerable coverage to questions of politeness. Such was the level of activity in the field that, by 1994, a bibliography on linguistic politeness (Dufon *et al*, 1994) had captured some 1000 items.

Many recent comparative studies have tended to take English as one pole of comparison in cross-cultural comparisons between two languages and cultures in an attempt to characterise the ethos of different language communities. For example, Maria Sifianou (1992: 41) argues that

> [t]he notion of face, consisting of the aspects of approval and non-imposition, seems to account for the motivation of politeness phenomena in Greek and to explain the differences between Greek and English. The English seem to place a higher value on privacy and individuality, i.e. the negative aspect of face, whereas the Greeks seem to emphasise involvement and in-group relations, i.e. the positive aspect.

Having discussed a survey devised and carried out by the author herself of what Greeks and English consider to be politeness, she concludes that

> there are basic differences in the conception of what politeness means, and, consequently, in its manifestations, and these two factors give evidence to my hypothesis that the Greek and English systems of politeness are different, the former being predominantly positive and the latter predominantly negative. (p. 94)

Similarly, in this volume, there is a general attempt to characterise the respective ethos or ethnostereotypes of the countries covered. For example, Araújo Carreira argues that in Portugal 'gregarious relationships, consensus and tact are favoured over confrontation, frankness or the protection of an individual's territory', a generalisation which could perhaps be applied to all the languages in the Southern Europe section. At the other geographical extreme, Yli-Vakkuri holds that Finnish politeness is withdrawing and evasive and that reference to the addressee is avoided at all costs. And while Scandinavian politeness might be characterised by the prevalence of thanking (Fredsted and Fretheim), many conventionalised politeness routines are either absent or used infrequently. For Fretheim, 'linguistic politeness in Norwegian society is characterised by a tendency toward parsimony; conventionalised indirectness in the performance of requests exists, but too much linguistic embroidery for the sake of mitigating requests is normally counter-productive'. Keevallik cites Giles *et al.* (1992) who identify 'differences in conversational style between East and West – Westerners talk for affiliative purposes, and in order to fill silences which are deemed stressful, while Easterners talk primarily for instrumental purposes and can remain in comfortable silence in other cases'. Given that, for example, Estonians tend to focus more on content than on relationships in interaction, she locates Estonia in the East alongside Germany. Interestingly, parallels can be drawn between these countries and our Northern European grouping. Much of the section on Eastern Europe is devoted to changes in social stratification largely subsequent to the Velvet Revolution of 1989 and a shift from more collectivist to more individualistic forms of self-expression whereby politeness is seen as instrumental rather than as a social semiotic.

Indeed, a number of contributors refer to Hofstede's (1984) characterisation of given cultures along such dimensions as 'uncertainty avoidance'. For instance, House argues that Germans achieve high scores on this particular dimension. Fredsted contrasts Danish with German politeness and her study shows that Danes score even more highly in avoiding uncertainty and 'getting to the point'. Kerbrat-Orecchioni rejects the view, popularised by Hofstede, that French society is essentially hierarchical and notes that France shares many characteristics with both Northern and Southern neighbours. Similarly, Kallen's study of Irish politeness examines the tensions between silence as a face need (typically generating negative politeness strategies) and hospitality and reciprocity, which call for positive politeness. Manno, writing of Switzerland with four official languages, suggests that, while the individual politeness systems of France, Italy and Germany influence to an extent politeness in communities speaking those languages in Switzerland, there is a specifically Swiss ethos characterised by preference for negative politeness and for autonomy. Most other chapters in this volume are equally concerned with attempting to characterise the 'ethos' of their society as well as examining on a micro-linguistic level the data on which they are working.

Issues of data collection have been prominent in the empirical studies published in this area. While it is relatively easy to collect valid samples of written texts, there are a number of difficulties associated with establishing corpora of naturally-occurring spoken discourse. Great difficulties are presented to the researcher by such factors as Labov's 'observer's paradox' (the possible distorting effect on the data of the researcher's very presence), the fact that audio and video can seldom capture all features of a speech event, the fact that certain speech acts – for example, compliments, commands or invitations – may occur only infrequently in any particular stretch of unprompted discourse, not to mention legal and ethical issues relating to whether it is legitimate to record other persons' conversations without informing them in advance or obtaining their permission to use any such recording afterwards. Furthermore, as we saw in the discussion over emic and etic perspectives, there are difficulties inherent in obtaining valid corpora for contrastive studies.

Consequently researchers have sometimes chosen to rely on rather artificial elicitation techniques, such as questionnaires, Discourse Completion Tasks or role plays of one kind or another. Some may tailor their research questions to the nature of the data available. In this volume, a wide range of data has been used: a number of researchers have drawn on recordings of service encounters (e.g. Kerbrat-Orecchioni and Fredsted) or of telephone conversations (e.g. Keevallik); others have used established corpora of spoken language (e.g. Kallen); some have drawn on written sources (e.g. Stewart and Fretheim); others have used Discourse Completion Tasks (e.g. Le Pair); and one has used the re-enactment of scenarios for comment by focus groups (Hickey).

This volume is about politeness in Europe but, if the concept and everything to do with politeness is problematical and uncertain, much more so is the concept of Europe. We have chosen to define Europe for the purposes of our volume as a loose geographical grouping which is, however, in continuous flux but with political considerations brought in to explain some of the boundaries. One of the interesting points is that, as Europe changes and transforms itself, then necessarily its politeness system or systems are also bound to be transformed. This is a point made with considerable force by a number of the contributors from Eastern Europe. One of our hopes, therefore, is that this book will be re-written every so often, say every ten years, to update politeness in Europe and *Politeness in Europe*.

References

Arndt, H. and Janney, R.W. (1985) Politeness Revisited: Cross-model supportive strategies. *International Review of Applied Linguistics in Language Teaching* 23 (4), 281–300.

Baxter, L.A. (1984) An investigation of compliance-gaining as politeness. *Human Communication Research* 10: 427–56.

Bayraktaroğlu, A (1991) Politeness and interactional imbalance. *International Journal of the Sociology of Language* 92: 5–34.

Bayraktaroğlu, A. and Sifianou, M. (eds) (2001) *Linguistic Politeness across Boundaries: The Case of Greek and Turkish*. Amsterdam/Philadelphia: John Benjamins.

Bell, A. (1984) Language style as audience design. *Language in Society* 13: 145–204.

Blum-Kulka, S. (1992) The metapragmatics of politeness in Israeli society. In R. Watts, S. Ide and K. Ehlich, *Politeness in Language. Studies in its History, Theory and Practice* (pp. 255–80) Berlin. Mouton de Gruyter.

Blum-Kulka, S. and Olshtain, E. (1984) Requests and apologies: A cross-cultural study of speech act realization patterns (CCSARP). *Applied Linguistics* 5 (3), 196–213.

Brown, R. and Gilman, A. (1960) The pronouns of power and solidarity. In T. Sebeok (ed.) *Style in Language* (pp. 253–276). New York/London: MIT Press.

Brown, P. and Levinson, S. (1978) Universals in language usage: Politeness phenomena. In E. Goody (ed.) *Questions and Politeness: Strategies in Social Interaction* (pp. 56–289). Cambridge: Cambridge University Press.

Brown, P. and Levinson, S. (1987) *Politeness: Some Universals in Language Usage.* Cambridge: Cambridge University Press.

Chen, R. (2001) Self-politeness: a proposal. *Journal of Pragmatics* 33, 87–106.

Culpeper, J. (1996) Towards an anatomy of impoliteness. *Journal of Pragmatics* 25, 3, 349–67.

Dufon, M., Kasper, G., Takahashi, S. and Yoshinaga, N (1994) Bibliography on linguistic politeness. *Journal of Pragmatics* 21: 527–78.

Edmondson, W.J. (1981) *Spoken Discourse: A Model for Analysis.* London: Longman.

Escandell Vidal, V. (1998) Politeness: A relevant issue for relevance theory. *Revista Alicantina de Estudios Ingleses* 11, 45–57.

Eelen, G. (2001) *A Critique of Politeness Theories.* Manchester: St. Jerome.

Ehlich, K. (1992) On the historicity of politeness. In R. Watts, S. Ide and K. Ehlich (eds) *Politeness in Language. Studies in its History, Theory and Practice* (pp. 7–107). Mouton de Gruyter.

Fraser, B. and Nolen, W. (1981) The association of deference with linguistic form. *The International Journal of the Sociology of Language* 27, 93–109.

Fukushima, S. (2000) *Requests and Culture.* Bern: Peter Lang.

Giles, H., Coupland, N. and Wiemann, J. (1992) 'Talk is cheap…' but 'My word is my bond': beliefs about talk. In K. Bolton and H. Kwok (eds) *Sociolinguistics Today: International Perspectives* (pp. 218–241). London & New York: Routledge.

Goffman, E. (1971) *Relations in Public: Microstudies of the Public Order*. New York: Harper Torchbooks.

Grice, H. P. (1975) Logic and conversation. In P. Cole and J. Morgan (eds) *Syntax and Semantics, 3: Speech Acts* (pp. 41–58). New York: Academic Press.

Grundy, P. (2000) *Doing Pragmatics* (2nd edn). London: Arnold.

Gu, Y. (1990) Politeness phenomena in modern Chinese. *Journal of Pragmatics* 14, 237–257.

Held, G. (1995) *Verbale Höflichkeit. Studien zur linguistischen Theorienbildung und empirische Untersuchung zum Sprachverhalten französischer und italienischer Jugendlicher in Bitt- und Dankessituationen.* Tübingen: Narr.

Hofstede, G. (1984) *Culture's Conseqences.* New York: Sage.

Holmes, J. (1986) Compliments – compliment responses in New Zealand English. *Anthropological Linguistics* 28: 484–508.

Holmes, J. (1988) Paying compliments: A sex-preferential strategy. *Journal of Pragmatics* 12: 445–465.

Holtgraves, T. (1986) Language structure in social interactions: Perceptions of direct and indirect speech acts and interactants who use them. *Journal of Personality and Social Psychology* 51: 305–14.

Ide, S. (1989) Formal forms of discernments: Two neglected aspects of universals of linguistic politeness. *Multilingua* 8: 223–48.

Kasper, G. (1990) Linguistic politeness: Current research issues. *Journal of Pragmatics* 14: 193–218.

Kerbrat-Orecchioni, C. (1990, 1992, 1994) *Les interactions verbales* (Vols I, II, III). Paris: Armand Colin.

Kerbrat-Orecchioni, C. (1997) A multilevel approach in the study of talk-in-interaction. *Pragmatics,* 7(1), 1–20.

Lakoff, R. T. (1973) The logic of politeness; or minding your p's and q's. In *Papers from the Ninth Regional Meeting of the Chicago Linguistic Society* (pp. 292–305). Chicago: Department of Linguistics, University of Chicago.

Matsumoto, Y. (1988) Reexamination of the universality of face: Politeness phenomena in Japanese. *Journal of Pragmatics* 12, 403–426.

Schulze, R. (1985) *Höflichkeit im Englischen.* Tübingen, Narr.

Searle, J. (1969) *Speech Acts: An Essay in the Philosophy of Language.* Cambridge: Cambridge University Press.

Spencer-Oatey, H. (2002) Managing rapport in talk: Using rapport-sensitive incidents to explore the motivational concerns underlying the management of relations. *Journal of Pragmatics* 34, 529–45.

Sperber, D. (1996) *Explaining Culture. A Naturalistic Approach.* Oxford: Blackwell.

Watts, R. (1989) Relevance and relational work: Linguistic politeness as politic behaviour. *Multilingua* 82–3, 131–66.

Watts, R., Ide, S. and Ehlich, K. (eds) (1992) *Politeness in Language. Studies in its History, Theory and Practice.* Berlin: Mouton de Gruyter.

Chapter 1

Politeness in Germany: Politeness in GERMANY?

JULIANE HOUSE

Introduction

Politeness in Germany? Is there any, people may ask. Are the two nouns, politeness and Germany, not a contradiction in terms? Yes, many will reply, thus confirming a widespread stereotype. But is there a factual basis to such a belief? Or are we here dealing with nothing but another nasty prejudice acting against those members of an unfortunate nation more often than not already filled with self-doubt, guilt and identity qualms? If, however, there is such a thing as politeness in Germany, what is it like? To find out, we might ask 'Lügt man im Deutschen, wenn man höflich ist?' (Does one lie in German, when one is being polite), as did Weinrich (1986) playing on a famous quotation from Goethe's *Faust*.

It is questions such as these that I will tackle in this chapter. I will also make a plea for an integrative socio-cognitive approach to politeness, uniting the individual and the social in Clark's (1996) sense. Politeness is so closely linked to both cognitive-intentional aspects and linguo-cultural expressions that are conventionalised in a linguaculture (Agar, 1994) that only an approach combining the two seems fruitful. Concretely, I will first briefly present my own view of politeness. In doing this, I will refer to some of the more recent innovative and critical work on politeness, passing by established politeness models, as covered in the Introduction to this volume. Second, I will discuss some aspects of the meaning of politeness in Germany mostly from a contrastive perspective. In conclusion, I will try to answer my initial question, i.e. whether politeness and Germany are mutually exclusive terms.

What is Politeness?

Politeness is one of the basic socio-psychological guidelines for human behaviour. As such, it is an integral part of all human interaction – the hallmark of abiding by the Gricean cooperative principle. Speaking politely is the unmarked way of speaking, as it tends to be expected and passes unnoticed, while overpoliteness or impoliteness tend to be noticed (cf. Escandell Vidal, 1996; Jary, 1998). Politeness can thus be regarded as the behavioural norm for speakers and it is, of course, speakers only – never utterances – who can be called polite (or impolite), to the extent that their utterances are in keeping with the particular rights and obligations holding in a particular interaction and reflect the contextually determined responsibility interlocutors have to one another.

Politeness is reflected in interactants' demonstrated consideration of one another. The word 'demonstrated' is meant to imply that this 'consideration' need not be genuine or sincere, rather 'it is the fact that an effort was made to go through the motions at all that makes the act an act of politeness' (Green, 1996: 147).

Given this common-sense view of politeness as a real-world human behavioural tendency, politeness can be regarded as reflecting a specific culture's behavioural norms. Politeness is then intimately connected with the realisation of conventional styles of communicating and levels of formality, often referred to as 'deference', a concept which is now regarded as an integral part of certain languages (e.g. Japanese), whose speakers are obliged to make appropriate choices in planning, formulating and articulating utterances. Much recent non-western research is concerned with this type of built-in choice and how it impacts on 'politeness' (e.g. Ide, 1989). But deference is also built into the system of all those languages that are characterised by a 'T/V subsystem' (*du* and *Sie* in German), and there are naturally many other cross-cultural differences in the realisation of politeness norms simply because languages differ, not so much in what they can, but what they must, express.

These differences have been the focus of many studies attempting to compare so-called politeness norms in different cultures. In many earlier contrastive studies, surface linguistic forms were used as indices of politeness norms, and with these, the impact of isolated social and contextual variables (Power, Distance, Imposition, Affect) on norms of politeness was investigated, and correlations with the enactment of particular speech act sequences were made (see, e.g., Walters, 1979). However, it is now accepted by many (e.g. Eelen *et al.*, 2002; Fraser, 2002) that it is misleading to assume that a particular linguistic form or structure is 'inherently polite'. Linguistic forms are always only part of the evidence which interactants use to assess their interlocutor's utterance and infer polite intentions. The complex interaction of various contextual and participant variables has also been contrasted: with reference to requests, for instance, Germans, Israelis and Argentinians were found to perceive participants' rights and obligations, their difficulty in performing the speech act and the likelihood of the interlocutor's compliance, in markedly different ways (see, e.g. Blum-Kulka & House, 1989).

In many recent studies of politeness, the focus of analysis has moved away from a Brown and Levinson-inspired focus on the speaker, on isolated speech acts and their face-threat towards relevance theory-inspired addressee orientation and investigations of politeness displayed in different discourse environments, such as everyday face-to-face interpersonal talk (House, 2000) or workplace communication (Clyne, 1994). There is a move away from the rather static and prescriptive idea of viewing some acts as per se face-threatening or face-enhancing regardless of the context in which they are performed; rather, as Sifianou (2002: 7) has pointed out, 'it seems more plausible that all acts include both aspects, one or both of which may surface in a specific situation'. Utterances cannot be analysed as though they were produced *in vacuo*, detachable from the contexts they are embedded in. They occur in specific sociocultural and linguistic contexts including (at least) the individual speakers (their intentions and expectations), the relationship between them and the ensuing acts.

Recognising the crucial role of context in describing interpersonal phenomena such as politeness is, of course, nothing new. It has a long tradition in philosophy, anthropology and social psychology, where meaning has always been described as inextricably linked to context: without context, words and actions, polite or impolite, have no meaning at all, which is, in Gregory Bateson's (1979: 15) words, 'true not only of human communication in words but also of all communication whatsoever, of all mental processes, of all mind'. Earlier definitions of context as a set of variables statically surrounding stretches of talk are consequently abandoned in favour of a dynamic psycho-social view of a mutually reflexive relationship between talk and context, with talk and the interpretive and inferential processes it generates shaping context as much as context shapes talk (see, e.g., Duranti & Goodwin, 1992).

The idea that instances of 'doing politeness' should be described and explained with reference to their context, also taking account of the interaction between individual and social phenomena, has recently been taken up and synthesised by Eelen (2001). Following his critique of 'mainstream' politeness theories, Eelen (2001: 240) sets out to sketch an approach to politeness which regards 'the social/cultural [as] the result of human (inter)action rather than vice versa'. His approach, drawing on Bourdieu's notion of *Habitus*, emphasises the empowerment of the hearer and individuals in general and aims at (re)uniting the individual and the social. In his suggestions for a future research agenda, Eelen gives pride of place to investigations of what ordinary people actually think of politeness and suggests working with real-life spontaneous conversational data. This is compatible with a line of research reflected in much current sociolinguistic work on 'communities of practice' (Wenger, 1998), a concept designed to break down notions such as 'the speech community' into a dynamic social construct characterised by shared goals and practices bridging intergroup and interpersonal behaviour and focusing on what members actually 'do' to indicate that they belong to a particular group. I myself strongly favour such a 'first-order first' approach (see the following section).

The theoretical implication of much of this new line of thinking about politeness is of course the thesis, mentioned earlier, that politeness is *the* norm underlying behaviour that is adequate in context. This thesis has recently been explored by Terkourafi (2001 and this volume) on the basis of a corpus of spontaneous offer and request realizations in Cypriot Greek. Terkourafi found analysing and explaining polite discourse with reference to universal principles à la Brown and Levinson very difficult, mostly because their formula implies that the polite import of an utterance is a function of its degree of indirectness assessed on semantic criteria out of a limited micro-level perspective – a perspective that ignores the nature of language as a culturally and linguistically shared medium, which makes it an infinitely 'grander' instrument than the mere sum of individual rationalisations. Terkourafi rightly concludes that a shift in perspective is essential ('politeness is a perlocutionary effect') and that utterances' embeddedness in the macro-context of culture must be recognised. Since speakers are rooted in their culture, they can resort to their individual, socioculturally generated knowledge in the form of 'frames' (acquired in primary socialisation though language in a specific culture) in which linguistic expressions are linked with extralinguistic features of the situation (setting, sociolinguistic variables etc.), which together make up a minimal context that sets up inferencing processes.

Terkourafi's approach is similar to Sperber's (1996) view of culture and his attempt to defend the very notion of culture as a collective, supra-individual, phenomenon against excessive relativising and atomising conceptualisations. Sperber views culture in terms of different types of (mental) 'representations' (which may be representations of ideas, behaviours, attitudes, etc.). A multitude of individual 'mental representations' exist in any group. Most of these representations are fleeting and remain individual. However, a subset of them can be overtly expressed in language and artefacts. They then become 'public representations', which are communicated to others in the social group. This communication gives rise to similar mental representations in others, which, in turn, may be communicated as public representations to others, which may again be communicated to different persons and so on. If a subset of public representations is communicated frequently enough within a particular social group, they may become firmly entrenched and turn into 'cultural representations'. The point at which a mental representation becomes sufficiently widespread to be called 'cultural' is, of course, a matter of degree and interpretation, i.e. there is no clear division between individual public, and cultural representations, which may be taken as an argument against assuming monolithic 'national mentalities' and stereotypes of various kinds.

The type of socio-cognitive explanation of individual and collective processes which characterise both Terkourafi's and Sperber's work is also a feature of my own attempt to set up a descriptive and explanatory framework capable of uniting universal aspects of politeness (such as the ones claimed in face- and maxim-oriented approaches) with culture- and language-specific aspects, such as the ones emphasized by non-western scholars. My attempt at such a theoretical framework can be displayed diagrammatically as follows.

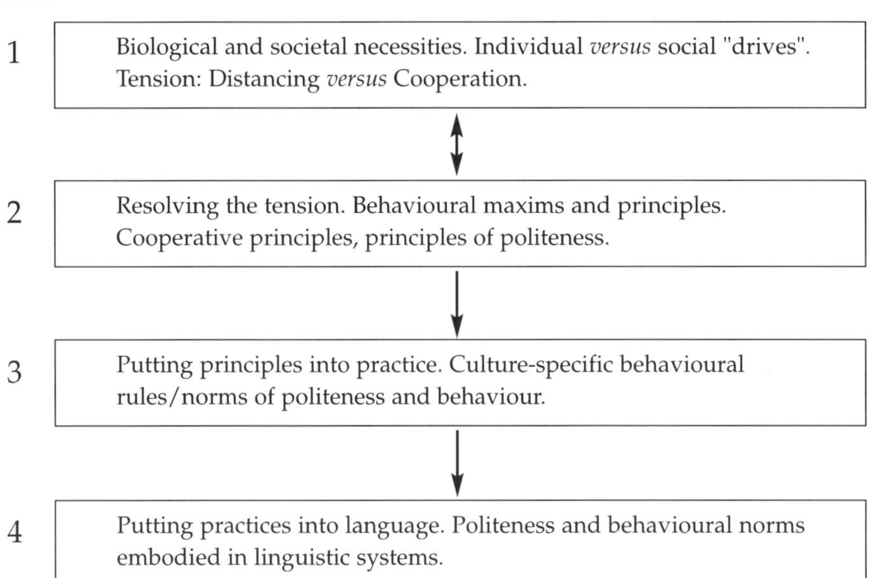

Level
1
Biological and societal necessities. Individual *versus* social "drives". Tension: Distancing *versus* Cooperation.
2
Resolving the tension. Behavioural maxims and principles. Cooperative principles, principles of politeness.
3
Putting principles into practice. Culture-specific behavioural rules/norms of politeness and behaviour.
4
Putting practices into language. Politeness and behavioural norms embodied in linguistic systems.

Level 1 is bio-social, level 2 is philosophical, level 3 is cultural, level 4 is linguistic. Levels 1 and 2 are universal: levels 3 and 4 are culture-specific.

Figure 1.1 A multilevel model of politeness

The model operates on four levels: first, a biological, psycho-social level focusing on the deep-seated tension between the individual and society which is based on the well-known animal drives 'coming together' *versus noli me tangere*, self *versus* other as opposed to self via other. This fundamental level is compatible with Brown and Levinson's conception of positive and negative politeness. The second level is what might be called the 'philosophical level', which seeks to capture human biological drives in terms of a finite number of principles or maxims. The third level is the level of culture-specific norms of behaviour arising out of a community's individuals' cultural representations or 'frames'. It is an empirically descriptive level, which pays tribute to the fact that, in certain cultures, politeness operates in terms of a particular (open-ended) set of norms, tendencies or preferences. The fourth level captures those linguistic phenomena which are built into or 'fixed' in the language system, such as honorifics or the T/V pronoun distinction. These are real-world, sociocultural phenomena 'crystallised', as it were, in language representing language-typologically givens.

Viewed in such a way, the universalist stance can be upheld if it refers to levels 1 and 2 only. At levels 3 and 4, one might wish to distinguish between relatively open-ended negotiable rules relating to the philosophical principles accepted at level 2 and other normative rules that are relatively closed or fixed. The distinction relates to the question how far the language system itself decrees or imposes certain politeness norms or choices (e.g. honorifics in Japanese). Working top-down, one might wish to hypothesise a procedure operating between levels two and three, which one might call 'negotiability'. This type of 'mega-parameter' would determine how flexible a given culture is in terms of degrees of freedom or constraint with regard to the realisation of certain maxims and principles and it might be used to explain why a particular parameter appears to be so linguistically differentiated in culture A but inflexibly hide-bound in culture B. If one works bottom-up, one may well arrive at principles and maxims that do not have universal validity. In practice, then, one may well need a theory akin to Chomskyan principles and parameter theory, which would explain how 'exotic' a given culture may be.

This model of politeness may serve as a guideline for the following discussion of what it means to be polite in Germany.

Politeness in Germany: Empirical Evidence and Explanatory Hypotheses

One of the most fruitful methods of characterising politeness in a particular linguaculture (such as Germany) is to contrast persons 'doing politeness' in the culture in question with the behaviour of members of another cultural group. This is what I have tried to do in the series of contrastive pragmatic analyses I have conducted over the past decades comparing German with English and American discourse norms. The assumption is that, through contrast, linguistic and cultural characteristics of politeness can be better described and explained. In what follows I will briefly characterise these empirical studies and indicate what their results may mean for answering the title question of this chapter: Politeness in *Germany*?

In my empirical work I have analysed and compared the discourse of German and English native speakers (for overviews see House, 1989a,b; 1996; 2000; 2002; House & Kasper, 1981). I have used a variety of data-elicitation methods. While it would of course be preferable to follow the previously-mentioned tenet of conducting analyses with naturalistic data from everyday conversations, the relationship between effort and outcome have made this idealistic demand unrealistic. The alternative I have therefore chosen is to use a variety of different data-collection methods, i.e.

(1) audio-taped open role-play interactions between English and German speakers followed by retrospectively-focussed introspections (200)
(2) author's own field-notes of naturally occurring 'critical incidents' (clashes of politeness) in English–German interactions (49),
(3) self-reflective diary-type records of naturally occurring critical incidents given to the author by colleagues, students, friends, where differences in politeness norms in German–English interactions were involved (81),
(4) audio-taped narrative interviews in which English native speakers describe critical incidents they experienced in a German cultural context (58) and
(5) audio-taped authentic interactions (+/- participant observation) of different speech events (23).

Apart from working with these oral data, I have also analysed and compared German and English written discourse, as well as translations in different genres (see House, 1981, 1997), with a view to revealing differences and commonalties in discourse structure and communicative preference. A recent analysis of translations of English children's books into German (and *vice versa*) (House, in press) has, for instance, revealed the operation of culturally conditioned communicative orientations and 'cultural filtering' had actually taken place as the texts travelled through time and space and from one linguaculture to another. Discourse analyses of these different data sets are all based on Edmondson's (1981) discourse model, his discourse-processing model (1987), Edmondson and House's interactional grammar (1981), as well as the categorical scheme developed in the Cross-Cultural Speech Act Realization Project (Blum-Kulka *et al.* 1989), which largely builds on Edmondson and House's work.

The discourse phenomena investigated include discourse phases, discourse strategies, gambits and speech act sequences.

Briefly, the analyses yielded the following results:

(1) *Opening and closing discourse phases*
German subjects tend to use fewer conversational routines and there is less reciprocity in the use of phatic moves. Germans are generally less likely and less willing to engage in 'small talk'. Indicative of this is the fact that there is no equivalent German expression for 'small talk'! This dispreference for 'empty verbiage' is also reflected in the written translation corpus. For instance, in the German translation of Michael Bond's *A Bear called Paddington (Paddington unser kleiner Bär)* the following sequence of phatic moves in the original – 'Hallo Mrs Bird', said Judy 'It's nice to see you again. How's the rheumatism?' 'Worse than it's ever been' began Mrs Bird – is simply omitted.

(2) *Discourse strategies*
German subjects tend to use more content-oriented strategies, e.g. introducing topics explicitly and expanding them; they also use fewer interpersonally-active strategies, such as anticipatory moves, e.g. availability checks, moves seeking pre-commitment or various disarming moves. Germans also prefer moves with explicit reference to self, such as, e.g., 'Kann ich...' *versus* 'Would you like me to…'. Further, there is more *ad hoc* formulation in German and more reliance on conversational routines in English.

(3) *Gambits*
In using gambits (discourse markers or elements that can occur in turn-initial, turn-internal or turn-final position), Germans tend to prefer both content-oriented and self-referenced gambits, such as 'starters' to preface their message or 'underscorers' to emphasise the content of a message. English speakers were found to prefer gambit types with which they explicitly address (and attempted to manipulate!) conversational partners (such as, e.g. 'cajolers' to coax interlocutors into heightened attention, sympathy or willingness to do something for the speaker) etc.

(4) *Speech act sequence*
Requests, complaints and apologies were analysed and compared and certain 'levels of directness' were suggested to capture differences in the execution of complaints and requests by German and Anglophone

subjects. There is converging evidence that Germans prefer more direct expressions when complaining or making a request. In making apologies, German subjects tend to be more verbose, selecting more self-directed strategies (such as grounders) in their attempt to express responsibility for an offence and in general, use expressions of responsibility more frequently than English speakers. Germans were also found to use a more varied range of tokens (displaying less routinised behaviour) than their English counterparts, who use one all-purpose token ('sorry') with overriding frequency.

From these results, a consistent pattern has emerged: German subjects tend to interact in ways that are more direct, explicit and verbose, more self-referenced and content-oriented; they are also less prone to resort to verbal routines than English speakers. The consistent pattern of cross-cultural differences in communicative norms emerging from these analyses can be displayed along five dimensions, as in Figure 2. The oppositions represent end-points on different clines, with German subjects tending to give preference to positions on the left of these dimensions. The dimensions are not to be mistaken for dichotomies, they simply display tendencies.

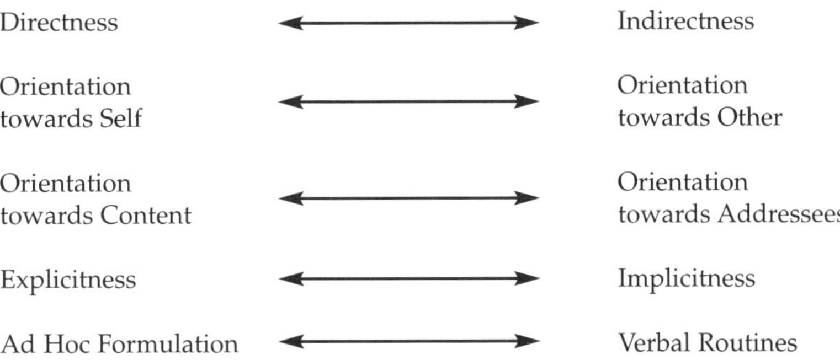

Figure 1.2 Dimensions of cross-cultural differences (German–English)

In terms of the hypothesised multilevel politeness model, we can say that the (claimed) universality at levels 1 and 2, i.e. the basic human drives of 'come together' *versus noli me tangere* and the ethical and moral principles and maxims of tact, agreement, cost–benefit etc. are clearly operative here too. However, the way these universals are interpreted and negotiated at level 3, where cultural-behavioural norms of politeness are captured, and at level 4, where these specifics are crystallised in linguistic form, clearly varies and it is at these two levels that the hypothesised dimensions are likely to operate.

As regards the tendency for German speakers to produce speech acts marked by directness such as the raw imperative in performing requests or uttering an unmitigated 'No, this is not true' rather than 'you must forgive me but this is simply not true' is reminiscent of Hofstede's (1984) dimension of 'uncertainty avoidance' and, indeed, according to Hofstede, Germans achieve high values on this dimension. In the words of one of my American informants: 'Germans say what they mean while we [Americans] dance around not to hurt anyone' (but see Kallen, this volume). According to Hofstede, members of a culture that leans towards uncertainty-avoidance would be generally more inclined to say directly what they mean, they feel a greater need for rules, structures, exactly defined topics, detailed instructions and timetables, all of which help them in their general flight from ambiguity.

Now, does the fact that German speakers perform certain speech acts such as requests, complaints, criticisms, refusals in a more direct way mean that Germans can be said to be 'less polite' or even that they are unable to be polite? Of course not! Both House (1986) and Blum-Kulka (1987) have shown that the relationship between indirectness and politeness is much more complicated than had been predicted by politeness models such as Brown and Levinson's. While conventionally indirect requests conventionally performed by preparatory strategies (can/could you) were rated as most polite in many different languages, non-conventionally indirect requests, i.e. hints, although clearly much more indirect, were rated as less polite, presumably because of the high processing load imposed on the receptor. These findings can be interpreted as indicating that one cannot simply equate indirectness with politeness regardless of the linguo-cultural context. What this also means is that German speakers' directness cannot be (mis)interpreted as impoliteness: it is just a culture- and language-specific convention. Further, Pike's distinction between emic and etic perspectives on culture-conditioned behaviour is relevant here. In other words, while an utterance like 'Go down to the basement and get it for me' may appear like an impolite order to a non-member of the German linguaculture, it may be perceived as perfectly polite by an 'ordinary German'.

The dimension Self- *versus* Other-orientation is reminiscent of Hofstede's Individualistic *versus* Collectivist parameter (and Talcott Parson's Self *versus* Collectivity orientation), 'I *versus* Us or Them' feeling. This dimension is clearly related to the directness orientation: if there is a tendency to speak baldly, the speaker tends to be more oriented towards self than alter. The German apology data features a pattern of justificatory grounders and other self-referencing discourse strategies absent in the English apologies.

The dimensions Content *versus* Addressee orientation and Explicitness *versus* Implicitness are clearly intimately connected and reminiscent of the Halls' (Hall & Hall, 1983) High *versus* Low content orientation. Such a strong focus on the subject matter and the concomitant need to 'fill it out with (often didactic) details' is reflected in the way written genres (e.g. academic and popular science articles) are conventionally composed (House 2002 b).

As regards the dimension Reliance on Verbal Routine *versus* Ad Hoc Formulation, German subjects seem less able to rely on an extensive stock of verbal routines than Anglophone speakers, with their interminable variety of phatic formula of the 'Nice talking to you' type. However, this pragmatic lacuna is currently being filled fast in German conversational discourse either with more or less literal translations or with loan words from English. So we now find Germans using routines such as *Man sieht sich, Wir telefonieren, Hi, Hallo* as well as *sorry* (the new all-purpose German illocutionary force indicating device) in contemporary German, unheard of 20 years ago. We also find a token which is now frequently used (especially among young people) to express both greeting and inquiry-after-alter, namely *Na* with rising intonation. Whether and how this influx of Anglophone routines will change German conversational style and politeness norms is, however, an open question.

The validity of these five dimensions is supported by the results of many other contrastive pragmatic German–English studies such as Byrnes (1986), Clyne (1987) or Watts (1989). Converging evidence also accrues from several postgraduate theses in which students of mine contrasted the performance of different speech act sequences in face-to-face or telephone talk, elicited judgements in interviews, metapragmatic tests or analysed and contrasted written discourse. The language pairs involved include German–American, German–British English and German–Irish English (Barron, 2001; Ebeling, 1994; Möhl, 1996), German–French (Probst, 1997), German–Spanish (Larrosa, 1998; Reising, 1997), German–Farsi, (Nouranian, 2000), German–Arabic (Harfmann, 2001). Taken together, these studies, using different methodologies, subjects, linguistic phenomena, again point to the hypothesis that German speakers in certain discourse environments tend (still) to underuse phatic small talk, are verbosely explicit, value propositional content over interpersonal accommodation and 'talk straight' as opposed to members of many other linguacultures.

Given these cross-cultural differences in communicative preferences in discourse behaviour which reflect politeness practices, one can hypothesize that the Gricean Maxims of Quantity and Relation tend to be interpreted 'idiosyncratically' in the German linguaculture, i.e. supplying just as much and no more information as the occasion requires and being 'relevant' to the perceived purpose of the discourse tends to be flouted more often than not in German discourse. The tendency in German to explicate content may then well set up different conditions for the performance of inferencing operations.

Within Lakoff's (1973) frame of reference, it seems to be the case that all of her three rules of politeness are interpreted differently in the German and Anglophone linguacultures: the politeness rule 'Don't impose' is given different values in German due to a preference for higher directness levels in the performance of certain speech acts. The Rule 'Give Options' is also interpreted differently due to a preference for higher directness levels and explicitness of content in German. The rule 'Be friendly', in particular, is interpreted and realised differently in the German linguaculture, given a preference for (explicated) content over a concern for addressees, self-referencing over other-referencing, reduced reliance on conversational routines and generally greater directness in speech act performance.

In looking for 'deeper explanations' for this German interactional ethos, we must consider the historical and cultural roots of German linguaculture. It is necessary to relate linguistic studies of discoursal style to the richer context of historial, political and philosophical developments, and we should also take legal and educational systems and other cultural practice into account. Only then might it be possible to see how German discourse patterns are anchored in shared cultural experience in the sense of Sperber's (1996) theory, and how the 'German *habitus*' which Norbert Elias (1990) describes, has developed over time. One would have to ask why, in German discourse patterns, transactional language use (message and topic-oriented) tends to be valued differently from interactional language use or, to put it in Hallidayan terms, why the ideational language function is so often given preference over the interpersonal one. Tentative explanations of the roots of some of these German discourse preferences point to the following German cultural phenomena:

(a) There has been a loss of a sense of national identity and the erosion of a feeling of 'Gemeinschaft' (community) after the catastrophe of the Nazi regime and the Second World War.
(b) There has been a breakdown of etiquette, i.e. a behavioural canon of generally accepted rules of politeness in the wake of the bourgeoisie's loss of influence in post-war Germany.
(c) The German educational system has traditionally placed greater

emphasis on the transmission of knowledge (*Bildung*), on developing 'inner virtues' and 'character formation' than on instilling a sense of community in the young or on shaping useful social skills, let alone the transmission of that particular brand of Anglo-Saxon 'Etiquette of Simulation' where rules of verbal behaviour implying that one 'must sound (and act) as if one meant what one said' when expressing, for instance, thanks, apologies, compliments and other 'face-lifts' are implicitly handed down from generation to generation. This kind of effective 'impression management' tends to be both underdeveloped and less strongly valued by German speakers.

(d) The German legal system is based (as in most of continental Europe) on prefixed statutes, laws and regulations, whereas the Anglo-Saxon legal system is characterised by a pragmatic, negotiable case law system (see the fascinating analysis by Legrand, 1996).

(e) There has been an 'idealistic' philosophical tradition in Germany as opposed to the more 'pragmatic' Anglo-Saxon way of 'doing philosophy'.

Linking discourse behaviour, in general, and politeness, in particular, with these cultural practices and tracing their mutual influence is a daunting task. At present, attempts such as the previous reflections must be regarded as highly speculative. Nevertheless, for a complete picture of the German *habitus* and the special brand of German politeness, such trans-disciplinary work is essential.

Conclusion

Politeness in Germany? Yes, it certainly exists – as I have tried to show – and Weinrich's provocative question must be answered in the negative: no, one does not actually lie in German when one is being polite. Being polite in German is different from being polite in an English-speaking country. It means following a secret comment which is probably less obvious than its Anglo Saxon counterpart: it often involves saying what one means and meaning what one says; engaging more and sooner in 'serious talk' than carefully preparing the ground with 'small talk'; it may mean referring in detail to matters relating to both self and the topic in hand, and it may mean omitting all-purpose formulae in favour of improvising and providing links to the particular speech event being shared with one's interlocutor. Knowing all this might make it easier to understand what one needs to do if one wants to count as 'polite' in Germany: simply behave in a way that is adequate to the specific cognito-social context in which you and your inter-locutor find yourselves. Showing such real-world politeness would also be in line with recent politeness theorizing.

References

Agar, M. (1994) *Language Shock. Understanding the Culture of Conversation.* New York: Morrow.

Barron, A. (2001) A longitudinal study of the effect of the year abroad on L2 pragmatic competence. PhD Dissertation, University of Hamburg.

Bateson, G. (1979) *Mind and Nature. A Necessary Unity.* Toronto: Bantam Books.

Blum-Kulka, S. (1987) Indirectness and politeness in requests: Same or different? *Journal of Pragmatics* 11, 131–46.

Blum-Kulka, S. and House, J. (1989) Cross-cultural and situational variation in requesting behaviour. In S. Blum-Kulka, J. House and G. Kasper (eds) *Cross-cultural Pragmatics: Requests and Apologies* (pp. 123–54). Norwood, NJ: Ablex.

Blum-Kulka, S., House, J. and Kasper, G. (eds) (1989) *Cross-cultural Pragmatics: Requests and Apologies.* Norwood, NJ: Ablex.

Brown, P. and Levinson, S. (1987) *Politeness. Some Universals in Language Usage.* Cambridge: Cambridge University Press.

Byrnes, H. (1986) Interactional style in German and American conversation. *Text* 6, 189–207.

Clark, H.H. (1996) *Using Language.* Cambridge: Cambridge University Press.

Clyne, M. (1987) Cultural differences in the organization of academic texts: English and German. *Journal of Pragmatics* 11, 211–47.

Clyne, M. (1994) *Intercultural Communication at Work. Cultural Values in Discourse.* Cambridge: Cambridge University Press.

Duranti, A. and Goodwin, C. (eds) (1992) *Rethinking Context.* Cambridge: Cambridge University Press.

Ebeling, S. (1994) Probleme in der interkulturellen Kommunikation. Eine exemplarische Untersuchung deutsch–amerikanischer Interaktion. MA Thesis, University of Hamburg.

Edmondson, W.J. (1981) *Spoken Discourse. A Model for Analysis.* London: Longman.

Edmondson, W.J. (1987) 'Acquisition' and 'Learning': The Discourse System Integration System. In W. Loerscher and R. Schulze (eds) *Perspectives on Language in Performance* (pp. 1070–1089). Tübingen: Narr.

Edmondson, W.J. and House, J. (1981) *Let's Talk and Talk About It. A Pedagogic Interactional Grammar of English.* München: Urban and Schwarzenberg.

Eelen, G. (2001) *A Critique of Politeness Theories.* Manchester. St Jerome.

Eelen, G, O'Driscoll, J. and Watts, R. (2002) Introduction to Symposium on First-order and Second-order Politeness: The Dispute over 'Modelling' Politeness. Fourteenth Sociolinguistics Symposium, Gent, 4–6 April 2002.

Elias, N. (1990) *Studien ueber die Deutschen.* (M. Schroeter; 4th edn). Frankfurt: Suhrkamp.

Escandell Vidal, V. (1996) Towards a cognitive approach to politeness. In K. Jaszczolt and K. Turner (eds) *Contrastive Semantics and Pragmatics* (pp. 629-50). Oxford: Pergamon.

Fraser, B. (2002) Whither politeness? Plenary Lecture given at the first Symposium on Intercultural, Cognitive and Social Pragmatics, Seville 11 April 2002.

Green, G. M (1996) *Pragmatics and Natural Language Understanding*. Mahwah, NJ: Erlbaum.

Hall, E.T. and Hall, M.T. (1983) *Hidden Differences. Studies in International Communication. How to Communicate with the Germans*. Hamburg: Gruner and Jahr.

Harfmann, M. (2001) Arabische und deutsche Schulaufsaetze im Vergleich. MA Thesis, University of Hamburg.

Hofstede, G. (1984) *Culture's Conseqences*. New York: Sage.

House, J. (1981) *A Model for Translation Quality Assessment*. 2nd edn. Tübingen: Narr.

House, J. (1986) Cross-cultural pragmatics and foreign language learning. In K.-R. Bausch *et al*. (eds) *Probleme und Perspektiven der Sprachlehrforschung* (pp. 281–95). Frankfurt: Scriptor.

House, J. (1989a) Politeness in English and German: The functions of 'please' and 'bitte'. In S. Blum-Kulka, J. House and G. Kasper (eds) *Cross-cultural Pragmatics: Requests and Apologies* (pp. 96–123). Norwood, NJ: Ablex.

House, J. (1989b) Oh Excuse me please... Apologizing in a foreign language. In B. Kettemann *et al*. (eds) *Englisch als Zweitsprache* (pp. 303–29). Tübingen: Narr.

House, J. (1996) Contrastive discourse analysis and misunderstanding. The case of German and English. In M. Hellinger and U. Ammon (eds) *Contrastive Sociolinguistics* (pp. 345–61). Berlin: Mouton de Gruyter.

House, J. (1997) *Translation Quality Assessment: A Model Revisited*. Tübingen: Narr.

House, J. (2000) Understanding misunderstanding: A pragmatic discourse approach to analysing mismanaged rapport in talk across cultures. In H. Spencer-Oatey (ed.) *Culturally Speaking* (pp. 145–164). London: Continuum.

House, J. (2002a) Universality *versus* culture-specificity in translation. In A. Riccardi (ed.) *Translation Studies. Perspectives on an Emerging Discipline* (pp. 92–111). Cambridge: Cambridge University Press.

House, J. (2002b) Maintenance and convergence in covert translation English–German. In H. Hasselgård, S. Johansson, B. Behrens and F. Fabricius-Hansen (eds) *Information Structure in Cross-linguistic Perspective* (pp. 199–211). Amsterdam: Rodopi.

House, J. (2003) Misunderstanding in university encounters. In J. House, G. Kasper and S. Ross (eds) *Misunderstanding in Social Life. Discourse Approaches to Problematic Talk* (pp. 22–56). London: Longman.

House, J. (in press) Linguistic aspects of the translation of children's books. In *Translation-Übersetzung–Traduction. International Handbook on Translation*. Berlin: Mouton de Gruyter.

House, J. and Kasper, G. (1981) Politeness markers in English and German. In F. Coulmas (ed.) *Conversational Routine* (pp. 157–85). The Hague: Mouton.

Ide, S. (1989) Formal forms and discernment: Two neglected aspects of linguistic politeness. *Multilingua* 8, 223–48.

Jary, M. (1998) Relevance theory and the communication of politeness. *Journal of Pragmatics* 30, 1–19.

Lakoff, R.T. (1973) The logic of politeness; or, minding your p's and q's. *Papers from the Ninth Regional Meeting of the Chicago Linguistics Society,* (pp. 292–305). Chicago: Chicago Linguistics Society

Larrosa Gracia, P. (1998) Kulturelle Prägung des kommunikativen Handelns beim Telefonieren. MA Thesis, University of Hamburg.

Legrand, P. (1996) European legal systems are not converging. *International and Comparative Law Quarterly* 45, 52–81.

Möhl, S. (1996) Alltagssituationen im interkulturellen Vergleich: Realisierung von Kritik und Ablehnung im Deutschen und Englischen. MA Thesis, University of Hamburg.

Nouranian, M. (2000) Konflikte und Missverstaendnisse in der interkulturellen Kommunikation Deutsch–Persisch. MA Thesis, University of Hamburg.

Probst, J. (1997) Komplimentverhalten im Deutschen und Französischen. MA Thesis, University of Hamburg.

Reising, M. (1997) Entschuldigungsroutinen im interkulturellen Vergleich. MA Thesis, University of Hamburg.

Sifianou, M. (2002) 'Don't do the FTA' to be extremely polite? Paper delivered at the Fourteenth Sociolinguistics Symposium, Gent, 4 April.

Sperber, D. (1996) *Explaining Culture. A Naturalistic Approach.* Oxford: Blackwell.

Terkourafi, M. (2001) Politeness in Cypriotic Greek: A frame-based approach. PhD Dissertation, University of Cambridge.

Walters, J. (1979) Strategies for requesting in Spanish and English – structural similarities and pragmatic differences. *Language Learning* 9, 277–94.

Watts, R. (1989) Relevance and relational work: Linguistic politeness as politic behaviour. *Multilingua* 8, 131–66.

Weinrich, H. (1986) *Lügt man im Deutschen, wenn man höflich ist*? Mannheim: Bibliographisches Institut.

Wenger, E. (1998) *Communities of Practice.* Cambridge: University of Cambridge Press.

Chapter 2

Politeness in France: How To Buy Bread Politely

CATHERINE KERBRAT-ORECCHIONI

Introduction

It would be impossible, for a number of reasons, to give a comprehensive and accurate representation of what constitutes politeness in France. First, even if one reduces the definition of politeness to its verbal usage, the forms it can take in a given society still vary enormously. If one understands it as *all procedures that help maintain a minimum level of harmony within any exchange (despite the risk of conflict inherent in all exchanges*), politeness reveals itself to be multiform and all-pervasive in discourse, rather than a marginal phenomenon restricted to the well-known 'formulas' favoured by manuals on good manners and fine breeding.

Furthermore, 'manners' vary from one region to another within a country and depend on a number of sociolinguistic parameters, such as each speaker's age, social and cultural background. They vary, especially, according to the communicative situation and type of exchange going on: whether public or private, casual or institutional, face-to-face or by telephone, on radio or television, in writing or on the internet etc..

It has not yet been possible to collect empirical data for each and every type of exchange. Yet 'naturally occurring' data are, in my opinion, essential to get a clear idea of the workings of language. All other means of data-collecting (interviews, questionnaires, role plays, discourse completion tests, etc.) can, of course, highlight a number of pertinent facts[1] but the results obtained should not be taken as a faithful representation of reality – especially in France where pressure to conform to standards of correct speech remains strong[2] and where a gap exists between what people *think they say* and what they *actually say* (for example, we have noticed that statements produced 'artificially' contain more terms of address than real exchanges).

Rather than presume to give an all-encompassing overview of politeness, I will, therefore, examine how it functions in a particular setting, namely small shops.[3] Specifically, I will use the example of a bakery in a city centre part of Lyons, a relatively representative setting of 'ordinary' use of language, set mid-distance between the familiarity of casual conversation and the formality found within other types of institutional setting. I will conclude with some broader considerations linked to this.

Theoretical Framework: A 'Revamped' Brown and Levinson Model

Politeness as face-work

I will adopt the core idea of Brown and Levinson's (initially Goffman's) theory, in which politeness equals 'face-work', that is a desire to preserve one's territory ('negative face') and self-esteem ('positive face'): on the one hand, one finds all speakers carry within them a 'face-want'; on the other, most speech acts likely to be accomplished in our day-to-day lives are potentially 'threatening' in relation to one or more of the 'faces' of the interlocutors (consequently they are called Face-Threatening Acts, (FTAs)). This introduces a high risk in terms of exchanges going without a hitch. Hence, there is a need for the intervention of face-work, which smooths out and 'polishes'[4] the sharp edges of the FTAs we are likely to perform, making them less hurtful to our interlocutors' face. This work is made up, first, of indirect speech acts, alongside a wide range of *softeners* and *mitigators* which politeness experts have catalogued and described in detail. For example, there are: preliminaries, disarmers, grounders, hedges, downtoners, sweeteners, cajolers, diverse forms of repair and minimisation, etc., with each language showing a preference for this or that type of softener.

Face-threatening and face-flattering acts

This theory has been criticised for being overly pessimistic – verging on a 'paranoid' vision of exchanges[5] (a minefield of FTAs which need to be constantly defused) and of interlocutors (who have a siege mentality with constant threats hanging over their heads, faces and territories, and which they must eternally 'guard' against). While much so-called 'polite' behaviour fits this definition, on a more positive note, politeness also consists in producing 'anti-threats' (given that face-work aims both to save one's face and to expand on it). While many speech acts may be potentially threatening for the participants' faces, these same faces can also be enhanced via a 'thank you', a good wish or a compliment (which Brown and Levinson consider to be FTAs for the negative face of the receiver, when it is primarily an 'anti-threat' to the positive face of the same receiver). It is, therefore, of utmost importance to highlight, in this theoretical model, the role of these acts, which are like the positive side of the FTAs, acts that reinforce the other's face and which I suggest we call FFAs (Face-Flattering Acts).[6]

Every speech act could, therefore, be described as an FTA, an FFA, or a compound of the two. In correlation, two forms of politeness emerge from this theoretical base: *negative politeness,* which involves avoiding or softening the formulation of an FTA (as a way of saying 'I wish you no harm'); and *positive politeness,* which involves the production of an FFA, possibly reinforced (as a way of saying 'I wish you well'). Seen from this vantage point, the ebb and flow of an exchange involves a constant and subtle swinging back and forth between FTAs and FFAs as the following examples show.

(1) *Negative politeness.* A offends B via an FTA and instantly tries to patch things up via an apology (an FFA). The greater the 'weight' of the FTA is (measurable only in the context of the communicative framework in which the act is taking place), the greater the repair-work required to repair things again will be.
(2) *Positive politeness.* A does B some favour (FFA), and it is up to B to find the appropriate FFA ('thank you' or other sign of appreciation) as a way of re-establishing the ritual balance between the participants (in the logic of 'give and take' or 'one good turn deserves another'): the greater the weight of the initial FFA is, the greater the effort needed in the counter-FFA will be.

Introducing the notion of FFAs allows us to clarify further the notions of 'negative' *versus* 'positive' politeness (which, in the standard model, remain somewhat confusing[7]) and to re-examine the classification of politeness strategies.[8] It also allows us to make the model more coherent and, above all, stronger: linguistic facts explainable by such a model are numerous and diverse. For instance, the formulation of speech acts largely depends on the status of the act under consideration in relation to the system of faces (as well as a range of considerations linked to the specificity of each situation). Generally speaking, it would appear that the following can be found within polite communication:[9]

(1) FTAs tend to be softened, in particular, via an indirect speech act, 'conventionalised' or not. For example, a French waiter may ask customers what they want with *Vous prenez quelque chose?* (Are you having anything?) (a yes/no question which stands for a wh-question), whereas the customers cannot ask how much they owe with the formula *Je vous dois quelque chose?* (Do I owe you anything?): it is considered polite for the waiter to seem not to force the customer to

have something; but it would be impolite for customers to pretend that they have no obligation to pay.

(2) FFAs, by contrast, tend to need reinforcing. For example, a 'thank you' in French is very often upgraded: *merci beaucoup/ mille fois/ infiniment* (lit. thanks a lot/ a thousand times/ infinitely) but never downgraded: *merci un peu* (lit. thanks a little) would be considered incorrect from a pragmatic point of view – except when the utterance stands for a request or a reproach, that is an FTA: *Tu pourrais me dire un petit merci!* (lit. you could say a little thank you to me!).

(3) When it comes to 'mixed' speech acts, such as offerings, one notices that they are routinely both softened and reinforced. *Mais reprenez-en donc un peu!* (lit. But have just a little bit more) is an utterance in which the reinforcers *mais* and *donc* deal with the FFA component of the speech act (showing concern for the addressee), whereas the softener *un peu* deals with the FTA (due to the offering being an 'impositive' action).

Data Analysis: Politeness at the Bakery

For our first example, we transcribe a complete transaction while the second covers only the beginning of a different transaction. The elements that relate to face-work are in bold, showing the 'pervasive' nature of politeness.

Example 1

1 **B:** ***madame bonjour?***
2 **C:** *je **voudrais** un pain aux céréales* **[*s'il vous plaît***
3 **B:** [*oui*
4 **C:** *et une baguette à l'ancienne*
5 **B:** *et une baguette* (bruit de sac en papier) *treize soixante-dix* ***s'il vous plaît*** (C pose un billet de 200F) ***merci*** (C farfouille dans son porte-monnaie) *vous voulez me donner d'la monnaie?*
6 **C:** ***heu::*** *vingt centimes* ***c'est tout c'que j'ai***
7 **B:** ***heu*** *non ça va pas m'arranger* ***merci*** (**sourire**)
8 **C:** ***excusez-moi***
9 **B:** ***oh mais c'est rien j'vais me débrouiller*** *alors sur deux cents francs ça fait cent quatre-vingt-six trente (.) cent cinquante soixante soixante-dix hum quatre-vingt-cinq quatre-vingt-six (.) vingt et trente* ***voilà on y arrive***
10 **C:** ***je vous r'mercie***
11 **B:** ***c'est moi (.) merci madame bon week-end au r'voir***
12 **C:** ***merci au r'voir***

1 **B:** **good morning madam?**
2 **C:** **I would like** a multigrain loaf [**please**
3 **B:** [yes
4 **C:** and a regular breadstick
5 **B:** and a breadstick (*sound of paper bag*) thirteen seventy **please** (*C puts down 200F*) **thank you** (*C searches in her purse*) are you looking for small change?
6 **C:** **er::** twenty centimes is **all I've got**
7 **B:** **er** no that won't quite do it **thanks** (***smile***)
8 **C:** **sorry about that**
9 **B:** **oh never mind I'll manage** so with 200 francs that's one eighty six thirty (.) a hundred and fifty sixty seventy hum eighty five and six (.) twenty and thirty **see we made it**
10 **C:** **thanks a lot**
11 **B:** **No my pleasure (.) thank you madam have a good week-end good bye**
12 **C:** **thank you good bye**

Example 2

1 **B:** *madame?*
2 **C:** *une baguette **s'il vous plaît***
3 **B:** *les baguettes elles sont au four y en a pour cinq **p'tites** minutes **y en a pas pour longtemps hein** il manque **un tout p'tit peu** d'cuisson **simplement***

1 **B:** madam?
2 **C:** a breadstick **please**
3 **B:** the sticks they're in the oven for another five **little** minutes **it won't be long eh just a tiny bit more** baking **that's all**

The politeness is concentrated in the opening and closing sections (whose function is essentially 'ritual'), but remains to a lesser extent throughout the transaction.

The opening section

The opening occurs largely via the *greeting act,* which is nearly always offered first by the baker (B), and happens in 90% of the exchanges that make up the corpus (60 exchanges in total).[10] The initial greeting can take one of two main forms:

- *Bonjour!* (Hello!)[11] (with the option of a term of address preceding or following the greeting): The exclamation mark, in this case, signals a descending intonation, making it a genuine greeting. It is used mainly in 'take your time shops' (eg. a shoe-shop), and secondarily in 'stream-of-customers shops', when the saleswoman acknowledges a new customer arriving even though she is currently involved in serving a previous customer. This type of initial greeting is usually followed by a response from the customer arriving.
- (*Madame*) *bonjour?* (Hello (Madam)?): the rising intonation gives the utterance a questioning value (May I help you?) added to the initial value of the greeting. At the same time as having these two illocutionary values, the formula has two functions: ritual and transactional. This 'pragmatic compound' allows for a speeding up of events (via the application of the 'celerity principle', which governs most exchanges in service encounters).[12] In this case, a reply is optional and the customer can go straight into his/her request without the shortcut giving any sense of truncation.

The closing section

Closing rituals are usually even more conspicuous than opening rituals and they are more drawn out. Beyond the swapping of greetings (generally via a pair of *au revoir*), the closing of the transaction carries within it other ritualised reciprocated acts charged with a light-heartedness which aims to brighten up the moment of parting.[13] We find the following mostly:

- The expression of a wish: *Bonne journée* (Have a nice day), *Bonne fin de journée* (Have a nice evening), *Bonne soirée* (Have a good evening), *Bon week-end* (Have a good week-end), *Bon dimanche* (lit. Have a good Sunday, etc.). In our 'Bakery' corpus, one out of two examples makes use of such a wish. Generally, it has become the custom, in France, to have a wish element in exchange closures: on the phone, especially, it is now very rare not to find a wish component at the end of the conversation, always following the same syntactic structure (*Bon X*) but varied in its lexical choices: *Bon courage* (Be brave), *Bon Mac* (Good Macintosh), *Bonne salade* (Good salad), *Bonnes courses* (Good shopping), *Bon cinoche* (Good movie), *Bon Woody Allen* (Good Woody Allen), etc. Depending on the situation, one often reacts to the wish by reciprocating it (*vous aussi* [you too], in the French spoken in the Hexagon[14]) or by a mere *merci*. Let us note that this last option is not available after a greeting, hence the difference between *Bonne soirée!* (wish) – *Merci* and *Bonsoir*! (greeting) – **Merci*: the initial greeting is

not considered to be an FFA carrying enough 'weight' to justify the manifestation of gratitude in 'thank you'. Although the wish formula may sometimes act as a substitute for the greeting (*Au revoir madame – Bonne journée!* (Good bye madam – have a nice day)), the two speech acts should not be seen as being totally equivalent.
- Beyond the 'thank you' responding to a wish, the closing greeting can also contain a speech act or an exchange of 'thank yous' that function as a summing up or endorsement of the transaction (meaning, for customer and vendor respectively, something like: 'Thanks for the great deal' and 'Thanks for preferring us over the competition – come back soon!').

For the seller, the most complete closing routine (where the order of these components varies considerably) would, therefore, be:

- *Merci bonne journée madame au revoir* (thank you have a nice day madam good bye)
- *Passez une bonne journée au revoir madame merci!* (have a nice day good bye madam thank you!)

'Thank yous'

This speech act appears five times in the first excerpt (three from B and two from C). In the corpus recorded at the bakery, the number of 'thank yous' rises to an average of 3.6 per transaction, a considerable number given the brevity of the encounters. The 'thank yous' appear, as we have seen, in the closing sequence (after a wish or as a closure device). They occur also within the encounter, after receiving the product and possibly the change (C) and after being paid (B).

It is worth emphasising that in this context not only are the 'thank yous' numerous but also reciprocated: in France, shopkeeper/customer relationships are seen as ones of *mutual indebtedness*[15] which is far from universal.

Asking for the product

During the transaction, politeness manifests itself in different places and forms. In our survey we will examine, first, the act that sets off the transactional sequence: the request for the product.

This request can be seen as both an initiating and a reactive act in that it is a response to the salesperson's inquiry either in the form of a question-greeting or as a genuine question: *Qu'est-ce qu'elle veut la dame?* (lit. What does the lady require?), *Vous désirez?* (What would you like?), *Qu'est-ce que je vous sers?* (What can I get you?) or the more elliptical: *Dites-moi!* (Tell me!), *À nous!* (Our turn!) or *À nous deux!* (It is down to us!) (one can see in the first example the use of the third person to indicate the addressee[16] and, in the last two, the 'we of solidarity').

When it comes to the formulation of the customer's request, what stands out is that *it is systematically softened*:

- The direct formula (*Donnez-moi X* (Give me X)) is very rarely found and it is always accompanied by *s'il vous plaît* (please);
- This softener also invariably accompanies the elliptical phrase (*X s'il vous plaît!)*, whose interpretation is very problematic. Is the missing bit a *Donnez-moi* (Give me), a *Je veux* (I want) or a *Je voudrais* (I would like)? Is this phrase 'brutal' or the opposite – a form of politeness where the abbreviation is a time-saving device, taking into account the other people's needs (the salesperson and other customers)?
- In most cases the request is expressed indirectly,
  – either in the form of an assertion: *Je vais prendre X* (I am going to take X) or, more frequently*: Je voudrais X* (I would like X), an affirmation of a want couched in the conditional mode,[17] which has to be seen, in French, as the softener 'par excellence' for requests and other 'directive' acts;
  – or as a question on the availability of the product: *Vous avez X?* (Have you got X?), *Je voudrais savoir si vous avez des meringues au chocolat* (I would like to know if you have chocolate meringues), etc.

These different wordings are not necessarily interchangeable. The question form is used when the product is not instantly visible on the shelves or there is a doubt about its availability. By contrast, *Je vais prendre X* is used when the product is in evidence or readily available. Finally, *Je voudrais X* can be seen as the most 'passe-partout' wording for a request.

These request wordings warrant further examination given that, while a request would generally be considered an FTA (intruding on the receiver's territory), one cannot but imagine that the commercial context strips it of this 'threatening' quality, since the request is imposed by the 'script' of the exchange (indeed making no request might be threatening) and the receiver has more to gain than the person making the request (in this economic system of open competition). In this rather special case, one might suppose that the request may be perceived more as an FFA than an FTA. But the facts cannot be ignored and they force us to acknowledge that *even in this situation, the request retains some of its 'threatening' nature*, given that the speaker finds it necessary to soften the wording – a rather mild threat, however, since it is compensated by the benefits it suggests for the seller in an imminent sale: all it takes to make it polite is the use of the conditional form, whereas overdoing the softening via an apology (appropriate for 'repairing' genuine disruptions or offences) would seem too much (it would only be as a sort of ironical joke that one might contemplate using 'Pardon me for disturbing you, would you have any bread?', for example when faced with an overly-sluggish salesperson; here, 'hyper-politeness' would become impoliteness).

Apologies and other forms of 'beyond the basic routine' politeness

The apology manifests itself when the weight of the FTA increases beyond a certain point or when the customer has special requirements; for example, within our shop-based data, in relation to an elaborate flower arrangement: *Je vous embête excusez-moi* (I'm being a pain, forgive me); or when purchasing a pair of shoes: *Il me faut beaucoup de choses voyez pour me satisfaire excusez-moi!* (Forgive me but it takes a lot to get the perfect fit!). Apologies also appear in situations where the request goes beyond the predefined boundaries of the obligations understood to exist within the exchange script, like asking for directions or other 'services' – examples from our 'Garage' corpus: *Excusez-moi est-ce que vous auriez un jerricane vide?* (Excuse me would you have an empty petrol can?), or *Pardon madame c'est juste un p'tit service c'est juste pour euh régler l'air dans les pneus parce que j'sais pas faire marcher l'truc* (Excuse me madam I just need a bit of help to adjust the air in my tyres and I don't know how this thing works). The apology appears also in some 'incident', when something relatively unforeseen or 'off-script' occurs, as can be illustrated within our previous two examples.

In Example 1, there is the small change episode. When it comes to paying, C does not have the modest sum of 13.70F but rather a 200 franc note. She also offers, on the off chance (*heu*), an approximate amount, which she knows is unlikely to satisfy B (*vingt centimes c'est tout ce que j'ai* (twenty centimes is all I've got)); an offer which B refuses. Given that the refusal is a 'dispreferred choice' (being an FTA), it needs to be softened (*heu, merci*, smile). As for C, she has to face up to the failure of her attempt at being helpful to B. In turn, she needs to soften this 'offence' via an apology (*excusez-moi*), to which, as expected, B reacts by minimizing the affront (*oh mais c'est rien je vais me débrouiller* [oh never mind I'll manage]). Hence, this episode clearly illustrates how C and B vie with each other in politeness in order to neutralise the mini-FTAs that they have been driven to commit upon each other.

In Example 2, the 'incident' is of a different nature (while remaining just as typical): with the product not being immediately available, the situation has become an FTA for C (due to the increased waiting time), which B then tries to soften via the use of no fewer than four different expressions of minimisation. (Soon afterwards, B tries to lighten the FTA via another process: the offer *si vous voulez vous asseoir deux petites minutes* (lit. Why don't you have a seat for two little minutes)), an invitation in which the five minutes have miraculously shrunk to two...).

Conclusions

French-style politeness in small shops

From our observations on the way politeness works within an everyday transaction like buying bread, a number of conclusions emerge.

In the first, politeness reveals itself to be an all-pervasive, rather than a peripheral, component of social encounters: *more than half of the verbal material in our two examples has a ritual, rather than a transactional, function.*

In the second, the main strategies of politeness 'à la française', within our data and generally speaking, reveal themselves to be the 'thank yous' associated with positive politeness; the use of the *conditional* (mainly attached to requests) associated with negative politeness and the *minimizers* spread throughout all the recorded commercial exchanges gathered, going with all sorts of speech acts, and consisting principally of the adjective *petit* (lit. 'little') as conveyed in the translations of the following examples, in spite of the oddness of the English corresponding phrases), and secondarily of the adverbs *un peu* (a little) and *juste* (just).

Example from a pharmacy:

Je vous ai collé votre petite vignette (I've pasted your little sticker on your health form for you).

Example from a shoe-shop:

des petites choses comme ça sans talon (little ones like that without a heel); *les petites noires* (those little black ones); *un petit modèle* (a little model); *des petits mocassins* (little moccasins); *le petit décolleté* (the little open shoe); *des petits trous d'aération* (little air holes); *une petite semelle* (a thin little sole); *des petites socquettes* (little ankle socks); *un petit lacet* (little laces); *je prends un petit siège hop!* (I'll take a little seat right!); *c'est un peu grand là* (it's a bit big there); *elle est un peu plus lourde* (it's a bit heavier); *votre pouce il déborde un peu* (your big toe sticks out a bit); *ça me serre un peu* (it's a little tight); *peut-être un petit peu plus échancré* (perhaps a little bit more low-cut); *un tout petit peu plus haut* (just a little bit higher); *ils sont un peu chers* (they're a bit dear); *elles sont un tout petit peu plus chères* (they're just a little bit more expensive); *je vous laisse marcher un petit peu* (try walking round a little bit); *je vous montre juste la pointure* (I'll just show you the size); *juste pour voir* (just to see); *juste pour comparer* (just to compare).

Example from a newsagent's
(le client va prendre le journal *Le Pays Roannais* et le pose sur le comptoir)
C: *un p'tit Pays*
B: *un tout petit Pays des familles*
C: *un p'tit gris*
(B prend le paquet de tabac qu'elle pose sur le comptoir-caisse)
B: *un p'tit gris*
C: *et une grosse boîte d'allumettes*

(the customer picks up the paper *Le Pays Roannais* and puts it on the counter)

C: a little 'Pays'
B: a little 'Pays' for families
C: a little grey
(B takes a pouch of tobacco and puts it on the counter)
B: a little grey
C: and a large box of matches

(for the box of matches, it would not be possible to use *petit* as a softener as this would lead to a misunderstanding over the size required).

Hence, the adjective *petit* is polysemic in French: beyond its usual role in defining size, it is likely to carry a 'ritualised' meaning which has nothing to do with size, as illustrated in the following example, recorded at the butcher's:

C: *je voudrais un petit bifteck*
B: *un gros?*
C: *moyen*

C: I'd like a little steak
B: a large one?
C: medium-sized

It is worth noting that these minimisers also turn up, with approximately the same value, in other Romance languages such as Italian and Spanish; but in these languages, they most often take on a morphological form (diminutive suffix). In French, minimisation involves lexical choice.

Other relevant observations

From the observation of other exchange situations, the following facts (among others) emerge:

(1) During private *conversations on the telephone*, in France, it is the caller who identifies the two parties to the exchange. Contrary to telephone etiquette in Germany and Switzerland (including the French-speaking part), in France the person called does not feel the need to introduce him or herself when answering the telephone but merely answers 'hello' (which can sometimes lead to mistaken identity).
(2) *Greeting questions* are used to guarantee a smooth exchange between acquaintances. Both *comment allez-vous?* (how are you?) and the more familiar *ça va?* (you OK?) play an important role. They function as 'complementary greetings' without losing all of their original question-value. Used in this way, they pave the way for a smooth transition from the greeting exchange, which functions on a purely phatic level, to the main part of the conversation (see Kerbrat-Orecchioni, 2001: 110–22; Traverso, 1996: 70–5).
(3) *Terms of address* (first names or *Monsieur/Madame*,[18] depending on the relationship between the speakers) are rarely used nowadays in most French communicative situations. Beyond their traditional use for identifying and calling, they seem to arise preferably when 'tension' mounts within an exchange, becoming loaded with a polemic tinge. Anyhow, it would be wrong to interpret systematically as impolite the absence of a term of address alongside a greeting or a 'thank you', despite what 'proper etiquette' manuals are still recommending.

In search of a French 'ethos'

Having collected a broad range of examples of politeness in France, it is tempting to try to deduce a set of overall principles from the data. It seems reasonable to think that the various behavioural trends observed within the same community obey an underlying uniting principle. So, one could imagine that a systematic description of these behaviours within the data might add up to a 'communicative profile' or 'ethos' for that community. At this point there are difficulties in generalising in this domain.

For instance, it is worth asking if France tends more towards negative politeness (as in northern Europe) or positive politeness (as in southern Europe). There can be no doubt that negative politeness is well represented in France: apologies are systematically used to 'repair' the slightest territorial intrusion (physical touching that is 'out of place', lateness and other kinds of disturbance) and, as we have seen, requests are regularly softened by indirect formulation, justification or some distancing device (e.g. the use of the conditional or the 'polite past': *Je voulais vous demander si…* (I wanted to ask you if...), *Je vous appelais parce que…* (I was ringing you because...)). And yet *everything is relative* in this area: our French request formulas may seem rather blunt to the English ear (instead of *Vous pourriez fermer la porte?* (Could you close the door?)), they might prefer even more softening as in 'Would you mind closing the door?'); and our respect for others' time seems moderate to Germans who have a stricter concept of what constitutes punctuality.[19] However, positive politeness also plays an important role in the daily lives of the French, given the ongoing frequency of compliments, thanks and good wishes.

The situation is just as confusing when it comes to the management of interpersonal relationships:

(1) On the 'vertical' relationship front, the work conducted by Hofstede has popularised the view that French behaviour is greatly influenced by a sense of hierarchy. This is undoubtedly true amongst business people and administrators but should not be generalised for all communication. In the French academic world, for example, addressing people by their official title has virtually disappeared (which is not the case in some of the countries around France). It is worth noting also that, overall, situations where an asymmetric use of the pronoun of address (*tu–vous*) serves to express a hierarchical relationship are becoming very rare, the pronoun being essentially used symmetrically, to express distance or familiarity.
(2) On the 'horizontal' relationship front, the number of situations in which one chooses to use *vous* rather than *tu* is greater in France than in most neighbouring countries. And yet our proxemics (interpersonal distance) is closer than in northern Europe and eye-contact and body contact remain more frequent (starting with our famous French 'bise' or kiss on the cheek).
(3) Finally, the French have a reputation for being more inclined to veer towards conflict than consensus. There is their self-assertive style (*moi je pense que...* (lit. me I think that...)), the bluntness of their disagreements (illustrated in the frequency of expressions such as: *oui mais* (yes but), *oui mais attends* (yes but wait), *oui mais justement* (yes but precisely), *mais non* (of course not) or *oui mais non* (yes but no)), the stubbornness of their counter-attacks, their inability to compromise and, above all, their lack of respect for the other person's right to speak and be heard (permanent interruptions, repeated overlapping with other people's turns)[20] – leading one to conclude that the French are, indeed, rather arrogant.

I will not dare to take a stand on the validity of this stereotype. Nevertheless, I would point out that, when it comes to interruptions, one should not see them as solely serving the cause of impoliteness: very often they help speed up the tempo of a conversation, they can brighten up an exchange and make it sparkle, give it warmth, spontaneity and a sense that everyone is fully involved (for similarities with Spanish politeness, see Hickey, this volume) – all qualities that are much appreciated in our society. In contrast, a conversation where turn-taking is meekly and mechanically maintained without any interruption and overlapping is seen as boring. But our northern neighbours have a different set of cultural values through which they continue to see this tendency to interrupt as aggressive and unbearable. Hence, *it is not just behaviour that varies from one culture to another but also the way it is judged in relation to the value system that supports it.* The unfavourable judgements that regularly arise in relation to other cultures (according to a recent survey, 19% of the English see the French as the most impolite nation on earth[21]) are often based on a set of misunderstandings.

In conclusion, I will note that the French conversational style seems, on many fronts, to be halfway between that of the northern and the southern European countries. However, we must remain cautious about generalisations, since we do not possess comprehensive empirical evidence. Authentic data will continue to be a vital safeguard against stereotyping and 'preconceived ideas', which can help to advance intercultural research – while being its worst enemy.

Notes

1. See, for example, the work of the CCSARP (Cross-Cultural Speech Act Research Project) on requests and apologies in different languages and societies (Blum-Kulka *et al.* 1989), collected via discourse completion tests.
2. The existence of institutions such as the Académie Française (founded in 1634) effectively illustrates the importance the French place on the linguistic norm.
3. Our research team, GRIC (Groupe de Recherche sur les Interactions Communicatives, CNRS-Université Lyon 2 now ICAR), has been working on this type of exchange for several years now and has, at its disposal, considerable data on the subject.
4. In French, the term *politesse* ('politeness') is derived from the verb *polir* ('to polish').
5. Cf. Kasper (1990: 194): 'The theory represents an overly pessimistic, rather paranoid view of human social interaction'.
6. Others use the similar expressions 'Face-Enhancing Act' or 'Face-Giving Act'.
7. Defined in a far clearer way by Leech (1983: 83–4): 'Negative politeness therefore consists in minimizing the impoliteness of impolite illocutions, and positive politeness consists in maximizing the politeness of polite illocutions.'
8. See Kerbrat-Orecchioni (1992).

9. Bearing in mind that not every type of exchange pertains to this kind of communication. We can, however, consider as 'marked' exchanges those that are fundamentally 'impolite'.
10. Without taking into account non-verbal greetings, given that only sound was recorded.
11. In French there are two main formulas for greeting, *bonjour* and *bonsoir*. It is worth noting the rarity of *bonsoir* (good evening) in our corpus (despite the data having been recorded during the winter months) : the term is clearly 'marked', making it a more formal alternative. Moreover, there is a tendency for the customers to use it more than the salespeople, no doubt due to their coming regularly in from outside carrying with them a greater awareness of time passing and fading daylight.
12. An even more economical variation: just the term of address with a rising melody (*Madame?*), used in Example 2.
13. For more information on this aspect of closing rituals, see Kerbrat-Orecchioni, (1990: 22–3).

    Regarding the attempts at 'departure brightening' one could also mention the fact that, in French, *adieu* (which implies that the two persons are not going to meet again) is somewhat 'taboo': the use of this form is automatically avoided by the speaker even if he/she thinks there is not any chance for him/her to see the other speaker ever again. It is as though our ritualistic conventions dictate that, at the moment of separation, we must 'make believe' that there *is* a chance that the current conversation could be picked up again later. The greeting must remain merely an *au revoir* and nothing final. (Of course, in some parts of France and French-speaking Switzerland where *adieu* means in fact *au revoir*, the word is regularly used).
14. In other varieties of French (for example in French-speaking Switzerland), one finds *merci pareillement* (lit. thank you equally), which has the same meaning.
15. This indebtedness is, however, less of a burden for the client than for the salesperson who tends to thank the other more often and who systematically says *C'est moi (qui vous remercie)* (lit. it's me [who should thank you]) when the first 'thank you' is uttered by the client.
16. This third person usage is found mainly amongst shopkeepers.
17. The conditional present, and politer still, the conditional past (*J'aurais voulu...* [lit. I would have liked...]), which corresponds to the 'pessimistic strategy' according to Brown and Levinson (1987: 183).
18. At times accompanied by the family name (*Bonjour madame Martin!*). This usage, generally banned from 'proper French', is a typical habit amongst French shopkeepers who use it to show that they recognise their most faithful customers.

    Overall, the degree of politeness within a given utterance in French is less based on terms of address than in other languages such as Russian or Brasilian Portuguese. In these languages, politeness within an utterance will be transmitted via the use of 'cajoling' terms of address rather than by an indirect speech act.

19. For a comparison of how the French and Germans view their spatial and temporal territories, see Hall and Hall, (1990).
20. This behaviour is just as evident in the context of casual conversations as in professional ones (see Geoffroy, 2001).
21. Mentioned in the newspaper *Libération*, 23 January 2002.

References

Blum-Kulka, S., House, J. and G. Kasper (eds) (1989) *Cross-cultural Pragmatics: Requests and Apologies*. Norwood, NJ: Ablex.

Brown, P. and Levinson, S. (1987) *Politeness: Some Universals in Language Usage*. Cambridge: Cambridge University Press.

Geoffroy, C. (2001) Anglais et Français partenaires de travail. Regards croisés sur quelques pratiques linguistiques et communicatives. In G. Paganini (ed.) *Différences et proximités culturelles: l'Europe* (pp. 137–52). Paris: L'Harmattan.

Goffman, E. (1974) *Les rites d'interaction*. Paris: Minuit.

Hall, E. T. and Hall, M. R. (1990) *Guide du comportement dans les affaires internationales. Allemagne, Etats-Unis, France*. Paris, Seuil.

Kasper, G. (1990) Linguistic politeness: Current research issues. *Journal of Pragmatics* 14: 193–218.

Kerbrat-Orecchioni, C. (1990, 1992, 1994) *Les interactions verbales* (Vols I, II, III). Paris: Armand Colin.

Kerbrat-Orecchioni, C. (2001) *Les actes de langage dans le discours*. Paris: Nathan.

Leech, G. N. (1983) *Principles of Pragmatics*. London: Longman.

Traverso, V. (1996) *La conversation familière*. Lyon: PUL.

Chapter 3

Politeness in Belgium: Face, Distance and Sincerity in Service-exchange Rituals

EMMANUELLE DANBLON, BERNARD DE CLERCK
AND JEAN-PIERRE VAN NOPPEN

Wedged between the North Sea, The Netherlands, Germany and France, Belgium has earned the dual status of battlefield and crossroads between cultures and languages. It straddles the frontier between Germanic and Romance languages and consequently is split into three language communities – Dutch (in its Belgian variety), French and German, the first two being in constant 'contact and conflict' (Nelde, 1997). This affects (or infects) almost every aspect of political, economic and social life (Baetens Beardsmore, 1981), including patterns of politeness.

Of course, not all differences in politeness behaviour in Belgium can be attributed to the binary contrast between Dutch and French: massive immigration in recent decades, for instance, may explain observable differences and occasional clashes between civility and politeness patterns of groups with different cultural and religious backgrounds (Gajjout, 1997; Janssens, 1999). But within the limited purview of this chapter we wish to draw attention to a few aspects of politeness linked to this situation where two languages, (Southern) Dutch and French, enjoy a relationship of interaction and interference. Van der Wijst (1996, 2000) has compared politeness strategies in French and Dutch, albeit within the context of business negotiations, where the need to achieve optimal understanding naturally encourages mutual accommodation (cf. Giles & Powesland, 1975: 157–66), thus playing down the potential for confrontation inherent in the choice of language.

The Choice of Language

> When I spoke to her in French, she answered me in Flemish,
> with an air the reverse of civil. (C. Brontë: *The Professor*).

In bilingual situations, especially in Brussels, where language is both instrument and symbol in a shifting power situation (Baetens Beardsmore,

1999), the question 'who speaks what language to whom and when' (Fishman, 1965; O'Driscoll, 1999) is a strategic one. Anecdotal accounts report on forms of non-accommodating behaviour whereby speakers demand to be served or addressed in their own language, and/or respond to someone's failure to do so with irritation, anger or even insults, showing that language choice is a negotiable demand in a potentially conflictive situation.

From a Brown and Levinson perspective, S should adopt H's language to save H's negative face. However, a *de facto* imbalance prevails because speakers of Dutch are often more motivated to learn and speak French than the other way around. In this context, one may imagine a situation where F is French-speaking but tries to address the Dutch-speaking D in Dutch or Flemish. D, noticing F's limited command of Dutch, may resort to either of two strategies: respond in French to save F considerable effort, leading to an unsatisfactory result, or pretend not to notice F's poor performance, and continue in D's own language. Both strategies may be interpreted as polite, with the speaker intending to respect the interlocutor's face-wants, thus conditioning the affective climate of the exchange as a whole; but, paradoxically, the same choices may also be read as face-threatening, since addressees may interpret the use of one linguistic code rather than another as a curtailment of their freedom (and, hence, as potential damage to their negative face); likewise it can threaten positive face, since the lack of accommodation may indicate a refusal to claim common ground and solidarity. Even accommodation might be perceived as a patronising face-threatening act (FTA), implying that the efforts of one's interlocutor are not appreciated and/or insufficient for effective interaction.

In practice, however, such research as has been done on language use and attitudes in workers and students tends to show that, in a society where bilingualism is a highly rated skill, speakers of Dutch, though acutely aware of their right to speak and be addressed in their own language, will not infrequently shift to French when the interlocutor's skill seems uncertain (Baetens Beardsmore, 1988; Panowitsch, 1996), thus deriving an indirect advantage by maximising the cost to themselves while saving the addressees' positive face.

More typical of the Belgian situation, however, are those cases where politeness strategies in one language are conditioned by transfer or interference from the other. Lexical, grammatical and phonological interference between Dutch and French works both ways. The transfer of politeness strategies, however, seems to take place especially from Dutch to French. Van der Wijst (2000) states that in exchanges between members of different language communities, deviance in the marking of politeness is likely to be caused by the speaker's mother tongue or culture; but, in Belgium, some transfers, though originating in Germanic language habits, have also found their way into the French of non-bilinguals.

Van der Wijst has highlighted differences in the distribution between French and Dutch of downtoners, understatements, diminutives and other forms of tentativeness. A typical transfer of one such difference is the appearance of the adverbial phrase *une fois* (once) in Belgian French, a modal phrase frequently mocked, but poorly imitated, by French comedians (Baetens Beardsmore, 1971: 247–8). In Dutch and German, the corresponding particles (*eens* and *mal* respectively) are not always, or necessarily, used as downtoners: their politeness function is only one of several possible contextual interpretations, which hints that the timing of an order, request or suggestion may be inconvenient, but that the action solicited must be performed eventually if not immediately (Foolen, 1993; Weydt, 1969). In his study of the Brussels equivalent *une fois*, De Vriendt (1985) has shown that this is an Illocutionary Force Indicating Device potentially marking a request but that, in this function, it must operate in conjunction with other markers like negation and interrogation: *tu [ne] veux pas une fois ouvrir la porte pour le chat?*, whereas with imperatives, it acts as an illocutionary force softener.

In this study we will focus specifically on a set of politeness markers whose frequency is noted by foreign visitors as typically Belgian, i.e. the 'ritual' interchanges (Goffman, 1967) taking place during service encounters, everyday routines during which goods are exchanged (Merritt, 1976: 321).

Kuiper (1996) has shown that, at the centre of any formulaic tradition, there are discourse-structure rules and an inventory of formulae. Among the characteristic formulae appearing in service-encounter scenarios, the Dutch and French equivalents of 'please' and 'thank you' (*alstublieft/alsjeblieft, s'il vous plaît/s'il te plaît, dank U wel/dank je wel, merci*) are prominent. When asking lay people to define politeness, they are very likely to answer 'saying please and thank you'. These forms of first-order politeness (Kienpointner, 1999), taught to children, affect subsequent behaviour so overtly that foreigners (and even some Belgians) comment on their frequent, almost compulsive, use in everyday service exchanges.

Ideally, speakers' choices should, in a sociopragmatic perspective (Martiny, 1996), correlate with variants like the relationship between participants, sex, age, social and economic background, presence of an audience, nature and function of the speech act, recourse to other linguistic devices (e.g. collocation with different terms of address) and non-linguistic resources (like body language). In this chapter, however, we restrict ourselves to only a few parameters in this complex configuration, focusing notably, but not exclusively, on the formula *alstublieft / s'il vous plaît*.

Alstublieft/S'il vous plaît

Youngster to barman: *Donnez-moi un whisky.*
Barman (who has several brands of whisky): *Un whisky comment?*
Youngster (sheepishly): *Un whisky, s'il vous plaît, Monsieur.*

Etymologically, both *alstublieft* and *s'il vous plaît* originate in a sentence construction which (like the English 'please') literally means 'if you please' or 'if it pleases you' but whose use, though diachronically rooted in negative politeness, has today become totally formulaic. These formulae interrelate with other politeness markers as in both Dutch and French they include second-person pronouns: French marks the difference between *tu* and *vous* (Brown & Gilman, 1960) and standard Dutch between *jij* and *U*, which allows a choice in terms of interpersonal status (distance, age, familiarity, politeness and power/solidarity). Southern Dutch and the Flemish dialects display a more complex three-pronged system *Jij/Gij/U*, where *Gij* distinguishes neither number nor status. Given the widespread diglossia, however, the three forms are frequently mixed and sometimes indistinguishable, with some overlapping (De Vriendt, 1995). In the situations we observed, however, the contrast between familiar and polite pronouns was only of marginal importance.

In Dutch, *alstublieft* can accompany both requests and acts of giving, unlike standard French, where *s'il vous plaît* is used only in requests (for requests and thanks see Kerbrat-Orecchioni, this volume). It has been observed that Belgian French, however, uses *s'il vous plaît* similarly to *alstublieft*, i.e. both when asking and when giving something.

The Data

Our observations are based on a total of 300 real-life (unscripted, non-experimental) service encounters, 100 from each region (Flanders, Wallonia, Brussels), recorded/observed in different shops at different times. In Flanders, the exchanges were recorded in several village bakeries; in Wallonia, at a neighbourhood grocer's shop; in Brussels, in a variety of situations (sandwich shop, post office, chemist's, butcher's, baker's, pastry shop and fast-food outlet) in middle-class areas. Precautions were taken to avoid interference from the recording/observation situation, respecting the informants' right to privacy. The salespersons were mostly aware of our activity and initially may have been somewhat self-conscious, though they were told the object of the research only after each session.

The results, compiled in one large chart (van Noppen *et al.*, 2002), are presented region by region, divided into use of the various politeness markers by shop assistants and customers during their turns in the interactions. The scenario used is a maximal one, with all turns being represented: request, giving and taking goods, request for payment, giving and taking payment, giving and receiving change, final greetings. Not all these turns appear in all exchanges, nor in that order: they may overlap or be telescoped, as when the request for payment accompanies the handover of goods, the customer knows the price and gives the exact amount, or payment precedes the handover of goods. In other cases, interactants may be untalkative or use only body language, especially when, say, a non-service-related conversation is going on between them. Furthermore, not all turns in the exchange may be marked for politeness, whether formulae or terms of address, modals, downtoners, tentativeness, indirectness etc.

Of course, 100 encounters per region cannot be very representative of a whole country. Especially in Brussels, where a variety of exchanges were observed, it became clear that shops have different styles and different visits might have yielded different results. It is prudent, then, to focus mainly on the patterns that clearly emerge from a comprehensive view of the data, regarding comparisons between regions as more tentative indications.

Region, language and interference

Obviously, the service exchanges in Flanders were in Dutch/Flemish, and in Wallonia in French. Of the 100 exchanges observed in Brussels, only one was in Dutch. Exchanges in different boroughs might have yielded different proportions; but some salespersons and customers were clearly Dutch speakers who switched to French in a 'polite' effort to identify with their addressees or with the prevailing linguistic environment.

In Flanders, the typical marker accompanying handovers of goods, money or change was *alstublieft*, without a term of address or, more rarely, a phonologically-adapted form of the French *voilà*. The appearance of *voilà* and *merci* shows that interaction between the two languages here takes the form of lexical borrowing. No similar borrowing of Dutch politeness markers by French speakers was observed either in Brussels or Wallonia. Both languages offer their users the same politeness potential (formulae to mark requests, handovers, thanks, with embedded personal pronouns to mark interpersonal relationships). Whether Belgian regions honour different politeness policies is doubtful and could not be established by the limited evidence provided here. We may infer, however, that there is a marked difference between behaviour patterns in village and city shops.

The Flemish bakers and the Walloon grocer knew many of their customers and shopping, besides its instrumental role, seemed to fulfil a social function, together with gossip and friendly banter. This was particularly noticeable in the grocer's shop, whose owner would use customers' first names and *tu* during the conversations, though rarely in the service exchanges themselves; while in Brussels, many of the encounters were reduced to the minimal requirements of the situation, with the *tu* form altogether absent. In Flanders and Wallonia, recourse to politeness markers was, respectively, 1.5 and 1.25 times higher than in Brussels. If this behaviour is to be accounted for in terms of Brown and Levinson's theory, then we shall have to allow for the fact that, contrary to what their theory suggests, decreasing Distance between participants correlates with increased Politeness.

Requests for goods or payment

Not all sale requests contained politeness formulae. In Flanders, about 60% of the 100 requests contained them, in Brussels a little less than half, and in Wallonia 42%. Among these marked items, the most frequent politeness formula was *alstublieft/s'il vous plaît*, followed by modal indicators of tentativeness like *je voudrais/ik zou graag* (I would like) or *pourrais-je/mag ik...* (Could I ...). Unmarked requests were mostly plain statements: *Un fromage, un thon* (one cheese [sandwich], one tuna); or, more rarely, imperatives: *donnez-moi* (Give me). If one postulates that salespersons are expected or 'obliged' to serve their customers (Merritt, 1976: 321), a sales request will, theoretically, be perceived as a threat to their negative face; however, customers grace the shop-owner with their patronage and the sales request will prove more commercially beneficial than threatening to the provider. Our theory will have to account for this tension.

Similarly, customers are expected to pay for the goods or services they receive. In Brussels, many customers presuppose or accept this, and not infrequently, payment – even correct change – is tendered without any verbal incentive from the shop assistant. However, in shops where one person serves and another is at the till or where the price is not known in advance, requests for payment are dressed up in much politeness, as if making customers part with their money were a face-threatening act or a favour to be solicited. Here, the only politeness marker is *alstublieft/s'il vous plaît*, most often without a term of address. The unmarked requests take the form of statements: *Dat is dan vier Euro twintig* (That will be 4 Euro 20, then).

Giving and receiving goods or money

In general, the shopowners and assistants use more politeness markers than their customers (see Kerbrat-Orecchioni, this volume). The exchange of goods is a clear example: in the 300 transactions observed, 243 salespersons used politeness formulas when handing over the merchandise, while only 75 customers responded with thanks.

In Flanders, the most frequent formula is, again, *alstublieft*, with the less formal *zo zie* and the French *voilà* (there you are) as infrequent alternatives. This use of *alstublieft* (if you please) is standard in Dutch. In Brussels and in French-speaking Belgium, we find not only *voici* and *voilà*, which correspond to standard French usage, but also *s'il vous plaît*, which is not used for this purpose in France. Had the proportion of *s'il vous plaît* over *voici/voilà* been higher in Brussels than in Wallonia, one might have presumed a transfer, not of the Dutch lexical item, but of the cultural habit, on to French by virtue of the language-contact situation in the capital (Van Uytfanghe, 1978: 86; Baetens Beardsmore, 1998: 96). However, the relative proportion of *s'il vous plaît* proved to be higher in the Walloon village grocery than in the Brussels shops. The village being part of Walloon Brabant, not far from Brussels, we asked shopkeepers elsewhere in French-speaking Belgium, unacquainted with Dutch or Flemish, about their habits. They confirmed that the use of *s'il vous plaît* with handovers was customary. Rather than direct interference from Dutch, then, one may hypothesise a more widespread form of interference across the Germanic–Romance border, whereby a 'behavioureme' present in Northern and Southern Dutch (*alstublieft*), German (*bitte*), Luxemburgish (*wann ech glift*, cf. Kramer, 1996 and this volume) and Alsatian (*wenn's beliebt*), i.e. the use of the same politeness marker in requests and handovers, has affected French usage in contact areas.

The formulae whereby customers acknowledge receipt of goods are the French *merci* and the Dutch *Dank U* but, in Flanders, the formula more often takes the form *ja* (yes), which acknowledges without thanking (for something similar in Spanish, see Hickey, this volume). Generally, the exchange of money, including change, follows the same *please/thank you* routine, with the difference, however, that giving or receiving change is more heavily marked for politeness, and customers thank the salespersons more profusely for their change than for the goods. We can suggest two explanations for this. The first, considering the politeness procedures with which some assistants ask for payment, and the fact that only half of the customers thus solicited use a politeness formula when paying, might suggest that people are loath to part with their money, albeit in exchange for goods or services, and happy to retrieve part of it in the form of change. A more optimistic hypothesis would be that these final stages of the transaction lead to its eventual completion, making further thanking unnecessary and making way for the final farewells.

Leave-taking

Leave-taking is a popular, reciprocal activity. While thanks are not always expressed, farewells seem to constitute an almost indispensable conclusion of the ritual, combining politeness with friendliness. They may be adapted to the time of the day (*bonne fin de journée*), the activity (*bon appétit* in the fast-food outlet) and/or 'personalised' through use of a term of address (*Au revoir, Madame*) or the name (*Allee, bedankt, hee, Jan*). Friendliness (or solidarity) is marked in both languages by the interjection *hein* (in French) *hè* or *hee* (in Dutch), which not only acts as an intensifier but (like the English 'huh?' or 'y'know') suggests that some common ground or knowledge may be assumed. In the Liège area, the French equivalent of 'you know' is used by somewhat older people for the same purpose: *Au revoir, sais-tu*!

Routines

What a piecemeal discussion of stages in the shopping scenario fails to show is how the turns interrelate. The bulk of the data is too scant to warrant hard and fast conclusions; but there are several indications that turns may 'echo' each other and thus politeness triggers politeness, or, conversely, unfriendly impatience, a gruff response. Thus *alstublieft Mijnheer* might trigger *dank U wel Mevrouw*, etc. In this respect, one might say that shops have a 'house style': one Brussels bakery in the early morning was very silent, with hardly a word exchanged. The butcher's wife next door, in contrast, compulsively marked every single stage of the transaction with a formula and a term of address, delivered routinely, almost mechanically, in a singsong manner: *Bonjour Madame, oui Madame, s'il vous plaît Madame, trois Euro cinquante Madame, merci Madame, au revoir Madame*.

Discussion

Brown and Levinson's (1987: 76) formula $W_x = D(S,H) + P(H,S) + R_x$ represents their view that the higher the face-threat, the more likely that S will attend to H's face-wants. The idea of 'calculating' *Wx* is a metaphor, since the only arithmetical relationship presumably prevailing between the factors is plain (i.e. non-proportional) addition, and no real, calculable

values are assigned to *D*, *P* and *R*. In fact, they are values perceived or assumed by the protagonists and, for that reason, they must be viewed as a dynamic equilibrium which may fluctuate as the interaction develops and may, therefore, be 'calculated' in terms of a fuzzy logic. While, on the one hand, this is not a very promising procedure for someone who wishes to reach a reliable, and ideally quantifiable, assessment of the degree of threat involved in an FTA; on the other hand, it might be sufficiently adaptable to allow for non-canonical, deviant cases of politeness management.

Reversing the premiss that 'the stronger the face threats, the higher the likelihood of S's attending to H's face wants' (Brown & Levinson, 1987: 76), one might presume that, given the massive, continual, amount of linguistic output aimed at doing politeness, service encounters must be perceived as heavily face-threatening and the many politeness markers employed are aimed at redressing that threat. However, the various stages of the buying/selling scenario seem to be face-threatening to the shop assistants and customers only in very general ways (i.e. inasmuch as any interaction, regardless of the relationship between the participants, is intrinsically face-threatening and, therefore, all requests, etc. must, in theory, constitute FTAs (Brown & Levinson, 1987: 65–6)). However, in our service encounters, they are willingly and deliberately engaged in, and ultimately beneficial to both parties, inasmuch as they guarantee income for the provider and goods or services to the customer. One might, then, assume that in our consumer society, R_x in these service encounters is practically nil.

P, the asymmetrical power relationship between interlocutors, is dependent on the situation and on the roles being played within and outside that situation. In the case of service encounters, the roles of seller/shop assistant and buyer/customer are easily defined. Bearing in mind the definition of service encounters, we know that shop assistants are 'obliged to provide service' to customers and to satisfy their service-related demands (Merritt, 1976: 321). In our regions, 'the customer is always right': French and Dutch idioms even say that the customer is 'king'. In their service role, assistants must, therefore, treat customers well and one aspect of this can be 'polite behaviour'. In the roles of buyer and seller, the relative power relationship is rather stable but, of course, other roles might penetrate, or even override, the context of the service encounter. Customers, for example, may be doctors, lawyers, priests or police officers, children, immigrants or beggars, thus enjoying some personal status affecting the assistants' perception of a stronger or weaker *P*. However, the impact of this parameter is not such that there is likely to be a marked contrast between a high *P*, entailing the use of politeness markers, and a low *P*, allowing them to be dispensed with. On the contrary, although customers

enjoy different social statuses, politeness markers prevail throughout, relativising the impact of varying values for *P* on the choice of politeness markers. *P*, then, seems more situation- than person-related. Likewise, the presumed asymmetry of *P* fails to account for the fact that customers do politeness as well, although it may account for our general observation that salespersons spend more verbal energy on politeness than customers.

If we take *D* to be the social distance between the interlocutors, we may take this parameter to be assigned a relatively low value in the provinces, where customers and shop assistants are familiar with each other and interact both in and outside the shop. Of course, there will be fluctuations in this social distance, as some people will be real friends, neighbours or relatives, while others are people known by sight only. During the encounters observed in Flanders and Wallonia, the atmosphere of familiarity in these frequent, informal contexts was evident. In Brussels, contacts were generally more impersonal and business-like and, therefore, more 'distant' but also less marked for politeness. Following Brown and Levinson's thinking, a higher *D* should have entailed a higher W_x and consequently an increased output of politeness strategies. In our data, however, a low rating on the D scale did not preclude a high output of politeness markers. We, therefore, infer that Brown and Levinson's postulate 'higher familiarity leads to lower use of politeness strategies' does not apply here, as familiarity was expressed in a number of ways which did not supersede politeness.

The notions of face and distance might here be viewed in a more ethical perspective, wherein one's interlocutor might be viewed as a persona (a 'face' in the sense attributed to that word by Lévinas, [1991]) regardless of the status or distance sanctioned by society. Politeness, in this perspective, would no longer be accounted for in terms of face management with regard to a putative threat but as a response to a deeper-seated ethical demand. This might provide a more plausible explanation for the widespread use of thanks, which most often are not sincere tokens of gratitude but rather moves in a socially coded ritual in which the issue of sincerity is irrelevant.

These observations lead us to envisage an explanation less dependent on the notion of negative politeness seeking to redress a putative face threat.

An alternative account

In this view, neither customers nor shop assistants intend their use of politeness markers as strategies aimed at redressing a face-threat but as part of a display of friendliness, good manners and conventional courtesy, i.e. face-payment formulae aimed at dialogically affirming the relationship

between two social personae (Kuiper & Flindall, 2000: 186). In this perspective, the politeness markers can be labelled together with speech acts such as greetings, farewells, jokes, compliments and congratulations as supportive interchanges belonging to 'the ritualization of identificatory sympathy', 'rituals of ratification' (Goffman, 1971: 65, 67), which function as displays of reassurance between interlocutors and provide signs of involvement in, and connectedness with, another person in society. Thus, rather than redressing a negative face-threat, the display of verbal energy in these situations constitutes an act of doing positive face (Lakoff, 1973: 298), as it emphasises goodwill to bring the interaction to a successful end.

In this way, the politeness behaviours function as verbal routines marking the stages of mutual engagement in a social interaction viewed as a kind of joint enterprise. As such, they can (as we have observed) easily be replaced by other verbal (or even non-verbal) means fulfilling the same pragmatic function. This also suggests that the use or non-use of a given formula is not polite or impolite in its own right but is dependent on the evaluation of that utterance within a certain interactional context and, hence, on the expectations of the speakers themselves within a given social situation.

A Possible Synthesis

One might, on this basis, suggest that Brown and Levinson's model stands at the intersection of two different conceptions of politeness: on the one hand, a rational cooperation-based view and, on the other, one entirely determined by social convention (cf. Escandell Vidal, 1998: 45–57). Let it be remembered that Brown and Levinson's model envisages two degrees of 'sincerity' in its interpretation of off-record strategies. The first level may be paraphrased as 'I want your wants', where S represents H's desires as her own but where the utterance is insincere. But there exists another level, paraphrasable as 'I want your positive face to be satisfied' where, according to Brown and Levinson, the speaker *is* sincere. Regarding the first level as insincere, however, blinds one to the complexity of the interactive mechanism involved. It would be psychologically unrealistic to suppose that S should 'pretend' to have the same desires as H. Yet, requests marked by *alstublieft/s'il vous plaît / if you please* seem to do just that. In this ritual, however, the paraphrase 'I want your wants' is not insincere but simply false and, what is more, recognised as such by both S and H. And it is precisely this shared recognition which gives rise to politeness routines aimed at cooperation between individuals, that is routines in which face management acts as a

condition for the interaction to continue but is not a goal to be pursued in its own right. If this reasoning is correct, then one should dispense with an over-behaviouristic interpretation of politeness. In this respect, Brown and Levinson (1987: 3–4, 57–8) suggest that the politeness principle acts at a level prior to Grice's cooperative principle. This should not be taken to mean that a politeness principle restricted to the description of face-management processes is hierarchically superordinate to any principle of cooperation; but we must recognise that, for interaction eventually to result in cooperation, the condition of face management should previously be fulfilled and that, in this respect, politeness is, if not *a sine qua non* precondition of cooperation, at least the socially most desirable one.

References

Baetens Beardsmore, H. (1971) *Le français régional de Bruxelles*. Bruxelles (Institut de Phonétique: Conférences et Travaux 3): Presses Universitaires.

Baetens Beardsmore, H. (1981) Linguistic accommodation in Belgium. In H. Baetens Beardsmore and R. Willemyns (eds) *Linguistic Accommodation in Belgium* (Brussels Pre-Prints in Linguistics 5) (pp. 1–28). Brussels: Université Libre de Bruxelles.

Baetens Beardsmore, H. (1988) L'emploi du français dans la minorité néerlandophone à Bruxelles. *Présence Francophone* 33, 49–60.

Baetens Beardsmore, H. (1998) Language shift and cultural implications in Singapore. In S. Gopinathan *et al.* (eds) *Language, Education and Society in Singapore – Issues and Trends* (pp. 85–98). Singapore: Times Academic Press.

Baetens Beardsmore, H. (1999) Bruxelles. *Terminogramme*, 93–94 (pp. 85–102). Québec: Office de la Langue Française.

Brown, R. and Gilman, A. (1960) The pronouns of power and solidarity. In T. Sebeok (ed.) *Style in Language* (pp. 253–76). New York/London: MIT Press.

Brown, P. and Levinson, S. (1987) *Politeness. Some Universals in Language Usage*. Cambridge: Cambridge University Press.

De Vriendt, S. (1985) Tu (ne) veux pas une fois ouvrir la porte pour le chat? In J.-P. van Noppen and G. Debusscher (eds) *Communicating and Translating. Hommages à Jean Dierickx* (pp. 201–10). Brussels: Editions de l'Université.

De Vriendt, S. (1995) De pronomina van de tweede persoon. In *Van geen kleintje vervaard* (pp. 31–3). Brussel: VUB Press.

Escandell Vidal, V. (1998) Politeness: A relevant issue for relevance theory. *Revista Alicantina de Estudios Ingleses* 11, 45–57.

Fishman, J.A. (1965) Who speaks what language to whom and when? *La Linguistique* 2, 67–88.

Foolen, A. (1993) De betekenis van partikels. Doctoral Dissertation, Catholic University of Nijmegen.

Gajjout, H. (1997) Strategic politeness enactment in first and foreign language acquisition, with special reference to Moroccan learners of English. Doctoral

Dissertation, Université Libre de Bruxelles.

Giles, H. and Powesland, G.F. (1975) *Speech Style and Social Evaluation* (European Monographs in Social Psychology 7). New York: Academic Press.

Goffman, E. (1967) *Interactional Ritual: Essays in Face-to-Face Behavior.* Garden City, NY: Doubleday.

Goffman, E. (1971) *Relations in Public: Microstudies of the Public Order.* New York: Basic Books.

Janssens, R. (1999) Aspecten van het taalgebruik in Brussel. In E. Witte *et al.* (eds) *Het statuut van Brussel /Bruxelles et son statut* (pp. 283–307). Brussels: Larcier.

Kienpointner, M. (1999) Ideologies of politeness. *Pragmatics* 9 (1), 1–4.

Kramer, J. (1996) Entre français, allemand et néerlandais: quelques formules de politesse luxembourgeoises. *Travaux de linguistique et de philologie* 33–4, 201–9.

Kuiper, K. (1996) *Smooth Talkers. The Linguistic Performance of Auctioneers and Sportscasters.* New York: Lawrence Erlbaum.

Kuiper, K. and Flindall, M. (2000) Social rituals, formulaic speech and small talk at the supermarket checkout. In J. Coupland (ed.) *Small Talk* (pp. 183–208). Harlow: Pearson Education.

Lakoff, R. (1973) The logic of politeness; or, minding your p's and q's. In *Papers from the Ninth Regional Meeting of the Chicago Linguistic Society* (pp. 306–19). Chicago: Chicago Linguistic Society.

Lévinas, E. (1991) *Entre nous. Essais sur le penser-à-l'autre.* Paris: Grasset.

Martiny, T. (1996) Forms of address in French and Dutch: A sociopragmatic approach. *Language Sciences* 18 (3–4), 765–75.

Merritt, M. (1976) On questions following questions in service encounters. *Language in Society* 5, 315–57.

Nelde, P.H. (1997) Language conflict. In F. Coulmas (ed.) *Handbook of Sociolinguistics* (pp. 285–300). Oxford: Blackwell.

O'Driscoll, J. (1999) Inter-national communication and language choice in modern Europe. Doctoral Dissertation, University of Ghent.

Panowitsch, D. (1996) Het taalgebruik in het bedrijfsleven. In P. Van de Craen (ed.) *Mondig Brussel.* (Brusselse Thema's, 3). Brussels: VUB Press.

Van der Wijst, P. (1996) Politeness in requests and negotiations. Doctoral Dissertation, Katholieke Universiteit Brabant (Tilburg).

Van der Wijst, P. (2000) Beleefdheid in het Nederlands van Franstaligen. *Leuvense Bijdragen,* 89 (1–2), 251–265.

van Noppen, J.-P. *et al.* (2002) Politeness in Belgium: Face, distance and sincerity in service–exchange rituals. Numerical Data, per Region. On WWW at http://homepages.ulb.ac.be/~jpvannop/POLITENESS.html

Van Uytfanghe, M. (1978) Belgisme ou belgicisme? Esquisse d'une étude linguistique du français de Belgique. Undergraduate Dissertation, Vrije Universiteit Brussel.

Weydt, H. (1969) Abtönungspartikel: Die deutschen Modalwörter und ihre französischen Entsprechungen. Bad Homburg: Gehlen.

Chapter 4

Politeness in Luxemburg: Greetings from Foreign Parts

JOHANNES KRAMER

To write on linguistic politeness in Luxemburg is virtually an impossible task, because the country is so small and its ties with neighbouring countries are so close. There has never been a Luxemburgish way of being polite, in the sense in which there are typical German, French or English ways of behaving with other people. Luxemburgers are more or less fluent in at least three languages, French, German and, of course, Luxemburgish, which linguistically is close to German but has its own grammar, its own vocabulary, full of French words which have never crossed the German border (cf. Kramer, 1992) and, important in our context, its own stylistics and pragmatics (Berg, 1993).

As more than one-third of the 432,000 inhabitants of Luxemburg have not been born and raised there, as about 90,000 foreign commuters (50% from France, 30% from Belgium, 20% from Germany) come in every morning and leave every evening, and as most Luxemburgers have spent longer or shorter periods of their life abroad, we can imagine how heterogeneous the population of the small Grand Duchy (2586 km^2) is. In contact with people from France, Belgium or Germany, native Luxemburgers not only use foreign languages to a high degree of perfection and correctness but also adapt to the relevant foreign politeness codes – with the French they speak French and behave according to French conventions, with the Germans they speak German and respect German conventions (Christophory, 1992).

From this point of view, Luxemburg is a small territory in a French-speaking or German-speaking world and, therefore, to speak of politeness strategies in Luxemburg raises the question of: which Luxemburgers, speaking to whom, when and where? Yet, of course, we cannot compare Luxemburgish politeness to that of a region like Burgundy or Bavaria because, while the average Burgundian belongs unmistakably to a French politeness area and the average Bavarian belongs unmistakably to a German politeness area, albeit with some regional extras, Luxemburgers have the ability to change linguistic roles. When speaking French, they are expected to behave like a French person and when, moments later, they speak German, they are supposed to behave as Germans do – indeed, normally this act of mimicry works perfectly.

Politeness strategies are acquired or learned with the language and, unconsciously, Luxemburgers adapt their behaviour to the language they are using at any given moment (Christophory, 1992: 183–84).

Under these circumstances, it makes little sense to describe the politeness of Luxemburgers when they are using French or German. Real characteristics can be expected only in their own language, Luxemburgish. Before I present some formulas, I shall give a brief description of this language together with the conditions of its use (for more detail, see Berg, 1993; Hoffmann, 1979; Kramer, 1984: 155–213; 1994; 1998, Scheidweiler, 1988; Weber, 1994).

Luxemburgish, deriving from the regional variety of Mosellan Franconian, is the normal language spoken between people born and educated in Luxemburg (regardless of the families' ethnic background) but the average Luxemburger is reluctant to write or read it, even though there is an established (liberal) norm and it is taught (a little) at school. The written press is traditionally in German with some articles in French (some 10%, mostly on French politics and literary culture) with, every now and then, a short article in Luxemburgish on strictly local topics: the last few years have seen the emergence of two daily and one weekly newspaper written exclusively in French and aimed at the intellectual élite, at commuters from France or Belgium and at the first generation of immigrants from Romance countries who usually know little German. Most books sold in Luxemburg come from Germany but the more a person tends to behave as an intellectual, the stronger the tendency is to read French books.

There is a domestic literary scene with text production in all three languages but the reading public for these works is small and Luxemburgish literature, in particular, is read only by enthusiasts. In daily life the normal spoken language between Luxemburgers is Luxemburgish (in local variants which do not impede communication) but when non-Luxemburgers join in, there is a language switch to French or German (only if German-speaking persons are involved) or even, more recently, to English. The average Luxemburger feels it is impolite to continue speaking Luxemburgish in the presence of French- or German-speaking foreigners.

Officially the status of languages within the Grand Duchy is regulated by the 1984 Language Law (Loi du 24 février 1984 sur le régime des langues; see Dahmen *et al.*, [1992: 164]). Article 1 states that 'the national language of the Luxemburgers is Luxemburgish [La langue nationale des Luxembourgeois est le luxembourgeois])'. But the next paragraph restricts the position of the *langue nationale*, because in the legal system only French texts are valid (*'Les actes législatifs et leurs réglements d'exécution sont rédigés en français. Lorsque les actes législatifs et réglementaires sont accompagnés d'une traduction, seul le texte français fait foi'*). Paragraph 3 lays down that the languages of the administration (including legal affairs) are French, German and Luxemburgish (*'En matière administrative, contentieuse ou non contentieuse, et en matière judiciaire, il peut être fait usage des langues française, allemande ou luxembourgeoise').*

When citizens come into contact with the administration, it is they who determine the language of procedure, because the public services must respond as far as possible in the language used by the applicant assuming it is Luxemburgish, French or German (*'Lorsqu'une requête est rédigée en luxembourgeois, en français ou en allemand, l'administration doit se servir, dans la mesure du possible, pour sa réponse de la langue choisie par le requérant'*). The most important phrase in this paragraph is *dans la mesure du possible* (as far as possible): of course any public authority in Luxemburg is able to write a letter in French or in German but, since written Luxemburgish requires skills which are not entirely self-evident, this reservation makes it possible to avoid official written use of Luxemburgish (Hoffmann, 1988: 57).

These legal provisions reflect the attitude Luxemburgers have towards their languages (Fröhlich, 1992): Luxemburgish is one of the symbols of nationhood and constitutes an important factor in daily life, as the spoken communication medium for people belonging to a more or less familiar circle of acquaintances but it is not seen as the equal of written literary languages like French, German or English. The highest prestige goes to French. Traditionally, a good knowledge of French – which, in fact, has some peculiarities typical of Luxemburg – (cf. Bender-Berland, 2000) is a sign of a solid intellectual background and Luxemburgers who were really fluent in French were considered to belong to the social élite. Things have changed a lot in the last decade and today we find many speakers of French in the lower strata of the social scale, because immigrants from Southern European countries have always used French as their medium of communication.

So today we find French both at the top and towards the bottom of the social scale; however, the general esteem in which French is held still reflects the period when being fluent in French meant automatically belonging to the Grand Duchy's élite. And whereas there is a sort of love story between Luxemburgers and the French language, we do not find the slightest trace of eroticism in the relationship between Luxemburgers and

German – German generally being considered a necessary evil, unloved but unavoidable in daily life. German is the normal reading and writing language and German television programmes are more popular than French (not only because of linguistic factors, of course). For 75% of Luxemburgers, German constitutes the gateway to the outside world but, for historical reasons (German occupation during First and Second World Wars), it is painful to admit this fact. Since Hitler used the argument of Luxemburg being a German-speaking area in order to incorporate it into his Third Reich, participation in any language-planning measures with countries which have German as their official language is a taboo subject. Some time ago, for example, when German orthography was reformed, representatives of the German minorities of Belgium, Denmark, Italy and even Namibia took part in the discussions but Luxemburg declined to attend because it did not want to be seen to be involved in German language politics.

Still today, the use of German is virtually taboo in all matters referring to national identity – speeches in parliament, addresses on the occasion of the national holiday (23 June), street- and place-name signs, even formal announcements of births, deaths and marriages (Hoffmann, 1979: 50; Kramer, 1984: 207).

The unequal prestige of Luxemburg's three official languages has had its impact on the use of politeness formulas. French is the most respected and so it is the language in which well-educated people will begin a conversation. A person one does not know is normally addressed in French. The usual greeting is *bonjour* or *bonsoir*, or, less formally, *salut*. People are always addressed as *Madame* or *Monsieur* (also written *Mossiö*), and even *Mademoiselle* is still often used when speaking to a young woman, although more and more liberated women do not like this 'sexist' form of address, especially those acquainted with the situation in Germany where *Fräulein* is unused and perceived virtually as an insult. (The situation in France is different, and *Mademoiselle* is a common address form.) In this respect, too, Luxemburg forms a transitional zone between German and French pragmatics. As in French (and unlike German) you can address a person whose name you do not know: *S'il vous plaît, Madame; excusez, Monsieur*. It is normal to add this form to most politeness formulas: *Merci, Mademoiselle* (in German, *Frau* or *Herr* require the family name, and evasive formulas like *mein Herr* or *gnädige Frau* have become obsolete).

Luxemburgish ranks second in the list of languages of address. Normally, Luxemburgish is only used when there is reason for assuming that all conversational partners have a Luxemburgish background – or, in unknown surroundings, it serves as a solidarity marker between all

Luxemburgers present. At any time of the day, the normal Luxemburgish greeting is *Moiën*: this has nothing to do with the German *Morgen* (Lux. *Mueren,* in contrast to its German counterpart, is rarely used as a greeting formula) but is to be connected to Dutch *mooi* 'nice' (< **e moiên Dag* [a nice day], cf. Kramer, 1996: 203). The formula *gudde Moiën* is due to popular etymology, formed in imitation of the German *guten Morgen* and by analogy with *gudden Owend*. Normally, people are adressed as *Mossiö* and *Madame* but less formally it is possible to say *Här Bestgen*. It is, however, impossible to say *Fra Bestgen* – here *Madame Bestgen* is inevitable, because, in contrast to German *Frau* (Luxemburgish *Fra*) its only meaning is 'wife' (*méng Fra,* cf. Remus, [1997: 56]).

When speaking of a person one calls by their family name, it is normal to preface the name by the definite article + *Monsieur* = *Här* or *Madame*: *d'Madame Bestgen léisst merci soen* (Ms Bestgen expresses her thanks); *dat as de Monsieur Bestgen* = *dat as den Här Bestgen* (This is Mr Bestgen). The Luxemburgish equivalent of *Mademoiselle* is *Joffer* (which has none of the pejorative connotations of the regional German *Juffer*). Waitresses, female clerks and, above all, teachers are normally addressed as *Joffer* (Remus, 1997: 55) – this is so normal that *Joffer* can even be used as a job title in the sense of 'teacher', regardless of the marital status of the woman in question (*eis Joffer as bestuet* [Our Miss is married], *LW* 2: 242). On introducing yourself, you must preface the first name by the definite article: *Ech sin de Pol Kramer* (I am [the] Paul Kramer) (Remus, 1997: 57).

In most cases, *Monsieur* and *Här* are synonymous but the higher prestige of French implies that *Monsieur* + family name is felt to be a little pedantic in Luxemburgish, whereas *Här* + family name seems better suited to the always rather familiar tone of the Grand Duchy's vernacular (Kramer, 1996: 204). A number of expressions (*LW* 3: 171) may confirm this observation: *en huet d'Mossiö erausgekéiert* (he has acted the high-up), *en trëtt op ewéi e Mossiö* (he plays the big noise), *e fäine Mossiö* (a shady figure).

Genuine German formulas are never used, whether formal *Guten Morgen, Guten Tag, Guten Abend* or colloquial *Morgen, Tag, Nabend* (*Nowend* being the abbrevation of the Luxemburgish *gudden Owend, [LW* 3: 302]). One of the sharpest linguistic differences between Germany and Luxemburg lies in the farewell formula: east of the border you say *tschö,* west of the border it is *äddi* (*LW* 1: 53). Both formulas have the same French root, *adieu,* but, in the German Rhineland, the borrowing is from standard French, while Luxemburg has taken its *äddi* from neighbouring Wallonian (Kramer, 1993: 43–44). This loan-word belongs to the older stratum of Romance elements in Luxemburg: in fact, the Wallonian form *adi* (< lat. *ad deum*), which etymologically is the basis for the Luxemburgisch *äddi* and the Limburgian Dutch *adi(e),* has been replaced in Belgium by *adiu* (Haust, 1933: 11), an adaptation of the literary French *adieu,* and neither the Luxemburgish umlaut (*a* > *ä* before *i*) nor the drawing back of the word accent (Wallon. *adi* has its accent on the second syllable, Lux. *äddi* on the first) occur in recent loan-words.

There is still another argument proving that the word acquired its Luxemburgish form before the end of the 18th century: in fact, according to the *Rheinisches Wörterbuch* (Vol. 1, col. 56, line 21) a form *dì* occurs in the Western Eifel (indeed only in the Western Eifel). It is a historical fact that large territories of the Western Eifel (Bitburg, Prüm, St Vith) belonged to the old Duchy of Luxemburg which was annexed to post-revolutionary France in 1795 and passed to Prussia in 1815: Luxemburgish words in this territory must have been present before 1795.

A more formal farewell in Luxemburgish is *awar,* formerly *arwar* and *arwuer.* This expression means the same as the French *au revoir* but etymologically we have to go to a form *à revoir,* which competed for a couple of years (first attestation: 1835) with the more successful *au revoir* and has now fallen into disuse. So the distinguished Luxemburgish farewell is a distant reflection of a French formula which never had any real acceptance in its language of origin (Kramer, 1996: 202).

I would like to conclude with an example (Kramer, 1996: 205–06) that proves the uniqueness of Luxemburgish, where French and German pragmatics merge in a new unity which could not possibly have emerged in any other part of the world. This is a case in which we have, besides French and German, a tiny Dutch addition. To say 'please', you have to fall back on a rather awkward formula, *s'il vous plaît* or, if you are on more familiar terms with the interlocutor, *s'il te plaît*: this expression was translated into Dutch (although not into German) in the course of the 18th century and still today you say *alstublieft* (< *als het U belieft*) and *alsjeblieft* (< *als het je belieft*). Now, this formula was introduced into Luxemburgish at the time of Dutch rule which began in 1815 and ended formally in 1890, with the accession to the throne of a Grand Duke who was no longer in personal union with the King of The Netherlands. However, in reality, the Dutch influence had ceased to be of any importance half a century earlier. The Dutch formula was slavishly translated into Luxemburgish: *als het U belieft* is reproduced to the latter as *wann iech glift,* with a verb *gelieven* that occurs only in this formula and reflects a Dutch verb *gelieven,* parallel to *believen.*

But the story does not end here: we are not only concerned with a French formula transmitted to Luxemburgish by Dutch mediation but the formula is used according to German pragmatic rules. In fact, in Luxemburgish French *s'il vous (te) plaît* and Luxemburgish *wann iech glieft* are used in the same way as Germans use *bitte.* In France, you say *voilà Monsieur* or *voici Madame,* if you give something to someone. In Germany, the usual expression in these circumstances is *bitte, bitte schön* or *hier bitte.* On the same occasion in Luxemburg you would say *s'il vous plaît, Madame,* speaking French, and *wann iech glift, Madame,* speaking Luxemburgish – German *bitte* dressed up *à la Luxembourgeoise.*

But there is still more: in German, if one has not understood something another person has said, the normal interrogative clause would be *wie bitte?*, very often abbreviated to *bitte?* In France, the equivalent would be *pardon, vous dites?* In Luxemburg, you hear *s'il vous plaît?* (which, in this situation, makes absolutely no sense to a Frenchman) or *wann iech glift?* And the height of 'unidiomatic' use of French is constituted by the formula *pardon, s'il vous plaît,* a perfect translation of German *Entschuldigung, bitte.* No wonder that Luxemburgish *entschëllegt, wann iech glift* reflects the same expression!

I hope that these few examples will have shown that there are no linguistic expressions of politeness in Luxemburg which we do not also find in the neighbouring countries – perhaps this is to be expected in such a small country. Rather, all sorts of influences have amalgamated in this unique linguistic and cultural crossroads giving formulas which either do not exist elsewhere or else are used in pragmatically different ways.

References

Bender-Berland, G. (2000) Die Besonderheiten des Französischen in Luxemburg. *Romanistik in Geschichte und Gegenwart* 6, 33–50.

Berg, G. (1993) *'Mir wëlle bleiwe, wat mir sin'. Soziolinguistische und sprachtypologische Betrachtungen zur luxemburgischen Mehrsprachigkeit.* Tübingen: Max Niemeyer.

Christophory, J. (1992) Angewandte Linguistik in einem Luxemburger Kulturinstitut. In W. Dahmen *et al.* (eds) *Germanisch und Romanisch in Belgien und Luxemburg* (Romanistisches Kolloquium VI) (pp. 165–87). Tübingen: Gunter Narr.

Dahmen, W. et al. (eds) (1992) *Germanisch und Romanisch in Belgien und Luemburg* (Romanistisches Kolloquium VI). Tübingen: Gunter Narr Verlag.

Fröhlich, H. (1992) Hierarchisierung und Kategorisierung im sprachrelevanten Alltagswissen. Anmerkungen zur sozioliguistischen Situation Luxemburgs. In W. Dahmen *et al.* (eds) *Germanisch und Romanisch in Belgien und Luemburg* (Romanistisches Kolloquium VI) (pp. 188–202). Tübingen: Gunter Narr.

Haust, J. (1992) *Dictionnaire liégeois.* Liège: Imprimerie H. Vaillant-Carmanne. 1933.

Hoffmann, F. (1979) *Sprachen in Luxemburg.* Luxemburg: Institut Grand-Ducal.

Hoffmann, F. (1988) Sprachen in Luxemburg. Unter besonderer Berücksichtigung der Situation nach 1945. In *Jahrbuch für Internationale Germanistik* 20, 45–62.

Kramer, J. (1984) *Zweisprachigkeit in den Benelux-Ländern.* Hamburg: Helmut Buske.

Kramer, J. (1992) Einige Bemerkungen zum Französischen in Luxemburg. In W.

Dahmen *et al.* (eds), *Germanisch und Romanisch in Belgien und Luemburg* (Romanistisches Kolloquium VI) (pp. 203–23). Tübingen: Gunter Narr.

Kramer, J. (1993) Von Versailles über Wien an die Donau und in die Alpen: Zum Wanderweg von Gruß- und Dankesformln. In J. Kramer and G. A. Plangg (eds) *Verbum Romanicum. Festschrift für Maria Iliescu* (pp. 41–52). Hamburg: Helmut Buske.

Kramer, J. (1994) Lëtzebuergesch – eine Nationalsprache ohne Norm. In I. Fodor and C. Hagège (eds) *Language Reform* 6 (pp. 391–405). Hamburg: Helmut Buske.

Kramer, J. (1996) Entre français, allemand et néerlandais: quelques formules de politesse luxembourgeoises. In D. Kremer and A. Monjour (eds) *Travaux de linguistique et de philologie* 33/34, *Studia ex hilaritate. Mélanges de linguistique et d'onomastique sardes et romanes offerts à Monsieur Heinz Jürgen Wolf* (pp. 201–09). Pris: Klincksieck

Kramer, J. (1998) Die Dreisprachigkeit in Luxemburg. In F. Landthaler (ed.) *Dialekt und Mehrsprachigkeit* (pp. 61-77). Saarbrücken: Elisabeth-Selbert-Akademie.

LW (*Luxemburger Wörterbuch,)* 5 volumes. Luxemburg: Buchdruckerei P. Linden, 1950–1977.

Remus, J. (1997) *Lëtzebuergesch Wort für Wort.* Bielefeld: Reise Know-How Verlag Peter Rump.

Scheidweiler, G. (1988) Glanz und Elend des Luxemburgischen. *Muttersprache* 98, 226–54.

Weber, N. (1994) Sprachen und ihre Funktionen in Luxemburg. *Zeitschrift für Dialektologe und Linguistik* 61, 129–69.

Chapter 5

Politeness in The Netherlands: Indirect Requests

ROB LE PAIR

Introduction

Besides linguistic competence – command of syntax, vocabulary, idiom and pronunciation – communicative competence is at least as important for linguistic performance, in general, and especially in contexts with speakers of different mother tongues (see Thomas, 1983). In interactions between speaker and addressee, the choice of words and phrasing may indicate, among other things, how speakers perceive their relationships with addressees or would like them to be perceived. Clearly, communicative competence is not just linguistically correct usage: it also presupposes an insight, and an ability to use it, into when, how and for whom speech acts are appropriate and effective. As part of their communicative competence, interlocutors consciously and unconsciously use communication strategies that affect the appropriateness and effectiveness of their interaction. The use of politeness strategies to formulate requests appropriately and effectively, for example by choosing direct or indirect ways of wording them, shows the interpersonal function of linguistic usage. Generally, speakers will want to phrase requests as clearly and explicitly as possible, in accordance with Grice's (1975) 'Cooperative Principle' but will also wish to ensure that their relationship with the addressee is not harmed by making the request.

A request may be seen as a speech act through which the speaker wants to get the addressee to do something (or commit themselves to doing something) that is generally in the interest of the speaker and demands a certain effort or exertion on the part of the addressee (Haverkate, 1979; Le Pair, 1997; Searle, 1969, 1976). Therefore, the addressee is imposed upon, to a lesser or greater extent. Depending on the degree of imposition of the request, the speaker will have to show a degree of face-support, in order to protect the hearer's negative face. Brown and Levinson (1978, 1987) describe these negative face-wants as the need 'to be left alone', to retain the freedom to act, to see one's individual independence unthreatened. The threat to the addressee's negative face is inherent in the request. This provides a broad outline of the field of tension in which the request utterance is realised.

> 'Clarity' in conversational behavior is conceptualized as a concern about achieving a primary goal in the most explicit and the shortest way possible; 'face support' is conceptualized as a concern about achieving a primary goal without hurting the hearer's desired social image and feelings. (Kim, 1993: 137)

The idea that preferences for certain request strategies may differ from culture to culture is based on two assumptions: first, that in culture A there may be a *general* preference for more directly worded requests (clarity-oriented) in comparison with culture B (face-support-oriented); and, second, that speakers in culture A may, *in concrete situations*, prefer indirectly-worded requests and more face support, while speakers in culture B in the same situation would phrase requests more directly and with less face support. As it happens, situational factors (for example 'power distance', 'social distance' and 'situational context') affect the choice of strategy in any interaction situation. However, the roles these factors play in culture A may be different from those in culture B.

This chapter has two objectives: first, to examine differences and similarities between Spanish and Dutch regarding the strategy choices made for the production of requests and the way the request production of Dutch learners of Spanish relates to that of the two groups of native speakers. In other words, if there are differences between Spanish and Dutch in the use of request strategies, do Dutch learners of Spanish adapt to the request behaviour of the Spanish native speakers and, if so, in what respect? Second, to examine the roles that situational factors play in the request production of the three groups of speakers. The pragmalinguistic competence of learners of Spanish is central to this, belonging in the domain of interlanguage pragmatics (Kasper, 1996; Kasper & Blum-Kulka, 1993; Kasper & Dahl, 1991).

Theoretical Background

The indirectness of speech acts and Leech's tact maxim are the two criteria on which request strategies are ordered in this chapter. The degree of indirectness is determined mainly by the way in which speech acts are given the illocutionary force of a request. An important criterion for this is the reference to the 'felicity conditions', which a speech act has to meet in order to be 'valid as a request' (Gordon & Lakoff, 1975; Labov & Fanshel,

1977; Leech, 1983; Morgan, 1978; Searle, 1975). (For a discussion of indirect speech acts and politeness, see Le Pair (1994: 41–3, 1996, 1997: 61–83.)

A request is 'felicitous' if the following conditions are met.

- Reasonableness condition: the request is based on a rational motive,
- Sincerity condition (speaker-oriented): the speaker genuinely wishes the listener to comply with the request,
- Non-obviousness condition (act-oriented): the request should refer to a future action, which the hearer – without the request having been made – would not have carried out as a matter of course,
- Willingness condition (listener-oriented): the speaker must have the expectation that the addressee is willing to comply with the request,
- Ability condition (listener-oriented): the speaker must have the expectation that the addressee is able to comply with the request.

Table 5.1 Request strategies in increasing degree of indirectness

Strategy	*Reference to felicity condition + example*	*Regulating effect of the tact maxim*
1. Imperative	Most direct form to encode illocutionary force: the request is directly expressed by the mood of the verb. 'Open the window.'	None. The imperative does not allow optionality
2. Performative verb	Direct form to encode illocutionary force: the request is directly expressed by a semantically 'relevant' verb. 'I request that you open the window.'	'I demand/ask/request that you' is a declarative sentence: the semantic aspect and the mood of the verb make the request less impositive than the imperative mood
3. Statement of obligation	No direct/explicit reference to an essential condition but implicitly through a condition of reasonableness. 'You have to open the window.'	The directness of 1 and 2 is missing but ignoring the request is difficult because it is presented as a (moral) obligation

4. Want statement	Request power is implied because the speaker refers to a speaker-oriented sincerity condition. 'I want you to open the window'	Optionality does exist, but it implies ignoring the speaker's wants
5. Suggestion	Power of request/suggestion through reference to a reasonableness condition: more or less conventionalised directive, not impositive *per se*. 'Shouldn't you open the window' 'Why don't you open the window?'	The 'cost–benefit dimension' can be manipulated: the action requested may be presented as if in the interest of the addressee.
6. Reference to preconditions	Reference to preconditions: (a) non-obviousness (action) 'Will you open the window?' (b) willingness (addressee) 'Would you open the window, please?' (c) ability (addressee) 'Can you open the window?'	The interrogative structure gives the addressee optionality because s/he has the possibility of doubting or denying: (a) the future action (b) willingness of H (c) ability of H
7. Hint	The speech act is only interpreted as a request if the hearer has sufficient contextual information. 'It is sweltering in here.'	The hearer is given a lot of optionality: he or she does not have to interpret the speech act as a request.

Depending on how these felicity conditions are referred to, seven main strategies may be distinguished (see Table 5.1), ranked in increasing order of indirectness (see, e.g., Blum-Kulka, 1989; Blum-Kulka *et al.*, 1989; Trosborg, 1995). This order is based on Leech's (1983) analysis and order of request utterances. An important ranking criterion is the optionality scale: the extent to which the addressee is provided with options not to comply with the request. A display of face protection is involved (respect for the addressee's negative face), since the speaker suggests or pretends that he or she is not certain that the addressee will, can or wishes to comply with the request (Table 5.1, strategy 6(a)–(c)).

Research Questions and Research Method

Research questions

The dual objective described earlier may be translated into four research questions.

(1) What direct strategies are chosen by 'native speakers of Dutch in Dutch', 'native speakers of Spanish in Spanish' and 'Dutch learners of Spanish in Spanish' when they formulate requests?
(2) What indirect strategies are chosen by the three groups of speakers to formulate requests?
(3) To what extent do the three groups of speakers differ with regard to the degree of directness of their request utterances?
(4) What influence do the situational factors 'power distance', 'social distance' and 'situational context' have on the degree of indirectness in the request utterances of the three groups of speakers?

Subjects

Subjects with similar backgrounds were selected for the language production tasks, giving the following three groups.

A group of 92 native Spanish speakers performed the language production tasks. These subjects, aged between 19 and 23, 77% of whom are women, are of Spanish nationality, born and raised in Spain, speak Spanish as their mother tongue and study a language (English, German or Spanish) at the universities of Valencia, Barcelona or Alcalá de Henares.

A group of 63 native speakers of Dutch took part in the task. These subjects are of Dutch descent, aged between 20 and 24, 78% of whom are females, born and bred in The Netherlands, speak Dutch as their mother tongue and study a language at the Business Communication Studies Department at Nijmegen University.

The group of Dutch learners of Spanish consisted of 36 subjects, aged between 21 and 25, 83% of whom are women, of Dutch nationality and with Dutch as their mother tongue. At the time of the experiment, they had done between 2.5 and 3.5 years of Spanish with an intensity of 4.5 hours a week, involving grammar, listening and speaking skills, text comprehension and writing skills, oral and written business language and cultural background.

Method and data collection

Variables in the research

Since it is assumed that the choice of request strategies depends on socio-cultural factors and on the situational context in which the request is performed, the degree of indirectness of requests is defined as the dependent variable in this study. The core of the request is coded on a scale of increasing indirectness, from 1 (most direct strategy) to 7 (most indirect strategy), as shown in Table 5.1. The role of internal and external markers, such as the conditional mood, the use of 'please' and mitigating particles such as 'just' and 'perhaps', is not taken into account here. The independent variables (see Figure 5.1) are – besides the culture and mother tongue of the subjects – the situational factors that are assumed to have an effect on the speaker's choice of face-supporting strategies accompanying the request (Brown & Levinson, 1978).

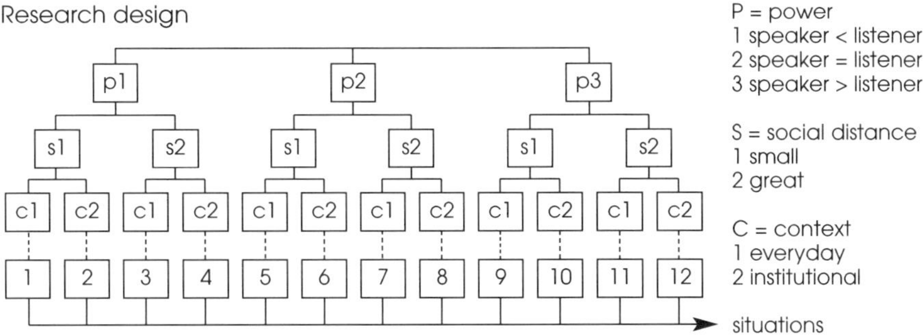

Figure 5.1 Twelve situation types, each with a unique 'PSC combination'

The independent variables are P (power distance; three values: speaker has equal, more or less authority than the hearer), S (social distance; two values: speaker and hearer know each other well or do not know each other) and C (situational context; two values: a business/institutional or an everyday, non-institutional context).

Research instrument and data collection

To compare the request production of Dutch and Spanish reliably, a language production task was developed for two groups of subjects. This task is an oral *Discourse Completion Test* (DCT), in which a subject gives an oral reaction to a written stimulus. In this way, a number of objections made against other forms of the DCT were compensated for (Bardovi-Harlig &

Hartford, 1993; Hartford & Bardovi-Harlig, 1992; Rose, 1992, 1994). The oral reactions were recorded on audiocassette tapes. The stimulus consisted of a written description of a situation with, usually, two persons. The respondent was to project him/herself into the role of one of these, namely the person acting as the speaker who makes a request of the addressee. Every subject reacted to 12 request situations. To avoid subjects producing requests 'on automatic pilot', eight 'distracter' situations were interspersed in which a speech act different from a request was evoked.

The respondent in situation type 6, for example, plays the role of the speaker who makes a request of the addressee on the basis of the following written situation and the question asked at the end:

> You and your colleague, John Miller, are both advertising managers and are currently working for the same customer. Your customer has organised a short presentation to introduce a new product; the presentation takes place tomorrow. It is important that one of you goes to this presentation. You are very busy this week and unable to go yourself. What do you say to your colleague?

In this example, the power balance between speaker and addressee may be characterised as 'status equals' (both are advertising managers), the social distance between them is small (they know each other well) and the context in question is an institutional one. Of each situation in the DCT, a Dutch version (for the native speakers of Dutch) and a Spanish version (for the learners and the native speakers of Spanish) were made. To make comparison of the request production between Dutch and Spanish subjects reliable and to ensure that the possible influence of power distance, social distance and situational context may be analysed systematically, these factors are controlled in every situation as represented in Figure 5.1. In this way, every situation is characterised by a unique combination ('PSC combination') of power distance, social distance and situational context.

Results, Conclusions and Discussion

Use of relatively direct request strategies

A comparison between the native speakers of Dutch, native speakers of Spanish and learners of Spanish shows that, on the level of relatively direct strategies (1–5), a number of important differences occur (see Table 5.2).

The most direct strategy, using an imperative, was chosen frequently by native Spanish speakers (in 8.7% of all request utterances) in comparison with native Dutch speakers (whose use of the imperative is negligible), while the learners of Spanish reached a little over 3%. The use of the imperative by native speakers of Spanish occurs in 11 out of 12 situation types; half of these cases, moreover, are in the 'party at home' situation (characterised by authority resting with the speaker, small social distance, everyday situation). The imperative was also used in 87% of the cases in situations where the speaker has authority over the addressee (P3) or in which the speaker and the hearer are status equals (P2). In almost 80% of the situations, the social distance (S1) is small. The impression is that native Spanish speakers feel less need to show face-support when there is small social distance and/or when the addressee does not have more authority than the speaker.

Table 5.2 Frequencies of request strategies used by native speakers of Dutch (NS-NL), native speakers of Spanish (NS-ES) and non-native speakers of Spanish (NNS-ES)[a]

Strategy	*Total (%) (N=2216)*	*NS-NL (%) (N=689)*	*NS-ES (%) (N=1098)*	*NNS-ES (%) (N=429)*
1. Imperative	5.4	0.1	8.7	3.3
2. Performative	0.7	0.3	1.0	0.2
3. Statement of obligation	2.1	0.3	3.2	2.8
4. Want statement	4.4	2.6	5.6	4.7
5. Suggestion	11.8	2.3	17.4	2.8
6. Precondition	74.8	93.0	63.6	84.6
7. Hint	0.8	1.3	0.5	1.6
	100	99.9	100	100

[a]Strategies above the dotted line are relatively direct; below the dotted line they are indirect.

With regard to the other relatively direct strategies, i.e. performative, obligation, want statements and suggestions, the same tendency is seen as with the imperative: for each of these strategies, the Spanish native speakers use considerably more of these than the Dutch native speakers, and the frequency of use by learners of Spanish is a little higher than among Dutch native speakers. The learners of Spanish lag behind considerably in directness compared with the Spanish native speakers.

For the various strategies that can be characterised as relatively direct (1–5 in Table 5.2), the largest discrepancy between the native speakers of Dutch and the Dutch learners of Spanish, on the one hand, and the native speakers of Spanish, on the other, was found in their use of suggestions (2.3% and 2.8%, respectively, against 17.4% for the Spanish native speakers). We believe that this may be explained at least partly by a number of pragmalinguistic differences between Dutch and Spanish. A difference certainly occurs in suggestions of the type *a ver si …* (let's see if …), a construction that does not exist in Dutch as a request but is frequently used in Spanish (not mentioned by Koike, 1996). In suggestions of the type 'why … not', there also seems to be a cross-linguistic pragmatic difference between Dutch and Spanish, since in Dutch, a 'why … not' utterance often expresses impatience or irritation, which is far less often the case in Spanish.

Furthermore, utterances of the type 'if you …' are unusual as requests in Dutch, but relatively popular in Spanish: 8.5% of all request utterances consisted of a construction of the type *si podía mirarme el resumen que he realizado de las prácticas* (if you could check the report that I've made on the placement).

Use of precondition strategies

What immediately stands out in the distribution of main strategies (see Table 5.2) is the very frequent use of strategy 6, e.g. 'could you …?' / 'would you …?' / 'would you mind …?', etc. In many languages, this is the most common strategy used to realise a request (see, e.g., Blum-Kulka, 1989; Blum-Kulka & House, 1989; Fukushima, 1996; Van Mulken, 1996; Van der Wijst, 1996). Since, in this strategy, explicit reference is made to the listener-oriented willingness condition or ability condition, the addressee is offered some measure of freedom to act when these types of request utterances are used (i.e. he can decide not to comply with the request without excessive loss of face), although the speaker transmits the illocutionary force of the request in no uncertain terms: this is an example of 'conventionalised indirectness' (Geis, 1995; Haverkate, 1994; Morgan, 1978; Searle, 1975) or of utterances that have reached 'idiom status' (Brown & Levinson, 1978; Sadock, 1974).

Comparability of directness and indirectness between language speakers

For every situation, the degree of indirectness of the request was determined for the subjects involved; low scores reflect a direct, high scores an indirect, strategy. Since the distribution of the degree of indirectness is not a normal distribution – the greater majority of speech acts is 'on the right side of the indirectness scale', i.e. the area with the most indirect strategies – a transformation was realised by calculating scores of the degree of indirectness. The statistical calculations were done with these *z*-scores. A repeated measures analysis revealed a significant main effect for 'language' ($F(2,188) = 81.28$; $p < 0.01$), which means the three groups are significantly different on the dependent variable 'indirectness'.

A post hoc analysis (Bonferroni) showed that the group of Spanish native speakers alone was responsible for the significant main effect. The groups of native speakers of Dutch and Dutch learners of Spanish did not differ significantly as regards the directness variable, whereas the native speakers of Spanish were significantly more direct in wording requests than the native speakers of Dutch ($F(1,188) = 132.96$; $p < 0.01$) and also more direct than the learners of Spanish ($F(1,188) = 81.17$; $p < 0.01$). This result is illustrated in Figure 2, which also shows that this result is true for the individual situations, with the exception of the 'supermarket situation', in which Spanish and Dutch native speakers did not differ in indirectness.

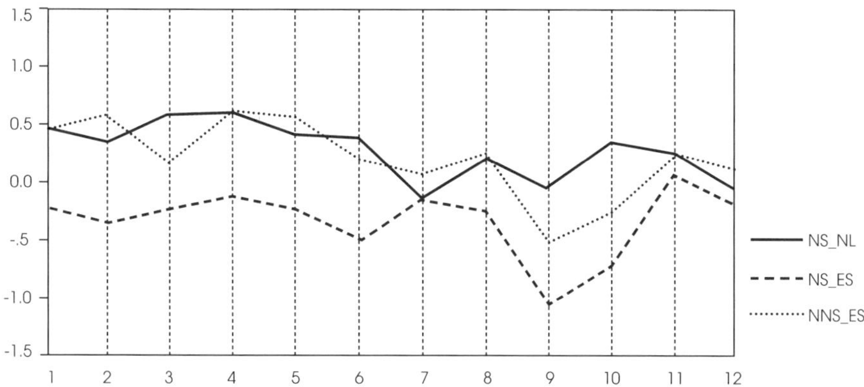

Figure 5.2. Average *z*-scores of the degree of indirectness of native speakers of Dutch (NS-NL), native speakers of Spanish (NS-ES) and learners of Spanish (NNS-ES); a higher *z*-score indicates a more indirect strategy. Situations: 1, 'Customs'; 2, 'Elderly person'; 3, 'Working overtime'; 4, 'Party at home; 5, Paper supply; 6, Supermarket; 7, Advertising campaign; 8, Neighbours; 9, Parcels; 10, Travel agency; 11, Placement report; 12, Homework help

Directness and indirectness related to situational factors

The situational factors 'power distance between speaker and addressee' (P), 'social distance between speaker and addressee' (S) and 'situational context' (C) (business or everyday context) were predicted to have an influence on the level of indirectness of a request utterance. A central issue in this study is the extent to which the three speaker groups differ with regard to the effect of the situational factors on the indirectness of their request utterances. The factors P, S and C are within-subject factors; moreover, each subject produced requests in 12 situations all characterised by a combination of P-, S- and C-values that occur *at the same time* in each of those situations (see Figure 1). A repeated measures analysis was carried out, with one between-subject factor ('group') and three within-subject factors (P, S, C) and indirectness as dependent variable. This yielded the following results.

No significant effect for the 'situational context' (C) factor was found, which means that in formal situations (C2), no more indirect strategies are used than in everyday situations (C1).

Significant main effects were found for the 'power distance' ($F(2,187) = 40.28$; $p < 0.001$) and 'social distance' ($F(1,188) = 16.61$; $p < 0.001$ factors. A significant interaction was found between 'power distance' and 'social distance': $F(2,187) = 28.80$; $p < 0.001$. Significant effects were also found for the interaction between 'power distance' and 'speaker group' ($F(4,374) = 3.72$; $p < 0.01$) and 'social distance' and 'speaker group' ($F(2,188) = 25.62$; $p < 0.001$). Finally, it turned out that there was a three-way interaction between 'power distance', 'social distance' and 'speaker group' ($F(4,374) = 6.04$; $p < 0.001$). Since this three-way interaction provides the most differentiated (though also most complicated) image of the influence of situational factors on the indirectness of the request utterances per speaker group, this influence is illustrated with the help of Figure 5.3.

Figure 5.3 shows the importance of distinguishing situations with a small social distance between the speaker and the addressee (S1) and situations in which there is a greater social distance between them (S2).

The speaker and the addressee know each other well (S1)

In S1 situations, the use of direct strategies increases for native speakers and learners of Spanish in situations in which the speaker has authority over the addressee (P3), in comparison to P1 and P2. Native speakers of Dutch barely show this tendency. In situations in which the addressee has authority over the speaker (P1), none of the three speaker groups shows a higher proportion of indirect strategies in comparison to situations in

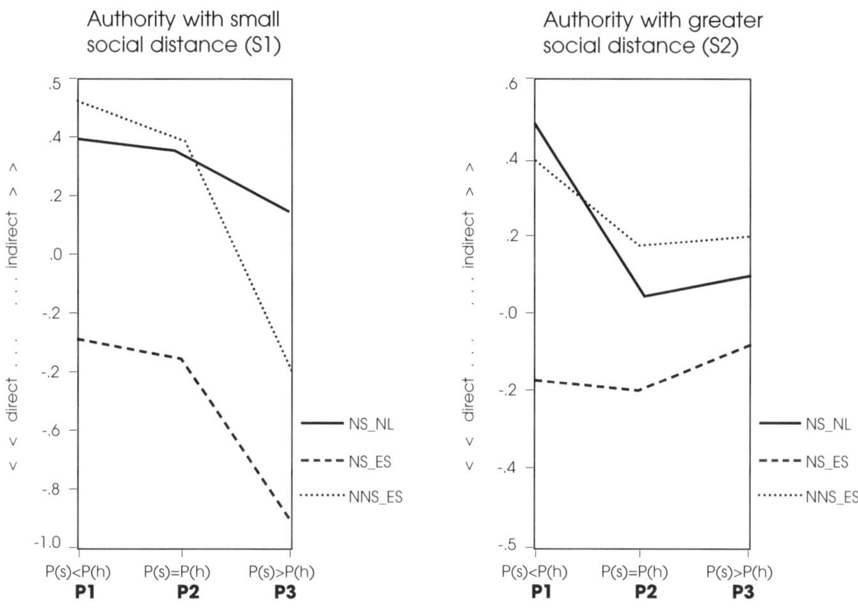

Figure 5.3 Direct and indirect strategies influenced by power distance and social distance in the three speaker groups

which the speaker and the addressee are status equals (P2). Apparently, native speakers of Spanish are sensitive mainly to authority on the side of the speaker. Dutch learners of Spanish 'follow' the native Spaniards in this tendency, even though the request utterances of the Dutch learners of Spanish remain on a more indirect level than those of the Spanish native speakers in all situations.

Speaker and addressee do not know each other (S2)

In S2 situations, the learners of Spanish do not 'follow' the tendency found in the native Spaniards, i.e. a more or less stable degree of indirectness in all S2 situations. In this type of situation, the two 'Dutch groups' show the same tendency: if speaker and addressee are status equals (P2), more direct strategies are used than in P1 situations, in which the addressee has authority. This increasing directness with increasing authority of the speaker does not occur in the native Spanish group, which does not appear to be sensitive to a different authority relationship between speaker and addressee in these situations. Also in the absolute sense, the 'Dutch groups' hardly differ with regard to their levels of indirectness. In contrast with the S1-situations, all three groups seem barely sensitive to 'speaker-authority' (P3) if this is compared to 'speaker and addressee are status equals' (P2): the indirectness even increases slightly in the three groups. As in all the S1 situations, however, the Spaniards are more direct in their requests than the Dutch.

To sum up from the viewpoint of the learners of Spanish, it may be concluded that they 'follow' the sensitivity to authority of the speaker over the addressee shown by the native speakers of Spanish in situations in which the speaker and the addressee know each other, although not reaching the degree of directness shown by the native speakers of Spanish; they do, however, relinquish some of the indirectness shown by native speakers of Dutch in favour of more direct strategies. If speaker and addressee are strangers, however, learners of Spanish seem to perform their request behaviour much like native speakers of Dutch.

Conclusion

The answers to the first three research questions posed in this chapter relate to the request strategies used by the three groups of subjects. It is shown that the Dutch learners of Spanish use request strategies in Spanish that are similar, as regards their degree of (in)directness, to those used by native speakers of Dutch in Dutch. Native speakers of Spanish use more direct strategies, in particular more imperative constructions and a larger range of suggestions uttered as requests. The impression that 'Spaniards are more direct' is heightened when we realise that Spanish does not possess any mitigating particles such as 'just' and 'perhaps', which allow Dutch imperatives to be expressed in a 'mitigated' manner. It must be stressed that indirectness is not the same as politeness, however (Blum-Kulka, 1987). To achieve more insight into the measure of politeness, research on the perception of the use of direct and indirect strategies is needed. In addition to this, the effect of all kinds of lexical markers (such as the use of 'please') and syntactic markers (such as the use of the conditional mood 'would you …') needs to be analysed.

The fourth research question refers to the role of situational factors in the performance of requests. The analyses show that the context in which interaction takes place (everyday *versus* business) has no influence on the degree of directness of the request. The 'power distance' and 'social distance' factors, however, do affect the directness level of the request utterance. This influence turns out to be quite complex in character, making itself felt in different ways for the different speaker groups. This result modifies the conclusion that Spaniards are simply more direct in their requests. The influence of authority between speaker and addressee, as well as the social distance between them, should be viewed accurately and in their mutual interaction, before any firm conclusions may be drawn. This Spanish directness (see Hickey, this volume) can only be interpreted correctly in the context of situational variation. Not until we know more about the perception and situational appropriateness of (in)directness can we draw valid conclusions about politeness.

References

Bardovi-Harlig, K. and Hartford, B. (1993) Refining the DCT: Comparing open questionnaires and dialogue completion tasks. *Pragmatics and Language Learning* (Monograph Series 4). 143165.

Blum-Kulka, S. (1987) Indirectness and politeness in requests: same or different. *Journal of Pragmatics* 11, 131–146.

Blum-Kulka, S. (1989) Playing it safe: The role of conventionality in indirectness. In S. Blum-Kulka, J. House and G. Kasper (eds) *Cross-cultural Pragmatics: Requests and Apologies*. Norwood, NJ: Ablex.

Blum-Kulka, S. and House, J. (1989) Cross-cultural and situational variation in requesting behavior. In S. Blum-Kulka, J. House and G. Kasper (eds) *Cross-cultural Pragmatics: Requests and Apologies* (pp. 123–154). Norwood, NJ: Ablex.

Blum-Kulka, S., House, J. and Kasper G. (eds) (1989) *Cross-cultural Pragmatics: Requests and Apologies.* Norwood, NJ: Ablex.

Brown, P. and Levinson, S. (1978) Universals in language usage: Politeness phenomena. In E. Goody (ed.) *Questions and Politeness: Strategies in Social Interaction* (pp. 56–89). Cambridge: Cambridge University Press.

Brown, P. and Levinson, S. (1987) *Politeness: Some Universals in Language Usage.* Cambridge: Cambridge University Press.

Fukushima, S. (1996) Request strategies in British English and Japanese. In K. Jaszczolt and K. Turner (eds) *Contrastive Semantics and Pragmatics,* II (pp. 689–702). Oxford: Elsevier Science.

Gordon, D. and Lakoff, G. (1975) Conversational postulates. In P. Cole and J. Morgan (eds) *Syntax and Semantics, 3: Speech Acts* (pp. 83–106). New York: Academic Press.

Geis, M. (1995) *Speech Acts and Conversational Interaction.* Cambridge: Cambridge University Press.

Grice, H. P. (1975) Logic and conversation. In P. Cole and J. Morgan (eds) *Syntax and Semantics, 3: Speech Acts* (pp. 41–58). New York: Academic Press.

Hartford, B. and Bardovi-Harlig, K. (1992) Experimental and observational data in the study of interlanguage pragmatics. *Pragmatics and Language Learning,* (Monograph Series 3) 33–52.

Haverkate, H. (1979) *Impositive Sentences in Spanish.* Amsterdam: North-Holland.

Haverkate, H. (1994) *La cortesía verbal: estudio pragmalingüístico.* Madrid: Gredos.

Kasper, G. (1996) Introduction: Interlanguage pragmatics in SLA. *Studies in Second Language Acquisition 18*, 145–48.

Kasper, G. and Dahl, M. (1991) Research methods in interlanguage pragmatics. *Studies in Second Language Acquisition 13*, 215–47.

Kasper, G. and Blum-Kulka, S. (1993) Interlanguage pragmatics: An introduction. In G. Kasper and S. Blum-Kulka (eds) *Interlanguage Pragmatics* (pp. 31–7). New York/Oxford: Oxford University Press.

Kim, M.S. (1993) Culture-based interactive constraints in explaining intercultural strategic competence. In R. Wiseman and J. Koester (eds) *Intercultural Communication Competence: International and Intercultural Communication annual, XVII* (pp. 132–50). Newbury Park, CA: Sage.

Koike, D. (1996) Transfer of pragmatic competence and suggestions in Spanish foreign language learning. In S. Gass and J. Neu (eds) *Speech Acts Across Cultures: Challenges to Communication in a Second Language* (pp. 257–81). Berlin/New York: Mouton de Gruyter.

Labov, W. and Fanshel, D. (1977) *Therapeutic Discourse: Psychotherapy as Conversation.* New York: Academic Press.

Leech, G. (1983) *Principles of Pragmatics.* London: Longman.

Morgan, J. (1978) Two types of convention in indirect speech acts. In P. Cole and J. Morgan (eds) *Syntax and Semantics 9: Pragmatics* (pp. 261–80). New York: Academic Press.

Mulken, M. van (1996) Politeness markers in French and Dutch requests. In K. Jaszczolt and K. Turner (eds) *Contrastive Semantics and Pragmatics* II (pp. 689–702). Oxford: Elsevier Science.

Le Pair, R. (1994) 'Pedir algo': communicatiestrategieën vanuit een pragmalinguïstisch perspectief. In C. van Esch and M. Steenmeyer (eds) *Symposium Spaans in onderwijs, onderzoek en bedrijfsleven* 5 (pp. 38–56). Nijmegen: Katholieke Universiteit Nijmegen.

Le Pair, R. (1996) Spanish request strategies: A cross-cultural analysis from an intercultural perspective. In K. Jaszczolt and K. Turner (eds) *Contrastive Semantics and Pragmatics, II* (pp. 651–70). Oxford: Elsevier Science.

Le Pair, R. (1997) Verzoekstrategieën in het Spaans. Een cross-cultureel en intercultureel perspectief. PhD thesis, University of Nijmegen.

Rose, K. (1992) Speech acts and questionnaires: The effect of hearer response. *Journal of Pragmatics* 17. 49–62.

Rose, K. (1994) On the validity of discourse completion tests in non Western contexts. *Applied Linguistics* 15, 1–14.

Sadock, J. (1974) *Toward a Linguistic Theory of Speech Acts.* New York: Academic Press.

Searle, J. (1969) *Speech Acts: An Essay in the Philosophy of Language.* Cambridge: Cambridge University Press.

Searle, J. (1975) Indirect speech acts. In P. Cole and J. Morgan (eds) *Syntax and Semantics 3: Speech Acts* (pp. 59–82). New York: Academic Press.

Searle, J. (1976) A classification of illocutionary acts. *Language in Society* 5, 1–23.

Thomas, J. (1983) Cross-cultural pragmatic failure. *Applied Linguistics* 4, (2), 91–112.
Trosborg, A. (1995) *Interlanguage Pragmatics: Requests, Complaints and Apologies.* Berlin/New York: Mouton de Gruyter.
Van der Wijst, P. (1996) *Politeness in Requests and Negotiations.* Dissertatie Katholieke Universiteit Brabant. Dordrecht: ICG Printing.

Chapter 6

Politeness in Austria: Politeness and Impoliteness

SILVIA HAUMANN, URSULA KOCH AND KARL SORNIG

Various kinds of (communicative) behaviour serve either to express solidarity and friendliness or to show more or less rudeness. Besides linguistic modes, there are non-verbal modes which also express either solidarity or social distance, such as bodily stance, proximity, gestures, facial expressions, eye contact and even (becoming or unbecoming) dress. All of these are elements of behaviour that members of any social group are supposed to know and remember, either to comply with or to ignore.

We shall base our discussion here on linguistic material available from our studies into the colloquial use of Southern German, as spoken and recorded in the various provinces of Austria (1977–2000). These data will, therefore, be used for an exclusively intra-cultural study of our subject.

Topic

Communicative activities are never quite exempt from considerations of politeness, relating to stylistic decisions regarding expressive means to choose and how exactly to use them. Such stylistic decisions governing and allowing for diversity in communicative behaviour depend broadly on the following distinctions: the subject matter (topic) to be negotiated and the speech act to be realised, dependent on the role relationship between the interlocutors, especially the risks and costs of the interaction for either participant.

The right to select and deal with a certain topic is a prerogative that derives from the rank of the participant. This of course poses the problem of turn-taking (see later) and turn usurpation, the latter being liable to be used (and understood) as an element of impolite behaviour (but see Hickey, this volume).

Besides, there are – in any society – topics that ought to be avoided altogether. Needless to say, these restrictions are subject to change over the course of time. For example, in Austria one should avoid mentioning one's interlocutors' financial position or political affiliation while the taboo on erotic topics has been weakened in recent years.

Role Relationship

Of primary importance is the positional and/or emotional relationship between interactants.

Role-governed behaviour signals and realises either intimacy, belonging and egalitarian solidarity, or formal social distance: 'Sympathy is extended or withdrawn' (Brown & Gilman, 1972: 277). Of considerable importance is social and affective distance, in other words, constellations of power *versus* solidarity, resulting from differences in age, sex or social status. Apart from these pre-eminently permanent role relationships according to status, there are situationally-governed relationships,[1] where considerations of politeness may be of even greater relevance, such as patient–doctor or parent–offspring communication, which are examples of extremely non-egalitarian, asymmetric relationships.

In certain conversational situations, it is necessary to be familiar with the assumptions about what kind of contributions (small talk, gossiping, joking etc.) will be regarded as cooperative in the circumstances. However, there are specific relationships where role-governed behaviour is, to a certain extent, suspended, e.g. 'among members of the same political creed, fellow students, or people who share the same hobby: mountaineers above a certain critical altitude shift to the mutual T' (Brown & Gilman, 1972: 262).

Mitigating and redressive steps (see later) exert great influence upon the perlocutionary effect of conversational moves. These steps can be gradually reduced in accordance with the development of an egalitarian balance between the partners. This even holds (nowadays) for the (traditional) behaviour of males in the presence of, or towards, female participants.

There is another important element responsible for different choices in communicative behaviour, that is the absence or presence of an audience, of bystanding and overhearing parties.

Naturally, conversations within the hearing of by-standers will be conducted differently from dyadic conversations; role relationships are likely to be camouflaged in conversations if outsiders are present:

Example 1

Mother: *Wie führst du dich auf vor den anderen Leuten!* (How do you behave in the presence of other people!) (Penzinger, 1985:161)

Example 2

Mother: *Stell dich nicht so blöd an, wenn Besuch da ist!*
(Don't behave so stupidly when we have guests!) (Penzinger, 1985:122)

Normal constellation reversed with the familiar partner regarded and treated as intruder:

Example 3

Mother: *Du, die Mutti möcht jetzt mit dem Onkel was redn. Sei jetzt brav – und quatsch nicht immer dazwischen.* (Let mum talk. Be a good girl and don't interrupt.) (Penzinger, 1985: 26)

Mishaps and Failures

Any kind of conscious and regulated behaviour should be analysed against a background of possible improper (impolite) demeanour and the mishaps (misunderstandings) that might occur in conversational procedures. Any communicative action may fail. For one thing, role relationships (e.g. kinship deference) may restrict otherwise possible and acceptable steps. Mistakes and errors are most easily discernible on the lower levels of linguistic realisation, e.g. in the use of terms of address: 'T, once extended, is almost never taken back for the reason that it would mean the complete withdrawal of esteem' (Brown & Gilman, 1972: 280).

Of course, doing things can be wrong but the alternative, namely not doing anything, is not particularly effective as a *vademecum* against communicative failure, e.g. keeping silent when you are expected to say something. Here we are confronted with the communicative relevance of pauses and silence in general.[2]

Mistakes in the use of pronouns may be regarded as rude, even insulting.

Rejecting the T-pronoun of solidarity:

Example 4

Sau gholtn habn ma noch net miteinand, göll, eingruckt a net miteinand. (We haven't been in the army together, have we?) (GU)

Example 5

Reporter, asking a girl who has won a 100m race:
Wie heißt du bitte?– Das geht Sie gar nichts an! (What's your [T] name? – Mind your [V] own business!) (Sammer, 1985: 153)

Speech Act Level

It is at speech act level that social and/or affective relationships are expressed most conspicuously.

Speech acts vary according to several aspects, amongst which are the costs, or the risk of face-loss, for the recipient (as well as the speaker) and the need for deference and/or mitigation as well as diverse preparatory steps as an introduction. This is where considerations of tact and politeness take on much more importance than mere cooperative maxims can explain.

Moreover, there are various acts that ought to be avoided altogether, i.e. speech acts that constitute forbidden ground for certain participants: never inquire about the age of women; do not argue with police officers, etc.

Opening and closing steps

Terms of address and moves to initiate a conversation are prominent opportunities to express politeness, presumably because they explicitly acknowledge rank and pay respect. Terms of address do not carry information beyond the acknowledgement of the other's social position, e.g. age, personal relationships or whether previously acquainted. Mention of the time of day and inquiry into one's interlocutor's health, family etc. are not really requests for information:[3]

Example 6

Wie geht's, wie steht's, Herr Kollege? (How is it going, how are things?) (Quite usual among colleagues)

Opting out of a conversational interaction also necessitates means of phatic communication and signals of politeness:

Also dann / Alles Gute / Auf bald/ Grüß mir deine Frau / etc. (So long / Best wishes / So long / Give my love to your wife / etc.)

These formulas usually try to implicate unanimity.

Greetings

There are various specifically Austrian forms and formulas:
(1) Ways of saying hello:

- *Grüß Gott* with its variants from formal to familar: *'sGott, Grüß Sie (Gott)*, sometimes even *Grüß Ihnen, Grüß dich/euch, Begrüße; Servus, Hallo, Haile* (Vorarlberg), *Hoi* (Vorarlberg) etc.; and *Küß die Hand* (to ladies) and *Habe die Ehre* (among gentlemen) are both very formal and old-fashioned but are still sometimes heard.

(2) Ways of saying goodbye:

- *Grüß Gott etc.* (except *Begrüße*), *Wiedersehn, Wiederschaun;*
- *Pfiat di/euch (Gott) < Behüt dich* (etc) *Gott*, which is never used with *Sie* but may be used with the dialectal pronouns *enk/Eahna (=euch/Ihnen);*

and

- *Servus, Baba, Haile, Hoi* etc., each with its specific indications of role. Sometimes they are combined (*Grüß dich servus, Servus baba* etc.), the more intimate usually in second position. Foreign but quite popular (among intimates): *Hi, Ciao, Tschüss.*

When and whom not to greet is a decision of great significance: whereas in rural areas everybody usually greets everybody else, strangers included, this does not apply to urban environments.

Pronouns of address

Speakers are required to select a pronoun of address: T (*du*), V (*Sie* or even *Ihr*). The use of pronouns of address differs from the Eastern to the Western provinces of Austria. This is partly due to the dialectal differences separating the two areas. Consequently, the use of pronouns of address – as well as other lexical items – is distributed differently. Whereas in Tyrol and Vorarlberg the T-pronoun *du* is the usual and almost only pronoun of address, the distinction between *du* and *Sie* (in some rural areas even *Ihr* is in use) is strictly observed in the rest of the country.

Vocatives and imperatives as parts of verbs in speech addressed to one's interlocutor may serve the same purpose to indicate social distinction. This is a consequence of their grammatical/morphological distinctness: *Schau! Hörst? Gell?* (note the peculiar form *Gölln'S* with the enclitic pronoun of respect *Sie*).

When interlocutors change, a switch in pronoun-use may result:

Example 7

Bank clerk asks the telephone operator to connect him with a colleague: *Ja, Herr Kollege, ich möcht gern den Herrn Schönwetter habn, geh'bitte! – Servus Erwin, grüß di Gott. Du, ich hob jetzt diese gaunzn Sochn kriegt wegn der Obänderung, gö ...* (Can you please put me through to Mr. Schönwetter. – Hi Erwin, howdy. You know, I've got these things concerning the...) (Sornig, 1983: 241) (Note the phonological switch from standard German to the vernacular.)

The following examples combine respect with intimacy:

Example 8

Herr Sornig, du hast unlängst selber g'sagt ... (Mr. Sornig, you (T) yourself said only recently ...

Example 9

Landlady: *Herr Zoller, werst no was (Herr Z., wirst du noch etwas (trinken))*? (Mr Zoller, are you (T) having another one (drink)?) (Overheard 29 December 2001)

Norms have changed over recent decades, especially among younger speakers. The use of first names, accompanied by the second person singular (*du*), is regarded as an obvious sign of intimacy. A change from one pronoun of address to another – usually from V to T – is practically irreversible and irrevocable. A change from the intimate *du* to the formal *Sie* is regarded as utterly impolite and even insulting (see earlier).

Honorifics, titles etc.

In contrast to usage in Germany, titles and honorifics are still a prominent and specific characteristic of formal conversation in Austria. There is a whole gamut of titles at the disposal of Austrian speakers: *Herr/Frau* (even old-fashioned *Gnädige Frau* is still in use), academic titles like *Magister, Doktor, Professor, Primarius*, administrative and purely honorific such as *Direktor, Hofrat, Präsident* and political ranks – *Landesrat, Nationalrat*, etc.

Misapplications may cause conflict. This is reflected in controversial misuse when surnames are used without a title or even without *Herr* or *Frau*.

Example 10

die Neutralität ist anders als hier Haider suggeriert ... (the neutrality is different from what Haider is insinuating here ...) (Halwachs, 1991:40)

Example 11

was meint also das Vier-Punkte-Programm des Vranitzky... (so what does the Four-Point-Programme of Vranitzky say ...) [uttered in the absence of Haider and Vranitzky] (Halwachs, 1991: 41)

This can be compared with the following examples:

Example 12

Herr Bundesgeschäftsführer Voggenhuber verdrehen Sie doch nicht die Statistik ... (Mr Bundesgeschäftsführer Voggenhuber, please don't distort the statistics ...) (Halwachs, 1991: 46)

Example 13

Ich glaube Herr Doktor Swoboda, lieber Herr Doktor, verehrter Herr Doktor Swoboda ... (I think Mr Swoboda, dear Doctor, dearest Doctor Swoboda ...) (*Öslerreichischer Rundfunk* [ORF] 22 February2001)

As a side-effect of the Austrians' extensive use of honorifics,[4] ambiguous exploitation of titles may even function as make-believe, i.e. ironic politeness, and thus be far from polite[5]. (For a discussion of titular honorifics, see Huszcza, this volume.)

Hardly surprisingly, the time-honoured Austrian preference for the use of titles has quite a respectable tradition in our satirical and parodic literature. Nicknames are special signals of intimacy, despite their sometimes seemingly face-threatening propositional content: it is precisely this fictitious aggressive intention that constitutes their effect of intimacy.

Responses

Communicative contact is inefficient without the hearer's acknowledgement. The speaker expects some indication that the message has got across, i.e. the hearer's reactions are essential parts of phatic communication. Phatic steps such as back-channelling have one characteristic in common: they cannot be questioned or challenged. They have no propositional meaning beyond their discursive function, their vagueness is essential:[6]

ja / mhm / wirkli? / (aber) geh! / eben = äbe (Vorarlberg) */ gö(l), gell / ah so? / jo genau / jo sicher(lich) / klar / freilich.*

The speaker might elicit some kind of reaction from the hearer by saying

Nicht wahr? / Net? / Verstehst? / Weißt? / Oder? = Odr! (Vorarlberg)

The following is an example of a doctor's callous, unresponsive, reaction, seen in an abrupt change of topic, to his patient's utterance:

Example 14

Patient: *jetzt bin ich total fertig, weil ich hab das net gwußt ... das hat mich schon* ... [I'm really shattered now, 'cause I didn't know ... it sort of has ...]
Doctor: *Haben Sie irgendwelche Fragen jetzt?*
[Do you have] any more questions [right now]? (Gstettner, 2001: 141)

Hearer responses may manifest themselves in various ways: repetition of the speaker's statement is especially responsive and face-saving because of its high degree of adjustment:

Example 15

Customer A: *Milch bitte auch* (And milk, please)
Shopkeeper: *Milch, ja* (Milk, yes)
Customer A: *Liter Milch* (One pint of milk)
Shopkeeper: *Einen Liter, bitteschön. Ein Liter Milch, bittesehr* (One pint, yes. One pint of milk, very well) (GU)

Example 16

Shoe-shop customer refuses shop assistant's offer:
Customer: *Na, die g'falln mir net* (No, I don't like these)
Shop assistant: *Gfällt Ihnen nicht* (You don't like them) (GU)
(Note the alternate usage of standard and colloquial forms.)

Paraphrasing the speaker's utterance has a similarly appeasing effect.

There are, of course, many other possibilities, even formulas, for expressing agreement:

Stimmt / Ja, da haben'S recht / Hast recht / Ja sicher / Da bin ich Ihrer Meinung / Nanet /Ja wirklich / Ja freilich / Freili wohl / etc.

Example 17

is mir schon klar ... (I quite understand) (*ORF,* 14 February1995)

Example 18

nein, nein, vollkommen richtig, ...Herr Kollege selbstverständlich ... (no, no, you're perfectly right, ... of course ,... exactly ...) (*ORF,* 23 February 2000)

Example 19

Ich bin voll auf Ihrer Seite... (I quite agree [with you] ...) (*ORF* 23 February 2000)

Turn-taking

Turn-taking strategies and manouevres are transparent reflections of power relations and rivalries. In cases where a speaker does not organise a change of turn beforehand, rivalry cannot always be subdued or suppressed:

Example 20

Insurance clerk: *Warten'S, was ich Ihnen sag* … (Wait, let me tell you …) (Sammer, 1985: 278)

Example 21

Insurance clerk: *Passen'S auf! Jetzt lassen'S mich auch was sagen.* (Now wait a second, let me also say something.) (Sammer, 1985: 147)

Example 22

Insurance clerk: *Jetzt seien'S amol ruhig!* (Now be quiet for a moment!) (Sammer, 1985: 336)

Example 23

gestatten Sie, daß ich, gestatten Sie, daß i fertig rede ? (would you please, would you please be so kind as to let me finish my sentence?) (*ORF*, 30 April 1995)

Example 24

jetzt red amal tschuldigen'S … daß amal i red. (it's my turn, excuse me …that's me talking now.) (*ORF*, 30 April 1995)

Example 25

Jetz hör amål zua! (Now listen for a moment!) (Overheard 16 January 2002)

Requests

Requests for information or for help, warnings, directives etc. are examples of differing degrees of imposition on the territory of the recipient. They may or may not be accompanied by mitigating pre-sequences.

Offering help

Example 26

Shop assistant: *Womit kann ich dienen?* (old-fashioned), *kann ich Ihnen helfen?* Can I help you? (Usual)

Ordering a meal

Example 27

Seien'S so gut und bringen'S mir… (Be so kind as to bring me …) (GU)

Introducing a question

Example 28

Entschuldigen Sie, gleich a Frage … (Excuse me, let me ask you a question to start with …) (*ORF*)

Example 29

Herr D., an Augenblick, eine Sachfrage … (Mr. D., just a moment, there's a question regarding …) (*ORF*, 22 November 1994)

The length of these introductory pre-sequences is indicative of the degree of the speaker's consideration for the face of the interlocutor.

Maternal warning/admonishment intensified by an ethic dative (see later):

Example 30

Daß du mir das nie wieder tust! (Don't you ever try and do that again!) (Penzinger, 1985: 80)

Example 31

Schatzi, aba du steigst mir nicht ins Wasser, gel? (You are not going to step into the water, dear, are you?) (Penzinger, 1985: 70)

Contradictions, interdictions, reprimands, threats

Requests, demands, commands, advice and similar acts all have the aim of inducing one's interlocutor to act in a certain way (or to refrain from acting in a certain way) which may involve varying degrees of threat to face.

Acts that oppose the interlocutor's interests and thwart his/her intentions are particularly face-threatening: e.g. contradiction, complaint, protest, criticism, reprimands, reproach, insults (bald on record or hedged). Some of these speech acts, despite constituting serious impositions, may sometimes be extended beyond camouflage to the point of really giving offence, remedial strategies becoming more and more rare.

Disagreement with one's interlocutor's opinion or statement (note the length of the introductory steps):

Example 32

Insurance clerk: *Ja, aber … trotzdem … trotz allem …*(Yes, but … still … nevertheless …) (Sammer, 1985: 270)

There are many formulas for questioning what one's interlocutor has said:

Ja aber / Ehrlich gesagt / Wenn'st mi fragst / Nein, bitte / Das seh ich anders / Ja schon, aber / Ja sicher, seh i ein, aber / Sein'S mir net ungehalten / Net bös sein, aber

Example 33

I will jå nix sågn, åba ... (I don't want to argue but ...) (overheard, 16 January 2002)

Example 34 Maternal order repeated and stressed

Mach die Tür zu...Ich hab dir gesagt, du sollst die Tür zumachen...Was hab ich dir gesagt?...Wenn du nicht sofort...Ich sag das nicht noch einmal... (Close the door...I've just told you to close the door...What did I tell you?...If you don't at once...I'm not going to repeat myself ...) (Penzinger, 1985: 158)

Example 35 Imperative, bald on record, assisted by reasoning

Komm!...Du, komm her jetzt! Wir kommen sonst zu spät nach Hause! (Come on!...Right away! Otherwise we'll be late!) (Penzinger, 1985: 40)

Example 36 Maternal order, intensified by threat

Du sollst nicht laufen. Hörst, aber jetzt kriegst du von mir eine! (I've told you not to run. You've been asking for it, now you're going to get it [a smack] from me!) (Penzinger, 1985: 42)

Remedies, repairs, apologies

Any expression, notwithstanding its polite intention, may nevertheless be misunderstood, e.g. cases of exaggerated politeness where a more modest form of expression would have been appropriate. The need for redressive and corrective steps is always imminent.

Misunderstanding as well as any kind of misguided behaviour (intended or unintentional) is liable to be redressed in order to avoid undesirable effects and feelings; this is usually done by apologies, justifications and all kinds of appeasing responses:

Mei(n Gott) entschuldigen'S / des hab i net so g'meint ... (I'm really sorry / I didn't mean to ...)

Of course, compliments and self-denigration are important ways of minimizing face threats.

Expressions of Respect

Means of expressing (or denying) respect may be either direct (bald on record) or indirect (hedged). In direct speech acts, formulaic speech plays a considerable role since formulas have unequivocally fixed meanings and cannot easily be misinterpreted. Moreover, expressions of respect tend to be strikingly long since verbosity seems to be a politeness marker. Depending on the costs and risks of threat to face, preparatory elements will vary considerably.

Preparatory steps

Also, nämlich, folgendes, ja bitte function as preparatory steps.

Example 37

Was ich Sie gerne abfragen will … (What I would like to ask you …) (Gstettner, 2001:135)

Example 38

Ja grüß Gott, …ich hätte eine andere Frage an den Herrn Hofrat, und zwar bezüglich… (Good morning, ...now there is another question I would like to ask Mr X,….) (*ORF*, 26 June 1990) (For further examples see earlier)

Orders

In parental (or military) orders, imperatives are the most direct means, they are short and usually lack any mitigating or redressive elements:

Example 39

Father: *Und bleib rechtzeitig stehn mit dem Roller…gleich bremsen und aufpassen.* (And don't forget to stop…do use your brakes.) (Penzinger, 1985: 42)

Talking to Foreigners

The way we sometimes talk to foreigners is a special case of openly displayed disrespect (talking down to somebody): its deficiencies (pidginisation) are intended not only to reduce complexities of grammar or vocabulary in order to assist comprehension but also to demonstrate disrespect, even contempt. If pronouns are used, it is usually second person singular (*du*) demonstrative of condescension, not of solidarity:

Example 40

Wo du wohnen? – Du hier unterschreiben. (Where you [T] live? You here sign.) (Fasch, 1993: 54)

Indirectness

Any culture or society acknowledges subject matter and conversational steps that ought to be handled with care, with some areas subject to taboo restrictions. Some of these necessitate extenuation, achieved usually by indirectness. Indirectness is widely used as a camouflaging expedient to avoid threat to face. Though indirect means (e.g. conversational implicatures) necessitate some decoding effort on the recipient's part, their use is omnipresent and well established. (cf. Brown & Levinson, 1987: 132ff).

Some of these hints, hedges and off-record allusions ('It is cold in here' as a request to close the window) are quite conventionalized so that they require no more effort to be understood than their more direct equivalents.

Refusing to buy something:

Example 41

Customer (shoeshop): *Na, der is schon sehr ...Ich glaub der is eher für ältere Damen, ha?* (Well, this one is rather ... I think it's for elderly ladies, isn't it?) (GU)

Impersonalisation

Haase (1998: 92) discusses 'Impersonalisierungsmechanismen (z.B. Passiv), die Sprecher und Hörer von der Sprechhandlung distanzieren...'.

Example 42

Bank clerk: *Wie ist der werte Name?* (Would you please give us your name?) (GU)

Example 43

Waitress: *Was trinkt der Herr?* (What is the gentleman going to drink?) (GU)

Example 44

Waitress: *Die Herrschaften werden schon bedient?* (Are you [= they] being served?) (GU)

Sociable plural

What we call the 'nurses' plural' (also used in 'motherese') serves as a mitigating strategy: instead of bald imperatives or some kind of whimperative, the sociable 'we plural' is used to get children or similarly power-dependent persons, e.g. elderly patients, to submit to activities they would not choose on their own initiative.[7]

Example 45

Mother: *Jetzt gehen wir dann in unser Betterl.* (Let us go to bed now, shall we.) (Overheard) (Note the use of diminutives as another means of mitigation.)

Apart from the function as a 'nurses' plural', this may serve to avoid direct address:

Example 46

Greengrocers' market:
Nehmen wir mit ein Sträußerl? (Why not have a bunch of flowers?) (Sammer, 1985: 160) (Note the use of diminutives.)

Example 47

Police officer: *Und wo wohn'ma (wohnen wir)?* (And where do we (=you) live?) (GU)

Interrogatives

Interrogative sequences can replace direct requests and directives. Rhetorical question and particles (maternal):

Example 48

Willst du nicht (endlich einmal / vielleicht wenigstens) dein Zimmer aufräumen? (You don't believe in tidying up your room, do you?) (Overheard)

Grammatical Deviations and Peculiarities

Use of the dative case (see earlier)

'Der Dativ, der als Kasus für weniger zentrale Aktanten, nämlich *Rezipienten, Benefizienten* usw. vorgesehen ist, übernimmt die Funktion familiärer Bezugnahme ... ' (Haase, 1998: 49) (compare with Examples 30 and 31)

Example 49

Paß mir ja auf, hörst du? (Watch out, will you?) (Overheard)

Example 50

Na, hören'S mir auf! Das ist nicht richtig. (Come on, stop it. That's not true.) (GU)

The conditional instead of a main clause

This gives the interlocutor the opportunity to avoid a request which would have been expressed in the main clause:

Example 51

Shop assistant: *Wenn Sie ein bisserl Platz nehmen* ... (If you would take a seat?) (GU)

Syntactic reductions

Example 52

Doctor: *Gut. Irgendwelche früheren Erkrankungen?* (Good. Any previous illnesses?) (Gstettner, 2001: 17)

Indirect statements accompanied by particles

To mitigate face-threatening acts, statements and questions are often accompanied by one or more particles: *Du liest zuviel* becomes: *Ich glaube, du liest ja wohl eigentlich auch zu viel.* (Don't you think your reading a bit excessive.) (Haase, 1998: 95)

Silence

To refrain from saying anything at all is a specific – perhaps the last – expedient to avoid face-threatening acts. However, silence, being non-cooperative, may easily be regarded as impolite and reacted to as such (see above).

The Connotative Power of the Vernacular

Languages like German, with non-standard varieties in addition to the accepted literary norm, offer another means for signalling solidarity and intimacy, i.e. using colloquial, dialectal, even slangy forms of expression. The choice between stylistic variants, either of a more colloquial or a rather formal register, is unavoidable and ubiquitous.

The power of the vernacular as a symptom and sign of belonging and camaraderie has strong emotional and affective connotations. Slang elements evoke 'all the shared associations and attitudes' (Zöllner, 1997: 85).[8]

However, these connotational elements may not only have a friendly and solidary effect, they may equally manifest aggression and insult (cf. features of this kind in the following examples).

Example 53

wann Sie's so genau wissn, sågn'S ma's. (…if you know it so well, why don't you tell me.) (*ORF,* 30 April 1995)

Example 54

i man, des find i wirklich årg (this is really too much.) (*ORF,* 20 April 1995)

Putting somebody in their place:

Example 55

jo wo samma denn überhaupt? (where do you think we are?) (*ORF,* 25 February 2000)

A switch back to standard usage means, in any case, a greater degree of formality.

Example 56

Insurance official: *…können'S ma glaubm…Eines können Sie mir glauben* (believe me … there is one thing of which you can be sure) … (Sammer, 1985: 280)

Example 57

weil so a gmahte Wiesn is auch das nicht gewesen… (the problem was not really settled by …) (*ORF*, 30 April 1985)

Example 58

jå i waß schon, Sie verteidigen sich da alle miteinander a bissl, åber i find man sollte aber schon ein bisschen … (I know, you're sort of trying to defend yourselves, all of you, a little bit, but I think one should) (*ORF*, 30 April 1985)

Imitation of baby talk (or 'motherese') is another signal of close intimacy:

Example 59

Doctor: *Darf ich Ihnen a bissi erklären, wie das läuft?* (Let me tell you a bit …) (Gstettner, 2001: 170)

Infantilizing leave-taking terms such as *Baba, Ciao-li, Tschüss-i* and the like have become extremely popular recently in Austria among young people as well as adults, even between officials. They serve similar socialising purposes to traditional greetings like *Servus, Herr Hofrat*.

In Austria, as we have seen in the case of the influx of infantilising leave-taking terms, there is innovation at the same time as there is an adherence to traditional norms as evidenced in the retention of a wide range of titles and honorifics. There is no shared norm and factors such as domain may determine a range of linguistic choices. For example, a knowledge of whether one is in a rural or urban domain may determine when and whom to greet, which form of pronominal address one uses, which titles and honorifics are appropriate and whether one adopts a non-standard variety.

Notes

1. 'Role relationships and ranking of subject matter (topic) need not be regarded as preordained configurations.' Coupland *et al.* (1988: 258f) argue in favour of a more dynamic appreciation of role-orientated activities.
2. 'Perhaps because it functions at a lower level of consciousness than speech, many (perhaps most) otherwise fluent bilinguals retain a foreign 'accent ' in their use of silence in the second language, retaining native silence patterns even as they use the new language' (Saville-Troike, 1985: 13).
3. 'While in Nigeria, the inference is made that someone who asks about one's children, wife, and relations in a greeting is concerned and caring, the inclusion of the same propositional content in greetings in Germany could result in the inference that the speaker is intruding in the addressee's private life. ' (Adegbijac, 1993: 9)
4. It is not unusual in Austria for wives or widows to ask to be addressed by their husband's title.
5. '(i) *Wünscht der Herr Doktor zu speisen?*
   (ii) *Zum Abrocknen ist sich der Herr Doktor wohl zu schade?*
   Während Satz (i), im Restaurant vom Kellner zum Gast gesprochen, ehrerbietig aufgefaßt wird, ist Satz (ii) als Bemerkung einer Ehefrau zu ihrem Mann ganz und gar nicht höflich. In diesem Kontext wäre Satz (i) ebenfalls kaum ehrerbietig gemeint. Die indirekte Anrede, die auf der Höflichkeitsskala des Deutschen eine hohe Position einnimmt, kann je nach Situation besonders höflich, aber auch ausgesprochen unhöflich wirken. ' (Haase, 1998: 18)
   'He [Captain Hook] was never more sinister than when he was most polite. ' (Barry, 1995: 55)
6. Be vague. Indeed 'one powerful and pervasive motive for *not* talking maxim-wise is the desire to give some attention to face. ' (Brown & Levinson, 1987: 95)
7. '[p]oliteness phenomena in nurses' talk to institutionalized elderly people ...' (Coupland *et al.*, 1988: 258)
8. 'In-group identity markers' (Brown & Levinson, 1987: 100ff.)

References

Adegbijac, E.(1993) *Greeting Norms in Nigeria and Germany, Their Place in International Understanding and Misunderstanding*. Düsseldorf: Linguistic Agency Univiversity of Düsseldorf (LAUD).

Barry, J.M. (1995) *Peter Pan*. London: Penguin.

Brown, P. and Levinson, S. (1987) *Politeness: Some Universals in Language Usage*. Cambridge: Cambridge University Press.

Brown, R. and Gilman, A. (1972) The pronouns of power and solidarity. In P. Giglioli (ed.) *Language and Social Context* (pp.252–82). Harmondsworth: Penguin.

Coupland, N., Grainger, K. and Coupland, J. (1988) Politeness in context: Intergenerational issues (Review article on Brown and Levinson 1978/1987). *Language in Society* 17, 253–62.

Fasch, Ch. (1993) Foreigner talk. Analyse eines soziolinguistischen Phänomens auf empirischer Basis. Unpublished Bachelor's thesis, University of Graz.

GU (Grazer Protokolle zur (österreichischen) Umgangssprache) (1975–1990) Mimeo.

Gstettner, A. (2001) Die Götter in Weiss und ihr 'Fall'. Kritische Diskursanalyse zur Kommunikation zwischen Arzt und Patient anhand von Erstgesprächen an einer onkologischen Ambulanz. Eine empirische Untersuchung. Unpublished Bachelor's thesis, University of Graz.

Haase, M. (1998) *Respekt. Die Grammatikalisierung von Höflichkeit. Unterschleissheim b.* München: Lincom Europa.

Halwachs, D. (1991) Persuasiver Sprachgebrauch in der Politik. Versuch einer Stilanalyse anhand von TV-Gesprächen. Bachelor's thesis, University of Graz.

Penzinger, Ch. (1985) *Soziostilistische Sprachstrukturen in der Mutter–Kind-Interaktion an Beispielen aus der Grazer Umgangssprache*. Frankfurt/M.: P. Lang.

Sammer, I. (1985) Fehler in Sprechakten. Unpublished PhD thesis, University of Graz.

Saville-Troike, M. (1985) The place of silence in an integral theory of communication. In D. Tannen and M. Saville-Troike (eds) *Perspectives on Silence*. Norwood, NJ: Ablex.

Sornig, K. (1983) Indikatoren der Rollendistanz in Alltagsgesprächen. In B. Sandig (ed.) *Stilistik II. Gesprächsstile*. (*Germanistische Linguistik* 5–6) (pp. 223–60). Hildesheim: Olms.

Zöllner, N. (1997) *Der Euphemismus im alltäglichen und politischen Sprachgebrauch des Englischen*. Frankfurt/M.: P. Lang.

Chapter 7

Politeness in Switzerland: Between Respect and Acceptance

GIUSEPPE MANNO

Introduction

Switzerland does not correspond to the (romantic) idea of 'one nation – one language'. Its constitution recognises four official national languages (German, French, Italian and Romansh) and the 'territorial principle' guarantees four (monolingual) linguistic areas: *Deutschschweiz* (DS), *Suisse Romande* (SR), *Ticino* and part of the *canton Graubünden*). In spite of Switzerland's small size, therefore, it is culturally complex and diverse.[1] Furthermore, each area has, except for the Romansh, a nation with a corresponding national language behind it: for instance, SR is politically Swiss but linguistically and culturally French.

Each area's speakers actually see big differences between themselves and others. Büchi (2001), for example, summarises the differences between SR and DS as follows:

> les Alémaniques s'étonnent parfois de l'urbanité courtoise qui règne dans la société romande. Les Romands n'hésitent pas à s'interpeller par 'cher ami'; à assurer quelqu'un qu'ils connaissent à peine de leur 'amitié'; à boire force 'verres de l'amitié' même avec des gens qu'ils abhorrent, et à s'embrasser plutôt trois fois qu'une. Ils se donnent du 'Madame' et du 'Monsieur', même 'Mademoiselle' n'a pas encore été banni, malgré les protestations féministes. Les Alémaniques, en revanche, ont souvent l'air emprunté quand ils doivent saluer quelqu'un, car leurs coutumes les obligent à dire le nom de leurs interlocuteurs. Alors ils préfèrent parfois leur donner du 'Herr Doktor' ou ... changer de trottoir.
>
> (... the German-speaking Swiss are occasionally surprised at the courteous manners which prevail in French-speaking Switzerland. The French-speaking Swiss are happy to call each other 'dear friend'; to profess their 'friendship' for a bare acquaintance; to drink copiously to each other's good health even with people they detest and to kiss each other on the cheek three times rather than once. They address each other

with 'Madame', 'Monsieur' and even with 'Mademoiselle', which despite protests from feminists, has not been eradicated. The German-speaking Swiss, in contrast, often look awkward when they are to greet someone as their customs require them to pronounce the name of the person to whom they are speaking. Therefore they sometimes prefer to call them 'Herr Doktor' or... cross the road.)

Furthermore, even within each area there are deep differences between the individual cantons. This reflects the country's federalist system, Switzerland being a Confederation of 26 cantons, and the situation of *diglossia*, for instance, in DS, where a common standard German is used for written discourse, while several Swiss dialects appear in spoken discourse (e.g. the greeting formula in Zurich is *Grüezi*, and in Basel it is *Guete Daag*). Despite political unity, it is thus rather problematical to speak about Switzerland as a whole from both a linguistic and cultural point of view.

It might, therefore, be thought useful to examine the corresponding nations (Germany, France and Italy) to get an idea of the politeness systems in each Swiss area. Unfortunately, strong evidence suggests that differences are as numerous as the similarities deriving from common cultural and linguistic backgrounds. Löffler (1989: 208) claims that nationality is more relevant than sharing a language, with particular differences between DS and Germany in their conversational styles. He suggests that Switzerland's 'direct democracy' and special situation as the meeting point of several cultures, languages and traditions are responsible for these differences. Guggenbühl (1967, quoted by Hauser, 1998: 130f), claiming that the Swiss digress from the cultures around them, speaks of 'Swiss impoliteness' deriving from their 'cultural consciousness' reinforced by an element of defiance and contrariness. Yet, despite the language divisions, there seem to be some features shared by most Swiss people, due to belonging to one nation with its own traditions and history. The most practicable way to study Swiss politeness, therefore, is to focus upon these common features. I will deal mainly with the SR and the DS, generalising, inevitably, to some extent, since any statements about the DS or the SR may not necessarily apply to the Italian-speaking part or to Romansh.

Theoretical Considerations and Methodology

The concept of politeness implied here is very close to the framework outlined by Kerbrat-Orecchioni (see Kerbrat-Orecchioni, 1997 and this volume; Manno, 2000). I assume that politeness consists not only of minimising face-threatening acts, (FTAs) (negative politeness) but that it has a positive counterpart: producing polite acts (face-flattering acts, FFAs), such as compliments, greetings, etc. (positive politeness), in line also with Leech's assumptions (1983: 83f). Furthermore, politeness does not concern only the addressee's (A) face (e.g. tact, compliments) but also the speaker's (S) face (e.g. modesty). In outlining the 'Swiss ethos', I shall also follow some of Kerbrat-Orecchioni's (1994: 62ff.) other distinctions, such as the concept of interpersonal relationship and politeness, the role of speaking in society, etc. (see also Traverso, 1999).

My data are threefold. First, I shall review some pragmatic studies of politeness in Switzerland. Second, I will use a corpus of recent letters received both from SR and DS and some data on face-to-face interaction previously elicited for other purposes. Finally, to compensate for any over-impressionistic views, I submitted a questionnaire to about 30 Swiss people both from SR and DS on their own and their neighbours' politeness routines, following which some foreigners living in Switzerland (Germans, Italians and French) were also asked about Swiss politeness.

Interpersonal Relationships

The horizontal dimension (proximity versus distance)

The Swiss have rather an ethos of distance, shown in their forms of address (pronouns, greeting formulas), physical distance and eye contact. As for pronouns of address, the distinction between formal or distant modes (*Vous/Sie* = V) and informal or intimate modes (*Tu/Du* = T) is common to both areas.[2] There is resistance to T/V but one finds a reduction in V/V because of the expansion of T/T among young people who, in DS, systematically use T to each other. They start using V, normally after leaving secondary school, when addressing people of a different age (Hauser, 1998: 132), with DS seeming to be less 'progressive' than Germany. The Gesellschaft für deutsche Sprache of Wiesbaden found that, in Germany, T is advancing among all classes, especially among speakers under 30. There seems to be some consensus that this new tendency came from Germany (Hauser, 1998: 116). The difference between Germany and Switzerland seems to be illustrated by German TV presenters' and sports reporters' frequent use of T, unlike their Swiss counterparts, who have an internal arrangement: no T on screen (Hark, 1998: 82).

There is some evidence that T is more widespread in DS than in SR. In a study of T/V in Lausanne (SR) based on socioprofessional status, age and sex, the results among informants at university show that S's age affects the choice, with the opposite results between students and others over 50: T is most common among students, whereas V is the usual form among the older speakers. While young people use V especially in formal contexts, older speakers choose T only in informal situations or when addressing colleagues (Schoch, 1978: 59–61). The use among 35–50 year olds shows the transition between younger people's 'expansive use of T' and the 'formal stiffness' of older people, with the choice of T or V seeming to depend on one's interlocutor's age: 75% of students choose T when addressing people of the same generation, while 100% of those between 50–65 choose V. Schoch (1978: 63) postulates a general evolution towards a less formal and rigid pronoun system but who knows whether today's youth will continue using T.

Some results from Schoch's study show that, in SR, older people, in particular, continue to use V. There are couples among the Lausanne bourgeoisie who still use symmetrical V to each other and not all young students use T to their friends (87.5%); among 50–65 year olds, only 37.5% use T. Although strangers may be addressed with T by young people if there is some connection between them (e.g. all students use T when introduced to a friend's friend), everyone over 50 prefers V in that situation. (Note that Schoch's study dates from 1978.) Finally, Swiss Germans living in SR feel that it takes longer in SR than in DS to change from V to T. However, SR seems more 'progressive' than France, probably relating to the fact that the transition from V to T usually takes longer than in the surrounding nations (see Kerbrat-Orecchioni, this volume), but one has to note that the corporate use of T is more 'natural' in France than in Switzerland – perhaps a sign of France's more egalitarian attitudes.

Both in DS and SR, greeting formulas still reflect the relationship between S and A through the distinction between the formal (DS: *grüezi, ade;*[3] SR: *bonjour, au revoir*, etc.) and the intimate alternatives (DS: *hoi, tschau, tschüss;* SR: *salut, ciao*, etc.).[4] The physical distance kept by the Swiss corresponds to the European average and to the 'cultures without contact': 'no closer than necessary' on buses or trains, with eye contact avoided between strangers. Perhaps surprisingly, in greeting, Swiss Germans exchange three kisses on the cheek (men–women, women–women), which seems to be an innovation, at least in DS (Büchi, 2001): according to Hauser (1998: 163), in 1975, people in Zurich used to exchange only one kiss. The same applies to shaking hands, which reduces physical distance and usually occurs in formal settings, between relative strangers and persons who meet seldom or have not met for a long time.

The vertical dimension (hierarchy versus solidarity)

Despite the resistance to the T/V distinction, there is a tendency away from the asymmetric and towards the reciprocal use of T/V in address pronouns, corresponding with the evolution described by Brown and Gilman (1972) from 'power semantics' to 'solidarity semantics', a clear exception being adult children interaction, especially in asymmetric settings (e.g. school), where age is a decisive factor: children may receive T but address their interlocutor as V. In addressing students over 17, teachers in Zurich are supposed to use V + first name, while students must use V + *Herr* + last name, which does not completely neutralise the asymmetry. In intimate (e.g. family) settings, children may use T to anyone, including all close adults, such as neighbours and their parents' acquaintances.

Guggenbühl (quoted by Hauser, 1998: 133) recommended even in 1967 that the exaggerated use of titles should be dropped. The practice of conferring their husbands' titles on wives, still common in Austria, has been obsolete for over 50 years. Swiss Germans never liked to use forms such as the very deferential *Gnädige Frau*. Some attribute this to the Swiss concept of democracy and mistrust of the nobility, while others think it proves that politeness in Switzerland has never been very elaborate, unlike the more 'aristocratic' Austria. For instance, it is claimed that, unlike the French system, Switzerland shows no big gap between formal and intimate styles.

Perhaps titles in address, (to be distinguished from reference, see Braun, 1988: 11), are about to disappear. A university professor may be addressed by his students orally or in writing as *Herr Meier,* with *Herr Professor* being rather exceptional, although in some formal settings titles still appear. At university conferences, they are used especially for reference, i.e. to designate or to introduce someone (*Ich übergebe jetzt das Wort Frau Dr. X,* [I now leave the floor to Ms Dr X]). In formal written communication, titles are still used both in the address and greetings at the beginning of letters (*Sehr geehrter Herr Dr. X* [Esteemed Mr Dr X]). However, titles are beginning to disappear nowadays in direct greetings, though still appearing as part of the address.[5]

Despite their decline in DS, titles in SR seem to be even less frequent than in DS. Whereas in DS in certain contexts their absence may be marked, in SR their use is rather the exception. It seems that titles are relegated to professional self-presentation, e.g. letterheads (Dr First name Last name *PD Service de psychiatrie de liaison* Address). Here, the linguistic and cultural background seems to influence the corresponding Swiss areas. In Germany, titles are clearly more important than in France, where their use (except for *Docteur*) is rare (Kerbrat-Orecchioni, 1992).

In everyday conversation, titles tend to be replaced by generalised or 'democratic' address forms: *Herr, Frau/Monsieur, Madame* (corresponding to English Mr/Mrs/Miss/Ms). [6] *Mademoiselle* (Miss) has not yet disappeared in SR (Büchi, 2001: 8), whereas in DS *Fräulein* is only used for waitresses. There is a slight difference between DS and SR regarding the use of patronymics in greetings and addressing. In DS, *Herr/Frau* must be followed by the surname (e.g. *Grüezi Frau A,* [Good day (V) Mrs A]). In close relationships, A's first name should also be mentioned (cf. Züger, 1998: 113, 267), showing perhaps that the Swiss like personalised relationships. This rule seems to be less observed nowadays, as the following exchange shows, where B does not greet A by her surname:

A: *Grüezi Frau B...* (Good day = I greet you (V), Mrs B...)
B: *Grüezi* (Good day (V))
A: *Wie gohts?* (How are you ?)
B: *Guet und Ihne?* (Fine and you ?) (Züger, 1998: 111).

In SR, however, as in France, *Monsieur/Madame* without the surname is considered polite in greeting (see Kerbrat-Orecchioni, this volume; Weil, 1983: 12). Furthermore, there seems to be a movement towards omitting any address form in greeting formulas. Whereas *Bonjour, Monsieur/Madame* is considered the polite formula, nowadays *Bonjour* can appear alone. This movement is confirmed by our survey: half of our informants claim to use only *Bonjour*, and others hesitate between *Bonjour Monsieur* and *Bonjour*. The same tendency is more striking in thanking: only one informant (of 12) considered using *Monsieur* after *merci*.

Conflictual versus consensual cultures

Whether Swiss culture is conflictual (like the German or French) or consensual (like the Scandinavian) is, apparently, undecided. Löffler (1989: 208–212), a German professor living in Switzerland, observes differences between DS and Germany. For instance, in university seminars, the gaps before someone takes the floor are longer than in Germany, where long gaps would be embarrassing, showing, Löffler thinks, the Swiss respect for others' right to speak and their tendency not to interrupt each other. Löffler analyses two talk shows: *Zischtigsklub* (Switzerland) and *Moment mal* (Germany) and finds 1.9 turns per minute in the German show against 1.6 in the Swiss, where speakers hold the floor longer. Furthermore, Löffler (1989: 217) observes an academic topic development in the Swiss shows, while the Germans are characterised by continuous wrangling and confused attacks. Swiss shows seem 'excessively harmonious' to Germans, with everyone letting the others speak. Finally, Löffler (p. 218) wonders what a Swiss argument would be like, if such a style exists, since even controversial topics are treated 'smoothly' and with good manners. Germans tend to intensify the force of their speech acts in conflict situations (House & Kasper, 1981) while the Swiss prefer consensus and agreement to competition (Kilani-Schoch *et al.*, 1992: 138),[7] this being related to the 'policy of consensus', so fundamental in Swiss (political) life, where rude battles of words are unknown.

It seems clear that interruption is scarcely tolerated by Swiss speakers even in controversial discussions (see examples in Luginbühl, 1999: 35), although Watts (1989) tends to refute the existence of this consensual Swiss conversational style. Watts (1989: 148) compared verbal interactions in a Swiss German and in a British family, showing certain cross-cultural differences. In the British family, intervention was rarely interpretable as violating another's conversational rights; topics were negotiated by the participants; no points put by others were challenged and participants frequently signalled agreement and attention. In the Swiss family, in contrast, the participants had fewer scruples about interrupting each other and topics were not negotiated by the participants but stated as positions to be accepted or contradicted.

Similarly, Kilani-Schoch *et al.* (1992: 139s.) explains that Swiss people are less silent or deferential than Bolivians and indeed some Bolivian students think the Swiss interrupt too frequently. In other words, if the Swiss seem rather non-competitive, on this continuum the Bolivians and British seem to be even more so. According to Kilani-Schoch *et al.* (1992), with Frenchmen, who are said to be competitive (Kerbrat-Orecchioni, 1994: 85), *Romands* are faced with the same problem as Bolivians have with the Swiss. This also applies to many Swiss Germans, who consider Germans arrogant. The Swiss, tending to avoid conflict situations, seem rather 'helpless' if such situations arise. Löffler (1989) claims, on the basis of several examples from Germany and Switzerland, that the latter lack any verbal conflict management strategy to cope with extreme situations of conflict.

The Concept of Politeness

Importance of speaker and addressee

Although Swiss society is clearly individualistic, it cannot be claimed that S's rights supersede A's. Individuals are supposed not to show off and the choice of some safe topics may illustrate this rule of modesty.[8] Although a common feature throughout Europe (Weil, 1983; de Salins,1992: 158), reticence to talk about one's income is particularly pronounced in Switzerland

(Dunand, 1987: 165) and this can be interpreted as a sign of modesty, not like the Japanese maximising dispraise of self but rather minimising praise of self. It is not verbal modesty – there are, for instance, no honorifics or humiliatives – but rather a tendency to keep 'a low profile', with rich people tending to avoid (verbal) ostentation of their wealth. In general, everyday behaviour confirms that Swiss people tend to hide their qualities and mistrust brilliant personalities. Their preference for 'mediocrity' may derive from the will not to make others feel inferior or to provoke jealousy or from the importance of non-imposition: one's own merits and wealth may risk disturbing others.

Nevertheless, Swiss speakers tend to claim their rights as soon as they feel that rules are being broken. They complain very quickly, especially about unrestrained behaviour, loud voices, etc. In fact, the need for smooth, well-organised interaction and peaceful cohabitation implies excessive respect for rules and conventions, with low tolerance of violations.

Negative face versus positive face

Swiss society values privacy and individualism, i.e. negative face. This differs from some non-Western and Mediterranean societies (civilisations of honour) where privacy is less important and isolation is viewed negatively (see Kerbrat-Orecchioni, 1994: 103). This becomes evident in attitudes toward unexpected visits, often interpreted by Mediterraneans as a welcome surprise but by the Swiss as a disturbance. Indeed, Swiss people seem to be more concerned by infractions of territory than by threats to positive face. While it is more threatening to ask someone personal questions, to telephone them late at night etc. than to criticise or even offend them, the importance of autonomy over acceptance (see Arndt & Janney, 1987: 378) means that to omit some FFA to positive face, such as compliments, expressions of solidarity, etc., seems less threatening than to disturb others.

Negative and positive politeness

As in other Western societies, in Swiss politeness 'abstentionist' or repair strategies (negative politeness for both negative and positive face) are more important than performance of FFAs (positive politeness). If we translate Leech's framework (1983) into Brown and Levinson's terms, we see that, for A's negative face, redress of FTAs (cost to A) appears to be a more powerful constraint on conversational behaviour than performance of FFAs (benefit to A). Moreover, in this type of culture of distance, the principle of minimising cost to A seems more important than the more positive principle of praising or benefiting A. In other words, the primacy of respect for the autonomy of others is so strong that it is preferable to avoid paying compliments or expressing sympathy to A, than to risk disturbing A. Any manifestation of interest by strangers – especially in public settings – is rare and is often interpreted as an intrusion or treated with mistrust. Furthermore, compared to Mediterranean cultures, the Swiss can hardly be said to value generosity or compliments very highly.[9] Some Swiss laws of hospitality show the importance of others' autonomy: it is safer not to impose on one's guests.

Let us now examine an official letter in order to see some negative politeness strategies:

Herrn (To Mr)
Dr X (title)
Address, place, date
Maturitätsprüfungen (Final examinations at Swiss secondary school)

(1) *Sehr geehrter Herr X* (Very honoured Mr X)

(2) *Als Folge der Verkürzung der Maturitätsausbildung finden nun die* [...] (As a consequence of the reduction of the secondary education, therefore take place the...)

(3) *Wie bisher sind wir auf zahlreiche* ***Expertinnen und Experten*** *angewiesen.* (As always we are dependent on various trained staff (experts))

(4) *Deshalb* ***möchten*** *wir Sie* ***gerne*** *anfragen,* (Therefore we would like to ask you)

(5) *ob* ***Sie bereit sind****, am (DATE) eine Klasse im Fache Italienisch zu betreuen.* (if you are willing to cover a class in the subject of Italian on the (Date)).

(6) *Zur Tätigkeit der Experten gehört [...]* (The responsibilities of the experts are ...)

(7) *Bei Unsicherheiten oder für weitere Informationen können Sie* ***uns selbstverständlich gerne*** *anrufen.* (If you have any doubts or require any further information please feel free to contact us (lit: you can certainly phone us))

(8) ***Wir freuen uns auf*** *Ihre* ***möglichst*** *umgehende Antwort und* (We are looking forward to hearing from you at your earliest convenience (lit: your hopefully immediate reply) and

(9) *danken Ihnen* ***herzlich*** *für Ihr Engagement.* (we thank you warmly for your commitment)

(10) *Mit freundlichen Grüssen* (With friendly greetings)

This request contains several mitigating devices. The head act (4) is realised indirectly (expressing S's desire to ask A if she is willing to do what is denoted in the proposition). The request itself has some internal modifications: there are some syntactic (subjunctive *möchten*) and lexical downgraders (*gerne,* 'with pleasure') and the request strategy is realised by a conditional clause with subordination (5), whose verb is hedged (S questions indirectly A's willingness). As for external modifications, we have some supportive moves: a grounder gives reasons for the request (3); an offer of help in case of any questions (7) strengthened by a commitment indicator (*selbstverständlich,* 'of course') and a lexical modification (*gerne,* 'with pleasure'). The request for an immediate answer (8) is introduced by *Wir freuen uns auf,* 'We are looking forward'; the time indication (*umgehend,* 'immediate'), interpretable as a strengthener, is mitigated by *möglichst,* 'possibly'. The closing section is very cordial and uses some FFAs: anticipated thanks (9) intensified (*herzlich,* 'cordial') and the final greetings (10). Finally, (3) shows concern in DS for political correctness, using both masculine and feminine forms of names of occupations (*Expertinnen und Experten*).

Even in face-to-face interactions, people prefer conventionally indirect strategies to others. In the following example, the request is realised by questioning the presence of a preparatory condition (possibility) (1), followed by a grounder (2):

> *[...] da isch ganz ä wichtigs Thema i dem – Artikel, (1)* ***chönd si – als Betroffänä – do no öppis däzuä sägä****, (2) si hend sich jo au kämpft däfür, das da Gsetz durächunnt [...]* (There is a really important subject in that article, (1) can you – as the person concerned – possibly tell us something about it, (2) for you have also fought for this law to be accepted) (Luginbühl, 1999: 32).

Past tense forms used with present time reference combined with lexical downtoners (*mol,* once, *eifach,* simply, just) are frequent downgrading devices (cf. Blum-Kulka *et al.*, 1989: 284):

> *ich* ***ha*** *dich etz* ***eifach mol welle*** *fröge* (Züger 1998: 161). (I just wanted to ask you now once...)

In SR or DS, even when asking for the bill in a restaurant, negative politeness and respect for territory prevail:

(a) *Monsieur, est-ce que je pourrais (vous) payer, s'il vous plaît?* (Sir, may I pay (you), please?)
(b) *Fräulein, chönnt i no zahle bitte?* (Miss, may I pay now, please?)

These formulas may vary but nevertheless in France or Germany no one would ask for a bill in this 'humble' way (Béguelin & de Pietro, 2000: 280).[10]

The Swiss seem less motivated by considerations of *positive politeness*, although, at least in closings, there is a high incidence of this and many researchers (both from SR and DS) have noted a frequency of *good wishes* (*bonne rentrée, bonne soirée, bon après-midi*, etc.: see Hauser 1998: 130 and Kilani-Schoch *et al.* (1992)). A distinction has to be drawn between conventional formulas in religious celebrations (Christmas, Easter, etc.):

A: *aso tschau, schöni – Zit* (so, bye and have a good time –)
K: *aso schöni Pfingschte dir au tschau A...* (so, good Whitsun to you too, bye A ...) (Züger 1998: 118)

and more personal formulas (*Chum guet hai,* [Get home safely] *schöns Wuchenend,* (have a) *good* weekend]) or even creative ones (e.g. *gueti Fahrt,* [(have a) good ride], *es schöns Fäscht* [(have) a good party]).[11] English people and Bolivians are struck by the frequency of these formulas and their 'superfluous character' when uttered even by people who will see each other (e.g. work colleagues) the following day (Hauser, 1998: 171; Kilani-Schoch *et al.*, 1992: 145). In 'impersonal' transactional exchanges, such as shopping, it is common for a cashier, after thanking the purchaser, to wish them good day/evening (*En schöne Tag/En schöne Abig*). The profusion of these formulas is also noticeable in official letters both in French and German (*Wir wünschen Ihnen einen schönen Frühling und Sommer,* [We wish you (V) a beautiful spring and summer]).

Individualism versus collectivism

The rather elaborate farewells that are almost obligatory in Switzerland may show some unease with human contact. Kilani-Schoch *et al.* (1992: 145) considers that the multiplication of these formulas is proportional to the anxiety created by the closing, perhaps indicating that individuals see themselves as separate from, rather than deeply involved with, others. Their individualism is also confirmed, she suggests, by greeting-questions such as *Qu'est-ce que tu racontes?* (What do you tell me?), a kind of question which offends people who have been socialised in collectivist societies (e.g. Ghanaians). Such individualism, commonly associated with some Western cultures, also appears in the importance of birthdays instead of Saints' days, as celebrated in collectivist societies like Italy or Greece. This feature may be reinforced by the fragmentation of the political and administrative system (confederation, canton, district and municipality), which prevents the Swiss from identifying with just one common entity.

The rather debt-sensitive character of individuals further confirms this individualism. In DS, invitations elicit a high frequency of thanks: one expresses thanks for the invitation[12]; on arrival, one repeats them; the same happens before starting to eat and again before leaving. To Mediterranean observers, this rather elaborate ritual seems to express embarrassment rather than the pleasure of 'communion'. In their view, it is sufficient to return the invitation at some time. More generally, this individualism and the importance of autonomy sometimes prevent people from exteriorising much empathy e.g. by sharing their feelings.

The Importance of Speaking in Society

Unlike other countries, such as France (*Oui Allô*) or Italy (*Pronto*), in Switzerland self-identification on answering the telephone (giving surname or forename and surname) is the norm. The caller must then greet the person called, present herself and indicate the reason for the call (*Bonjour, c'est X à l'appareil, est-ce que je peux parler à Y?*). Indeed, the Swiss believe that this procedure (also used in Germany and Austria) is universal and they often complain about foreigners who neglect it.[13]

Kilani-Schoch *et al.* (1992: 144ff.) claims that this procedure reflects the *transactional function* of the telephone in Switzerland, which serves to communicate information rather than to maintain interpersonal relationships. In other words, the telephone is not considered as a medium of 'normal' interaction,[14] unlike the French situation (see Carroll, 1987: 142), and the announcement of the reason for the call may be seen as over-direct and abrupt by outsiders.

This 'abruptness' seems more pronounced in DS, for Swiss Germans living in SR perceive the *Romands* as more inclined to indulge in small talk before introducing the reason for their call. Kilani-Schoch *et al.* (1992: 146ss.) relates this transactional concept of communication on the telephone to the general Swiss politeness system. Some Iranian students living in Switzerland, for instance, perceive Swiss requesting formulas (even for free goods) as insufficient. In fact, one of Brown and Levinson's (1987: 117) strategies of positive politeness is to 'claim common ground'. The value of S's spending time and effort in talking to A out of friendship amounts to the strategy of redressing FTAs. So, requesting something without small talk constitutes a brutal intrusion and may imply that S simply wishes to exploit A, without having any interest in maintaining a relationship with him. Yet this speedy procedure has advantages in the eyes of the Swiss, for it permits them to avoid wasting A's time. The motivation for this very direct behaviour seems, therefore, to lie in respect for A's basic claim to territories and accords with the high value placed on tact and autonomy.

More generally, it seems that speaking is considered by most Swiss

(Germans) as a tool for obtaining and conveying information, as a means to an end (problem-solving), rather than as a means of establishing and developing personal relationships: small talk between strangers on public transport is rather exceptional. In the 19th century, the Swiss writer Jakob Stutz described his compatriots as 'often grumpy and not very sociable' (my translation) and the Swiss researcher Hauser (1998: 106) writes that 'Swiss people seem to be grateful if one leaves them alone' (for Spanish attitudes to being left alone, see Hickey, this volume). Especially revealing in this context is that advisers on cross-cultural business communication tell Swiss businessmen to indulge in more relational work and to 'waste' their time with small talk before turning to business (for a discussion of small talk, see House, this volume). In this sense, Switzerland belongs to the average of Northern European cultures, where phatic communion is not highly valued (Kerbrat-Orecchioni, 1994: 67) and Kilani-Schoch *et al.* (1992: 138ss.) reminds us of the mistrust in SR of French conversational style and of 'beaux parleurs'. One of my informants summed the situation up by saying that in Switzerland 'almost everything is literal' with little room for irony or humour.

Conclusion

In attempting to treat Switzerland, though complex, as a whole, my examples confirm the existence of a specific Swiss ethos, whose most common features belong to the average Northern-European norms (preference for negative politeness and for autonomy). Although wishing formulas seem to represent an exception in this regard, they may be interpreted as further evidence of the individualistic character of this culture. Swiss politeness also presents some features of its own, such as modesty and avoidance of disagreement. The specificity of Swiss politeness is also manifested in some differences between the linguistic areas and their corresponding nations. Apart from these pan-helvetic features, there are also some regional phenomena due either to the federalist system or to the influence of the culture behind them. Still, one has to be very cautious about generalisations and the present study must be considered as at attempt at a working hypothesis which future research must confirm, both with regard to the linguistic areas of Switzerland scarcely discussed here and in seeking more empirical evidence for these phenomena.

Notes

1. Contrary to the myth of a multilingual Switzerland, individuals are not primarily multilingual. This is rather an attribute of the state.
2. Hauser (1998: 69) outlines the evolution of address forms in DS: 1, generalised T

(*Du*, second person singular); 2, T/V (*Ihr*, second person plural). (This form has been retained until now in the western Swiss dialects ex. Berne); 3, *Du/Ihr* or *Sie* (third person plural). *Sie* was imported from Germany in the 18th century; 4, System 1: *Du/Sie*; System 2: *Du/Ihr*.

3. *ade/adieu* is not the only French polite formula in DS. In the 18th century, there was the importation of plenty of them. This led a Frenchman who visited Zurich to write: 'I did not find any thing Swiss, but a lot of good French'. Even nowadays, when the prestige of this language has dramatically decreased, strangers are surprised to hear so many French polite formulas in Zurich (*salu/sali, ade/adieu, merci*, etc.) (Züger 1998: 109ss., 133).
4. It must be stated that *bonjour* and *au revoir* can also be used among familiars. These French formulas are, therefore, rather 'unmarked'. Finally, *salut* is more intimate than *ciao*.
5. A small survey shows that in some letter types, such as plea letters, frequently (12 of 15), titles are also used in salutations (*Sehr geehrter Herr Dr. X*). This is probably due to the fact that S does not want to 'annoy' a potential donor.
6. There is no unanimity as to what should be classified as a title. But these forms need not be regarded as particular titles (Braun, 1988).
7. Kilani-Schoch *et al.* (1992: 138) speaks about the 'ideology of consensus' in relation with safe topics, such as the weather and the systematic avoidance of politics. However, it must be added that the majority of my informants were willing to talk about politics. Finally, it must be stated that in Züger's (1998: 261) empirical study in DS, politics and institutions also appeared in phatic communion, although spare time, health, profession, friends, weather, etc. were more frequent topics.
8. Like in most European countries and in the USA, in Switzerland the weather is the safest topic for phatic communion (cf. Züger, 1998: 261). According to Kilani-Schoch *et al.* (1992: 138s.), the greeting question 'Il fait beau aujourd'hui' may, however, give rise to misunderstandings in cross-cultural communication.
9. Even the French, who are not said to be particularly generous (de Salins, 1992: 159), tend to consider them rather selfish and lacking in solidarity, as can be seen in the French proverb *boire/manger en Suisse* that means, according to *Grand Robert*, to eat or drink on one's own, without inviting one's friends.
10. In addition to this pragmatic difference, there are some well-known lexical differences between SR and France in politeness formulas: *adieu = salut, bonjour* (informal opening formula); *adieu = au revoir* (closing formula even if S considers that he or she is going to see A soon); *santé! = à tes souhaits!* (bless you); *faites seulement!* corresponds approximately to *je vous en prie* or *faites donc; merci pareillement = merci à vous aussi*, etc.
11. Despite the frequency of this ritual, it seems that these formulas are not as creative as the new phenomenon observed by Kerbrat-Orecchioni in France (this volume).
12. Swiss people tend to accept offers at once and to cover them with many thanks. But they do not necessarily return the favour as other cultures might do. This causes many cultural misunderstandings with Mediterranean people living in Switzerland.

13. This ritual is very strict in DS, whereas in SR, there is a degree of variation: *Oui, forename + surname; Allô, forename; Surname.* According to our informants, they could even answer *Allô!* and *Oui, Allô*, which is probably due to the French influence.
14. The transactional nature of telephone speech in Switzerland seems to have changed since the new wave of mobile phones.

References

Arndt, H. and Janney R. (1987) *InterGrammar. Toward an Integrative Model of Verbal, Prosodic and Kinesic Choices in Speech*. Berlin: Mouton de Gruyter.

Béguelin, M.-J. and de Pietro, J.-F. (2000) S comme Suisse, sans autre, schwentser, septante, séré, soccolis, sonderfall, souper, stamm, syndic.... In B. Cerquiglini *et al.* (eds) *'Tu parles!?' Le français dans tous ses états* (pp. 272–86). Paris: Flammarion.

Blum-Kulka, S., House, J. and Kasper, G. (eds) (1989) *Cross-cultural Pragmatics: Requests and Apologies*. Norwood, NJ: Ablex.

Braun, F. (1988) *Terms of Address. Problems of Patterns and Usage in Various Languages and Cultures*. Berlin: Mouton de Gruyter.

Brown P. and Levinson, S. (1987) *Politeness: Some Universals in Language Usage*. Cambridge: Cambridge University Press.

Brown, R. and Gilman, A. (1972) The pronouns of power and solidarity. In Laver and Hutcheson (eds) *Communication in Face to Face Interaction* (pp. 103–127). Harmondsworth: Penguin Books.

Büchi, C. (2001) *Mariage de raison. Romands et alémaniques: une histoire suisse*. Genève: Zoé.

Carroll, R. (1987) *Evidences invisibles. Américains et Français au quotidien*. Paris: Seuil.

de Salins, G-D. (1992) *Une introduction à l'ethnographie de la communication. Pour la formation à l'enseignement du français langue étrangère*. Paris: Didier.

Dunand, F. (avec la collaboration de l'Institut MIS) (1987) *Dessine-moi un Suisse*. Lausanne: Editions 24 heures.

Hark, U. (1998) Sag ganz einfach und ganz locker du. *Tages Anzeiger*, 29 September, p. 82.

Hauser, A. (1998) *Grüezi und Adieu: Gruss- und Umgangsformen vom 17. Jahrhundert bis zur Gegenwart*. Zürich: Neue Zürcher Zeitung.

Kerbrat-Orecchioni C. (1992, 1994): *Les Interactions verba*les, Vols. II, III. Paris: Armand Colin.

Kerbrat-Orecchioni, C. (1997) A multilevel approach in the study of talk-in-interaction. *Pragmatics* 7:1, 1–20.

Kilani-Schoch, M. Alamzad, N., Ayllon, P., Hauert, C. and Osei-Bonsu, A. (1992) Il fait beau aujourd'hui. Contribution à l'approche linguistique des malentendus interculturels. *Cahiers de l'ILSL* 2, 127–54.

Leech, G. (1983) *Principles of Pragmatics*. London and New York: Longman.

Löffler, H. (1989) Die Frage nach dem landessspezifischen Gespächsstil – oder die Schweizer Art zu diskutieren. In F. Hundnurscher and E. Weigand (eds)

Dialoganalyse II. Band 2: Referate der 2. Arbeitstagung Bochum 1988 (pp. 207–221). Tübingen: Linguistische Arbeiten 230.

Luginbühl, M. (1999) *Gewalt im Gespräch: verbale Gewalt in politischen Fernsehdiskussionen am Beispiel der 'Arena'*. Bern: Peter Lang.

Manno, G. (1997) Le travail régulateur et le travail de figuration dans les jeux télévisés: politesse et contrat communicatif. *SILTA*, XXVI (3), 529–560.

Manno, G. (1998) Politesse et typologie des textes. In B. Caron (ed.) *Actes du XVIe Congrès International des Linguistes* (Paris, 20–25 juillet 1997) (p. 348). Oxford: Elsevier Sciences (CD Rom).

Manno, G. (1999) La spécificité du travail de figuration dans la communication écrite. *Zeitschrift für Französische Sprache und Literatur* CIX (3), 256–276.

Manno, G. (2000) Le remerciement relève-t-il de la politesse positive? Pour une conception plus séquentielle de la théorie de la politesse. *SILTA*, XXIX (3) 451-469.

Schoch, M. (1978) Problème sociolinguistique des pronoms d'allocution: 'tu' et 'vous', Enquête à Lausanne. *La linguistique*, 14, (1) 55–73.

Traverso, V. (ed.) (1999) *Perspectives interculturelles sur l'interaction*. Lyon: PUL.

Watts, Richard J. (1989) Relevance and relational work: Linguistic politeness as politic behavior. *Multilingua 8* (2/3), 131–166.

Weil, S. (1983) *Trésors de la politesse française*. Paris: Belin.

Züger, K. (1998) *Säg öppis! – phatische Sprachverwendung: Eine linguistische Untersuchung anhand von schweizerdeutschen Gesprächen in öffentlichen Verkehrsmitteln*. Bern: Lang.

Chapter 8

Politeness in Britain: 'It's Only a Suggestion...'

MIRANDA STEWART

Introduction

British English, often referred to, along with the American variety, as 'old English' (see for example, Tupas, 2001) in contrast with the multitude of 'new' and post-colonial Englishes spoken throughout the world, is hardly homogeneous. Great Britain, comprising the three historic nations of England, Scotland and Wales, is enriched by a vibrant multiculturalism, especially within its major cities, with London bringing together speakers of more languages than any city in the world. Therefore, it is unsurprising that the resources used to convey linguistic politeness and the ways in which they are used vary considerably.

Simple linguistic conventions, such as a shop assistant asking 'Who's next?' (in England), or 'Who's first?' (in Scotland) may provide some clue to the complex ways in which we relate to other people through language. Here, personal deixis in England places the shop assistant at the centre of the interaction and the customer is positioned in relation to her. In Scotland, by contrast, the customer is placed centre stage, a positive politeness mechanism that may be played out through the ensuing interaction. Focusing devices, such as the use of 'see' and 'ken' (know), also provide speakers of Scottish varieties with positive politeness devices to intensify the interest of their tale as in 'See those old houses .... this area was all houses like that right round' and 'ken John Ewan – he breeds spaniels' (Miller, 1993: 134–5). Similarly, Scots English provides speakers with the diminutiviser 'wee', a powerful politeness hedge as in 'Could I ask a wee favour?' (see Terkourafi, this volume)

Folk linguistic stereotypes of the value given to language can also give some insight into quite considerable differences between different communities; for example, in Ireland (whose emigrants have populated large areas of Great Britain) a high premium is paid to verbal agility and the ability to entertain (often well over a regard for the prosaic truth) with 'she's good crack' (from the Irish 'craic') being a compliment of the highest order (see

Kallen, this volume). At the opposite extreme, there are communities within Britain where 'silence is golden' and 'children are seen and not heard'. The Japanese English writer, Kazuo Ishiguro (1989), provides a striking portrayal, in his novel *The Remains of the Day* set in post first World War England, of archetypal Englishness, albeit inflected for social class. His characters always say considerably less than they mean and every subtle nuance and inflection has to be scrutinised for its underlying meaning, and indeed potential for causing offence, creating an almost 'paranoid' (see Kasper, 1990) view of interaction. Negative politeness and non-conventional indirectness abound and are cast into sharp relief by the almost brutal directness of the housekeeper, Miss Kenton.

Address forms are often taken as an indicator of the social stratification of a given society and the English language, with no T/V distinction except perhaps as an historical relic in Quaker services, could be said to reflect a more egalitarian society. Yet the use of honorifics in British English mark it out very much as 'old English' in contrast with, say, more innovative varieties such as Hong Kong English, where Ms has supplanted both Miss and Mrs, or those countries which tend towards dispensing with address forms altogether, as reported in the Northern Europe section of this volume.

British English (BE) tends to be presented as essentially an avoidance-based, negatively-oriented culture. For example, Placencia (1992: 129), in a cross-cultural study of mediated telephone conversations, focuses on the prevalence of indirectness in BE in contrast with the use in Ecuadorian Spanish of both indirect and less indirect strategies accompanied by a display of deference. Fukushima's study (2000) of what Brown and Levinson (1987: 245) conceive of as two negative politeness cultures, the Japanese and the British, shows that, while both cultures use conventionally indirect and off-record strategies in requesting, the British use a narrower variety of strategies avoiding bald-on-record even when the threat is perceived to be low, and pay less attention to context (mainly power and distance) in selecting an appropriate strategy. The principal findings of Márquez Reiter's (2000: 171–2) study of requests and apologies by educated males and females in BE and Uruguayan Spanish suggest that, in the case of requests, users of BE use more conventional and non-conventional indirectness; they are more concerned with reducing the level of coerciveness in requests; they endeavour more to avoid naming the hearer as actor; and they call on a varied repertoire of external modifiers to accomplish their goals. In the case of apologies, they show a marked preference for intensifying 'I'm sorry' with a whole range of adverbs (e.g. 'dreadfully'); they give lengthy explanations; and they show a clear need to redress the addressee's negative face. While the interactional style in the variety of English chosen for this study (southern, middle class) is conceivably not representative of the many varieties available within the British Isles, what is interesting about Márquez Reiter's study is that the variable of language variety and consequently ethnic origin appeared to be more predictive of behaviour than that of gender given that class was held constant in both groups studied.

Further, it is the type of Britishness described earlier that is reported on in the majority of contrastive studies between BE and other languages (for contrastive studies with German, see House, this volume) and consequently the one I shall investigate here.

In this chapter I shall report on a micro-study of politeness in written interaction, looking at two specific features which typify a certain 'Britishness'. First, a preference for negative rather than positive politeness strategies (see, for example, Hickey, 1991, Sifianou, 1992, etc.) which is played out through a number of linguistic strategies, for example, personal reference, hedging and deictic anchorage. Second, the use of off-record politeness (Brown & Levinson, 1987: 211), also referred to as non-conventional indirectness, a strategy, not exclusive to British English, but yet exploited widely, which requires the hearer or reader to draw appropriate inferences.

The data are naturally–occurring, and, unusually for a case of politeness studies, written. Here Sell's (1991) distinction between the politeness in the text and the politeness of the text is relevant, and is a notion which Hatim (1998) has usefully applied cross-culturally in the field of translation studies. For while there are studies of politeness (Sifianou, 1992: 217) concerned with politeness *in* texts, that is 'relationships between personae and characters dramatised within the world of mimesis', there are fewer concerned with the politeness *of* texts, that is with the relationship between the writer and the reader(s) and the essential interactivity of the text. Useful examples of the latter are Myers (1989) and McLaren (2001) who have applied politeness theory to English language scientific articles and French and English language promotional literature respectively. In this connection, Sell (1991: 217) also draws our attention to the fact that it is frequently tempting to over-emphasise formal differences between speech and writing whereas there is considerable overlap between the two modes. Finally, while Brown and Levinson's face-saving model, within which we shall broadly locate this study, has generated more studies which focus on the face of the Hearer, we should also like to bear in mind that linguistic politeness frequently serves a face-protective function for the Speaker or, to use Chen's (2001: 87) term, is used as 'self-politeness'. Consequently, a preference for indirectness and non-conventional politeness may stem as much from a need to protect one's own face from potential attack as from any desire to be 'conventionally polite' to others.

The Data

Our data are taken from feedback provided by monitors to tutors on a high-level Spanish distance-learning course. The remit of a monitor is to sample the marking and feedback provided by tutors to their students and to provide constructive feedback designed to enhance the distance-learning teaching by each tutor. While the feedback was to be given in English (so that it was accessible to the quality assurance mechanisms of the institution) in a 'supportive and constructive tone' (institutional briefing for monitors), the vast majority of tutors and monitors were native speakers of Spanish. The issue which most exercised these Spanish-speaking monitors was how to adopt an appropriate interactional style in English, which would maintain the relationship specified earlier while carrying out what is potentially a face-threatening activity. They felt that there were significant ways in which the management of face differed between Spanish and English. This was the starting point for what is a wider study than that reported here. The speech community we shall essentially be concerned with is the educated native speaker of English working within a British Higher Education context and we shall contrast this, where relevant, with that of educated native speakers of Peninsular Spanish writing in English. This is not a contrastive study of English/Spanish politeness: the non-native speakers are merely used as a control group to cast light on certain facets of British politeness. The communicative event was the provision of a dual-purpose feedback: on the one hand, to provide formative training to the distance-learning tutor; and, on the other, to provide a transparent quality control mechanism for the institution. In terms of Bell's (1984) principles of audience design, there is an 'addressee' and 'auditors' (i.e. those known by the writer to read the text but to whom the text is not addressed). The mode is written.

The corpus for this chapter is drawn from a larger database of feedback in spoken and written English and Spanish and consists of 15,000 words of feedback in English by six native speakers of BE and six native speakers of Peninsular Spanish. The core face-threatening act is one of giving feedback on the tutor's performance; this, if negative, is potentially damaging to the tutor's positive face; and, if it is designed to bring about changes in tutoring practice, is potentially damaging to the tutor's negative face. It also threatens the positive face of the Speaker (S) in the case of negative feedback and this may further be threatened if the Hearer (H) decides to challenge the feedback. If positive, it may maintain or enhance the face of either S or H or both or, alternatively, also contain a threat to face, say, if H felt that S had no right to make 'personal comments' of this nature. While there are a number of contextual variables which could potentially impact on the expression of the feedback relating to Brown and Levinson's contextual variables of *power* (e.g. age, gender, status, knowledge), *distance* (e.g. whether monitor and tutor had met previously), and the *weight of the face threatening act (FTA (W_x)* (e.g. the degree of perceived shortcoming of the tutor), for the purposes of this study we shall focus principally on the single variable of native language, that is native speakers of BE and Peninsular Spanish non-native speakers of BE.

Wajnryb (1998: 531), in studying face-to-face supervision of teaching in Australia, found that 'the pressure that face concerns place on participants is reflected in the language used to negotiate the encounter. Specifically, supervisors frequently resort to a high degree of mitigation to ease them through the unenviable task'. She notes a 'tension between supporting morale and enabling better instruction' and argues that '(g)oing off-record by clothing criticisms ambivalently allows both goals to be pursued' (Wajnryb, 1998: 534). She investigates pragmatic ambivalence (that is an utterance where the hearer cannot be certain of its pragmatic force) as a strategy used by tutors in initiating FTAs (essentially criticisms of teaching technique) and shows how, by 'testing the water' in this way, if the tutor does not meet 'hearer acceptance', he or she has 'a path open for retreat'. Wajnryb (1998: 541) also points to evidence which suggests that subordinates are likely to read criticism into apparently innocent utterances such as fact-finding questions in situations such as the one we describe, being 'co-constructors' of their own social reality. Of course, when feedback is through the written mode, there is literally no negotiation of meaning (except on those occasions where a tutor formally challenges a monitor's comments) and it might be expected that clarity will override some of these considerations of politeness. However, a writer, depending on context, may attempt to predict and pre-empt possible reader response, a reaction which Bell (1984), in his theorisation of audience design, refers to as writer 'initiative' in opposition to writer 'reponsiveness'. The latter could, say, be a feature of an on-line chatroom (where the writer can respond to semi-instant replies) but it is not an option in this particular communicative event.

In this study we shall look at politeness both at the level of the text and at the level of the sentence, clause or word. To illustrate politeness at the level of the text, we could point to a commonly shared textual convention of this particular type of feedback: the overwhelming tendency in both native and non-native speakers of BE (in 97% of texts) to engage in considerable face-work designed to enhance the positive face of the Hearer (mainly through commenting on all the positive features of the tutor's work) before presenting any criticism or suggestion for improved practice. This is also observable locally within the text where there is a clear tendency textually for positive feedback to precede negative feedback.

In Example 1 below, positive feedback precedes marginally less positive feedback and the parallelism between 'very useful' and 'useful' acts as a trigger for the reader to draw an inference, in this case possibly that she should provide better advice on plagiarism.

Example 1

You give *very useful* advice to Jones on avoiding an overly descriptive approach to the essay and *useful* advice to Smith about 'lifting' expressions from sources. (NS1)

This example illustrates what Sell (1991: 221) would call 'presentational politeness' which operates at the level of the text and where the readers' awareness of the scenarios or schemata which relate to this particular text-type enables them to decode the text effectively. Here a reader acquainted with this genre of feedback might operate on the assumption that typically positive feedback precedes negative feedback and consequently be pleasantly surprised if no negative feedback ensues. Nonetheless, the British reader, like the archetypally English characters of Ishiguro's novel, may be primed to read the text closely for any implicature that may constitute negative feedback.

At the level of the word, we have what Sell (1991: 221) terms 'selectional politeness' where individual FTAs are identified and carried out through selected linguistic expression. For example, the following FTAs are carried out either directly (with or without mitigation) or through conventional indirectness, as in Examples 2 and 3 respectively:

Example 2

Just one small point: Smith's total score should be 72% and not 73%. (NS2)

Example 3

maybe sections such as p.6–7 *could* be commented on (NS1)

In example 2 the implicated criticism that the tutor has failed to add up the marks correctly is minimised by the introductory hedge and the elimination of the agent which effectively defocuses the tutor. In Example 3 we see similar impersonalisation, the conventional use of hedging (*maybe*) and modalisation (*could*).

Finally, at this level too we find non-conventional or off-record FTAs. In the following example, there is a non-conventional criticism of a tutor's failure to give oral feedback (the first set of feedback of the year) where the monitor takes 'the initiative' and actively pre-empts reader response.

Example 4

Lastly, I was a little surprised that you didn't provide any recorded comments about TMA2 on the cassette: this seems to be such a good opportunity to deal with language items – especially pronunciation ones – and to give the student a model. *I apologise* if this is something you normally do – it is a technique that other tutors use very effectively. (NS3)

Here, after expressing surprise that the tutor has not dealt with pronunciation, the monitor apologises using a performative verb, thereby confirming the face-threatening force of the whole previous utterance. He thus protects his own face from disagreement by offering a pre-emptive apology and gives the tutor an 'out' or 'deniability potential' (Weizman, 1993) as she can claim that indeed her normal practice is to give feedback on pronunciation (no evidence to the contrary being available). The pragmatic force of the final utterance is ambivalent; it could be a justification for the assumption that the tutor might usually give this feedback; alternatively, it could act as a justification for the implicated suggestion that the tutor adopt this practice. It is precisely these kinds of off-record indirectness and pragmatic ambivalence which appeared to characterise the feedback given by native speakers of BE but were rarely or never used by the non-native speakers in our sample. In the remainder of this chapter we shall first examine some elements of conventional indirectness before moving on to examine how non-conventional indirectness appears to function in this corpus.

Conventional Indirectness

Hedging

A key linguistic resource for face–protection (whether that of the self or the other) is hedging (see Brown and Levinson, 1987: 145). Brown & Levinson include hedges as part of the strategies available for both positive politeness, where 'intensifying modifiers fulfil the sub-strategy of exaggerating (interest, approval, sympathy with H)' (p. 104), and more normally for negative politeness, where they modify the expression of communicative intentions (p. 145). As Schröder and Zimmer (1997) show, hedges have generated considerable research activity.

The British English data appeared to feature speaker reference predominantly in the context of hedging and displayed a greater incidence of first person singular hedging than the NNS data.

Example 5

I felt that they could *perhaps* have been given more information (NS3)

Example 2

I felt your marking was *slightly* generous (NS3)

What we have here are examples of the type of negative politeness that typified a lot of the feedback from the BE native speakers: hedges (in italics), the use of the modal *could*, the defocusing of the criticism from the tutor by foregrounding the students (*they*) and the evaluative adjective *generous*, all of which are protective of the face of both speaker and hearer and clothe what are essentially criticisms in considerable face-work.

As we have seen, all feedback from tutors paid considerable attention to the positive face of the addressee. Yet here there also appeared to be differences between the strategies adopted by native and non-native speakers of English which serve to point up the more negatively-polite interactional style of this variety of BE. What was striking was the use of main clause verbs by non-native speakers as a positive politeness strategy often allied with the interpersonal use of the first name of the tutor and the 'vivid' use of the present tense, reminiscent of the positioning of the Scottish shop-assistant mentioned earlier.

Example 7

I like *your* very personal and friendly tone. (NNS1)

Example 8

Overall *I* am very pleased with *your* supportive and detailed marking. (NNS2)

Example 9

María, I've enjoyed both *your* wonderful 'tutoring'… (NNS3)

The non-native speaker data showed a greater 'involvement of S and H' which is a central element of Brown and Levinson's positive politeness and displays a degree of personalisation not present in the native speaker data.

Similarly, the interpersonal use of the second person *you* or *your*, as can also be seen in the data above, was considerably more likely to co-occur with reference to the speaker in the NNS data than in the British English data. For example,

Example 10

I am sure your students feel very fortunate in having *you* as their tutor! (NNS3)

This is an approach which exposes the speaker's face to a considerable degree; an uncooperative hearer might well respond 'and who are you to 'like', 'enjoy' or 'be pleased'?' and find such an approach patronising.

Conversely, writers of British English appeared to avoid drawing attention to their interpersonal relationship with the student. The use of first person reference in British English essentially for purposes of face-protection (as Myers [1989] has argued), that is for detachment from, rather than commitment to, propositions, is interesting when read against Luukka and Markkanen's (1997: 186) (see also Nikula, 1997) claim that Finnish texts tend to use impersonalisation as a form of hedging, English texts being slightly more explicit in their personal reference (see also Yli-Yakkuri, this volume). There may be evidence in a given society's preference for hedging and the nature of this hedging of a cline of personal investment going from more positively polite cultures to the more negatively polite.

Deictic anchorage

It is here that clear evidence may exist of tendencies towards positive and negative politeness in different cultures. Brown and Levinson (1987: 118–119) draw on Fillmore (e.g. 1971) to develop the relationship of participant role in the speech act and spatio-temporal and social location and strategies employed for positive and negative politeness. For example, 'the normal unmarked deictic centre is the one where the speaker is the central person, the time of speaking (or "coding time") is the central time and the place where the speaker is at coding time is the central place'.

The data suggest that, in the case of the NS, there is a greater tendency to displace hedges into the past tense, although this tendency did not appear to correlate overall with the degree of threat inherent in the speech act. For example,

Example 11

Overall, *I think* these students were given very effective follow-up to their work. In assessment, *I felt* you tended slightly towards generosity.... (NS3)

Such displacement is a clear example of conventional indirectness as a negative politeness strategy; not only does it distance the speaker from the FTA but it also provides the speaker with a greater 'out' than the present tense would; the speaker can always claim the provisionality of his or her view, which can be modified in the light of further evidence (I thought x but now I think y). (For use of the past tense see Fretheim, this volume). Use of the past tense is a common convention, for example, in politeness strategies in British English, as in 'I was wondering whether you could give me a hand', or, prior to leaving a room, 'I didn't think you'd mind if I just popped out for a moment'. The data for the non-native speakers showed that this strategy was virtually never employed.

As we argued previously, the data also suggest that BE native speakers show a greater tendency to shift from the 'I' of the Speaker to the 'you' of the Hearer, particularly in main clauses, whereas the NNS show a greater tendency to retain the anchorage of the self. Consequently, there is evidence of greater distancing from the speaker being the central person in the NS data and it is probable that the cross-cultural use of proximal and distal deictics is an area of deictic anchorage which could usefully be explored in future studies of cross-cultural politeness.

In this section we have argued that native speakers of BE tend, through hedging and deictic anchoring, to detach themselves more from their addressee, a key feature of negative politeness; conversely, they tend to avoid positively polite strategies such as the greater involvement of S and H.

Non-conventional indirectness

In the BE data, there was ample evidence of non-conventional indirectness. For example, in Example 12, the focus is shifted from the tutor (the text receiver) to the monitor herself (the text producer) with the result that the tutor might have to work quite hard to reconstruct one pragmatic force of the sentence, that is an implicated criticism of student performance, and the intended perlocutionary effect, i.e. that she should impress the need on the student to give a spontaneous oral presentation rather than read from a script and check for sound quality on the recording:

Example 12

You give constructive advice on each of the cassettes … . I thought Brown might have been reading aloud from a prepared script as her assignment didn't seem to flow naturally, but this is always difficult to prove. The sound quality wasn't too good, either – I had to turn the cassette player up to almost full volume! (NS2)

Here, after initial, hearer-oriented (*you give…*) positive feedback to the tutor about the quality of advice given, two criticisms are implicated. We can observe the refocusing from the tutor (*you*) to the monitor (*I*). The suspicion that the student was reading aloud is hedged with the cognitive verb *think*; a reason for this suspicion is provided; and crucially an 'out' to the tutor, as one implicature could be that the tutor has chosen not to comment on this shortcoming, not due to a failure to notice it, but due to lack of hard evidence. Similarly, the comment on the poor sound quality is non-conventionally indirect and indeed pragmatically ambivalent. Is the monitor commiserating with the tutor over having to mark in such circumstances; indirectly suggesting that the student should be told to monitor sound quality; or complaining about the position this has put her in? One benefit of this degree of non-conventional indirectness is that the monitor has amply protected her own face in the event, for example, that the student had in fact given a spontaneous presentation. The use of understatement 'wasn't too good' to implicate 'bad' or 'very bad' is similar to the Irish English usages discussed by Kallen (this volume).

In the following feedback, the juxtaposition, at the level of the sentence, between the first clause where there is positive feedback (the tutor has rightly instructed the student to work on adjectival agreement) and the second, where this positive reinforcement is denied, creates an implicature. The tutor must infer that he or she has failed to tutor her student in the use of written accents and consequently needs to pay attention to this in the future.

Example 13

Smith has a lot of work to do on adjectival agreements (as you point out!) *and also needs to check his use of written accents.* (NS2)

One implicature here is that the tutor has not 'pointed out' this misuse of written accents. As in the previous example, the responsibility for ensuring that Smith uses accents appropriately is defocused away from the tutor to the student.

Evidence that the writer is aware of the inherent pragmatic ambivalence of her feedback is to be found in the following sentence (also attested in instructional utterances in other settings) where a NS monitor was very careful to mark an otherwise pragmatically ambivalent utterance (directive 'It would be a good idea' or praise 'It was a good idea') as praise:

Example 14

Good idea to direct students, *as you do,* to specific sections of the course book for revision and consolidation purposes. (NS2)

Another related strategy is the off-record violation of Grice's maxim of quantity (Brown and Levinson, 1987:214) through scalar implicature (see Levinson, 2000) in the use of adverbial and adjectival hedges as illustrated by the following NS example:

Example 15

I felt that you gave **quite thorough** information, and **a lot of** encouraging support to this student (NS3)

Given the propensity already commented on in both the NS and NNS feedbacks to give praise wherever possible and the positive politeness feature of prefacing a dispreferred response (i.e. criticism) with positive feedback, what is striking here is the extent (often marginal) to which the writers in couching their criticism avoid 'the lower points of the scale' (Brown & Levinson, 1987: 218). The reader must be sensitive to British English conventions of politeness to draw the implicature that 'quite thorough' frequently means not thorough enough, an implicature which is supported by the juxtaposition of this comment with the fulsome praise of the support offered to the student. Further examples of this productive strategy are:

Example 16

You give *very useful* advice to McArthur on avoiding an overly descriptive approach to the essay and *useful* advice to McArthur about 'lifting' expressions from sources. (NS1)

The implicature generated by the mismatch between the positive evaluation 'very useful' and the next point down on the scale 'useful' could be read as an off-record suggestion that the tutor improve her feedback on plagiarism. This, again, was not a strategy which occurred in the NNS data.

Interestingly, in the data there were a number of instances of potential cross-cultural pragmatic failure (Thomas, 1983) due to the semantic difference between the English 'adequate' (just good enough) and the Spanish *adecuado* (appropriate).

Example 17

Your style of marking is *adequate* and correct... (NNS4)

Here a BE reader might pause to work out what appears to be implicated criticism ('adequate' implicating 'not good enough'), either finding that this interpretation is in conflict with the positive evaluation offered by 'correct' or redefining 'correct' as in some way deficient. Yet it is highly possible that no such criticism is intended.

Blum-Kulka (in Wajnryb, 1998: 540) argues that off-record strategies may be seen as imposing on the hearer by forcing on them an unwelcome burden of inference; Lakoff (1990 in Wajnryb, 1998: 536), however, points out that indirectness may suggest intimacy by signalling shared understanding. We would like to suggest that the degree to which on- or alternatively off-record strategies are acceptable is culture-specific and, further, that British society is relatively tolerant of the latter. A further area of study is the extent to which non-native speakers of the language are skilled in recovering implicatures and decoding pragmatic ambivalence in BE. Bouton (1994) has argued that while NNS of US English are able to learn stereotyped implicatures, they find idiosyncratic relevance-based ones much harder to process. This suggests that the socialization process in Britain, whereby speakers learn not only to use but to decode this type of off-record strategy, is complex.

Conclusions

In this chapter we have looked at a certain type of British politeness, indeed arguably the variety of politeness which Brown and Levinson largely exemplify. By focusing, on the one hand, on hedging and deictic anchorage, that is how individuals position themselves in relation both to the face-threatening act and to the hearer through language, and, on the other, on non-conventional speech acts which, indeed, may be pragmatically ambivalent, we hope to have added some more evidence to support the claim that, in certain circumstances at least, British English tends towards negative politeness and favours off-record strategies in carrying out certain face-threatening acts. It seems, at least, that to be British a healthy degree of paranoia can help.

Acknowledgement

This research was made possible thanks to a Small Research Grant from the British Academy.

References

Bell, A. (1984) Language style as audience design. *Language in Society* 13: 145–204.

Bouton, L.F. (1994) Can NNS skill in interpreting implicatures in American English be improved through explicit instruction: A pilot study. *Pragmatics and Language Learning Monograph Series* 5, 88–109.

Brown P. and Levinson, S. (1987) *Politeness*. Cambridge: Cambridge University Press.

Chen, R. (2001) Self-politeness: A proposal. *Journal of Pragmatics* 33, 87–106.

Fillmore, C. (1971) Toward a theory of deixis. *Working Papers in Linguistics*, Vol. 3 (4) Honolulu.

Fukushima, S. (2000) *Requests and Culture*. Bern: Peter Lang.

Hatim, B. (1998) Text politeness: A semiotic regime for more interactive pragmatics. In L. Hickey (ed.) *The Pragmatics of Translation* (pp. 72–102). Clevedon:

Multilingual Matters.
Hickey, L. (1991) Comparatively polite people in Spain and Britain. *ACIS Journal* 4, (2), 2–6.
Ishiguro, K. (1989) *The Remains of the Day*. London: Faber.
Kasper, G. (1990) Linguistic politeness: Current research issues. *Journal of Pragmatics* 14: 193–218.
Levinson, S. (2000) *Presumptive Meanings*. London: MIT.
Luukka, M.-R. and Markkanen, R. (1997) Impersonalisation as a form of hedging. In R. Markkanen and H. Schröder (eds) *Hedging and Discourse* (pp. 168–87). Berlin/New York: de Gruyter.
McLaren, Y. (2001) To claim or not to claim? An analysis of the politeness of self-evaluation in a corpus of French corporate brochures. *Multilingua* 20 (2): 171–90.
Márquez Reiter, R. (2000) *Linguistic Politeness in Britain and Uruguay. A Comparative Study of Requests and Apologies.* Amsterdam/Philadelphia: John Benjamins.
Miller, J. (1993) The grammar of Scottish English. In J. Milroy and L. Milroy (eds) *Real English* (pp. 99–138). London and New York: Longman.
Myers, G. (1989) The pragmatics of politeness in scientific articles. *Applied Linguistics* 10 (1), 1–35.
Nikula, T. (1997) Interlanguage view on hedging. In R. Markkanen and H. Schröder (eds) *Hedging and Discourse* (pp. 188–207). Berlin/New York: de Gruyter.
Placencia, M. E. (1992) Politeness and mediated telephone conversations in Ecuadorian Spanish and British English. *Language Learning Journal* 6, 80–2.
Schröder, H. and D. Zimmer (1997) Hedging research in pragmatics: A bibliographical research guide to hedging. In R. Markkanen and H. Schröder (eds) *Hedging and Discourse* (pp. 249–71). Berlin/New York: de Gruyter.
Sell, R. D. (1991) The politeness of literary texts. In R. D. Sell (ed.) *Literary Pragmatics* (pp. 208–24). London: Routledge.
Sifianou, M. (1992) *Politeness Phenomena in England and Greece*. Oxford: Clarendon Press.
Thomas, J. (1983) Cross-cultural pragmatic failure. *Applied Linguistics* 4(2), 91–112.
Tupas, T.R.F. (2001) Global politics and the Englishes of the world. In J. Cotterill and A. Ife (eds) *Language across Boundaries* (pp. 81–98). London and New York: BAAL/Continuum.
Wajnryb, R. (1998) Telling it like it isn't – exploring an instance of pragmatic ambivalence in supervisory discourse. *Journal of Pragmatics* 29, 531-44.
Weizman, E. (1993) Interlanguage requestive hints. In G. Kasper and S. Blum-Kulka (eds) *Interlanguage Pragmatics* (pp. 123–37). Oxford: Oxford University Press.

Chapter 9

Politeness in Ireland: 'In Ireland, It's Done Without Being Said'

JEFFREY L. KALLEN

Introduction

The speaker of the line quoted in the chapter title, a female undergraduate from Cork, is describing the differences between unsolicited compliments from unfamiliar American males and similar compliments from Irish males. To her and her friends, American males are insincere. Says one friend from Mayo, 'I think American guys anyway they can be nice to you just for the *sake* of it and not really mean it'. Agreeing, the first speaker comments, 'you know the way in Ireland, it's done without being said, like you know if they like you they don't start describing everything they like aboutcha, but in America they all do, don't they?... And if they don't like anything at all, they could just pretend". This chat, part of the International Corpus of English (ICE) project for Ireland (see later), articulates a powerful contrastive insight into politeness in Ireland. In Brown and Levinson's (1987) terms, the American approach could be characterised as bald on record, lacking any of the redressive actions which recognise that compliments are, as Brown and Levinson (1987: 65–6) say, face-threatening acts that represent a desire not to allow the listener to proceed unimpeded and may indicate a desire to obtain something from the listener. Lack of politeness here is equated with pretence and lack of sincerity, and evaluated negatively. In Ireland, however, 'it's done without being said': compliments take place off the record and allow the listener to feel no threat to her need to go through life unimpeded. The Irish politeness strategy is, in turn, equated with sincerity, not receiving the unfavourable assessment of American compliments.

This example is not an isolated or idiosyncratic evaluation but indicates, I suggest, a broad tendency in Irish politeness. Off-the-record and negative politeness strategies are elaborated and developed within a system of discourse that values *silence* as an integral part of the face needs that Brown and Levinson (1987) see as central to politeness (on silence in discourse, see Jaworski, 1993). Yet while high value is placed on negative politeness, salient strategies of positive politeness are equally ingrained in Irish culture. It is, therefore, the central hypothesis of this chapter that the full characterisation of Irish politeness must consider the contradiction between the competing demands of *silence* as a face need, which will tend to favour negative politeness strategies, and the demands of what I term *hospitality* and *reciprocity*, usually favouring positive politeness.

To examine this hypothesis, I rely on (a) the indirect evidence of published ethnographies and dialect studies, (b) insights from the unpublished thesis of Skiadaresi (1997), (c) my unpublished fieldnotes from an ethnographic study of Galway city in 1976–77 and from recordings and observations in Dublin and parts of the west and north of Ireland which I have made over the last 22 years and (d) the Irish component of the ICE project (ICE-Ireland). (For detail on ICE and ICE-Ireland, see Greenbaum, [1996], Kallen & Kirk [2001] and Nelson *et al.* [2002].) The ICE-Ireland project, co-directed by John M. Kirk and myself, based in The Queen's University of Belfast, is still under construction. The data used here come from raw data files of informal, face-to-face conversations recorded in the mid 1990s, mostly including college students from different parts of the Republic of Ireland, their friends and families. The size of this subcomponent of the corpus is approximately 80,000 words.

The picture of politeness presented here cannot purport to cover all social groups or be completely up to date. The data are weighted towards the west and south of Ireland, Dublin, and, to a lesser degree, Belfast and Newry. The ICE corpus does not include all types of English usage but, rather, 'standard' English – hence some variation will not appear. Social change, too, is a factor to be considered. Like most of Europe, Irish society is in a state of rapid change, stimulated in part by increased European integration and globalisation. Some of the economic basis for social relationships, described later, has lately yielded to a new, more impersonal, bureaucratic and globalised commercial basis. Increased urbanisation has also rendered some of the practices and relationships of rural life irrelevant and outdated. This report thus aims to capture an Irish tradition which reaches back several generations and captures aspects of the present but raises questions for future developments that cannot be answered now. In the rest of this introduction, I look briefly at the features of hospitality, reciprocity and silence which, I argue, receive primary weighting in the structure of Irish face needs and politeness.

Hospitality

Hospitality in the broad sense, of course, can involve more than talk, although talk may also be a prerequisite. Non-verbal indices of everyday hospitality in Ireland include the regular sharing of 'free goods' with relative strangers (e.g. an orange in a canteen or workplace lunchroom, offering cigarettes to a chance interlocutor in a pub or at a bus stop); laying out a relatively formal spread of tea, brown bread, butter, jam and biscuits for a casual drop-in visitor (possibly augmented by whiskey or sherry at festive times); and an elaborated practice of buying 'rounds' for others in the pub. These practices are not necessarily ways of solidifying existing friendships but of adhering to the values of hospitality even among relative strangers. We see this principle applied to talk in Elliot Leyton's description of 'decency' in social relations, based on his ethnographic work in Co. Down in the 1960s: 'to be a "decent" man is to carry out one's obligations to society in a style characterised by cheerfulness and friendliness, to pause willingly for a chat and, most importantly, to refrain – regardless of the provocation – from any display of overt hostility' (quoted here from Messenger, 1969: 80). Glassie (1982), writing about a small community in Co. Fermanagh, explicitly distinguishes ordinary talk 'about cattle and dunghills and ... the weather', which he claims is 'not pleasing, not beneficial, not entertaining' and sociable talk. Glassie (1982: 36) quotes a local man, Peter Flanagan, on the value of sociable talk: 'when the mouth's open, you must give it a wee consideration what you're sayin. And if it's beneficial in any way or respect – that's great. Entertainment is the greatest thing'. In other words, talk (like food or drink, I suggest) is not simply for its instrumental value, but is valued when it brings pleasure to others – when it adheres to the values of hospitality.

Reciprocity

Ethnographies of rural modern Irish life stress the means used to ensure reciprocity in social relations. The practice of mutual aid in the activities of farming (known as *cooring*, from Irish *comhar* 'cooperation') has long been an essential part of the social fabric in rural life. Arensberg (1968 [1937]: 69ff.) describes the practices of reciprocal lending of tools, labour and other goods for farm work. These cooperative relationships extend to the ties between small town shops and the surrounding countryside, for as Arensberg (1968 [1937]: 142) says, 'the country customer who brings his trade into the shop does so in response to the ties of kinship and friendliness. He "goes with" a shopkeeper or publican, most often, as he "coors" with his country friends. This is not his only incentive but it is his principal one'. In the realm of talk, reciprocity requires that a ready means be found by which the listener's point of view and positive face needs can be acknowledged, and by which any potential disagreement can at least be transferred to neutral footing.

Silence

'Silence' here is not simply absence of talk or noise but an interactive mode in which, roughly speaking, 'not saying' becomes a mode of saying in its own right (see Jaworski, 1993). Silence as part of the construction of face needs may include complete restraint from speaking; quite commonly, though, it allows indirect strategies for achieving discourse goals. These indirect strategies highly value off-the-record utterances (e.g. understatement, irony, rhetorical questions, ellipsis, etc.) and may even provide ways for speakers to accomplish certain discourse goals when they choose not to perform an explicit act of discourse at all. A 'silent' way of asking a face-threatening question arose in my encounter with a Galway official, who, in the more informal part of a business transaction, sized me up (accurately, as not native to Ireland) and simply stated: 'You're not from this part of the country'. His tone was not ironic or obscure: the obvious was being stated, the implicature being that I should state where I was actually from. But the phrasing of this query is deeply off-the-record. Not only is the question *Where are you from?* not asked but the phrase *this part of the country* (as opposed to *You're not from Ireland*) does not even permit the implicature *you are not Irish* – which would have broken conversational silence on a sensitive topic – to be voiced.

Brody (1973), too, illustrates the operation of negative comment by deeply off-the-record statements whose implicatures might be overlooked completely without inside knowledge. Brody (1973: 199) describes a family ('the Michaels') who have engaged in entrepreneurship in the local community and achieved economic success beyond the usual expectations. Some locals support this development, while others are 'less enthusiastic'. Says Brody:

> Hostile opposition or resentment are not expressed very easily or openly to strangers. ... The first minutes of any conversation about them [the Michaels] between a local farmer and an outsider are laden with circumspection and testing. Typically, the opening remarks involve mention of some success of the Michaels, some symbol of their style. 'It's a fine big house they have,' says the local farmer, waiting for the implications of tone and detail contained in a reply. Behind this cautious beginning lie

both hostility towards the Michaels and a strong desire to enlist visitors' support in criticizing.

Conventional Politeness in Contemporary Irish English

Having established some background to the operation of face needs in the performance of politeness in Ireland, I now consider the linguistic evidence. I focus here on conversational understatement, hedges, minimisation, conventional pessimism, reciprocity, reference to common ground, the use of in-group identity markers and conventional optimism. I do not imply that other politeness strategies are not found, or that these are unique to Ireland. Rather, I aim to concentrate on especially salient aspects of politeness, in particular because they are so well entrenched into everyday language that they constitute unmarked strategies of communication, liable to be encountered in everyday social routine.

Understatement

Understatement as a major part of Irish politeness should not be surprising: as an off-the-record strategy or as negative politeness it is highly congruent with the silence element of face needs while, as an aspect of positive politeness, it is highly congruent with reciprocity.

Simple everyday examples of understatement abound. 'How are you?' invites not a conventionally neutral reply such as 'Fine, thanks' or a more redressive 'Fine thanks, how are you?' but a response which is pitched further away from stating that the speaker is well. The following examples are routine replies to the question 'How are you?':

(1) Not too bad.
(2) Not the worst.
(3) Can't complain.
(4) Can't complain. Sure what's the use in complaining, no one would listen anyway.

The phrase *not the worst* and its companion, *not the best,* are regularly used in speech acts such as compliments, receipt of compliments, in complaints or refusals. Thus, in response to praise such as 'That's a great drawing, Robin', a common reply might be, 'Thanks, I suppose it's not the worst'; a common polite way of complaining about goods such as a pint of beer in a pub would be the observation that it was 'not the best'; and I have heard a radio traffic report warning motorists that traffic in a certain area was 'not the best'. In Skiadaresi's (1997) 'butcher' scenario, respondents were asked how they would address the butcher in order to express dissatisfaction with a particular piece of meat. Example 5 comes from an Irish informant (p. 83), while Example 6 was my own (successful) refusal in an actual shopping situation:

(5) Excuse me, but that meat doesn't look the best.
(6) Eh, it's not the freshest.

Related to (1)–(4), we might also cite conventional replies to routine offers such as 'Would you like a cup of tea?':

(7) I wouldn't say no.
(8) I don't mind.

Utterance (8) is the off-the-record statement *par excellence*: it neither requests nor refuses tea, and unlike (7), it carries no ready-made implicature but rather allows (or forces) the offerer to interpret the response. Likewise, the comment on winning a game show prize in (9), from the ICE-Ireland corpus, falls within Brown and Levinson's analysis of understatement, in that it fails to inform the listener fully of the speaker's opinion, but creates implicatures that the listener is expected to recover (for *like* as a sentence tag, see later).

(9) I wouldn't say no to it like.

A more extreme example of an off-the-record strategy that shifts the focus away from the intended implicature without eliminating it occurs in contemporary conversation, and was noted as far back as Joyce (1910). In discussing what he refers to as 'assertion by negative of opposite', Joyce (1910: 16–23) relates the rhetorical style to usage in the Irish language, also citing English examples such as the following (pp. 18–21):

> You remark that a person has some fault, he is miserly, or extravagant, or dishonest, etc.: and a bystander replies, 'Yes indeed, and 'tisn't to-day or yesterday it happened him' – meaning that it is a fault of long standing.
>
> 'There's a man outside wants to see you sir,' says Charlie, our office attendant, ... 'What kind is he Charlie? does he look like a fellow wanting money?' Instead of a direct affirmative, Charlie answers, 'Why then sir I don't think he'll give you much anyway.'
>
> A man has got a heavy cold from a wetting and says: 'That wetting did me no good,' meaning 'it did me great harm.'

Apart from minor linguistic features, there is nothing particularly out of date or unrealistic about Joyce's examples. Phrases like *it wasn't today or yesterday* or *not a million miles from here* (i.e. 'close-by') are still widespread.

What they demonstrate is the development of understatement as a simple device for implicature into a regular discourse style based on both set phrases and the general strategy of stating a point by stating something close to the opposite but not so close as to fall into irony. In Gricean terms, while the Maxim of Quantity is flouted by understating the speaker's intent, the Maxim of Quality is followed and the speaker can defend the literal truth of the utterance.

Hedges

The need for silence in discourse may be a motive for the use of understatement but, of course, the same face need can also motivate a host of hedging devices. Here, I concentrate on the use of modality and clause-final *like.*

In the ICE corpus, we find a number of performative verbs and verbs with similar structure, e.g. *accept, apologise, admit, say, swear, tell* and *think.* Most dramatic is the comparison between *say* and *think.* Both verbs can be used to express the speaker's point of view: *say* is nearly always hedged by modals or other devices, while *think* almost never is. Thus, when all non-performative uses of *say* (such as reported and hypothetical speech) are excluded from consideration, we find that, out of 57 performative uses, 44 (77%) are hedged by contracted *would,* as in (10)–(11). Of the remaining uses, seven contain additional hedges, three use the pronoun *we* instead of *I* (examples of positive politeness), and three use progressive aspect as a hedge. These types are exemplified in (12)–(14). There are no examples of bald on record expressions of the type *I say X.*

(10) I'd say that within Fine Gael there'll be a row about that
(11) I was out of my bed I'd say.
(12) It's a nice pub now, I'd hafta say.
(13) You'd be surprised how that builds up if they're not smoking ...for the women we'll say.
(14) I'm saying we're all lost.

The distribution for *think* is almost the reverse of *say*: while (15) is analogous to (10), there are only two tokens of this precise type in the corpus. There are, however, nearly 200 tokens in the corpus of the type in (16) and (17):

(15) I would think yes, yes there is money in medicine.
(16) I think you should tell us about that.
(17) He could live with that, I think.

The contrast between *say* and *think* is clear in politeness terms: the former is a bald on record performative verb which conventionally requires a hedge, while the latter contains enough hedging in its inherent semantic properties that it is usually hedged no further.

Contrasts between the tag elements of (11), (12) and (17) and matrix clause uses as in (10) and (16) suggest that syntactic placement may affect the politeness value of pragmatic elements. Though space limitations prevent a discussion of this question, we see the importance of syntactic placement in the Irish use of *like*, to which we now turn. Quotative *like* used with *be*, as in (18), and the use of *like* as a focus particle as in (19), both from the ICE-Ireland corpus, have received much attention in recent years (e.g. Dailey-O'Cain, 2000; Tagliamonte & Hudson, 1999).

(18) 'I was soaked, like they were a mess'.
(19) 'She was like, 'Ehm, well we're not. You could've asked me".

What concerns us here, however, is a tag marker used as a hedge which has not received attention elsewhere. Examples of tag *like* are common in the corpus, which includes roughly 130 tokens in affirmative clauses and 20 in questions. As in (20)–(23), these uses are clause or sentence-final and, therefore, not to be confused with quotatives or focusers (which introduce new information, rather than follow it). Just as modals may hedge the impact of performative or representative verbs, we see here that *like* can be used to hedge the strength of whatever proposition precedes it.

(20) It's such a tragic story like.
(21) He was a pure pole ['skinny person'] like, and he'd a belt on him.
(22) That happens so much like.
(23) But are they old fashioned like?

Minimisation

Minimisation of the imposition of a speech act is treated by Brown and Levinson (1987: 176–178) exemplifying negative politeness, though their discussion concentrates on particles and nominal minimisations. Irish politeness shows many verbal uses as well. Sentences (24) and (25) belong to hospital routine: (24) is a nurse's instruction to sit or lie on an examination bed, while (25) is a nurse's instruction for the listener to go into a private cubicle, undress and put on a disposable hospital gown. From the household and friendship domain come everyday utterances in (26)–(27), while (28) is a directive from a travel agent to a client who wants a travel brochure. The relevant verbs are italicised for clarity. Though these examples contain different speech acts, they coincide in their use of verbs denoting transient motion to minimise the nature of the activity referred to in the sentence. Such statements are neither understated nor ironic but, rather, minimisations of the imposition denoted in the sentence.

(24) Now, if you could just *pop* up here.
(25) Now, if you could just *slip* this on.
(26) Can I *steal* a bit of your drink?
(27) I'm just gonna *jump* into the shower, okay?
(28) You can just reach up there and *grab* one.

While nouns such as *drop*, seen in (29) from the corpus, encode respect for negative face needs by ostensibly reducing the magnitude of the goods offered or requested, by far the most salient aspect of Irish politeness in the nominal area is the use of *bit* applied freely to nouns and adjectives across a wide variety of speech acts. In (30)–(32), *bit* is used to reduce, respectively, the force of propositional content, the threat to the speaker's general esteem, and the emotional impact of the utterance. In all cases, *bit* operates as a minimisation of force but creates no new implicatures, e.g. that the accident in (32) was anything other than 'horrific'.

(29) Will you have another drop of wine?
(30) But you know it's a bit unfair if you were illiterate you wouldn't be able to vote
(31) Oh gosh I'm a bit mixed up now, that's me, on automation.
(32) It was a bit horrific now.

Other common minimisers include *wee* (strongest in the Ulster dialect zone), which, as seen in the non-redundancy of (33), does not necessarily equate referentially to 'small' (although it often does), *old* (seen in (34), a request for goods in a second-hand clothes market), and *just*, which features prominently in everyday usage. In Skiadaresi's 'certificate' question, respondents were put in the discourse frame of needing to ask a professor for a certificate of their student status, triggering the professor's response 'All right, I'll type it for you now'. In their requests for the certificate, two of the 20 Irish respondents (but none of the 20 Greeks) used *just* as a minimiser of imposition. Sentences (35) and (36), from Skiadaresi (1997: 57), contrast strategies in the placement of *just*. The free applicability of *just* in minimisation is also seen in (37) and (38).

(33) No, I've a few wee small potatoes and I have coleslaw and tomato.
(34) Have you any old light slacks?
(35) I just want a certificate …
(36) … to write a certificate for me just saying that …

(37) I'm just gonna have like a soft drink.
(38) No, it's just a conference, just goin' on for a few – a few days

Conventional Pessimism

By 'conventional pessimism', I suggest that pessimism acts not only as Brown and Levinson's (1978: 173–176) kind of politeness strategy, but that the frequency of pessimistic strategies and the elaboration of pessimism in everyday requests in Ireland is especially salient. The exchange in (39) is from a second-hand clothes dealer to a potential customer: both sides use minimisation strategies, while the conventional pessimism of the seller in the last line is a determined attempt to interest the listener in buying clothes without creating an imposition. Utterance (40) comes from the same market, this time as a request from a potential customer.

(39) Seller: Good morning sir
Buyer: Good morning
Seller: Any bit o' money this morning?
Buyer: Well not much
Seller: No. You don't want this suit or a coat or anything, no?

(40) Hey, gov'nor. You wouldn't have a nice pair of working boots for me, would you?

Reciprocity

Though the discussion thus far has focused on negative politeness strategies, it would be misleading to overlook positive face orientations, often grounded in hospitality and reciprocity. Even the simple question–answer adjacency pair in Irish English affords an enhanced opportunity to engage in conversational reciprocity. Speakers of Irish English frequently answer questions with phrases or full clauses that repeat the verb of the question, rather than using a simple *yes* or *no*. This pattern is generally taken to originate in substratal transfer from the Irish language, which has no word for *yes* or *no* but relies on repetition of the verb (see especially Filppula, 1999; see also Kallen, 1994, 1997). This conversational pattern may thus originate in the syntax, rather than in politeness, but its effect is that Irish responses will not appear as bald as simple *yes* or *no* responses. I consider (41)–(43) as examples of reciprocity rather than agreement, on the basis that agreement or sympathy is not necessarily inferred from the repetition of the verb: all we can really say is that the listener has attended to, and used, the speaker's verb, even to disagree. The following examples are from everyday home and shop situations. Speakers of dialects favouring (a) or (b) responses are of course free to add additional politeness markers but the point of the contrast here is that Irish English speakers have a mild degree of reciprocity built into the unmarked syntax of responses.

(41) Would you like some tea?
   (a) I would
   (b) Yes
(42) Are you going to the shops?
   (a) I am
   (b) Yes
(43) Have you any greaseproof paper?
   (a) I haven't
   (b) No.

Given the cross-cultural differences in the use of words like *thanks* and *thank you*, it is noteworthy that reciprocal *thanks* in Ireland is salient. A simple shop transaction frequently involves a high saturation of *thanks* exchanges. Handing over goods, money, change, credit or debit cards, receipts and a bag for goods offers opportunities for both customer and shop assistant to say *thanks*: though not all opportunities must be taken, I have counted 14 utterances of *thanks* in one transaction involving a simple purchase.

Common Ground

The search for common ground in Irish conversations very often leads to talk about the weather. Given the importance of not directly performing a speech act which could threaten the interlocutor's face, weather talk often becomes almost obligatory and may extend over several conversational turns. The climate contributes to the importance of weather talk, with no time of the year when rain, wind, and temperature remain unchanged for long. The comment in (44) contains more reference to shared knowledge than meets the eye. To my comment 'It's a great day today', the speaker agrees emphatically, but goes on to point out that this may be only a transient phase. Agreement with the transience of the good weather – accompanied by conventional pessimism – can be assumed by this speaker, and in the event, provided for more common ground in the discussion which followed.

(44) Tis powerful weather, powerful. I believe we – it's the best o' climate in Europe now, so far. But sure anything can happen. Overnight, yuh.

In (45), two speakers seek agreement over whether the weather is, in fact, cold or mild, where the commonly used weather term *changeable* allows for agreement.

(45) **A**: Very cold today
B: Well, at least it's not raining
A: True. Still, it's very changeable
B: It is indeed.

Some phrases are particularly widespread in highlighting shared knowledge, real or assumed (conversational markers are italicised):

(46) *As the man said to me*, one man hasn't, another man has
(47) That'll be a great day, *as the fella says*
(48) It's just gone too high, *you know yourself*.

In-group Identity Markers

The sociology of language in Ireland provides a ready-made source of in-group markers of linguistic identity which may figure in the politeness system. Most English speakers educated in the Republic of Ireland will have studied Irish throughout their school years, and many will have been to the Gaeltacht (areas where Irish is the main community language) or other Irish-speaking settings. Though knowledge of Irish is less widespread in Northern Ireland, it also functions as an identity marker for some. For others, the Ulster variety of Scots may provide an in-group function (see Mac Póilin, [1999] for an overview of language and identity in Northern Ireland). In (49), the speaker is telling the listener not to go further into a hallway until bottles are cleared from it. Irish *buidéal*, 'bottle', here has the English plural *-s* attached; note the use of *we* and *old* as additional politeness markers. In (50), a mother uses the Irish for 'wooden spoon', lessening the force of chastisement to a child, while in (51), the use of Irish *grá* instead of English *love* builds on an understatement to add a further level of politeness by using an in-group term:

(49) Wait till we get these old *buidéals* out of the way
(50) It's the *spúnóg adhmaid* for you, missy
(51) I've no great *grá* for her, anyway.

Even within Irish English itself, speakers are aware of the solidarity functions of well-known features of traditional dialect and urban vernaculars. Among these we may list, for example, use of /aʊ/ in *old, cold, bold* and a few other such words (conventionally spelled <auld>, <cauld>, etc.), retention of earlier historical /e:/ in words with Middle English /ɛ:/ now elsewhere usually raised to /i/ (e.g. *please* (as a verb), *meat*, *tea*, etc), and sporadic use of what Wells (1982: 370) calls the 'T-to-R rule' (shared with some British varieties), by which words such as *excited* take on /r/ instead of /t/ (hence the conventional spelling in (54)). Many speakers regularly distinguish between *old* and *auld* – the former can be minimising, while the latter can additionally indicate shared status – so that in (52), the effect of criticism is reduced by the use of *auld*. Similar effects of in-group marking are achieved in (53), and (54), where 'excited and delighted' is in a conventional dialect spelling.

(52) That's only an auld leaf.
(53) Would you e'r [ever] give us a cup o' tae.
(54) I would be excirrah and delirrah.

Conventional Optimism

Though we have discussed conventional pessimism in Irish English, we turn now, perhaps paradoxically, to the importance of conventional optimism. Just as pessimism may relate to silence, optimism may relate to hospitality and reciprocity. The widespread marker *sure* is extremely useful in this regard. Though not all uses of discourse-marked *sure* are expressive of optimism concerning positive outcomes or agreement with the speaker, optimistic uses abound, for example in (55)–(56) from the corpus. In all these cases, an assertion is made, to which the consent of the listener or listeners is elicited by clause-initial *sure*. *Sure* in these cases does not hedge or minimise the speaker's act of assertion. On the contrary, as seen in the tag usage of (57), it optimistically assumes agreement with the speaker, even if the facts have not been explicitly agreed.

(55) But sure, no party likes to be in opposition, anyway.
(56) Sure he'll be goin home as well won't he.
(57) You won't go just yet, sure you won't.

Conclusion

This discussion is, of course, no substitute for the in-depth ethnographic analysis needed in order to understand the complex relationships that unite discourse, language and culture in doing politeness work in Ireland. Despite the limitations of our current state of knowledge, however, I suggest that if we accept the idea of *hospitality*, *reciprocity* and *silence* as salient and distinctive elements in Irish politeness, we have the key to understanding the system and the tensions within it. No doubt there are other factors at work but it is to be hoped, at least, that this account will draw attention both to the visible factors that operate in Irish politeness and to those factors which lie beneath the silent and sociable surface.

Acknowledgement

ICE-Ireland has been supported by the Royal Irish Academy, the British Council, and the Arts and Humanities Research Board. I am indebted to John M. Kirk for assistance in using the material, to Mary Pat O'Malley for work on the ICE transcriptions, and to the students who contributed these ICE recordings

References

Arensberg, C. (1968 [1937]) *The Irish Countryman.* Garden City, NY: American Museum Science Books.

Brody, H. (1973) *Inishkillane: Change and Decline in the West of Ireland.* Harmondsworth: Penguin, 1974.

Brown, P. and Levinson, S. (1978) Universals in language usage: Politeness phenomena. In E. Goody (ed.) *Questions and Politeness: Strategies in Social Interaction* (pp.56–289). Cambridge: Cambridge University Press.

Brown, P. and Levinson, S. C. (1987) *Politeness: Some Universals in Language Use.* Cambridge: Cambridge University Press.

Dailey-O'Cain, J. (2000) The sociolinguistic distribution of and attitudes toward focuser *like* and quotative *like. Journal of Sociolinguistics* 4(1), 60–80.

Filppula, M. (1999). *The Grammar of Irish English: Language in Hibernian Style.* London: Routledge.

Glassie, H. (1982) *Passing the Time: Folklore and History of an Ulster Community.* Dublin: The O'Brien Press.

Greenbaum, S. (1996) *Comparing English Worldwide: The International Corpus of English.* Oxford: Clarendon Press.

Jaworski, A. (1993) *The Power of Silence: Social and Pragmatic Perspectives.* London: Sage.

Joyce, P.W. (1910) *English as We Speak it in Ireland.* Reprinted Dublin: Wolfhound Press, 1988.

Kallen, J.L. (1994) English in Ireland. In R. Burchfield (ed.) *The Cambridge History of the English Language, Vol. 5: English in Britain and Overseas* (pp. 148–196). Cambridge: Cambridge University Press.

Kallen, J.L. (ed.) (1997) *Focus on Ireland (Varieties of English around the World, G21).* Amsterdam: Benjamins.

Kallen, J.L. and Kirk, J.M. (2001) Convergence and divergence in the verb phrase in Irish Standard English: a corpus-based approach. In J.M. Kirk and D.P. Ó Baoill (eds) *Language Links: The Languages of Scotland and Ireland* (pp. 59–79). Belfast: Cló

Ollscoil na Banríona.
Mac Póilin, A. (1999) Language, identity and politics in Northern Ireland. *Ulster Folklife* 45, 108–32.
Messenger, J.C. (1969) *Inis Beag: Isle of Ireland*. New York: Holt, Rinehart & Winston.
Nelson, G., Wallis, S. and Aarts, B. (2002) *Exploring Natural Language: Working with the British Component of the International Corpus of English*. Amsterdam: Benjamins.
Skiadaresi, E. (1997) 'Will the Greeks ever learn how to be polite?' An interlanguage study of speech acts and politeness. M Phil thesis, Trinity College Dublin.
Tagliamonte, S. and Hudson, R. (1999) *Be like* et al. beyond America: The quotative system in British and Canadian youth. *Journal of Sociolinguistics* 3(2), 147–72.
Wells, J.C. (1982) *Accents of English*. Cambridge: Cambridge University Press.

Chapter 10

Politeness in Norway: How Can You Be Polite and Sincere?

THORSTEIN FRETHEIM

Introduction

Norwegian society is stereotypically believed to be rather more egalitarian than that of other West European nations. To the extent that this is not just a myth, maybe it partly accounts for the fact that so little research has been done on the way that politeness is reflected in the Norwegian language. Although it would be a gross misunderstanding to claim that Norwegians do not pay any attention to the negative or positive face wants (Brown & Levinson, 1987) of their interlocutors, verbal politeness in Norwegian is not of the conspicuous sort. Even if it may be true that linguistic politeness frequently passes unnoticed in many other languages as well (see, e.g., Kasper, 1990; Terkourafi, 2001), one may easily get the impression that in Norway it passes unnoticed because Norwegian contains relatively few conventionalised means of signalling concern for the addressee's face wants; at the same time there is a risk that use of non-conventional ways of displaying willingness to be polite will actually be misunderstood and interpreted as either ironical or servile.

Norwegian is remarkably short on conventional markers of positive politeness (Brown & Levinson, 1987). A polite address term corresponding to English *Sir* simply does not exist[1], and the vocative term corresponding to English *Madam* is hardly ever found except in written texts where the author tries to capture the spirit of olden times. There is no conventionalised use of diminutives or other terms of endearment. Greetings are never linguistically elaborate and are seldom accompanied by a vocative term. Titles or address terms referring to the addressee's occupation are banned in most sectors of society, and the most common vocative is the second-person pronoun *du* (you, sing.), which is used as an utterance-final parenthetical tag but also frequently as an attention marker initially in a discourse. The traditional V (*vous*)/T (*tu*) distinction, which is very much alive in Denmark and is undergoing a renaissance in Sweden, has largely disappeared. Most of what can be classified as obligatory markers of positive politeness in many other languages would be perceived as either comical or a sign of insincerity if transplanted into a Norwegian conversation. What is felt to be cajoling is generally resented.

There is one thing, though, at which Norwegians are good. They thank profusely (see Fredsted, this volume) and acknowledge their obligation even in situations which, in other cultures, would hardly call for a display of gratitude or where thanking would sound odd, have a humorous effect or even sound sarcastic (see Hirschon's [2001] observations, on the relative infrequency of the word ευχαριστω 'thank you' in Greek conversation). Typical Norwegian examples are 'Thanks for now', 'Thanks for today' or 'Thanks for the company' upon parting, followed by something which is literally 'Thanks in equal fashion' from the interlocutor. What is literally 'Thanks for yesterday' and 'Thanks for last time' are used as greetings upon your first encounter with the addressee after the event that took place the previous day or the last time you met. 'A thousand thanks for the food' is the right thing to say to the host(ess) after a meal. The most curious one, however, is probably 'Thanks for me', said to your host(ess) when the party is over.

However there is no Norwegian word or phrase that can be said to correspond directly to the English *please*. That multifunctional English word can be translated into Norwegian in a number of ways and often the translation is felt to be adequate only because we know it is a translation that purports to retain the tenor of the original English text. The same sort of Norwegian marker of politeness would be less adequate in ordinary conversation and even in fiction where the setting is Norwegian (see Yli-Yakkuri, this volume).

In recent years, a new marker of positive politeness has become conventionalised and has gained popularity, initially among people in service institutions but gradually in the population as a whole. This is the phrase *Bare hyggelig!* (Just a pleasure!) used in response to an act of thanking. Though it is still being parodied by some who consider this usage to be atypical of Norwegian behaviour, it has become entrenched in most parts of society – maybe a sign that Norwegians no longer feel quite comfortable with the traditional sparseness of ways of routinely communicating positive politeness. A few phrases already existed at the time in the 1990s when *Bare hyggelig!* started to gain ground, which were meant to serve a similar purpose and which could be translated as 'Don't mention it' or similar but these are considered rather quaint, belonging to the politeness code of the generation who were already middle-aged during the Second World War.

The rest of this chapter will be devoted entirely to requests. My concern is to what degree Norwegians feel a need to communicate a concern for the hearer's negative face in acts of requesting and how this is achieved.[2]

Politeness in Norwegian requests: 'Don't Overdo It!'

The auxiliary *få* + infinitive construction

Like other nations in Europe, Norwegians use conventionalised indirectness in requests, as exemplified in (1) and (2), where instead of an imperative, the speaker decides to use an interrogative in which the proposition described as desirable to the speaker is embedded under the modal auxiliary corresponding to English *can* in the matrix clause.

Example 1

Kan du sende meg smøret?
(Can you send me the butter)

Example 2

Kan jeg få låne en telefonkatalog?
(Can I get borrow a telephone directory)

Example 1 contains no marker of politeness apart from the indirectness involving the auxiliary *kan* (can). The sentences in Examples (1) and (2) – and (1′) – are taken from the English Norwegian Parallel Corpus (ENPC) at the University of Oslo (http://www.hf.uio.no/iba/prosjekt/), a bi-directional translation corpus containing fiction and non-fiction. The level of linguistic politeness appears to be stepped up considerably in the English translation (1′) of the Norwegian source text in (1).

Example 1′

Would you pass the butter, please?

The combination of the modal auxiliary *would* and the politeness marker *please* indicates a level of politeness which exceeds the level shown in the Norwegian (1). For a service as trivial and natural as passing the butter if the addressee is closer to it than the speaker, (1) is entirely sufficient in the Norwegian community and the most literal translation of (1′) back into Norwegian would indeed be somewhat excessive for such a tiny favour. In the Norwegian request of (1′), *ville* equals *would* and *være så snill* (be so nice) is the closest one can get to *please*.

Example 1″

Ville du være så snill å sende smøret?
(Would you be so nice to send the butter)

Because the linguistic marking of a polite attitude may be judged to be excessive for a particular occasion, there is always a risk that the audience will read an implicated message into the Norwegian request in (1″). Trying to sound even more polite than would be optimal under the circumstances is a well-known strategy if you intend to communicate indirectly that you are getting impatient, and possibly annoyed, because the addressee ought to have been perceptive enough to realise that he should have passed the butter without anyone telling him to do so. Hearing (1″), the interlocutor might begin to suspect that the politeness markers convey an implicit criticism, which is sure to damage that person's positive face. Or the phrase *ville du være så snill* (would you be so kind) might simply confuse the interlocutor, who may suspect that the speaker has some ulterior motive which is hard to deduce from whatever contextual clues might be available. The age of the speaker is a social variable that should be taken into account in an assessment of the relevance of an utterance of (1″). Coming from an older person, especially an old middle-class lady, it is not likely to sound as marked as if the speaker were a younger person, male or female.

Turning now to sentence (2) from the ENPC, we find the same Norwegian auxiliary *kan* as in (1) but, in addition, there is a modal verb *få* (get) – strangely, not customarily recognised as one of the modal auxiliaries in Norwegian – whose semantic function is to indicate that its subject referent is understood by the speaker to be a beneficiary. In the ENPC, there are a great many tokens (involving the syntactic construction with the modal *få* plus a bare infinitive) which have nothing to do with politeness but when *få* combines with a 'Can I' request, it normally enhances our feeling that the communicator is being polite. It does so in a very unobtrusive way, however, so speakers will never be perceived as being overly polite just because they use the opportunity to acknowledge that the fulfilment of the request would be beneficial to themselves. (2) was translated into English as (2′) in the ENPC, where the more formal *may* has replaced *can*.

Example 2′

May I borrow a telephone book?

Data of the sort presented in (3)-(5) suggests that the *få* + infinitive construction strengthens the recipient's feeling that the speaker is perceiving the fact that a face-threatening communicative act is being performed, an act which is in need of redress.

Example 3

Kan jeg sette fra meg kofferten min her?
(Can I set from me the suitcase mine here)
'Can I place my suitcase here?'

Example 4

Kunne jeg få sette fra meg kofferten min her?
(Could I get set from me the suitcase mine here)
'Could I place my suitcase here?'

Example 5

Tror du jeg kunne (få) sette fra meg kofferten min her?
(Think you I could (get) set from me the suitcase mine here)
'Could I place my suitcase here, do you think?'

The present tense modal *kan* is replaced by the subjunctive past *kunne* in (4) and the auxiliary *få* encodes the assumption that the speaker considers herself to be a beneficiary if the request is fulfilled. An utterance of (4) is more appropriate than (3) if the addressee is a stranger. In (5), the auxiliary construction is embedded under the verb of belief *tro* (think, believe), which emphasises the speaker's communicated attitude of uncertainty and leaves it to the addressee to judge to what extent the request might be an imposition which may have to be refused. We conclude that the parenthesised auxiliary *få* in (5) would not contribute as much to the overall relevance (Sperber & Wilson, 1986) of an utterance of (5) as *få* would in (4).

The auxiliary *få* + past participle construction

The same syntactic construction with the auxiliary *få* pointing to a benefactive subject appears with a past participle complement as well as the infinitival complement whose pragmatic implications were considered in the previous section. The past participle does not encode the information that the speaker is *not* the intended agent of the activity described but it strongly implicates that the agent is meant to be someone other than the speaker, probably the addressee or someone that the addressee has authority over. It is potentially more face-threatening, due to the fact that the addressee is actually being asked to see to it that the required action is carried out, instead of just being asked to grant the speaker permission to go ahead and do whatever is needed. Consider the difference between (6) and (7).

Example 6

Kan jeg få undersøke og sammenligne prisene?
(Can I get examine and compare the prices)
'Can I examine and compare the prices?'

Example 7

Kan jeg få undersøkt og sammenlignet prisene?
(Can I get examined and compared the prices)
'Can I have the prices examined and compared?'

The job requested by means of an utterance of (7) is not cost-free. If the speaker is a customer doing business with some firm that will be paid for their services, the fairly plain linguistic form of (7) is normally quite acceptable but, if the addressee is not under an obligation to comply with the request, then more redress work is required in order to avoid damage to the interlocutor's negative face. Nothing much in the way of a deviation from (7) is needed to achieve the desired level of politeness. A substitution of the subjunctive *kunne* (could) for *kan*, as in (7′), will suffice. An utterance of (7′) leaves the decision to either concur with the speaker's request or refuse it entirely in the hands of the addressee. Nothing corresponding roughly to *please* would work.

Example 7′

Kunne jeg få undersøkt og sammenlignet prisene?
(Could I get examined and compared the prices)
'Could I have the prices examined and compared?'

In order to step up the degree of politeness without impunity, the speaker of (7′) might do as in (6), embedding (7′) under *Tror du at* … (Do you think that …):

Example 7″

Tror du at jeg kunne få undersøkt og sammenlignet prisene?
(Think you that I could get examined and compared the prices)
'Could I have the prices examined and compared, do you think?'

'I wondered if P'

In asking for the addressee's attention to some matter or in asking for verbal information of various sorts, a politeness phrase involving the Norwegian verb meaning 'to wonder' is probably the most common device intended to reduce a potential negative face threat. This is primarily a linguistic formula used in addressing people you presuppose will be able to help out. Even at an information desk, a Norwegian customer will generally start with an indirect request which looks like a description of the speaker's past-time attitude to the propositional function expressed in the wh-complement structure but which is actually a polite request for information. Consider (8).

Example 8

Jeg lurte på hvor de selger billetter til matineen.
(I wondered on where they sell tickets to the matinee)
'I was wondering where tickets for the matinee are being sold.'

It is important that the past tense is used with this construction, otherwise the speaker will be heard as literally describing what is going on in her mind at the time of utterance; it would sound more like a question that the speaker is addressing to herself rather than to the person she is facing. Thus, (9) contains the appropriate kind of verbal redress when the speaker wants to order a taxi with the help of the addressee and (10) does not sound like a request at all, and would even be rude if it were intended as one.

Example 9

Jeg lurte på om det gikk an å bestille en taxi her.
(I wondered on if it went to order a taxi here)
'I was wondering if I could order a taxi here (with you).'

Example 10

**Jeg lurer på om det går an å bestille en taxi her.*
(I wonder on if it goes to order a taxi here)
*'I'm wondering if I can order a taxi here.'

(9) with its past tense forms is not just a slightly more polite expression because the past tense is used for a modal purpose; the version with the past tense form is the only one that could be a request. Again a word corresponding to *please* would be inappropriate in a request of this sort.

The verb *gå an*, meaning 'be possible' or 'be feasible', which appears in the 'whether'-complement of (9), is an important verb in Norwegian requests. An interrogative with the past tense of this verb will invariably be associated with a hypothetical context (subjunctive mood), and will be understood as a request for some service or for permission to act in a certain way. (9') is an unequivocal request which is pragmatically equivalent to (9), and this stimulus is arguably more relevant (Sperber & Wilson, 1986) than (9), because, by dispensing with one of the three clause levels of (9), the speaker succeeds in reducing the processing work for the addressee while maintaining the level of politeness.

Example 9′

Gikk det an å bestille en taxi her?
(went it to order a taxi here)
'Could I order a taxi here (with you)?'

The absence of 'please' in Norwegian

The following three parallel sequences from the ENPC are English source texts and Norwegian translations.

Example 11

E: Please don't take against Oliver like that.
N: *Vær snill og ikke døm Oliver så hardt.*
(be nice and not judge Oliver so severely)

Example 12

E: Please don't use language like that around me.
N: *Vær vennlig å ikke bruke denslags språk her.*
(be kind to not use that sort of language here)

Example 13

E: Please would someone, I asked the world in general, mind going down to the yard, ...

N: *Kunne noen være så snill å gå ned på parkeringsplassen, sa jeg ut i løse luften, ...*
(could someone be so nice to go down on the parking lot, said I out in the fresh air, ...)

There is indeed an expression corresponding to *please* in (11)–(13) and we have come across this phrase before in (1″). It appears in various shapes: in (11) it is formed as the imperative *vær* (be) followed by the adjective *snill* (nice, kind, good) plus the coordinating connective *og* (and), in (12) as the same imperative followed by the less colloquial adjective *vennlig* (kind, friendly, amiable) plus an infinitival complement, and in (13) as a modal auxiliary *kunne* (could) plus the copular infinitive *være* (be) and a discourse particle *så* (so) pointing cataphorically to the proposition of the complement of *være ... snill* (be ... nice). The ENPC sequences in (14) and (15) represent Norwegian source texts and English translations. There is a cataphoric particle *så* in both cases, representing a degree of kindness to be specified in the following infinitival complement, but while (14) is syntactically of the same imperative type as (12), (15) is a declarative sentence with the present-tense copula form *er* (are).

Example 14

N: *Vær så snill å hente en halvflaske.*
(be so nice to fetch a half bottle)
E: Please fetch half a bottle.

Example 15

N: *Imens er De kanskje så snill å samle damene og underrette dem om at fru Olsrud er død, … .*
(in the meantime are you-3.pl. perhaps so kind to gather the ladies and inform them about that Mrs Olsrud is dead, …)
E: Perhaps in the meantime you'd get the rest of the ladies together and tell them that Mrs Olsen [*sic*] is dead, …

There is a transparent reason for the writers' vacillation between using a coordination of imperative phrases, as in (11), and using constructions involving an infinitival complement, as in (12)–(15). Many authors whose fictional texts are represented in the ENPC prefer the infinitival complement alternative across the board, even when the sentence type is imperative, as in (14) or the verb is in the present tense, as in (15). Hardly any author or translator uses a coordination of verb phrases when the copula is in the infinitive. An exception is seen in (16), taken from a novel published as recently as 2001, which means it is not part of the ENPC. (16) illustrates the rarely-occurring case of two infinitival phrases coordinated by means of *og* (and).

Example 16

Arnold, kan du være så snill og sette deg på plassen din?
(Arnold can you be so nice and seat yourself on the seat yours)
'Arnold, could you please sit down on your seat?'

The coordination of infinitives in (16) and the infinitival complement in (13) ought to be the same grammatical construction – apart from the difference between present tense *kan* in (16) and past tense (subjunctive) *kunne* (could) in (13), but (16) and (13) represent mutually exclusive 'lay' analyses of the syntactic structures involved. The same applies to the coordinated imperatives in (11) compared to the imperative followed by an infinitival complement in (12). While (12) is necessarily a syntactic blend, the cataphoric *så* in all these examples is arguably easier to reconcile with an infinitival complement than with coordination.

One important source of syntactic confusion is the fact that the co-ordinating connective *og* and the infinitive marker *å* are pronounced in the same way in present-day Norwegian: it is just a back, mid, rounded vowel in both cases. At the same time one can observe certain tendencies in speech to handle *værsåsnill* as if it were on its way to becoming a politeness particle with no internal syntactic structure. It can constitute an utterance of its own just like *Please* and it can be tagged on to an imperative but the most remarkable point about the incipient particle *værsåsnill* is that in child language it is often used with a first person rather than a second person subject, illustrated by (17).

Example 17

#Kan jeg værsåsnill å få en kjeks til?
(can I be so nice to get one biscuit more)
'Can I please have another biscuit?'

We adults succeed in eradicating this usage, because for us it is illogical to say 'Can/could **I** be so nice ...', etc. While small children in Norway find it natural to experiment with a politeness particle resembling English *please* (even before they have acquired any English), the crucial step toward lexicalisation of *vær så snill* in the standard language code is prevented by adult users' appeal to logic and systematic correction of children who, in their spontaneous speech, combine *værsåsnill* with a first person pronoun. To the extent that *vær* in *vær så snill* is still perceived as a verb by Norwegians, the phrase cannot fulfil the function of English *please* and similar markers in other languages. Obviously the final step toward development of a politeness particle also implies getting rid of the infinitive marker *å* in (17), as the modal auxiliary *kan* only takes a bare infinitive. To date I never heard anyone saying *Kan jeg værsåsnill...* followed by a bare infinitive.

It was noted earlier that a sentence like (7') cannot be made more polite by the addition of the infinitival phrase *være så snill* after the modal auxiliary *kunne*. The subject of *kunne* in (7') is a first person pronoun, hence the following expanded version of (7') is rejected because it is judged to be illogical and therefore unacceptable, as is (17).

Example 7'

Kunne jeg (#være så snill og) få undersøkt og sammenlignet prisene?
'Could I please have the prices examined and compared?'

It would be naïve to assume that if Norwegians were to develop a word analogous to *please*, it would have to be a lexicalisation based on the expression *vær så snill*. This is admittedly the default choice in translations of *please*, as illustrated by the metalinguistic ENPC sequences in (18) where the source text is English and the translation Norwegian but there are other candidates for the development of something closely related to *please*.

Example 18

E. He'd thank me for meals and habitually used the word 'please'.
N: *Han takket bestandig for maten, og sa som regel 'vær så snill' når han ba om noe.*
(he thanked always for the food and said as a rule 'be so nice' when he requested about something)

One alternative translation of *please* as a tag appended to an imperative is *er du snill* (are you nice), whose origin is a conditional clause – 'If you are nice' – formed in the same way as an interrogative with inverted word order. In the ENPC, *er du snill* is only found in Norwegian translations of *please*, including two occurrences where the English source had no specific politeness marker: in Norwegian source texts, there was not a single occurrence of this parenthetical phrase. My conclusion is that *er du snill* belongs to the past, like so many other conventionalised markers of politeness in Norwegian.

Very often the word *please* in English source texts included in the ENPC is omitted altogether in the Norwegian translation, or is rendered in some more oblique way. An example of the former is seen in (19), while the latter is exemplified by (20).

Example 19

E.: Listen to me carefully, please.
F: *Følg nå godt med.*
(follow now well with)

Example 20

E: Moments later he murmured, 'Could you please clear that bed?'
N: *Litt etter mumlet han: 'Kunne du ikke rydde sengen litt?'*
(a little later murmured he could you not clear the bed a little)

The Norwegian translation in (20) involves the use of a negative 'Couldn't you' interrogative to compensate for the absence of *please*. A negative interrogative is not particularly polite in either language, though it is also disputable whether *please* would be perceived as a sign of sincere politeness in (20).

There are translations of *please* as *vær så snill* in the ENPC which are downright unidiomatic, as when an utterance-initial *please* is followed by a wh-question. *Vær så snill*, whether it occurs parenthetically in initial or final position, does not sound right with an interrogative. Moreover, quite a few instances of *vær så snill* in translations of English source texts seem stilted, or sound as if they are trying to capture the culture in which the English-speaking fictional characters are embedded: this is definitely a legitimate goal for a translator, and maybe even a requirement, but it still does not make the translation fully idiomatic Norwegian.

While English *please* serves as a go-ahead signal to the addressee when the speaker accepts an offer from him, *takk* (thanks) is what a Norwegian will say under similar circumstances. Consider how offers are accepted in (21) and (22), taken from the ENPC.

Example 21

E: 'Yes, please,' I said.
N: *'Ja takk,' svarte jeg.*
(yes thanks answered I)

Example 22

E: But yes, please.
N: *Men tusen takk.*
(but thousand thanks)

Please in *Yes, please* indicates that the speech act shares an important component with canonical requests, and accepting an offer might actually be regarded as a request for the addressee to carry out the action referred to in the offer – if it pleases him/her to do so. The corresponding Norwegian utterance meaning 'Yes, thanks' instead communicates the speaker's gratitude. Thus, in Norwegian the same politeness marker – *takk* – is used in accepting an offer and in rejecting it. In English, in contrast, the difference between acceptance and rejection of an offer is underscored by the speaker's use of *please* for the former and *thank you* (*No, thank you*) for the latter.

A similar thing happens when a speaker places an order, as in *One American breakfast, please*, compared with its Norwegian counterpart *En amerikansk frokost, takk*. While the English perform what must be classified as a request, Norwegians thank in advance for the anticipated service. Norwegians do it differently from the English, probably not so much because they perceive the whole transaction differently but because Norwegian lacks a word meaning *please*.

It has been observed by Aijmer (1996) that *please* is not an appropriate device for making amends when the imposition is not of the trivial sort. Similarly, Norwegian *vær(e) så snill* should never be used for the purpose of mitigating impositions that constitute a potentially considerable threat to the addressee's negative face. Uttering (23) is a way of putting a bit of pressure on the addressee, so if you sincerely want him to be given the opportunity to opt out, you avoid the construction in (23) and say something like (24) instead.

Example 23

Kunne du være så snill å støtte Redd Barna?
(could you be so nice to support Save the Children)
'Would you like to support Save the Children, please?'

Example 24

Kunne du tenke deg å støtte Redd Barna?
(could you imagine yourself to support Save the Children)
'Would you like to support Save the Children, please?'

When mitigating conventions are absolutely required, *vær(e) så snill* sounds really 'bossy'. Example (25), uttered by one train passenger to another, sounds as if the speaker intends to be offensive while (26) is an example of verbal redress which is felt to be much more acceptable for this kind of request in a conversation between strangers.

Example 25

Ville du være så snill å bytte plass med meg?
(would you be so nice to change place with me)
'Would you please change seats with me?'

Example 26

Ville du hatt noe imot å bytte plass med meg?
(would you [have] had anything against to change place with me)
'Would you mind changing seats with me?'

Conclusion

The safest politeness strategy for a Norwegian performing an act of requesting information or some extra-linguistic service is to abandon the indicative mood. Although there is no morphological difference between indicative and subjunctive in Norwegian, the past tense can have a function similar to that of the subjunctive in other languages, it can be a sign that the state of affairs described is hypothetical rather than factual, as in English.

This subjunctive use of the past tense can be combined with various kinds of matrix clause reference to the speaker's propositional attitude ('I wondered whether ...'), the addressee's attitude ('Do you think ...?') or the addressee's ability ('Could you ...?'). There is no equivalent of *please* in Norwegian, and the closest equivalent has been argued to be of limited applicability. Linguistic politeness in Norwegian society is characterised by a tendency toward parsimony: conventionalised indirectness in the performance of requests exists but too much linguistic embroidery for the sake of mitigating requests is normally counter-productive.

Notes

1. In translations of English texts it is largely rendered as *Sir* to preserve the atmosphere of the original.
2. I acknowledge my indebtedness to Anne Wichmann for sharing with me her views on *please* (See Wichmann forthcoming), to Marina Terkourafi for giving me a copy of her dissertation on politeness in Cypriot Greek, and to Stig Johansson who gave me access to the ENPC (see 2.1) and encouraged me to do a search on *please* there.

References

Aijmer, K. (1996) *Conversational Routines in English*. London: Longman.

Brown, P. and Levinson, S. (1987) *Politeness: Some Universals in Language Usage*. Cambridge: Cambridge University Press.

Hirschon, R (2001) Freedom, solidarity and obligation: The sociocultural perspective. In A. Bayraktaroğlu and M. Sifianou (eds) *Linguistic Politeness Across Boundaries: The Case of Greek and Turkish* (pp. 17–42). Amsterdam: John Benjamins.

Kasper, G. (1990) Linguistic politeness: Current research issues. *Journal of Pragmatics* 14, 193–8.

Sperber, D. and Wilson, D. (1986) *Relevance: Communication and Cognition*. Oxford: Blackwell.

Terkourafi, M. (2001) Politeness in Cypriot Greek: A frame-based approach. Doctoral dissertation, Department of Linguistics, University of Cambridge.

Wichmann, A. (forthcoming) Ways of saying *please*: Attitudinal marking in *Please*-requests.

Chapter 11

Politeness in Denmark: Getting to the Point

ELIN FREDSTED

Introduction

Compared with certain other languages and cultures, Scandinavian cultures appear rather informal, at least if you take the dominant Scandinavian self-image at face value. An important part of political correctness during the period of Social Democratic government (beginning in the early 1930s), and especially after the student revolution of the late 1960s and early 1970s, has been that social hierarchies are not marked. It is not good 'tone' in the Scandinavian welfare states to show off, demonstrate wealth or superiority; hierarchies (even in businesses and organisations) are largely invisible or hidden, so you must be alert to subtle distinctions to discover differences in status and rank.

Consequently, you do not usually show verbal respect to people merely because they are placed higher on the social scale than yourself. On the contrary, a medical superintendent at a hospital in Jutland once told me that he would only use the formal address form (*De*) to cleaners and this to compensate for what he called his 'bad social conscience'.

So it is difficult to get to grips with a definition of politeness in Danish. I have, however, chosen to focus on three aspects: address forms, getting in and out of conversations and a comparative case study on politeness markers in a Danish and a German conversation.

This chapter is based on empirical data. In 1993–94 I collected about 120 conversations at Danish and German tourist information offices. Initially, these were written down on location; later, conversations and guided tours were audio-taped, and 18 conversations were video-taped. Speakers recorded were, of course, aware of being recorded, but not instructed in what to say or do (Fredsted, 1998).

Address Forms - A Valid Parameter?

Leech (1983: 126) uses an abstract scale to explain the pragmatic choice of address forms:

```
               v
               e
               r
               t
               i
               c
               a
               l
—-horizontal distance——
               d
               i
               s
               t
               a
               n
               c
               e
```

The vertical dimension measures the distance in relation to power/authority. The horizontal dimension measures social distance. However, this scale is not helpful if – as argued earlier – the vertical dimension is invisible; leaving only the horizontal scale. Focusing on the horizontal dimension, you could claim

- that you are closer to persons of your own generation than to those considerably older (or younger) than yourself,
- that you are closer to persons of your own sex than to those of the other, and
- that you are closer to people in an unofficial context than in an official one where you play a professional role.

Such parameters may also influence the choice of address forms in Danish. In my data, some employees use the formal *De*-form in an official context when guiding a group of tourists, whereas they use both the formal *De* and the informal *du* when giving information to individuals in a more informal situation.

We find few instances of the formal address form *De* in my Danish data. In the recorded tours, two of four Danish guides use it. The other two use the informal plural *I* (you), while the use of inclusive *vi* (we) predominates in all four. In the monologic guided tours, it is the guide who defines the appropriate degree of formality and distance from the audience. In the dialogic conversations, however, both guides and tourists are involved in defining formality and distance and here we find a consistent and mutual use of *De* in conversations between the guides and middle-aged or elderly tourists who speak Copenhagen Standard Danish. With tourists who speak a regional West Danish variety of Standard Danish, a dialect or the Low Copenhagen sociolect the informal forms of address are used.

This indicates that the dominant parameters are age, formality and (perhaps most importantly) the regional language variety used. The data were collected in Jutland mainly with interactants from Jutland. Data from speakers predominantly from Copenhagen might have given a different result. *De* gained a foothold in Danish during the 18th century as a formal polite form and as an equivalent to the German *Sie*. *De*, however, never became an integral part of the pronominal system of Danish dialects partly because these are attached to the close-knit society in rural areas where one seldom talks to outsiders. Consequently, people in the countryside never got used to *De* before it became largely outdated. Thus a dialect may only have the informal form (*du* singular, *I* plural), a regional variety of Standard Danish might have both forms but only Copenhagen Standard Danish definitely has both (informal *du* and *I*, formal *De*). This, of course, leads to uncertainty, especially among speakers of regional varieties of Standard Danish.

Generally speaking, if people are uncertain, they will either wait and see what their interlocutor does, and then do likewise, or choose an avoidance strategy, e.g. use the inclusive *we*, as seen in the tourist information offices. Some organisations, however, have internal rules concerning, for example, official occasions, business communication or communication with customers or clients. However, in general, no universal 'rule' exists for address forms in Danish. The relationship between nominal and pronominal forms of address in Danish and German is shown in the following (for German politeness, see House, this volume):

German	*Danish*
Sie + *Herr/Frau* + last name	*De* + *hr./fru* + last name
	De + first name + last name
	du + (*hr./fru*) + last name
	du + first name + last name
Du + first name	*du* + first name

This rough cross-linguistic scale, does not, however, explain pragmatic use. 'Distant' *versus* 'intimate address' is codified differently in Danish and German, but in neither language are there purely linguistic rules governing whether a certain kind of address form is polite or impolite *per se*. Certainly there is a correlation between the degree of distance and the form of address chosen. A popular idiom in Jutland goes 'People can be so mean that you only can say *De* to them'.

However, formal address forms have often been treated as being *eo ipso* more polite than the informal, as early sociolinguistic literature shows: the T-form and the use of first name express 'intimacy, juniority, low social status, inferiority' whereas the V-form, surnames or titles express 'distance, seniority, high social status, or superiority' (Braun, 1988: 35). This hypothesis does not fit Danish usage. It is more accurate to regard *both* forms (T and V) as realisations of appropriate language behaviour and examine the factors governing their choice in a given situation (Watts *et al.*, 1992: 58 ff.). Furthermore, the conventional form of polite address might not have the same status even in closely-related cultures. 'Tact' and 'formal politeness' represent different aspects of politeness, and each might carry a different range of social meanings for members of different regional cultures – even if they share the same national culture and speak (varieties of) the same language.

So while the field of address forms is not really the proper place to look for politeness in Danish, it helps to show the complexity of the issue.

Getting In and Out of Conversations

It became clear during the recordings in tourist information offices that Danish and German conversations were structured in different ways and that the transcripts of the Danish conversations seemed to be quite direct or even lack linguistic politeness markers in comparison with the German conversations. So was this first impression correct and, if so, what were the differences?

Typically, a Danish tourist would begin by asking 'What can I see here?'. The German tourist would perhaps start with a greeting, then make a pre-request and then ask a question. Could the explanation simply be that different language codes are connected with different cultural codes, that one culture prefers 'talking straight' while, in the other, a more elaborate code is preferred? At the same time, I observed that Danish tourists in Germany and Danish employees in Denmark seemed rather direct when speaking German as a foreign language. Both languages and cultures have certain expectations in respect to 'tact' and these expectations do not appear to match. Thus, my fundamental interest was to investigate similarities and differences between these two genetically closely-related languages.

I first analysed the structure of the Danish and German data and constructed the following pattern to cover almost all of the 120 conversations.

The structure of conversations in tourist offices

Initial phase	→	1. Dialogue opening signal/greeting
	→	2. Phatic interaction signal/pre-request
	→	3. Introduction of the topic
Medial phase		Negotiation of the topic →
		↕
		Introduction of a new topic →
Final phase		1. Conclusion →
		2. Thank you →
		3. Farewell greeting →

The conversation starts with an initial phase containing a greeting, a pre-request and the introduction of a topic. The next medial phase contains a negotiation of the topic and, perhaps, the introduction of a new topic for negotiation. The final phase may contain a conclusion, a thank you and a farewell. But the conversation may be opened without any greeting [arrow two] or without a pre-request [arrow three] introducing a topic immediately. The interlocutors may opt out of the conversation directly after negotiating the topic, or end with or without a conclusion, thank you or good-bye.

This model represents a prototypical conversational scheme but the real conversations do not follow it in the same way: Danish conversations show a clear tendency to start with the topic [arrow 3] and end with a conclusion [final phase 1]. German conversations show a tendency to start on the second arrow (pre-request) and end with a thank you [arrow 2] in the final phase. In short: the German conversations show more phatic language and conventional verbal politeness, the Danish conversations show almost exclusively referential language, pure 'negotiation' of the subject and little or no conventional verbal politeness markers. In other words, this structural analysis appears to confirm initial impressions.

Verbal and Non-verbal Cooperation in Conversations

A case study

I shall now further analyse these features by introducing two videotaped conversations, one Danish and one German, selected because they are almost identical in topic and content. (All participants speak their mother tongue.) A tourist visits the tourist information office to ask about the sights of a town. The employee responds by pointing out objects of historical and cultural interest on a city map. (The last part of the Danish conversation dealing with overnight accommodation has been omitted here. For full transcripts see [Fredsted, 1998: 238ff].)

I have analysed the following:

(1) verbal politeness markers,
(2) discourse markers,
(3) eye movement, eye contact and gestures and
(4) co-relations between verbal and non-verbal features.

Verbal politeness markers

Inspired by Brown and Levinson (1987), I looked for the following verbal politeness markers:

(A) personal pronoun selection (use of in-group identity marker (inclusive *we*), formal *versus* informal address form, impersonalise speaker and hearer, avoid the pronouns *I* and *you*),
(B) lexical downgrading (minimise imposition, be pessimistic),
(C) lexical upgrading (exaggerate interest),
(D) negation and hedges (interactional pessimism),
(E) switching point of view from S to H (attend to hearer's interest),
(F) indirectness (indirect questions and indirect requests),
(G) subjunctive as conventional polite form in German, past tense of modal verbs in Danish,
(H) syntactic downgrading, i.e. use of conditional clauses, and
(I) use of pre-requests.

In the Danish and German conversations, we find the following verbal politeness markers:

The Danish conversation

(A) Personal pronoun choice. Here we must differentiate between the tourist and the employee: while the tourist is in a relatively private or everyday situation, the employee is communicating professionally.

Accordingly, we find each selects different pronouns. The Danish tourist uses predominantly *jeg* (I) and also the impersonal *man* (one/you) when talking about her own wants:

> ***Jeg** er lige kommet til byen og (.) hhh **jeg** vil godt have et par tips om (.) hvilke ting **man** bør se når **man** nu er her* (**I** have just arrived in town and **I** would like a couple of tips about what **one** ought to see when **one** is here)

The employee acts in a more official and impersonalised mode avoiding *jeg* (I). Instead of 'I' and 'you' she prefers the inclusive *vi* (we) which she uses 16 times referring alternately to the whole city, the team of the tourist office (substituting *I*) or 'you and me', thus avoiding an explicit address form. As address form, she starts with the formal form of address *Dem* (oblique form of *De*).

> *Kan **vi** hjælpe **Dem**?* (Can **we** help **you**?)

Later in the conversation, however, she changes to *dig* (you, informal, oblique form of *du*, singular).

> *Der har **vi** lavet sådan en byvandring, som nok vil fortælle **dig** lidt mere omkring det* (There **we** have made such a city-guide which will tell **you** a little bit more about it.)

So the uncertainty concerning address form is clearly reflected in this conversation.

(B) Lexical downgrading is used by both speakers, but for different purposes: the tourist downgrades her requests by using modifying particles such as *lige* (just) and *ret* (quite, fairly):

> *Jeg er **sådan ret** interesseret i gamle bygninger* (I am **in a way quite** interested in old buildings)

The employee uses predominantly *lidt* and *lille* ('a little bit' and 'small/little') as a kind of understatement:

> *Ja **vi** har **vores** turistinformation som fortæller **lidt** om selve byen og **lidt** om hele området der er her.* (Yes **we** have got **our** information brochure which explains **a little bit** about the city and **a little bit** about the region here.)

(C) Negation and hedges are used only by the tourist, once to express insecurity, once to soften a request:

> *e:h I har **ikke sådan en** professionel guide på der kan (.) ta' én rundt?* (e:h you have**n't got a kind of** professional guide who can guide you around?)

(D) Lexical upgrading – generally characteristic of the language of tourist information brochures – is used very moderately, only twice by the tourist: ***meget** interessant* (**very** interesting) and *det ser **meget fint** ud* (it looks **very fine**). The employee also uses 'very' three times to upgrade the sights of the town, and once – very hesitantly – the superlative to describe sights of the city, in fact referring to the text of an information brochure.

> *så har vi udpeget nogle af de:* ***ældste*** *– nogle af de* ***mest*** *ø:h* ***interessante bygninger*** *der er her* (then we have pointed out some of the: **oldest** – some of the **most** e:mm interesting buildings here)

Apart from this, no other verbal politeness markers of the nine items A to I just mentioned appear in the Danish conversation.

	Tourist	***Employee***
Personal pronoun selection:	self-reference:	
	jeg (9 times),	*vi* (16 times)
	address form:	
	I, du	*Dem, dig*
	impersonal:	
	man (6 times)	*man* (4 times)
lexical downgrading	*godt lige, li:ge, ret*	*lidt,* (4 times), *lige, lille* (twice)
negation and hedges:	*er det ikke sådan en..* *I har ikke sådan en.*	
lexical upgrading	*meget, meget fint*	*meget* (twice) *ældste, mest interes-sante meget spændende, utroligt meget, store udstillinger*

The German conversation

In order to discuss politeness in Denmark, I will use the German conversations for comparison only.

As regards the use of personal pronouns, the pronouns used for self-reference by the German tourist are almost identical to those used by the Dane (*ich* [I] and *man* [one]). As an address form, he uses the formal *Sie*. The German employee is also very consistent in his use of this form (21 items of *Sie*). Accordingly, he does not use the inclusive *wir* (we) as often as his Danish counterpart, and he does not avoid using 'you and me'. Neither does he impersonalise with *man* (one) as often as the Danish employee and, consequently has a more personalised style as can be seen in the following examples:

German employee: *genau. und das können* ***Sie*** *hier unten in der legende, die beschreibung, die finden* ***Sie*** *hier in der legende wieder, damit* ***Sie*** *auch wissen, wo (.) was (.) ist.* (exactly. and **you** can see it down here in the legend, the description, **you** find it here in the legend, so that **you** can see where (.) everything (.) is.)

Danish employee: *ja, og der står så lige kort en lille notits om de forskellige bygninger, hvad de hedder og hvor gamle de er og hvor* ***man*** *finder dem henne.* (Yes and there is just a small notice about the different buildings, what they are called and how old they are and how to find them.)

As regards lexical downgrading and hedging, there is not much difference between the Danish and German conversations. The German tourist, unlike the Dane, uses conventional indirect requests (*können Sie* (could you)) and formal explicit politeness forms like the subjunctive (*würde gern* (would like to)). The German employee also downgrades syntactically using conditional clauses (*wen...dann* (if...then)).

The most striking difference is seen in lexical upgrading. Both German interlocutors stress their co-operation, common interest and approval of each other and of the sights of the town. The tourist stresses the beauty of the old city (*es gefällt mir ganz toll* [I like it very much]; *schöne schöne Wasserläufe* [Lovely lovely water-courses]) and his gratitude towards the employee (*prima! dann sage ich ganz herzlichen Dank* [wonderful! thank you very much indeed]). The employee stresses the quality of the sights (*sehr schön sehr schön sogar* [very beautiful, very beautiful indeed]) and of the information brochure:

> *wir haben* ***eine ganze breite palette an sehenswürdigkeiten****. das kann ich Ihnen* ***am besten*** *anhand unseres* ***schönen*** *stadtprospektes erläutern* (we have got **a great variety of sights.** I can explain them to **you in the best manner** by means of our **beautiful** city-brochure).

To create a good atmosphere, he jokes and is consistently optimistic about what the tourist can see (*oh da haben Sie Glück* [oh you are very lucky]) and how he can meet the tourist's needs (repeatedly *ja selbstverständlich* [yes, of course], in answer to the tourist's questions and requests). Finally, he expresses his good wishes when the tourist leaves (*einen schönen Aufenthalt wünsche ich Ihnen* [I wish you a very pleasant stay]).

	Tourist	***Employee***
Personal pronoun selection:	self-reference:	
	ich (7 times),	*ich* (3 times), *wir* (8 times)
	address form:	
	Sie (twice)	*Sie* (21 times)
	impersonal:	
	man (5 times)	*man* (once)
Lexical downgrading:	*ein bißchen*	*noch ein bißchen mehr, einen kleinen rundführer*
Lexical upgrading:	*ganz neu, ganz toll,*	*eine ganz breite palette, am besten,*
	oh ja das ist ja schön,	*unseren schönen stadtprospektes,*
	gut (twice), *schöne-*	*ganz neu, hübsch durchnumeriert,*
	schöne wasserläufe,	*ganz neu, oh ja da haben Sie glück,*
	prima! ganz herzlichen dank	*sehr schön sehr schön sogar, ganz individuell alleine, sehr schön beschrieben, prima! einen schönen aufenthalt*
hedges:	*irgendwie* (twice)	
Indirect questions with switch of point of view:		
subjunctive:	*können Sie*	
	würde gern	*da müßte ich, das wäre*
syntactical downgrading, conditional clauses:		*und wenn Sie lust haben, können Sie... und wenn Sie es dann mit dem tretboot machen*

Compared to the Danish data, we find a remarkable frequency of verbal politeness markers in the German, with the obvious conclusion that the German speakers express somewhat more verbal negative politeness and much more positive politeness compared to the Danes.

Discourse markers

Discourse markers are here considered as verbal markers which regulate turn-taking such as 'starters', appealers, hesitation phenomena, pauses within syntactic units, pre-closing and closing signals, back-channelling signals and asides. There is a very complex system of back-channelling and turn-taking signals, especially in the Danish conversation.

The German conversation shows more variation in the use of back-channelling (nine items of *ja* [yes], three items of *gut* [very well]) and two items of *mnn*). In the Danish conversation, the use of back-channelling is more frequent but consists mostly of *ja* (yes) (26 items) and *nå* (well) – the latter as a kind of astonished or disapproving back-channelling used by the Danish tourist, as the employee declines her request for a guided tour. The striking difference is, however, that the Danish conversation contains more hesitation markers *(e:h, ø:h, mm)* than the German one does (Danish, 9, German, 1) and a considerable number of pauses within syntactic units in connection with audible in-breath and out-breath. One could perhaps additionally interpret the use of repetitions and asides in the Danish conversation as hesitation (*hvad skal vi sige* [what shall we say]).

Eye movement, eye contact and gesture

Third, I examined the interlocutors' gaze, their eye movements and the frequency and length of eye contact measured in tenths of seconds. Dominating in both conversations is a gaze concentrated on a common object, a city map or a brochure. Eye contact does not occur as often as might be expected from other analyses of everyday conversation. I analysed eight conversations, four German and four Danish, on videotape and found that the interlocutors in the Danish conversations have more eye contact, i.e. 27% of the time on average compared with the Germans who only have eye contact 18% of the time. The 'referential' – gaze on a common object – in both Danish and German conversations is almost identical, making up about 46% and 47% of the conversations respectively (see the following diagram).

	Eye contact	*Gaze concentrated on a common object*
Danish conversations	27%	46%
German conversations	18%	47%

The percentages of eye contact and gaze concentrated on a common object for the conversations analysed in this chapter are:

Danish conversation	24%	48%
German conversation	7%	56%

Finally, I looked at indexical and deictic gestures and body, especially head, movements. Generally, there is considerable communication between the tourists and employees in highlighting and pointing with fingers and pencils on maps, models and pictures as an important support to the interaction: verbal communication and gesture can be seen as closely interrelated and interdependent with much verbal communication being redundant in light of the visual communication taking place at the counter.

Finally, let us return to the correlation between the features analysed so far.

Correlation between verbal and non-verbal features

In the following Danish examples, there is a correlation between eye contact, requesting, pausing or hesitating (T = tourist, E = employee):

Occurrences of eye contact

	Discourse markers	*Speech acts*
(1)	*ja. .hh* /aside (T)	(Introduction to) Greeting
(2)	*ja? hh* (.)/starter + hesitation (T)	Request
(3)	*ikke* (.) (.) /appeal + hesitation (T)	Question
(4)	*ja.* /back-channel (T)	
(5)	*ja, ja* / back-channel (T)	
(6)	*.hh ja* (E)	Closing signal
(7)	*e:h* (.) hesitation (T)	Question
(8)	*nå okay så* / back-channel (T)	Uptake
(9)	*ø:h* / hesitation (T)	Question
(10)	(.) [*på museet*]/hesitation (T) [*på på museet*] /overlap, as E interprets T's pause as a closing signal	Question
(11)	*a.* / back-channel (T)	
(12)	*ø:h* / hesitation (T)	Request

When the Danish tourist requests something, this coincides with eye contact and different forms of hesitation phenomena (pauses, hesitation markers [*ø:h e:h]* or in-breath/out-breath). I will interpret this coincidence between eye contact, hesitation and requesting as a kind of paralingual and non-verbal politeness, mitigating the weight of the imposition on the hearer. Not only does the tourist use this kind of non-verbal politeness marker, in one case the employee declines a request and does so (also) by hesitating/holding back her speech while she slowly knocks her pen twice on the table:

E: *jo: det har vi:: ø:h (.)* ((knocks her pen twice on the counter)) *om sommeren.*
yes: we have got that:: e:h (.) ((knocks her pen twice on the counter)) in the summertime. (The tourist is visiting the town in January.)

The following reactions are also characterised by hesitation:

T: *nå* (well)
E: *ja* (yes)
T: *nå, så det kan jeg altså ikke (.) få?* (well, then I can't (.) get that?)

There are five significant instances in the Danish conversation where the tourist shakes her head slowly while requesting something (the phases where she is shaking her head are in bold, overlaps in square brackets):

Example 1

T: *mm:: ja, den så jo meget interessant ud,* ***en typisk – er det ikke sådan en typisk vest(.)slesvigsk(.)*** *[kirke?]*
T: mm:: yes, it looks very interesting, **a typical – isn't it a typical West(.) Schleswig(.)** [church?]
E: *[en vestslesvigsk] kirke, jo, det kan man jo godt sige at det [er].* ([a West-Schleswig] church, well you might say [so])
T: *[ja. ja].* [yes, yes]

Example 2

T: *det ser meget fint ud.* ***ehh: I har ikke sådan en professionel guide på, der kan*** *(.) tage én rundt?* (it looks very nice. ***e:hh you haven't got a kind of professional guide who can*** (.) take you around?)

In the first two examples the head-shaking movement co-occurs with a downgrading *ikke* (not) as if a negative response is anticipated.

Example 3

T: *jeg er sådan ret interesseret i gamle bygninger.* ***hvad skal man [så]*** (I am kind of quite interested in old buildings. **What can you [then]**)
E: *[ja]* [yes]
T: ***=specielt kigge på.*** **(take a closer look at.)**

Example 4

T: ***hvad ø:h med museerne her i byen,* (What e:h about the museums in this town.)**
E: *ja?* (yes)
T: *hvordan ser det ud med det?* (how about it?)

Example 5

T: *ja. hvad er der* ***sådan specielt (.) på museet?*** (yes. what is **special there (.) at the museum?)**

In Examples 3–5, the tourist is requesting very cautiously. The shaking of her head can only be interpreted as non-verbal gestural downgrading and as interactional pessimism, as if she is withdrawing her request and showing that she will not be surprised if it is rejected. From the perspective of *face*, S's interactional behaviour allows the employee to give a negative response without threatening either the hearer's or her own *face*.

In German conversation there is not the same correlation between verbal and non-verbal features:

We find occurrences of:

Eye contact	*Discourse markers*	*Speech acts*
1.	*mn: ja:/* back-channel (E)	
2.	*oder?* / appeal (T)	question
3.	*ja?* / appeal (T)	question

Conclusion

We have seen rather different combinations of verbal, paralinguistic and non-verbal markers of politeness in the German and Danish data: the German data primarily contain elaborated verbal politeness; the Danish data, in contrast, do not show many forms of verbal politeness, but contain a higher degree of paralingual and non-verbal politeness markers, which are by no means easy to interpret. Politeness – or perhaps more correctly – consideration or regard for your interlocutor's *face* is expressed in rather different ways.

The 'deficit' in conventional politeness in the Danish verbal data is counterbalanced by non-verbal and paralinguistic politeness markers. Consequently, intercultural problems may occur when Danes do not make use of verbal politeness markers speaking a foreign language or when people from other cultures omit the non-verbal politeness markers used by Danes.

Referential communication predominates: consideration of other people is by 'getting to the point' and not wasting their time with unnecessary verbiage and beating about the bush.

On one point, however, Danish politeness is highly verbalised, the small word *tak* (thank you), which is used in many contexts – sometimes surprising for foreigners. You say thank you on almost any occasion in Danish: for food, coffee, change at the cash desk or on the bus, for an invitation, for the latest get-together (*tak for sidst*). The frequent use of *tak* may be interpreted as a highly ritualised politeness marker but seen from a conversational or interactional point of view it is also a kind of terminal signal (Braunmüller, 1999: 135). Since it also serves as a communicative 'border' signal signalling that an activity has reached its end I will conclude this paper by saying 'tak' for the reader's attention!

References

Braun, F. (1988) *Terms of Address: Problems of Patterns and Usage in Various Languages and Cultures*. Berlin, New York: Mouton de Gruyter.

Braunmüller, K. (1999) *Die skandinavischen Sprachen* (2nd edn). Tübingen, Basel: Francke.

Brown, P. and Levinson, S. (1987) *Politeness: Some Universals in Language Usage*. Cambridge: Cambridge University Press.

Fredsted, E. (1998) *Analyser af dansk og tysk talesprog*. Oslo: Novus.

Leech, G. N. (1983) *Principles of Pragmatics*. London: Longman.

Watts, R. J., Ide, S. and Ehlich, K. (eds) (1992) *Politeness in Language*. Berlin, New York: Mouton de Gruyter.

Chapter 12

Politeness in Sweden: Parliamentary Forms of Address

CORNELIA ILIE

Introduction

This investigation focuses on the interplay between different deictic and relational functions of pronominal terms of address, on the one hand, and face-work politeness strategies (deference markers, (de)focalisation markers, impersonalisation markers), on the other. The analysis is intended to capture the particular manifestations of parliamentary politeness in Swedish and the ways in which they are articulated at the interface between conventional and non-conventional politeness devices, positive and negative face-work, as well as positive and negative politeness.

The shape of a system of address forms is affected by, and has its effects on, the individual speakers' and interlocutors' awareness and perception of interpersonal relationships. The question that obviously arises is: do speakers from different speech communities perceive and evaluate interpersonal relationships differently because the systems of address in their languages are different or is it the other way round? This is a question with far-reaching implications. On the one hand, for example, the non-differentiating pronominal address form in English, *you*, does not necessarily make English speakers perceive each other as equal. On the other hand, the second person pronoun *you*, like the Swedish second person plural pronoun *ni*, may turn from an unmarked into a marked pronominal form when used in institutional settings where it is not normally expected to occur, as will be discussed later in this chapter.

Aim, Method and Corpus

Two sets of transcripts have been examined, namely official transcripts of proceedings in the Swedish *Riksdag* (selected from the *Rixlex* records) and, for purposes of comparison and/or contrast, some transcripts of proceedings in the British House of Commons (from the *Hansard* records).

A choice has been made deliberately to examine comparable corpora of parliamentary interaction, namely question–answer sessions, which are referred to as *Frågestund* (i.e. Question Time) in Sweden[1] and *Prime Minister's Question Time* (PMQT) in Britain.[2] They represent prototypical manifestations of question–answer-based confrontation in parliament. In both countries, Question Time is devoted to the questioning of prominent representatives of the Government, namely the Prime Minister and Government Ministers, by other Members of Parliament (MPs). The question–response sequences represent the default adjacency pairs of Question Time and often display exchanges of challenging, accusatory and also countering, defensive and ironical, speech acts between Opposition and Government MPs, as well as friendly and cooperative questions from MPs belonging to the Government party. In either case, the default institutional form of address in both parliaments is the third person singular.

Here I contrast two linguistic and cultural varieties of the same parliamentary event, focusing on the distinctive patterns of address forms that emerge at the interface between language-based politeness rules, culture-based politeness principles and institution-based politeness strategies. I draw on insights from institutional discourse analysis and pragmatic politeness theory. Two major issues are addressed from the start: the more generally valid characteristics of parliamentary politeness norms, on the one hand, and the more specific manifestations of politeness rituals in each parliament, on the other. What counts as an appropriate pronominal form of address in the Riksdag and the House of Commons, respectively? How do these pronominal usage patterns correlate with the debating styles and politeness strategies of MPs? To what extent and in what ways do particular politeness address strategies reflect institution-specific, culture-specific and individual-specific features?

Previous Politeness Studies

Forms of address have particular significance, reflecting and revealing the way in which interlocutors perceive and evaluate each other, as well as the relationships between them. Following Brown and Levinson (1987), Lakoff (1990) and Leech (1983), three politeness-related social variables have first been taken into account when examining parliamentary terms of address: P (the perceived power difference between interlocutors), D (the perceived social distance between them) and R (the cultural ranking of the speech act). Further studies by Arndt and Janney (1991), Blum-Kulka (1992), Gu (1990), Ide (1989), Ilie (2003a, b) and Watts (1992) have provided conceptualisations of politeness phenomena in explicitly culture-specific frameworks.

Apart from authority and social distance, two further variables are examined here. One is the notion of *reciprocity*, introduced by Brown and Gilman (1960), whereby address is reciprocal when two speakers exchange the same, or equivalent, form. Correspondingly, address is non-reciprocal when the forms used by the two speakers are different or non-equivalent. A relationship can also be partly symmetrical, if parts of the forms are used reciprocally. The other politeness variable, particularly relevant to parliamentary confrontational discourse (Ilie, 2001), is the notion of *vulnerability*. In verbal interactions, the participants' vulnerability is perceived as maximised or minimised due to the use of specific addressing strategies, because different forms of address are associated with varying degrees of deference and imposition.

Positive *versus* Negative Face-work

A major distinction between different culture-based face-work patterns appears to consist of the varying rankings of the concrete manifestations of negative and positive face. In other words, there are different ways in which the speaker's/addressee's claim to negative personal face (autonomy) interrelates with their claim to positive interpersonal face (acceptance). Kerbrat-Orecchioni (1991) has updated Brown and Levinson's face-work theory by setting up a politeness system of three axes, namely speaker/hearer orientation, positive/negative face and positive/negative politeness.

In parliamentary debates, which, by definition, involve FTAs aimed both at the interlocutors' negative and positive faces, it is relevant to examine three aspects in particular: (a) which of the two faces is socially and culturally more important to save and maintain; (b) which of the two faces is more threatened and therefore needs to be saved or redressed; and (c) which politeness strategies (negative or positive) are given priority with respect to the speaker's and to the addressee's faces. Depending on which procedures are considered more important or relevant, different cultures sometimes seem to resort to identical, similar or comparable politeness strategies and, at other times, to different strategies (Eelen, 2001).

Pronominal Address Forms in Parliament

In parliamentary settings, the use of addressee-oriented, speaker-oriented and audience-oriented terms of address is particularly sensitive to in-group membership, out-group positioning, institutionally hierarchical status and, to a certain extent, gender. This study focuses exclusively on pronominal forms of address. The use of pronominal address and reference forms is motivated by a number of factors, including

(1) conveying deference by using a distancing strategy (addressing the interlocutor in the third person),
(2) conveying deference (or lack of it) by directly addressing the interlocutor in the second person singular or plural and
(3) conveying deference and multiple reference by means of a defocalisation strategy, involving a shift from speaker self-reference in the first person singular to speaker co-reference (self-reference and audience-reference) in the first person plural through the plurality principle.

(1) One way of conveying deference in institutional settings is to use a particular distancing strategy, namely to address the interlocutor in the third person, thus avoiding the second person direct form. This strategy is typically illustrated by face-saving acts (FSAs) and face-enhancing acts (FEAs) whereby the addressee's negative face is indirectly targeted by means of positive politeness.

Third person indirect address was formerly used in colloquial Swedish to convey distinctions in social rank and/or age but nowadays it is little used by Swedish speakers (Schubert, 1984). Some recurring traces of it may still be found in the speech of service personnel, such as waiters: *Vad kan jag hjälpa damen/herren med?* (How can I help the lady/gentleman?). Another strategy is to avoid pronoun or noun selection, using impersonal constructions and circumlocutions, some of which are still in use: *Vad får det lov att vara?* (What is it going to be?), *Önskas det något till kaffet?* ([Is there a wish for] something to go with the coffee?), *Vad sägs/tycks?* (What is [your] opinion/impression?), *Känns det skönt?* (Does it feel comfortable/good?), *Sitter det bra?* (Does it fit well?).

Institutionalised distancing in the speaker–addressee relationship, involving indirectness, derives from the fact that members of both Parliaments address each other in the third person through the intermediary of the Speaker (Chairperson), the third person being the unmarked address form in interactions between questioning and answering MPs. (See examples 1 and 2.)

Example 1

Mr Hague: The Prime Minister once boasted that the dome would be in the first paragraph of the next Labour election manifesto. Had **he** proposed to start **his** election manifesto saying that **his** party shares this responsibility with the Conservative party? (PMQT, 8 November, 2000, Col. 311)

Example 2

Lars Hjertén *(m): […] Jag vill fråga försvarsministern hur* ***han*** *ser på situationen med den stora officersbristen och om* ***han*** *har några förslag till lösningar.*
Lars Hjertén (Con): […] I want to ask the Minister for Defence what **he** thinks about the present situation with big officer shortages and if **he** can suggest any solutions. (Frågestund, 21 September 2000, Anf. 26)

However, this institutional use of the third person pronoun does not apply as consistently in the Swedish Riksdag as in the House of Commons. Some deliberate, strategically motivated deviations occur and are automatically perceived as marked forms. Consider the following examples:

Example 3

Owe Hellberg (v): *Fru talman! Nu ska inte ministern komma undan så lätt. […]*
Statsrådet Lars-Erik Lövdén (s)*: Fru talman!* ***Owe Hellberg*** *(v) ska inte heller komma så lätt undan. Om* ***ni*** *har interna kommunikationsproblem i Vänsterpartiet får* ***ni*** *ta itu med det.*
Owe Hellberg (Left): Mrs Speaker! The minister is not going to get away with it so easily. […]
Minister Lars-Erik Lövdén (Sdem): Mrs Speaker! **Owe Hellberg** (Left) is not going to get away with it either. If **you** have internal communication problems within the Left Party **you** should start dealing with them. (Frågestund, 26 October 2000, Anf. 53)

Example 4

Statsminister Göran Persson (s): *Hela den sociala bostadspolitik har ju bestått i att göra det möjligt också för människor med låga inkomster att bo bra och bo centralt. Nu vill* ***ni*** *[kd] uppenbarligen införa en marknadshyra […]. Det är ju det systemskiftet som* ***ni*** *öppnar för när* ***ni*** *talar på det sätt som ni nu gör, och det är det som vi vill motverka.*
Prime Minister Göran Persson (Sdem): The whole social housing policy has consisted in enabling low income people to enjoy good and central accommodation. Now **you** [Christian-Dem] obviously want to introduce market rents […]. This is the change of system that **you** are promoting when **you** are talking like that, and this is what we want to counteract. (Frågestund, 26 October 2000 Anf. 98)

What is distinctive about the address forms in Examples 3 and 4 is the co-occurrence of both the third and second person pronouns during the same intervention and referring to the same addressee. In Example 3 Hellberg is first addressed by Minister Lövdén in the third person as an individual: *Owe Hellberg (v) ska inte heller komma så lätt undan* (Owe Hellberg [Left] is not going to get away with it either). Then, however, through a person shift from third to second person plural *ni*, he becomes less strongly focused, since he is now addressed collectively as a representative of the Left Party members: *Om ni har interna kommunikationsproblem i Vänsterpartiet får ni ta itu med det.* (If *you* have internal communication problems within the Left Party *you* should start dealing with them). Here, the pronominal shift from indirect to direct address is motivated partly by Minister Lövdén assuming a stronger confrontational attitude, and partly by his intention to mark the distance not only from one individual but from the latter's whole party, thus widening his target.

(2) A particular way of conveying deference or, often, lack of it, is to address the interlocutor directly in the second person. Since the parliamentary system is based on indirectness, i.e. third person address, any deviation from this convention acquires special significance and indicates a change in the speaker–addressee relationship concerning politeness orientation (positive or negative), reciprocity and/or vulnerability.

The second person plural pronoun, V, is used in many languages as an honorific form for important, respected or distant interlocutors. Conversely, the use of a singular non-honorific pronoun, T, to address a non-familiar interlocutor may signal a claim to solidarity. This distinction applies, of course, only to languages with two contrasting pronominal variants, such as French *tu/vous*, German *du/Sie* and Swedish *du/ni*.

In English the second person pronoun *you* is a marked parliamentary form of address, contrasting with the institutionalised third person. Although its use is, therefore, rather marginal, it is nevertheless highly significant and fulfils two opposite functions: on the one hand, as a positive politeness marker in FSAs performed by MPs when addressing the Speaker (Chairperson) of the House and on the other, as a negative politeness marker in overt FTAs, e.g. interrupting, challenging or apostrophising speaking MPs. The former use is illustrated in Example 5:

Example 5

Helen Southworth (Lab): May I welcome **you** to **your** post, Mr Speaker? [...] (PMQT, 25 October, 2000, Col. 217)

In this example, it is the positive face of the Speaker of the House that is addressed by means of a positive politeness strategy. All MPs use the second person to address the Speaker, who, in turn, addresses them in the third person, thus making the second person use non-reciprocal. Furthermore, since the Speaker is the only parliamentary interlocutor who is supposed to be politically neutral, his or her institutional relationship with the other MPs may be regarded as convivial and/or collaborative, except when reprimanding them or calling them to order.

In Sweden, a rather rapid change has occurred in the use of pronominal address forms during the latter half of the 20th century, with the T pronoun *du* gaining and the V pronoun *ni* losing ground (Paulston, 1976). As a consequence, younger persons nowadays address elderly people using *du* rather than the formerly preferred respectful *ni*. Indeed, a violation of this recent rule may now be an indicator of irony, anger or authoritativeness. Moreover, when used in everyday speech between adults who do not necessarily know each other well, *du* denotes group membership: speakers signal that they belong to the same group and respect its norms. When *ni* is used in Swedish Question Time, it functions exclusively as an address form to target several addressees or a collective addressee that includes the interlocutor.

Although Swedish parliamentary terms of address do not formally include the second person pronoun (singular or plural), the transcripts indicate that such cases do occur occasionally. Of the two forms of the second person pronoun, only the plural, *ni*, is used. Like the English *you*, *ni* is occasionally used as a marked parliamentary form of address, since the unmarked form is the institutionalised third person singular. Unlike English *you*, however, *ni* is motivated by different discursive and strategic intentions and occurs during the parliamentary interaction proper. Moreover, unlike English *you*, *ni* may also be reciprocal, in the sense that both questioning and answering MPs occasionally use it as an FTA, to challenge or question the position and actions of political opponents. This negative politeness strategy obviously increases the competitive and/or conflictual relationship between them. Also, unlike *you*, *ni* may be used in connection with a pronominal address shift from or to the third person during the same MP's intervention, as illustrated in Examples 6 and 7:

Example 6

Carl G. Nilsson (m): *Min följdfråga [till finansministern Ringholm] är: Har **ni** beräknat vad detta kommer att innebära för boendekostnaderna för en sådan normalfamilj?*
Carl G. Nilsson (Con): My follow-up question [to Finance Minister Ringholm] is: Have **you** calculated the effects of this [rise] on the housing costs for a normal family? (Frågestund, 21 September, 2000, Anf: 4)

Example 7

Statsrådet Lars-Erik Lövdén (s): *Fru talman! Owe Hellberg (v) ska inte heller komma så lätt undan. Om **ni** har interna kommunikationsproblem i Vänsterpartiet får **ni** ta itu med det. [...] Smit inte ifrån ansvaret, Owe Hellberg!*
Minister Lars-Erik Lövdén (Sdem): Mrs Speaker! Owe Hellberg (Left) is not going to get away with it either. If **you** have internal communication problems within the Left Party **you** should start dealing with them. [...] Do not run away from your responsibility, Owe Hellberg! (Frågestund, 26 October, 2000, Anf: 53)

A significant aspect of these examples is that, in both cases, the interlocutor is first addressed neutrally in the third person, while the second person is used only when the speaker adopts or reinforces a confrontational tone. Apart from assertive utterances, *ni* occurs typically in interrogative and directive utterances, as in Examples 6 and 7, which are normally perceived as stronger and more direct FTAs.

(3) Another way of conveying deference is by a defocalisation strategy. The term *defocalisation* was used by Haverkate (1992) to refer to the minimisation of the identity of a singular speaker or addressee through the use of plural personal pronouns. In parliamentary forms of address, the pluralisation process involves, not so much minimisation of speaker identity, as maximisation of speaker institutional function and authority.

Interaction between participants in institutional forms of dialogue, in general, and in parliamentary Question Time, in particular, is expected to meet basic requirements of upholding appropriate standards of civil behaviour and mutual respect, meant to counterbalance the face-threatening nature of institutional confrontation. Of particular relevance for the interpersonal relationship between participants is the shift from the singular to the plural forms of the first and second personal pronouns. The principle of respectful plurality is responsible for a variety of number-related pronominal shifts. Although, in general, this seems to be the case in both Parliaments, relatively significant deviations can, nevertheless, be noted.

The inclusive function of *we* in British parliamentary discourse is similar in many ways to the use of the first-person plural pronoun *vi* in Swedish parliamentary discourse. Basically, both pronominal systems display several mitigating effects in comparison with the use of the first-person singular pronoun. Typically, *we* is used in political settings to indicate the *plural of authority* or *power* (Brown & Gilman, 1960). Consider Example 8, where *we* conveys the accompaniments of high office, i.e. institutional prestige and responsibility, as well as personal authority.

Example 8

William Hague (Con): Can the Prime Minister confirm that the member of the Cabinet who insisted that the project should proceed and said that it 'could even make money' was him?
The Prime Minister (Tony Blair, Lab): It is certainly true that **I** said that it should proceed. It is also true, however, as **we** demonstrated conclusively last week, that funding for the dome … (was) all agreed by a Cabinet Committee… (PMQT, 15 November 2000, Col. 931-2)

Another function of the plural of authority is seen in the *we* pronoun of the group, i.e. a reminder that the speaker does not stand alone but has authority supported by institutional backing, as illustrated in Example 9.

Example 9

William Hague (Con): **We** set out **our** spending plans stage by stage. (PMQT, 20 December, 2000, Col 353)

As leader of the Conservative Party, William Hague uses the first-person plural both to show his authority within the group of Conservative MPs and to position himself as Opposition Leader in relation to the Government. MPs, particularly Party Leaders and Ministers, are expected to speak in several institutional capacities when they take the floor and the overlap of institutional roles may be indicated by alternative uses of the singular and plural pronouns, as illustrated in Example 10:

Example 10

The Prime Minister (Tony Blair, Labour): […] It is for that reason that **we** have taken measures that **I** think are sensible and right… (PMQT, 7 March 2001, Col. 294)

The use of the Swedish first-person plural pronoun *vi* in Swedish Question Time also displays the two major usage patterns mentioned earlier. First, the speaker's authority is shown to derive from their role as official spokesperson, due to holding high office and having acquired an influential position, as illustrated in Example 11. Second, the speaker's authority is shown to derive from their substantial backing of political supporters, as illustrated in Example 12.

Example 11

Finansminister Bosse Ringholm (s): ***Vi*** *återkommer i år med ett förslag som innebär att* ***vi*** *höjer energiskatten med lite drygt 3 miljarder.*
Bosse Ringholm, Finance Minister (Sdem): **We** will come back later this year with a proposition which implies that **we** will raise energy taxes by over 3 billion. (Frågestund, 21 September 2000, Anf: 3)

Example 12

Utrikesminister Anna Lindh (s): *Fru talman!* ***Jag*** *tog exemplet när det gäller utrikesfrågor. Tyvärr måste* ***jag*** *nog säga att* ***jag*** *tror att problemen är så pass stora att* ***vi*** *inte kommer att klara att lösa dem under det svenska ordförandeskapet.* ***Jag*** *kan garantera att* ***vi*** *gör allt vad* ***vi*** *kan för att minska dem under det svenska ordförandeskapet.*
Anna Lindh, Minister for Foreign Affairs (Sdem): Mrs Speaker! **I** gave that example with respect to foreign policy issues. Unfortunately **I** must say that **I** think the problems are so big that **we** are not going to be able to solve them during the Swedish [EU] Chairmanship. **I** can guarantee that **we** do whatever **we** can to reduce them during the Swedish chairmanship. (Frågestund, 21 September 2000, Anf: 9)

One particular use of *vi* in Swedish Question Time has a typically inclusive and mobilising function, the speaker's intention being to include, not only the interlocutor and the party-political group they represent, but all MPs in the Chamber. When making collective appeals to all MPs, Swedish MPs in general, and Government members in particular, resort to this use of the first person plural in order to reach a cross-party political consensus and to rally popular feelings into one common standpoint. Such an instance is illustrated in Example 13:

Example 13

Vice-statsministe Lena Hjelm-Wallén (s): *Fru talman! Som privatpersoner kan* ***vi****, både riksdagsledamöter och regeringsledamöter, säkerligen ha synpunkter på polisens arbete. Men* ***jag*** *tror att* ***vi*** *ska avhålla* ***oss*** *från att lägga* ***oss*** *i det direkt verkställande arbete som polisen gör.* [...]
Lena Hjelm-Wallén, Deputy Prime Minister (SDem): Mrs Speaker! As private persons **we**, both MPs and Government members, can have

opinions about police work. But **I** think that **we** should abstain from interfering with the executive work carried out by the police. [...] (Frågestund, 21 September 2000, Anf: 45)

The particular use of *vi* in Example 13 has a consensus-invoking function. It is symptomatic that it is correlated with one of the frequently occurring forms of the verb *skola*, namely *ska* (= shall), which can operate in Swedish both as an auxiliary that conveys a future meaning and as a modal verb that conveys the idea of 'will' or intention (Ljung & Ohlander, 1993/1971). Thus, in Example 13 the co-occurrence of *vi* and the verb *avhålla* (abstain) preceded by the modal auxiliary *ska* was rendered into English by means of the conditional *should*, which confers both a future meaning and a (programmatic) meaning of obligation on the main verb *avhålla*. A comparable example is provided in Example 14:

Example 14

Utrikesminister Anna Lindh (s): *Fru talman! Det som* ***jag*** *har sagt är bara att* ***jag*** *tycker att det är olyckligt att* ***vi*** *inte under den tid då* ***vi*** *faktiskt företräder EU på den internationella scenen och i EU kan visa att vi har ett gemensamt ordförandeskap. Just under dessa sex månader tycker* ***jag*** *att* ***vi*** *kunde avhålla* ***oss*** *från en debatt som enbart splittrar den svenska opinionen.*
Anna Lindh, Minister for Foreign Affairs (Sdem): Mrs Speaker! Only what **I** meant to say is that **I** think it is unfortunate that **we** cannot show a united chairmanship during the time *we* are representing the EU internationally and on the European stage. **I** think that **we** could, at least during these six months, abstain from a debate that would only have a disruptive effect on Swedish opinion. (Frågestund, 21 September 2000, Anf: 25)

Anna Lindh, Swedish Minister for Foreign Affairs, was a member of the European Union (EU) and European Monetary Fund (EMU) friendly Social Democratic Party. Here she makes an appeal to EU and EMU-sceptical MPs during the period of Sweden's EU-chairmanship for a temporary cross-party consensus in the Riksdag concerning abstention from debates on EU issues, because such debates would be embarrassing for Sweden as temporary chair of the EU. In her intervention, the consensus-oriented pronoun *vi* co-occurs with the same verb used by Wallén, i.e. *avhålla* (abstain) preceded by two forms of the modal verb *kunna* (can), namely the present *kan* (can) and the present conditional *kunde* (could).

Both Wallén's and Lindh's use of *vi* is a double appeal to both the positive and negative face of the addressees. It acquires thereby an inclusive and mobilising value, which may be explained by the fact that its major function is not exclusively deictic but also programmatic. Since the notion of consensus is firmly rooted and positively evaluated in Swedish political tradition, such appeals to parliamentary consensus on issues of national importance conveyed in the first-person plural with future-oriented verbs are not at all unusual or unexpected. There is no exact equivalent of this consensus-invoking and/or consensus-seeking use of the pronoun *we* in British Question Time, which displays a more confrontational tone, and it would be less realistic to imagine such an appeal being made in the House of Commons. Whereas the first-person plural tends to be used more programmatically under similar circumstances in Swedish Question Time, it appears to be used more strategically in British Question Time.

Concluding Remarks

This study has focused on the use of the pronominal address forms that emerge at the interface between language-based politeness rules, institution-based politeness strategies and culture-based communication principles in the Question Time sessions of the Swedish Riksdag, using the British Parliament for purposes of comparison and contrast. The goal of the investigation has been to examine the functions of pronominal forms of address as key elements in an interpersonal, programmatic and confrontational interplay of strategies, rather than the mere application of a strictly rule-governed institutional pattern of deictic markers.

The analysis has been carried out in terms of the following set of politeness variables: positive *versus* negative politeness orientation, positive *versus* negative face-work, speaker-addressee relationship, pronominal shift, degree of vulnerability and reciprocity. Since parliamentary interaction during Question Time displays more confrontational and competitive politeness strategies than collaborative and cooperative strategies, terms of address can often be seen to maximise, rather than minimise, face-threatening acts, albeit indirectly or implicitly.

Parliamentary politeness patterns have been envisaged in terms of an interplay of strategies based on both mandatory and optional choices, rather than the unfolding of a strictly rule-governed competitive game. It is suggested that politeness strategies based on MPs' mandatory choices should be regarded as unmarked features of parliamentary politeness, while those based on their optional or free choices should be regarded as marked features of parliamentary politeness.

In parliamentary settings, terms of self-reference (speaker-oriented), as well as addressee-oriented and multi-layered audience-oriented terms of address have been shown to be particularly sensitive to in-group membership, out-group positioning, institutionally hierarchical status, and, to a certain extent, gender.

Two kinds of pronominal shift have been found particularly relevant for the interpersonal and strategic relationship between MPs in the corpora: the shift from the first-person singular to the first-person plural (and *vice versa*), and the shift from the third-person to the second-person singular (and *vice versa*). Occurrences of the former shift exhibit comparable functions in both corpora, whereas the latter shift involves different discursive mechanisms, as well as institutional and interpersonal relationship patterns.

The English second-person pronoun *you* as a parliamentary form of address is a marked politeness form in relation to the institutionalised third-person pronoun. Precisely because the use of *you* is rather infrequent in this type of discourse, its rare occurrences are so much more significant. In the House of Commons this same address form may be used in two opposite ways: as an FSA performed by all MPs when addressing the Speaker of the House, and as an FTA performed by MPs in order to challenge and/or apostrophise speaking MPs. In both cases, the use of *you* is normally non-reciprocal, in the sense that the Speaker of the House addresses MPs in the third-person singular pronoun and speaking MPs also address their fellow MPs, including the ones who interrupt them, in the third-person singular.

The Swedish counterpart of *you*, namely the second-person plural pronoun *ni*, is also occasionally used as a marked form of address in Swedish Question Time, where the unmarked and institutionalised pronominal address form is the third-person singular, just as in the British Parliament. Unlike the use of the English *you*, however, the uses of the Swedish *ni* are often reciprocal, in the sense that both questioning and answering MPs occasionally use it as an addressee-targeted FTA, reinforcing the competitive and/or conflictual relationship between the interlocutors. Also unlike English *you*, Swedish *ni* is used in connection with a pronominal address shift from and to the institutional third-person address during the same MP's intervention.

Notes

1. The Swedish transcripts include the Question Time (= Frågestund) sessions that took place on the following dates: 21 September 2000, 12 October 2000, 19 October 2000, 26 October 2000, 16 November 2000, 30 November 2000, 18

January 2001, 25 January 2001, 1 February 2001. The total number of words is 76,000.

2. The English transcripts include the Question Time sessions that took place on the following dates: 25 October 2000, 8 November 2000, 15 November 2000, 22 November 2000, 29 November 2000, 13 December 2000, 20 December 2000, 10 January 2001, 17 January 2001, 24 January 2001, 31 January 2001, 7 February 2001, 14 February 2001, 28 February 2001, 7 March 2001. The total number of words is 75,6000.

References

Arndt, H. and Janney, R.W. (1991) Verbal, prosodic, and kinesic emotive contrasts in speech. *Journal of Pragmatics* 15, 521-49.

Blum-Kulka, S. (1992) The metapragmatics of politeness in Israeli society. In R. Watts, S. Ide and K. Ehlich (eds) *Politeness in Language: Studies in its History, Theory and Practice* (pp. 255–80). Berlin: Mouton de Gruyter.

Brown, P. and Levinson, S. (1987) *Politeness: Some Universals in Language Usage.* Cambridge: Cambridge University Press.

Brown, R. and Gilman, A. (1960) The pronouns of power and solidarity. In T.A. Sebeok (ed.) *Style in Language* (pp. 253–76). New York/London: MIT Press.

Eelen, G. (2001) *A Critique of Politeness Theories.* Manchester: St Jerome.

Gu, Y. (1990) Politeness phenomena in modern Chinese. *Journal of Pragmatics* 14, 237–57.

Haverkate, H. (1992) Deictic categories as mitigating devices. *Pragmatics* 2(4), 505–22.

Ide, S. (1989) Formal forms and discernment: Two neglected aspects of universals of linguistic politeness. *Multilingua* 8(2–3), 223–48.

Ilie, C. (2001), Unparliamentary language: Insults as cognitive forms of ideological confrontation. In R. Dirven, R. Frank and C. Ilie (eds) *Language and Ideology, Vol. II: Descriptive Cognitive Approaches* (pp. 255–261). Amsterdam/Philadelphia: Benjamins.

Ilie, C. (2003a). Insulting as (un)parliamentary practice in the English and Swedish parliaments: A rhetorical approach. In P. Bayley (ed.) *Contrastive Studies in the Confrontational Strategies of Parliamentary Problem-solving Practices* (pp. 45–86). Amsterdam: John Benjamins.

Ilie, C. (2003b). Parenthetically speaking: Parliamentary parentheticals as rhetorical strategies. In M. Bondi and S. Stati (eds) *Dialogue Analyses 2000* (pp. 253–264). Tübingen: Max Niemeyer.

Kerbrat-Orecchioni, C. (1991) La politesse dans les interactions verbales. In *Dialoganalyse III Actes du Congrès de Bologna 1990*, Vol I. (pp. 39–59). Tübingen: Max Niemeyer Verlag.

Lakoff, R. (1990) *Talking Power: The Politics of Language in Our Lives.* Glasgow: HarperCollins.

Leech, G. N. (1983) *Principles of Pragmatics.* London: Longman.

Ljung, M. and Ohlander, S. (1993/1971) *Allmän grammatik*. Malmö: Gleerups.
Paulston, C.B. (1976) Pronouns of address in Swedish: Social class semantics and a changing system. *Language in Society* 5, 359–86.
Schubert K. (1984) *Tilltal och samhällsstruktur* (Address and social structure). [FUMS rapport 122]. Uppsala: Institutionen för nordiska språk vid Uppsala universitet.
Watts, R. J. (1992) Linguistic politeness and politic verbal behaviour: Reconsidering claims for universality. In R. Watts, S. Ide and K. Ehlich (eds) *Politeness in Language: Studies in Its History, Theory and Practice* (pp. 43–69). Berlin: Mouton de Gruyter.

Chapter 13

Politeness in Finland: Evasion at All Costs

VALMA YLI-VAKKURI

Introduction

The great cultural emancipation of the 1960s changed speech culture in Scandinavian countries, among them Sweden and Finland. For historical reasons, society in these two countries is quite similar – although one is a monarchy and the other a republic – as Finland was annexed to Sweden for seven centuries, Russian rule only lasting from 1809 until 1917, when Finland became an independent republic. Finland is still a bilingual country, with both Finnish and Swedish as official languages. Therefore Finnish codes of behaviour and speech culture are very similar to those of Sweden – in spite of the languages belonging to different families, Finnish being a Finno-Ugric language, and Swedish being an Indo-European language.

We are well aware of the power of cultural contact. This is why the codes of politeness are, conversely, so different in Finnish and Estonian, despite being two closely-related Baltic-Finnic languages. Historically, Finland belongs to the Scandinavian cultural zone and Estonia to the Central European: the historical upper classes in Finland spoke Swedish, in Estonia German. Finnish abounds with metaphors and everyday phrases which are direct translations from Swedish – and through Swedish – mostly of Pan-European origin.

European standards of politeness originating from the court etiquette of the Byzantine Empire were adopted by the newborn European courts and gradually spread to the northern peripheries (cf. terms like *courteous* (Eng.), *höflich* (Ger.), *hövlig* (Sw.) *høflig* (Nor.).[1]). Thus, standards of formal politeness are, in principle, Pan-European: figures of speech literally translated from Swedish into Finnish. However, alongside this formal code there is a colloquial variety of Finnish used in informal speech. This code better reflects, so to speak, the national character and the characteristics of a language grammatically based on suffixation.

In this chapter, I will first deal with the standard formal code and then with the low variety, based on my own observations and material collected over 20 years of observation and reading.

Forms of Address

Finnish forms of address have been influenced throughout history by developments elsewhere in Europe. In Germany, for example, formal address using the second-person plural (2.pl.) (*Ihr*) was common already by the ninth century and this spread to Sweden and from there, initially as a freak of fashion among the upper classes, to Finland where, in the 18th century it began to spread among common people, initially when addressing civil servants and other members of the educated elite.

Having become so widespread, the use of 2.pl. started losing its effect as a token of respect, and it was gradually replaced by the use of third-person plural (3.pl.) in Central Europe towards the end of the 17th century. 3.pl. has remained a mode of address in some European languages, e.g. German (*Sie*), Danish and Norwegian (*De*). Address by title was characterised by the use of the third-person singular (3.sg.) verb form and, thereby, 3.sg. and the corresponding personal pronoun(s), were established as the correct expression of respect.

In Sweden, as late as the 17th century, younger and less powerful people still used 2.pl. when addressing older and more powerful persons but from that century onward the use of the 2.pl. alone was considered disrespectful when addressing strangers. In the middle of the 1800s, 2.pl. could only be used by older and more powerful persons when addressing younger and less powerful ones although even then there was the risk that this might be perceived as offensive. Only young members of the educated elite addressed each other with 2.pl.; for all other purposes the use of the third-person had become standard.

When 2.pl. became the official form of address in Sweden and Finland towards the end of the 19th century, the new mode of address conflicted with the customs of both the educated and the common people. The lack of an established and generally accepted address code could be one possible explanation for the rapid spread, starting in the 1960s, of 2.sg. as the prevalent address mode in Sweden and Finland.

Let us now look at the address forms available in Finnish. In conversation all can be used to refer to the addressee depending on the status and role of the interlocutors as well as the context of utterance, as shown in Figure 13.1. Let us first look at the Finnish system of personal forms.

In Finnish, a personal suffix is added to verbs: 1.sg. *-n*, 2.sg. *-t*, 3.sg. generally V^- (vowel extension) or Ø, 1.pl. *-mme*, 2.pl. *-tte*, and 3.pl. *-vat/-vät*. In addition, there is a personal form which has been called the passive or impersonal, and also the fourth person (the term used in this chapter): its meaning is human, undefined and plural: *-(t)t*V^-*n*. The corresponding personal pronouns are in 1.sg., *minä,* 2.sg., *sinä,* 3.sg, *hän, se,* and in 1.pl., *me,* 2.pl., *te,* 3.pl, *he, ne.* There is no corresponding pronoun for the fourth person.

Since Finnish verbs have a personal suffix, the personal pronoun in the first and second person is optional, and is only used in emphatic expressions in standard Finnish. The third person, however, normally requires the addition of a noun or a pronoun (*hän* and *he* refer to a person in standard Finnish, *se* and *ne* to inanimate objects, abstracts or animals; in colloquial Finnish both may also refer to a person: *hän/he* are emphatic, *se/ne* neutral). The subject is left out in generic clauses where the verb is in 3.sg., e.g. *Niin Ø saa maata kuin Ø petaa* (Lit. so Ø must lie as Ø makes Ø's bed. '[As a man makes his bed so must he lie']). Such forms are very common in everyday speech.

Ways of avoiding the mention of persons in formal standard Finnish are the same as in Pan-European languages (see figure 13.1). Exceptions are due to the fact that Finnish politeness is withdrawing and evasive and, carried to an extreme, reference to the addressee is avoided at all costs. This is possible, as Finnish grammar allows the use of verbs in the third and fourth persons without a noun or a pronoun; nor does the personal suffix of the verb provide reference to a particular person in the third and fourth persons.

One particular way of avoiding direct reference to persons is to replace the personal pronoun by an adverb indicating the addressee's location – *Ja sinne?* (pro *teille* – to you) (And there?) shop assistant to a customer. – *Hyvää pääsiäistä – Samoin sinne!* (pro *teille* – to you (Happy Easter! – The same there!) from a formal phone conversation. In *Onko tämä kynä sieltä?* (pro *teidän* – yours), (Is this pen from there?), the speaker is addressing the person sitting next to her.

However, the most common method of avoiding direct or even indirect reference to the addressee is by means of a kind of evasive transformation focusing on the subject of conversation; thus mention of the person is not grammatically required and may, therefore, be omitted. Differences between Swedish and Finnish may be illustrated by bilingual notices. Take the following reminder posted on the door of a changing room: *Unohtuiko jotain?* (Finnish: Was something forgotten?) and *Glömde ni någonting?* (Swedish: Did you (2.pl.) forget anything?) The Finnish equivalent of the Swedish *Unohditteko (te) jotain?* would sound too formal and artificial in this context, therefore the personal form has been lowered in the hierarchical value of the structure *unohtuiko* ***teiltä*** *jotain* (Was something forgotten by you?) and then omitted altogether: *unohtuiko Ø jotain.* Finns use many transformations to omit person, partly spontaneously or auto-

Sg.			
1.		*Voi kun mä olen sulonen* (Oh, how sweet I am!)	The addressee is a child or an animal.
2.		*Mitä etsit?* (What are you looking for?)	Addressee's inherent person
3.	a.	*Haluaako rouva muuta?* (Does madam want anything else?)	Title address (common with service personnel)
	b.	*Hänel on sit kaunei sireeni.* (She has such beautiful lilacs.)	Old fashioned politeness form, still used in dialects.
	c.	*Mitä se nyt kävi tekemään?* (Now, what did it (=he/she) start doing?)	Colloquial, unemphasised personal pronoun. *Se* in familiar speech, possibly jesting.
	d.	*Ø Saa huuhtoa. Nyt Ø voi purra.* (Ø May rinse.) (Now Ø can bite.)	Dentist to patient.
Pl.			
1.		*Emme ota nyt kenkiä pois.* (We won't take off shoes now.)	Inclusive 1.pl., nursery language. Sometimes also in nursing homes. More common in Finnish is the use of fourth person forms; often a first person pronoun is added to fourth person verb form: *Nyt (me) syödään puuroa.* (Now [we] eat porridge.)
2.		*Oletteko jo syönyt?* (Have you eaten already?)	Conventional, correct politeness form in standard Finnish.
3.		*Milloin he aikovat lähteä?* (When are they planning to leave?)	Archaic politeness form. Appears as a rarity in dialects.
The 'fourth' person:		*Syödäänkö täällä vai tuleeko tää mukaan?* ([Will the food be] eaten here or [will it be] taken away?)	Hamburger waitress to a customer.
		Miten tääl on jaksettu? - Jaa, mitä? - Miten on jaksettu nyt? (How's [it] been going here? - Eh, what? - How's [it] been going now?)	Dialogue in an old people's home.

Figure 13.1 The indirect use of personal address forms in Finnish

matically, partly by design. Students surveyed have reported that they resort to such methods when unsure whether to use the familiar *sinä* (2.sg.) form or the formal *te* (2.pl.).

This genuinely discreet way of refraining from referring to the addressee has been very useful over recent decades. When the use of 2.sg. as an address form started becoming prevalent in the 1960s, conflict was unavoidable. Some were offended by this address form, which they found too familiar, while others considered it too egalitarian.

According to a study which I made in the 1980s of letters to the editors of newspapers, the advocates of formal address (mostly elderly and educated people, particularly women) justified their preference on the grounds of traditional 'good manners', while those advocating the familiar form emphasised its connotations of freedom, equality and ease of communication.

People engaged in the service industry have quickly learned to judge their customers' preferred mode of address by their appearance and behaviour. However, every now and then, a misjudgement may occur, leading to a breach of the cooperative principle from the addressee's perspective, who may then humiliate the speaker by commenting on the use of the 'wrong' form. This seldom happens from a lower to a higher status person (in such a case it would be put down to arrogance). Thus, this is essentially a question of power – and, indeed, there is an ongoing power struggle in modern Finnish. There are people who, regardless of the situation, use and demand the formal address form or, on the contrary, the familiar form. On the other hand, there are people who follow the cooperative principle by accommodating to the addresser, also using address forms which defocus the latter.

As service industry workers are subject to the power of others, regardless of the status of the customer ('the customer is the king'), I shall use the account of a service worker to illustrate what an art selecting the appropriate mode of address has become in Finland: 'Having myself been in customer service I know that there is a generation of people, perhaps approximately 28–38 years of age, who perceive *teitittely*[2] (the use of 2.pl.) as pestering. Older people expect this as a matter of course and even some young people – perhaps due to the modern trend of conservatism – seem to have the attitude that *teitittely* is quite natural. There you are, then, scrutinising people, trying to figure out whether they are one of those '"Beatles generation" types who expect *sinuttelu*[2] (the use of 2.sg.) to make things glide.' The following newspaper headline is from 1991: 'The sixties generation are angered by the use of *teitittely* while yuppies use *teitittely* in search of success' (my translation). However, in work communities the collegiate use of 2.sg. has evidently come to stay.

The addresser's attitude in a speech situation also becomes apparent from the different forms used for self-reference. In most situations these are personal forms encoded in the verb. But, significantly, evasive expressions are frequently used for self-reference, in line with the formality of the context. In principle, the method is the same as when choosing the personal form for the addressee. Linguistic evasiveness directed at the addressee tends to be called tactfulness while it is considered to be modesty when self-directed.

The use of 2.sg. has increased enormously among young people for self-reference, a custom sometimes condemned as anglicisation, although its use has also older roots in Finnish (see Figure 13.2). Nevertheless, many older Finns consider its use both un-Finnish and impertinent.

More commonly, a Finnish speaker will use for self-reference a 3.sg. verb form without a noun or a pronoun. Particularly common is a formula where the pragmatic adverb, *sitä* (3 b.), is linked to a 3sg. verb form. Common also is the use of *meikäläinen,* (one of us), a derivative of the pronoun *me,* with connotations of humbleness, even of belittling oneself. It is also symptomatic that this and some other derivatives and compounds are used in boastful speech, either playfully or disguised as such. In this context *meikäläinen* is also used, when the speaker, while seemingly belittling himself (this is typically male talk), is actually boasting. The corresponding derivative of the pronoun *te, teikäläinen* (one of you) bears a slight negative connotation.

Terms of Address

In Finnish, terms of address are used relatively less frequently than in many other European languages, as their purpose is mainly to attract the addressee's attention. To take the addressee into consideration in a polite manner, terms of address are only used in solemn, ceremonious speeches: *Pyydän teitä, herra pääministeri / arvoisa vastaväittäjä.* (I beg you, Mr Prime Minister / honoured opponent) – or in intimate affectionate speech: *Voi, kulta pieni, mitä teen sinun kanssasi!* (Oh, little darling, what shall I do with you!).

In unofficial formal speech, terms of address do not generally appear. This is perhaps due to the fact that address by title has become obsolete, as well as to the nature of general terms of address, such as *herra* (Mr/Sir), *rouva* (Mrs/Madam) or *neiti* (Miss). *Herra* and *rouva* are loan words from Swedish and have never had the same wide importance in Finnish. Second, they have always had negative connotations in agrarian Finland. These terms of address were last in general use when addressing envelopes as late

Sg			
1.		*Olin ihan hiljaa* (I kept all quiet)	(Addresser's inherent person)
2.		*Vaan on se leipäkin siinä elinaikainen, ja kun huonoksi* ***tulet****, niin (puoliso) hoitaa.* (But bread is there for life, and when **you get** poorly, (the spouse) will care for you.)	Passive *you*, especially favoured by young people.
3.	a.	***Meikäläinen*** *oli ihan hiljaa.* (**One of us** kept all quiet.)	A derivative of the pronoun *me*.
	b.	*On ollut kosijoitakin, ei sen puolesta ettei Ø* ***olisi*** *miestä* ***saanut****.* (Sure, [there] have been suitors, not that Ø **didn't get** a man.) *Ø Pitänee tästä lähteä.* (Ø **should perhaps** leave.) *Sitä* (pragmatic adverb) *Ø* ***juoksee*** *kuin hullu koko päivän.* (So Ø **runs** like mad all day.)	The general method of self-reference when ordinary people speak in public. Used for instance by sportsmen when giving interviews.
Pl.			
1.	a.	***Olemme*** *antaneet kertoa itsellemme.* (**We have** let ourselves be told.)	A commentator's (exclusive) plural has perhaps originated in the fact that the writer has in a way taken over the role of court jester.
	b.	*Edellä* ***olemme*** *tehneet selkoa…* (Above **we have** accounted for…) *Seuraavassa* ***ryhdymme*** *tarkastelemaan…* (Below **we will begin** to examine…)	A rhetorician's (inclusive) plural. This has become more widespread in recent decades. The most prevalent form in this position is, however, the use of the fourth person. (cf. 4 b. below), as in 'nursing language'. It has also otherwise largely superseded the use of 1.pl..
2.		–	
3.		–	
The 'fourth' person	a.	*Nyt sisään ja äkkiä! - No,* ***tullaan****,* ***tullaan****.* (Inside, now, and quickly! - Well, **coming**, coming.) ***Mene*** *jo! - No,* ***mennään****,* ***mennään****.* (- Go now! - Well, **going**, **going**.)	Conceding, giving in to commands, requests, etc.
	b.	*Edellä on* ***tehty*** *selkoa…* (Above, [it] has **been accounted** for…) *Seuraavassa* ***ryhdytään*** *tarkastelemaan…* (Below [it] **will begin** to be examined…)	A rhetorician's fourth person used typically in a 'matter-of-fact' style.

Figure 13.2 Self-reference

as the 1950s but even then *herra* was used only if the addressee did not have any other title: it thus became the title of the 'titleless'. From the 1960s, it has been customary only to write the addressee's name, except when the context is especially ceremonious when the professional title is used.

Nowadays *herra* and *rouva* are encountered mainly in shops or at the hairdresser's (or other such service establishments where the customer is treated with politeness which dates back to class society), in political or similar debates, where one wishes to offend the addressee, and in intimate speech, where one jokingly or ironically addresses a member of the family, for instance a child: *Koulussakos herra on noin viisaaks tullu?* (Is it school that's made the master so clever? – to a child who has spoken impudently to an adult).

In familiar speech, one may use not only the surname, first name, petname or nickname but also relationship terms denoting the addressee's relationship to the speaker, e.g. *Päivää – Päivää vaan, naapuri. Mitä kuuluu?* ([Good] day. Day there, neighbour. How are you?).

In my data, in one conversation, where the participants were unacquainted, one speaker referred to the person next to him saying: *Naapuri tässä on sitä mieltä että...* ([My] Neighbour here is of the opinion that...). The cashier in a hardware store addressed a customer, when the price tag of an item was missing, saying: *Asiakas varmaankin tietää hinnan.* ([You, the] Customer surely know[s] the price). Since modern Finnish lacks an appropriate general term, address is influenced by situation and, if a term of address is used, it indicates the relationship between the interlocutors. This may pose a problem in, for instance, a TV programme where the participants do not know each other (an unofficial formal situation).

The use of kinship terms has also undergone an interesting development during the cultural transition period of the 1960s onwards. When demands for equality reached children, child emancipation was reflected in the ways in which family members were addressed. In young families, children started calling their parents, and even grand-parents and other relatives, by their first names – often at the latter's request – the ideal being equality at all levels. Besides, the older generation felt that established kinship terms – e.g. derived from terms for old woman, *mummo* > *mummi* (grand-mother) and old man, *ukko* > *ukki* (grand-father), bore unpleasant connotations of old age. However, this fashion has now passed its peak.

So, on the one hand, Finns use terms of address in official, ceremonious speech, where Pan-European practice prevails, and, on the other, in intimate speech. In such situations, interlocutors have accurate information about each other. In unofficial, formal speech contexts, the situation is, however, quite different. The interlocutors frequently do not know each

(A)	OFFICIAL FORMAL (ceremonial)	2.pl. forms titles respectful epithets
	⇓	⇓
(B)	UNOFFICIAL FORMAL	2.pl. forms (formal address terms), generic verb forms (ellipsis), fourth person forms, 2.sg. forms
	⇑	⇑
(C)	FAMILIAR / INTIMATE/ INFORMAL / PRIVATE	2.sg. forms, nicknames, petnames, abusive, kinship etc. terms

Figure 13.3 Degree of formality in speech situations and pertinent address forms

other or each other's status. While the general terms *herra, rouva* and *neiti* have become inappropriate, two possibilities remain: either to omit the term of address altogether or use a temporary one (cf. *naapuri, asiakas*) if necessary.

Figure 13.3 gives a rough classification into three categories of different speech situations and the most typical forms of address attached to them. The thick arrows demonstrate the direction of pressure on unofficial, formal address (B). Part of the Finnish population demands the use of the official formal code of politeness also in this speech context (see (B) top row). This address mode is also in line with the higher code of spoken Finnish (A). Another part of the population uses familiar modes of address according to the lower code of spoken Finnish (C) also in unofficial, formal situations (B bottom row). In the middle of this controversy are the address modes which defocus the person (B middle row). The thin arrows to the right indicate the additional affective meanings caused by change of rank. The use of official, formal address, and especially the use of address terms (A), in an unofficial formal (B) or in informal (intimate, familiar) situation (C) is quite conspicuous: it might be considered snobbish or even offensive, because it goes against the principles of solidarity. In an intimate or familiar situation (C), expressions of the high code may be used to express playfulness or irony.

Greetings and Farewells

Expressions used in these situations have also undergone changes during the 20th century and vary considerably.

Greetings and farewells based on verbs still in use today (*tervehtiä* (<*terve*, healthy, sound) – to greet and *hyvästellä* (<*hyvästi* <*hyvä*, good), to bid farewell) are no longer in common use. *Terve* was a greeting which older people (born in the 19th century) widely used: today the term has made a comeback especially in young people's relaxed ways of speaking, giving *terve* (hello), when meeting, *terve (sitten)*, (bye [then]), when parting. (A contributory factor might be the Estonians' common greeting *tere*, which has become familiar to Finns after Estonia became independent in 1990.)

The official Finnish general greeting is *hyvää päivää* (good day). However, it is primarily used in ceremonious situations: *Hyvää päivää, sotilaat* (Good day, soldiers.); *Hyvää päivää, herra/rouva presidentti.* (Good day, Mr/Mrs President); or emphatically *Päivää, naapuri* ([Good] Day, neighbour.); *No, hyvää päivää!* (Neighbour, glad or surprised) (Well, good day!). The neutral unemphatic, *päivää* (day, afternoon), may be recognised as a greeting by its suffix *(päivä+ä).*

In addition to the general greeting, *päivää,* others are used such as *(hyvää) huomenta, iltaa, hyvää yötä* ((good) morning, evening, good night). Even these sound somewhat formal in modern use, especially among the younger generation. In everyday speech both when meeting and parting loan words such as *hei* (Sw.) and *moi* (German Dutch; cf. also the Finnish verb *moikata* – to say hello, hi) have taken over as general forms.

The general, previously so common, farewell, *hyvästi,* has also moved up the scale to become a ceremonious form, acquiring in everyday speech the implication of a final farewell. It has a connotation of 'I never wish to see you again'. As a formal farewell it has been replaced by *näkemiin* (cf. *auf Wiedersehen* in German, *på återseende* in Swedish – lit. until reseeing), *kuulemiin* on the telephone (lit. until rehearing, cf. *auf Wiederhören*, German). Therefore, younger people use other expressions: *hei, heippa, moi, moikka, terve sitten* etc. New forms of farewell are: *hyvää (päivän) jatkoa,* (lit. [have a] good continuation [of the day] 'have a nice day/all the best'), *nähdään* (fourth person) (see you) (cf. *vi ses*, Sw.).

Regrets, Apologies and Thanks

In ceremonious parlance Finns say: *pyydän* or *suokaa anteeksi* (lit. I beg [your] pardon or grant [me your] pardon) although in everyday practice they use the shorter *anteeksi* (pardon, excuse me). In formal situations it may also be used as a kind of address form to attract the addressee's attention. The loan word *sorry* is also gaining ground as a term of apology.

The term of gratitude, *kiitos* (thank [you]), is in extensive use as are its variants such as *paljon kiitoksia* (many thanks) (for thank you in Danish see Fredsted, this volume). In addition to expressing gratitude, *kiitos* is also used in the same sense as the English term 'please': *kyllä, kiitos* (yes, please) – *Sherry?* – *Kiitos* (Please) – *Ei, kiitos* (No, thanks).

In telephone conversations, for instance, *kiitos,* may also function as a farewell when the addressee is an official of a public office, agency, bank, etc. whom the speaker is not likely to meet, see or hear of again. Thus, the speaker wishes neither to use a term which implies seeing again, *näkemiin,* or hearing again, *kuulemiin,* nor *hei* or one of the alternatives, which would seem too familiar.

Mitigating Strategies in Finnish

Finnish has fewer politeness phrases than many other European languages. This arises from the nature of the language, based on the use of suffixes and, therefore, many of the mitigating strategies are grammatical. Finnish phrases are usually translations or loans from other languages, especially from Swedish and nowayadays also from English, e.g. *sorry*.

For instance, the English 'please' is usually either expressed by different phrases in Finnish: Daddy, please! Fi. *Isä kiltti!* (lit. Father kind! Cf. Sw. *snälla pappa*). May I sit here? Please do!, *Ole/olkaa hyvä!* (lit. Be [2.sg./pl.] good, cf. Sw. *var så god*) Alternatively, it may be omitted altogether and, instead, politeness is expressed through different sentence constructions and moods.

It seems that Finns are embarrassed to use even the few polite phrases that they have adopted, as loans, into standard Finnish. In familiar conversations many people, especially men, make their own playful, phonetic variations and puns, and may even add some pragmatic suffixes: *kiitos* > *kiitti, kiittipä kiitti; ole hyvä* > *olepa hyvä, olepa höveli; höveli* is dialect and sounds quite amusing.

A typically Finnish way of expressing politeness is to leave the choice to the addressee when presenting suggestions, requests or commands. They are presented in a questioning mode and suffixes which imply indecision or uncertainty are added to the verb: (conditional) *Saisiko olla lisää kahvia?* (Would Ø like more coffee?), *Hakisitko postin?* (Would you fetch the mail?), *Ottaisit vähän herneitäkin* (appeal) (You ought to have some peas, too.); (past tense) *Saiko olla lisää kahvia?* (Did Ø like more coffee?), *Kävikö Nortti?* (lit. Was a Nortti suitable? – the addresser offers a North State cigarette). The question may even be formed as a negative: ***Ei*** *päätoimittaja* ***ole*** *tavattavissa?*

(Is not the editor-in-chief available?) The unusual word order reveals the function of the sentence, the normal word order being: *Päätoimittaja* ***ei ole*** *tavattavissa.*

Variation between nominative, accusative and partitive cases occurs in Finnish, where the nominative/accusative cases express something which is complete, finalised, exact, etc., while the partitive expresses the opposite. It is notable that the partitive appears remarkably frequently in polite conversation in such structures where the nominative or accusative would be natural in neutral speech: *Saanko mä kuittausta* (pro *kuittauksen*) *tuohon?* (May I get [your] signature there?), *Takkia* (pro *takin*) *voi panna tuonne naulakkoon.* (The coat may be put in the rack over there.), *Kiitosta* (pro *kiitos*) *kaverit!* (Thanks, pals!). These examples are from colloquial speech but the rule also applies to standard Finnish: *Kutsukaa syytetty* (acc.) *sisään* (Call the accused), *Kutsukaa arkkipiispaa* (part.) *sisään* (Call [=invite] the archbishop in). The use of an accusative in this context would be seen as arrogant.

The adverbs *vähän* ((a) little) and *vain* (only) are used frequently in everyday speech and may even be combined with each other: *Minä* ***vain vähän*** *vilkaisisin* (conditional) *tätä.* (I would like to glance at this *only a little*).

Nykysuomen sanakirja (Dictionary of Modern Finnish) gives the following definitions, among others, of the previous expressions: '*vähän* mitigates an expression, giving the expression an air of caution or vagueness; *vain* gives an expression an air of vagueness, indifference, evasion, humbleness, etc.' (my translation).

Pragmatic clitics are also widely in use. A popular one is *–han/-hän*, which the same dictionary defines as 'appealing to the addressee in order to indicate that the matter in question is obvious and well known; mitigating the expression; expressing indifference; in polite, friendly encouragement.' (my translation).

Conclusion

Finnish politeness, as we have seen, is withdrawing and evasive, avoiding direct reference to hearer or speaker, for example by using deictic expressions, generic clauses, the so-called fourth verbal person or stress on the topic of the conversation. This tact or modesty has proved very useful since the cultural emancipation of the 1960s, when forms of address changed and 2.sg. verbs became prevalent. Titles (Mr etc.) are little used except ceremoniously, in shops or when joking. Greetings and farewells have also become less formal (nowadays mainly *hei* and *moi* in everyday speech). Finnish has relatively few 'smoothing' formulas (of the 'please' type); suggestions, requests and commands are often formulated as questions, leaving the addressee freedom in responding and a number of different mitigating grammatical structures, such as the pragmatically marked use of suffixes, are in frequent use.

Finns are seldom the first to speak in unfamiliar company and seldom start arguing or disagreeing with others' opinions; rather, they acquiesce, remain silent or change the subject. Even when simply informing, they often do so as if the addressee already has the information. Yet Finnish politeness is not homogeneous: Eastern Finns are more talkative and inquisitive than their western compatriots, and the 'common people' perceive some standard politeness formulas, mostly borrowed from Swedish, as artificial or even humiliating.

The tendency to avoid emphasising the person is conspicuous. When referring to the addressee or to oneself, the addresser readily uses impersonal, ambiguous or vague expressions. Wishes are communicated in roundabout ways, using ambiguous pragmatic adverbs, suffixes and clitics which imply humbleness and belittle the addresser. These are methods to which Finns are supposed to revert even when boasting.

A Finn will not willingly start arguing or presenting differing opinions (except in intimate or familiar contexts) but instead will acquiesce, if possible, and if not, will keep quiet or change the subject. Confronted by expressive politeness, a Finn will often become embarrassed and may even doubt the addresser's purpose. When conveying information, a Finn will often present facts as if they were already known to the addressee (by using suffixes such as *-han/-hän*).

In unfamiliar company, a Finn will not readily be the first to make contact (in compliance with traditional court etiquette: conversation should only be started after formal introductions). Thus, individuals not familiar with Finnish speech culture may misinterpret Finnish behaviour as being impolite.

In Finnish popular culture, there is a clear distinction between the Eastern Finnish spontaneous and the Western Finnish reserved speech culture. Politeness norms in standard Finnish are largely based on loans from other languages. Therefore, common people may consider this style artificial and, at worst, even humiliating.

Notes

1. The Finnish term for politeness, *kohteliaisuus* (n.), *kohtelias* (a.), however, is derived from the verb, *kohdella* (to treat).
2. Finnish has special verbs for the use of 2.sg. and 2.pl., derived from the respective pronouns, which are impossible to translate, as English uses the same pronoun in both cases.

Reference

Yli-Vakkuri, V. (1987) Aspect and the affective attitude of the speaker: Usage and meaning in grammatical case variation in Finnish. In M. Koski et al. (eds) *Fennistica Festiva in Honorem Göran Karlsson Septuagenaria* (pp. 189–205). Åbo: Åbo Akademisförlag

Yli-Vakkuri, V. (1989) Suomalaisen puhuttelun piirteitä. (Features of address in Finnish.) In A. Kauppinen *et al*, V. Yli-Vakkuri and K. Kylliki (eds) *Äidinkielenopettajain liiton vuosikirja XXXVI* (The 36th Year Book of the Association of Teachers of Finnish as the Mother Tongue) (pp. 43 – 74). Helsinki: Association of Teachers of Finnish as the Mother Tongue.

Chapter 14

Politeness in Estonia: A Matter of Fact Style

LEELO KEEVALLIK

Introduction

Linguistic politeness is intimately connected with social norms. Estonian society has gone through considerable change over the last ten years. It has regained independence and, at the same time, switched from a planned to a market economy as well as from dictatorship to democracy. A decade is most probably not long enough for linguistic norms to change drastically: as we know, the structure of a language often takes much longer to change. Politeness, however, may to some extent be subject to deliberate influence, as witnessed, for example, by the reform of Swedish *du* (you, sg.) where the recommendations of some left-wing organisations on the usage of mutual *du* (T) have won general social acceptance (Paulston, 1976: 365–66). It is, thus, not unlikely that change is taking place in Estonian politeness at present.

Several new phenomena connected with the market economy have had a relatively direct impact on patterns of politeness. It is widely known that marketing was unnecessary in the planned economy and service was non-existent. Due to the general shortage of goods, clients were treated as if the sellers were doing them a favour. Therefore, there was no need for selling strategies to be developed or for shop assistants to be trained to behave politely. During the last ten years, western-style service and marketing programmes have gained in popularity and although Estonian tourist brochures still warn westerners not to expect *hi* and *thank you* (not to mention *how are you?*) in shops in Estonia, change in service culture has been inevitable, at least at local level.

Another change has been towards informality throughout society, particularly in the media. The media had been under close scrutiny by the Soviet authorities and a special very formal style had evolved in reports on political, economic and other sensitive matters. This style has now disappeared along with strict political censorship. Also gone are the previously common language editors whose main task was to eliminate anything not in accordance with the established language standard. Less normative and more democratic language use in the media has resulted in numerous outcries by the general public and even by some linguists concerning the vanishing knowledge of 'correct language'. The current more informal style of public language use has meant that especially the older generations may sometimes feel that they are not being treated politely.

Regardless of these changes towards what could be seen as a more involved style (see later), Estonians are still quite reserved. We will first look at address forms and strategies, mainly attending to positive face (use of first names, compliments). Then we shall consider more elaborate negative face strategies: commanding and requesting. Our definition of politeness is consequently broader than the use of explicit linguistic indirectness and is, in part, due to the nature of our data.

The Data

Our corpus consists of 324 naturally-occurring telephone conversations of two types: telemarketing calls from one of the biggest daily newspapers in Estonia (109 conversations), and everyday calls between family members, relatives, friends and colleagues, recorded at the informants' homes. The corpus comprises more than 10 hours of conversational language (about 103,000 words) and includes representatives of both sexes and all ages, although there is somewhat more data from younger females who were our primary informants.

The majority of the data is informal. Everyday conversations comprise about two-thirds of the corpus data in terms of time (about 6.5 hours) and the telemarketing calls are not particularly formal. Telemarketing reached Estonia with re-independence and at the time of the recordings (1997/98), the sellers were doing their job on an intuitive basis – the informants of this study had no training whatsoever. There is no flattering or pushiness, no aggressive tactics. There are no scripts involved. Sometimes the telemarketers even feel free to argue with their clients' opinions. Consequently, the corpus should provide a relatively good basis for politeness research in Estonian as practised by ordinary people in everyday settings.

Singular and Plural Address

Address is a sensitive way of expressing social relations between interlocutors, as perceived by themselves. In Estonian speech, it is possible to address a person using either 2.sg. (T) or 2.pl. (V), the latter being more formal. The system involves the pronouns (*sina/sa* you, sg., *teie/te* you, pl.) as well as the respective verbal suffixes.

It seems that, at present, usage of T and V is symmetrical: parents are not addressed as V by children, let alone elder brothers, and grandparents receive V extremely rarely. Doctors, lawyers and professors do not automatically have the right to address their inferiors as T. Shop assistants and waiters are typically addressed as V, as are the representatives of 'lower' occupations such as cleaners and maintenance workers. In the adult world the unmarked variant is V, which is mutually used until the parties agree upon T. The right to initiate T, however, is supposed to be granted according to power relations, i.e. the older and/or higher status (female) speaker can suggest mutual T.

There may be a correlation between type of society and symmetry of address usage. Brown and Gilman (1960: 257–261) had already observed that in several European cultures the power dimension was losing ground as far as the usage of different address pronouns was concerned, and that in egalitarian societies T and V were used instead for marking intimacy/distance and informality/formality with symmetrical address patterns prevailing, and asymmetrical patterns disappearing. It is hard to know whether there has been any such change in Estonia – we now live in a democracy but society has actually become more differentiated economically during re-independence. However, according to one judgement from the end of the 1980s, asymmetrical address was still 'disturbingly common' back then and was even propagated on TV and radio (Erelt, 1990: 37).

A traditional and still surviving domain of asymmetrical usage is between children and adults. For example, at school the degree of acquaintance between teachers and students should usually require mutual T; however, while teachers generally use T at least until high school, the students are expected to use V.

Singular and plural address patterns have been studied by means of a questionnaire to 8–9, 14–15, and 17–18-year-old informants (Keevallik, 1999). This demonstrated that even these young people choose address forms more on the basis of solidarity judgements (degree of acquaintance) than the hierarchical dimension of power. They would, for example, use T with higher-ranking officials if they knew them personally.

Among other influential factors was area of residence, i.e. whether the informant lived in the city or the countryside. Interestingly, the smaller the settlement was, the more the students preferred to hear T from their teachers and to respond similarly. In the capital Tallinn, the oldest students expected considerably more mutual V than in the rural township of Kadrina (40% and 10% respectively wanted the teachers to use V, 36% and 65% respectively wanted to use T themselves to the teacher, [Keevallik, 1999: 135–36]). These results are not counterintuitive if we consider that social networks tend to involve more multiple ties in smaller places (Malmberg & Nordberg, 1994).

The Estonian second-person address system is rigid: once a pattern is established between two people, it is likely to persist. As one informant put it, he would never use V to his classmates even if one of them became the President of the Republic. The established pattern can only be temporarily changed for strategic reasons, e.g. a teacher who wants to express irony towards an inattentive student may say *Kas ma võiksin teid segada*? (May I disturb you: pl?). A marked T may be used to be derogatory or express anger towards somebody usually addressed as V (the teacher). This contrasts with, for example, Russian usage of T and V where much more dynamic switches have been reported (Friedrich, 1972: 288–98).

In accordance with the trend towards informality in the Estonian speech community, universal T seems to be spreading (for a journalistic account, see Laanem, 1999). At university, symmetrical T may be used between students and younger teachers. The new corporate culture also apparently involves addressing every insider as T, a pattern that is unfamiliar and sometimes uncomfortable for the older generation. The spread of T may be supported by the two most popular foreign languages at the moment – Finnish and English, that only have one address pronoun (as opposed to Russian, the previously most common second language). Even if younger people are certainly leading the shift to T, informants in our study generally rejected the possibility of eliminating V altogether. Many said that they wanted 'politeness to be preserved' in society, they wanted to be able to express deference and receive respectful V themselves. V also seems to be a handy means of keeping unpleasant people (amongst them teachers) at a safe distance.

In addition to second-person address, there are some fixed address patterns in third-person singular involving the respectful titles *proua* (Mrs), *preili* (Miss), and *härra* (Mr). These forms can mostly be encountered in service situations: *Kas proua soovib teed või kohvi?* (Does Madam want tea or coffee?). At present they are experienced as new due to the overtly unfavourable attitude towards them during Soviet times, when official attempts were made to introduce the solidary *seltsimees* (comrade) instead. According to Braun's (1988: 57–61) hypothesis about the universal tendency of polite forms to recede, these expressions may appear especially polite because of their relative novelty.

First Names and Personal Reference

Cultures differ in the frequency of usage of names. In Estonian, they are certainly used less often than in the American or Swedish speech communities. First, identification sequences on the phone rarely involve names. In our corpus, institutional callers and answerers only introduced themselves by first and/or second name 24 times (out of about 150). Instead, merely the name of the company, newspaper, etc. was used. Rääbis' study (2000) on a different corpus confirms this result. She also notes that private persons do not usually introduce themselves when calling institutions if they do not expect to be recognised by the representative (Rääbis, 2000: 413–14). In private homes, however, in our corpus, 39 answerers gave their names as a response to the call, 29 of them first names (out of about 250).

More interestingly, the construction *tere* (hi) + first name was used altogether 60 times. The use of the interlocutor's first name can be seen as a means of satisfying positive face wants, especially when it involves recognition of the other (Brown & Levinson, 1987: 38; Schegloff, 1979; 1986). This is the place in Estonian conversations where positive face can quite regularly be attended to. In Example 1, neither of two friends gives her name but they both express recognition of the other by name.

Example 1

1 **M:** *halloo* (hello)
2 **L:** *tere Merilin* (hi Merilin)
3 **M:** *tere Liina* (hi Liina)

Outside the opening sequence, names were hardly used. In the telemarketing calls, the name of the (potential) client was never used outside the identification sequences. This is certainly unusual in comparison with many other western cultures where (first) names are very often used manipulatively in this type of encounter. In American society, even young children are able to use names as mitigators (Ervin-Tripp *et al.*, 1990: 326, 329). Swedish children are socialised from the very beginning to add the name to *tack* (thanks), e.g. *tack Klara*. Unfortunately, there are no comparative quantitative data available but 21 cases in 10 hours of this corpus does not seem to be a high frequency. First names may occasionally precede requests, as in Example 2.

Example 2

1 **P:** *.hh Ragne hh* (Ragne)
2 **R:** *no:h* (yeah)
3 **P:** *mul on vaja ärakuulajat hh* (I need a listener)

Furthermore, when talking about closely related third persons, names are used sparingly. Parents and grandparents are called by their names extremely rarely and are mostly referred to with kinship terms, e.g. 'your mother'. Even children are often referred to as e.g. 'my child' rather than by name. Direct reference to those present may be avoided altogether by using first-person plural, impersonal or generic forms (Erelt, 1990). For example, after surrendering to her friend's insistence on going out late at night, a girl says: *ahh jumal jumal vana inimene aetakse välja* (oh god, an old person is forced to go out) jokingly referring to herself as an 'old person'. By using the impersonal form of *aetakse* (force, drive: impersonal), she avoids putting the blame explicitly on her friend. Reference avoidance is supposedly very frequent, similar to what happens in Finnish (Hakulinen, 1987). We could thus conclude that positive face is not primarily attended to via reference in Estonia.

Openings and Closings

Conversational openings and closings can allow ritual exchange of polite formulas. What appears to be most striking in Estonian openings and closings is their brevity. According to Schegloff (1986: 129–30), we would normally find 'how-are-you' sequences in American phone-call openings. In Estonian openings these are rare. Furthermore, they are usually not reciprocal as they are in America (Rääbis, 2000: 418). The greeting does not always have to be returned either, especially between close acquaintances. In Example 3, there is no space provided for the immediate return of the greeting – the caller Ene continues her turn by introducing herself. This is acknowledged with the particle *jah*, which is a mere go-ahead for the caller to give her reason for calling.

Example 3

1 **A:** *Aili kuuleb* (Aili listening)
2 **E:** *tere Aili Ene siin* (hi Aili, Ene here)
3 **A:** *jah* (yeah)
4 **E:** *kudas teil läks täna* (how did it go today)

Like the openings, Estonian conversation closures may be very brief. Terminating an informal conversation in Estonian does not usually involve numerous good wishes and greetings to relatives (in comparison with Sweden, where sending greetings to each other's intimates is a norm). The difference from the American closures seems to be that goodbyes need not be reciprocal or even present (see Example 4, cf. Schegloff & Sacks, 1973).

Example 4

1 **T:** *siis me:: saame kokku onju* (we'll meet then, won't we)

2 **O:** *okei* (okay)
3 **T:** *okei* (okay)
4 **O:** *tšau* (bye)

In many cultures, emotional 'presents' can conventionally be made to the interlocutor during the closings. In contrast, a short opening and closure are indications of intimacy in Estonian calls, while institutional calls tend to end with good wishes.

Complimenting

Attending to the positive face of the interlocutor is probably not prevalent in Estonian, just as in Finland (Saari, 1990, 1995). Speakers feel embarrassed about close interest in personal topics, exaggerated emotions and praise. Even if all Brown and Levinson's positive politeness strategies are represented, e.g. in marketing encounters with trained informants (Vellerind, 2000), they are certainly not as dominant as in, for example, the Swedish or American speech communities.

On the basis of our corpus, we can suggest that complimenting is a rare and not especially elaborate activity among Estonian interactants. The corpus involves 11 cases, many of them consisting of only one word, e.g. *tubli*, approximately 'brave, good'. Even if it is possible to accept a compliment with a *aitäh* or *tänan* (thank you), it only happens once in the corpus. In two cases the content is explicitly denied, which is what researchers have noticed even in other cultures (Pomerantz, 1978). Most often, however, the praise goes unacknowledged, i.e. the receiver of the compliment changes the topic. Apart from our corpus, which may not be representative in terms of compliments, Estonians who have been interacting in cultures more oriented towards positive face have reported uneasiness with compliments.

There are other research results pointing in the same direction – Estonians are not good at getting verbally involved. Compared to Canadians, Estonians have been shown to be less likely to initiate conversations, attribute negative characteristics to untalkative people, and feel uncomfortable with silences in conversations (Kivik, 1998: 76). Talkativeness is the negatively-evaluated target of numerous proverbs (Heinsoo, 1999). Estonian mothers prompt children's conversational participation less often than Swedish and American mothers do from the age of two to their teens (Junefelt & Tulviste, 1997; 1998; Tulviste, 1998). There are thus many indications that Estonians are verbally quite reserved.

Commands and Requests

Explicitly targeting negative face needs seems more frequent in our corpus (and in the Estonian speech community) and is evident in cases where one interlocutor wants the other to do something – acts that have been called *intrinsic FTAs* (Brown & Levinson, 1987: 65–8).

It is not easy to distinguish between commands and requests in conversational data since the difference mostly appears to be in the degree of politeness. As already noted by Brown and Levinson (1987: 94–101), direct imperatives are used mainly in activities that are urgent or where the recipient is in some way a beneficiary (e.g. *oota korra* [wait a second], *võta nii palju kui tahad* [take as much as you like]). In addition, commands to third persons are not necessarily modified for politeness, e.g. *las ta elistab siis Enele kui ta tuleb* (let him call Ene when he comes) (*las* is a particle that is, among other things, used for giving mediated orders), especially when the imposition on the interlocutor is small.

At the other end of the continuum, there are off-record strategies where the command/request is only implicated. For example, when the speaker wants to talk to someone other than the person on the phone, she may say *siis ma räägin Nelega oma jutud ära* (I'll talk to Nele then), which implicates that the present interlocutor has to go and get Nele – there is no other way for the content of this statement to become true. The implicit request is expressed in the form of a statement about what the speaker is planning to do, namely to speak to Nele.

Another implicit way of making a request is to produce a statement about some shortcoming of the speaker herself. In the following Example 5, a request for information is carried out in the form of a statement. The speaker, who is supposed to be on his way to his interlocutor, claims that he does not know the address.

Example 5

1 **H:** *[ee ee] tähendab e me ei tea ju kus te elate* (you know, we don't know where you live)

2 **K:** *aa (0.2) Ranniku neliteist seitsekend kaks* (oh, Ranniku fourteen seventy two

In this example, the first word of H's turn is the formulation particle *tähendab*, (approximately. 'you know'), which may foreshadow something face-threatening to follow. Furthermore, the particle *ju* indicates that according to H this piece of information is not new to the interlocutor, i.e. that K is aware that his address is unknown to H. This clearly implicates that it is K's duty to provide the necessary information, which he does immediately in the next turn.

Another way to make a request off-record is to ask about the prerequisites of request compliance. For example, when the caller wants somebody else on the phone, she may ask whether the person is present, rather than actually carrying out the FTA (see Example 6).

Example 6

1 **M:** *tere ega Helenit ei ole* (hi, isn't Helen [there])
2 **O:** *jaa kohe* (yes, one moment)

Naturally, this way of asking for a third person is conventionalised and the question about somebody's presence is usually not treated as a question. In this example, O promises to fetch Helen without actually answering the question (*jaa* 'yes' is not a grammatically appropriate answer here). The speech act in line 1 is clearly interpreted via a conversational implicature.

Most interestingly, however, when working with interactional data, we notice that potential FTAs are rarely carried out in one step. FTAs need not even be carried out by the same speaker. As has been shown in conversation-analytic work, awkward interactional steps may be preceded by the so-called pre-sequences (e.g. Schegloff, 1980; 1988). In the case of requests, they may be used for checking whether the prerequisites for the request are fulfilled (the question about Helen's presence in Example 6 can also be seen as the initiation of a pre-sequence). Pre-sequences come into being because of face concerns – they allow the off-record negotiation of business with face implications well in advance of the possible on-record transaction (Brown & Levinson, 1987: 40). The recipient is politely given the possibility of resigning without being directly confronted with an unwelcome offer, request etc. Thus, what in speech act theory we would see as one single act may actually be a series of actions and still recognizable by the interactors as, for example, doing requesting.

We have evidence that the interlocutor often already understands during the pre-sequence that a request or a proposal is due. In Example 7, K pursues M's plans for the evening. At first, M misinterprets K's question as being about the present moment and K has to put it more precisely. In line 4, M answers that she will be at *Püve* (a street address) for some time. Asking about interlocutor's plans may function as a pre-sequence for a request or a proposal and it is probably recognisable as such by M after line 3. However, when K proceeds to ask about the exact time of M's stay at *Püve*, M can already guess that a request is to come.

Example 7

1 **K:** *=ahah .h aga: kas sa oled Püves vä* (okay but are you at Püve)
2 **M:** *ei ma olen siin töö juures @* (no, I'm here at work)
3 **K:** *ei kuidas su plaanid on õhtuks* (no, what are your plans for tonight)
4 **M:** *öööö jaa ma mingi ajani olen Püves jah* (yes, I'll be at Püve for sometime)
5 **K:** *mingi ajan* (for some time)
6 **M:** *jah* (yes)
7 K: *[mis (su)]* (what)
8 **M:** *[tahad] värvimist* (you want dyeing)
9 **K:** *tahaksin küll jaa* (I would, yes)

In Example 7, we can see how a request sequence is formed in collaboration between the interlocutors. Even if it is one of them who actually wants a favour (her hair dyed), the receiver of the request is the one who actually utters it in line 8. The pre-sequence has thus made it clear to the receiver that a request is to follow and instead of letting K do the FTA she almost turns it into an offer, which is a preferable action (Brown & Levinson, 1987: 38; Heritage, 1984; Levinson, 1983: 307–08; 332–45). At the same time, it is still a mere guess at what K wants and K has to confirm it, which she does in line 9. The confirmation is done in the conditional form, which could be seen as a grammatical mitigating device for requests in general. Only after the confirmation can the request be seen as carried out. It is the joint action of the interlocutors that eventually results in a request for hair to be dyed.

Speech act theory and politeness theory, however, enforce a sentence-based speaker-centered mode of analysis. When working with conversational data from everyday interaction, it seems inevitable to use a methodology enabling us to account for the real-time emergence of the patterns. Apart from requests which are transformed into offers, parts of what we could consider to be requesting activity can occur after the request has been complied with, especially hedges and attending to positive face. Consider Example 8 where a compliment follows M's affirmation that she can lend an article to L (see appendix for transcript conventions).

Example 8

1 **L:** *ja sa saad <@ selle mulle @anda onju= @>* (and you can give it to me, can't you)
2 **M:** *=saan* (yeah)
3 **L:** *sa oled nii musi* (you are such a sweetie)

In order to incorporate sequences into their model, Brown and Levinson (1987: 233) suggest that politeness should be understood as a higher level intention, in fact, the reason why these sequences are designed in this particular way. That is what the common-sense scope of politeness is and several researchers have also claimed that politeness is simply a means of reaffirming and strengthening relationships (Bayraktaroğlu, 1991: 5; Holmes, 1995; Lakoff, 1973: 298). At the same time, in Brown and Levinson's model, positive and negative politeness are almost exclusively reduced to indirectness strategies striving against the cooperation principle in the case of FTAs (for similar points, see Held, 1992: 131; Meier, 1995). Thus, politeness is, according to them, a technical concept applying to acts with inherent potential for conflict and which, furthermore, presupposes constant awareness of the most efficient ways of saying things.

If politeness were a higher-ranking (social) principle, we should not take the different linguistic expressions as a starting point for the model of politeness, as Brown and Levinson do. Rather, we should keep the social and the lingustic levels of analysis apart by talking about negative and positive face needs as opposed to various (linguistic) strategies used to satisfy these needs. Among other things, not committing the FTA by remaining silent can target either the positive or the negative face (Sifianou, 1995: 107) and off-record strategies are often likely to be used to attend to negative face needs.

This does not mean that it is not possible to note explicit linguistic strategies that are often used specifically, for example, in order to maintain the negative face of the interlocutor, such as avoidance of imperatives by using (as directives) conditionals, negations and questions in Anglo-Saxon cultures (Wierzbicka, 1985). Politeness, however, could probably be treated as an omnipresent aspect of all social activities, so that everything done and said will be experienced as either to some or other degree polite, impolite or as quite neutral in a particular culture (Sell, 1992: 114). Seeing politeness as adequacy for the situation (e.g. Braun, 1988: 49) or appropriateness (Meier, 1995: 390) would also be in better accordance with our common-sense usage of the word.

Conclusion

The classic way of treating politeness phenomena in linguistics might not be the best way to handle conversational data, since what might have been considered single speech acts may actually be better accounted for as a series of conversational steps. Brown and Levinson's influential model of politeness seems to capture politeness in a single calculation on the basis of a couple of stable variables. Dissatisfaction with this view has resulted in attempts to make the model more dynamic and account for extended discourse (e.g. the interactional imbalance view of natural conversations by Bayraktaroğlu, [1991]; the constantly renegotiable conversational contract by Fraser [1990], Fraser and Nolen, [1981]; or work on literary dialogue by Buck, [1997]). Looking more closely at the mechanisms of conversation may reveal new facets of politeness. As Heritage (1984: 265) puts it, there is a general bias intrinsic to many aspects of the organisation of talk which is favourable to the maintenance of bonds of solidarity between actors and which promotes the avoidance of conflict. Face wants are a generative mechanism of human interaction and this is reflected in conversation.

In an attempt to generalise and interpret the above results on Estonian, we could say that the interlocutors do not seem to attend very much to face needs. Positive face is not attended to as frequently as in several adjacent cultures and caring about each other is implicit rather than actively expressed. Estonians are somewhat more oriented toward negative face but directness may be tolerated to quite an extent. For example, the preferred utterance type of Estonians for regulating children's attention and physical activity is the imperative (Tulviste, 1995). Intuitively, the results of certain quantitative comparative studies into German could apply to Estonian: Germans use higher levels of directness in complaints and requests compared to speakers of English (House & Kasper, 1981: 159–166), and fewer phatic utterances in personal relationships compared to speakers of Greek (Pavlidou, 1994: 507). Like the Germans in Pavlidou's study, Estonians seem to focus more on content than relationships in communication. Directness need not be offensive or impolite. Considering the length of German occupation and presence on Estonian territory, it would not be too surprising if politeness patterns were similar.

Interestingly, Giles *et al.* (1992: 220) have concluded that there are differences in conversational style between East and West – Westerners talk for affiliative purposes, and in order to fill silences which are deemed stressful, while Easterners talk primarily for instrumental purposes and can remain in comfortable silence in other cases. If this crude generalization is true, in terms of communicative patterns, Estonia still seems to belong to the East.

Appendix:

Transcription conventions

underlining	–	main stress
.h(h)	–	in-breath
hh	–	out-breath
:	–	lengthening
[xxx]	–	overlap
(0.2)	–	length of pause
@	–	laughter syllable
<@ xxx @>	–	the stretch of talk produced with a 'smiling voice'

References

Bayraktaroğlu, A. (1991) Politeness and interactional imbalance. *The International Journal of the Sociology of Language* 92, 5–34.

Braun, F. (1988) *Terms of Address: Problems of Patterns and Usage in Various Languages and Cultures.* (Contributions to the Sociology of Language, 50). Berlin, New York, Amsterdam: Mouton de Gruyter.

Brown, P. and Levinson, S. (1987) *Politeness: Some Universals in Language Usage.* Cambridge: Cambridge University Press.

Brown, R. and Gilman, A. (1960) The pronouns of power and solidarity. In T.A. Sebeok (ed.) *Style in Language* (pp. 253–76). Cambridge, MA: Technology Press of MIT.

Buck, R. A. (1997) Towards an extended theory of face action: Analyzing dialogue in E. M. Foster's *A Passage to India. Journal of Pragmatics* 27 (1), 83–106.

Erelt, M. (1990) Kõneleja ja kuulaja kaudse väljendamise võimalusi eesti keeles. (The possibilities of expressing the speaker and the listener in an indirect way in Estonian). *Keel ja Kirjandus* 38 (1), 35–9.

Ervin-Tripp, S., Gu, Y. and Lampert, M. (1990) Politeness and persuasion in children's control acts. *Journal of Pragmatics* 14 (2), 307–31.

Fraser, B. (1990) Perspectives on politeness. *Journal of Pragmatics* 14 (2), 219–36.

Fraser, B. and Nolen, W. (1981) The association of deference with linguistic form. *The International Journal of the Sociology of Language* 27, 93–109.

Friedrich, P. (1972) Social context and semantic feature: The Russian pronominal usage. In J.J. Gumperz and D. Hymes (eds) *Directions in Sociolinguistics: The Ethnography of Communication* (pp. 270–300). New York: Holt, Rinehart and Winston.

Giles, H., Coupland, N. and Wiemann, J. (1992) 'Talk is cheap...' but 'My word is my bond': Beliefs about talk. In K. Bolton and H. Kwok (eds) *Sociolinguistics Today: International Perspectives* (pp. 218–41). London & New York: Routledge.

Hakulinen, A. (1987) Avoiding personal reference in Finnish. In J. Verschueren and M. Bertuccelli-Papi (eds) *The Pragmatic Perspective: Selected Papers from the 1985 International Pragmatics Conference* (pp. 141–53). Amsterdam, Philadelphia: John Benjamins.

Heinsoo, H. (1999) Talkative as a Finn or an Estonian? In A. Künnap (ed.) *Indo-European-Uralic-Siberian Linguistic and Cultural Contacts. Fenno-ugristica* 22 (pp. 77–84). Tartu: Department of Uralic Languages, University of Tartu.

Held, G. (1992) Politeness in linguistic research. In R.J. Watts, S. Ide and K. Ehlich (eds) *Politeness in Language: Studies in its History, Theory and Practice,* Trends in Linguistics. Studies and Monographs 59 (pp. 131–53). Berlin, New York: Mouton de Gruyter.

Heritage, J. (1984) *Garfinkel and Ethnomethodology*. Cambridge: Polity Press.

Holmes, J. (1995) *Women, Men and Politeness*. London, New York: Longman.

House, J. and Kasper, G. (1981) Politeness markers in English and German. In F. Coulmas (ed.) *Conversational Routine: Explorations in Standardized Communication Situations and Prepatterned Speech* (pp. 157–85). The Hague, Paris, New York: Mouton Publishers.

Junefelt, K. and Tulviste, T. (1997) Regulation and praise in American, Estonian, and Swedish mother–child interaction. *Mind, Culture, and Activity: An International Journal* 4 (1), 24–33.

Junefelt, K. and Tulviste, T. (1998) American, Estonian and Swedish mothers' regulation of their children's discourse construction. In M. de Lyra and J. Valsiner (eds) *Construction of Psychological Processes in Interpersonal Communication* (pp. 137–54). Stanford, CA: Ablex.

Keevallik, L. (1999) The use and abuse of singular and plural address forms in Estonian. *International Journal of the Sociology of Language* 139, 125–44.

Kivik, P.-K. (1998) What silence says: Communicative style and identity. *Trames* 2 (1), 66–90.

Laanem, T. (1999) Sinatamine tikub eestlaste kõnepruuki. (Saying *sina* 'you: 2sg.' is spreading among Estonians), *Eesti Päevaleht* 14. August, 14.

Lakoff, R. T. (1973) The logic of politeness; or minding your p's and q's. In *Papers From the Ninth Regional Meeting of the Chicago Linguistic Society* (pp. 292–305). Chicago: Department of Linguistics, University of Chicago.

Levinson, S. (1983) *Pragmatics*. Cambridge: Cambridge University Press.

Malmberg, A. and Nordberg, B. (1994) Language use in rural and urban settings. In B. Nordberg (ed.) *The Sociolinguistics of Urbanization: The Case of the Nordic Countries* (pp. 16–50). Berlin, New York: Walter de Gruyter.

Meier, A. J. (1995) Passages of politeness. *Journal of Pragmatics* 24 (4), 381–92.

Paulston, C. B. (1976) Pronouns of address in Swedish: Social class semantics and a changing system. *Language in Society* 5 (3), 359–386.

Pavlidou, T. (1994) Contrasting German–Greek politeness and the consequences. *Journal of Pragmatics* 21 (5), 487–511.

Pomerantz, A. (1978) Compliment responses: Notes on the co-operation of multiple constraints. In J. Schenkein (ed.) *Studies in the Organization of Conversational Interaction* (pp. 79–112). New York: Academic Press.

Rääbis, A. (2000) Telefonivestluse sissejuhatus. (Phone conversation opening). *Keel ja Kirjandus* 48 (6), 409–18.

Saari, M. (1990) Interaktionsstrategier i Helsingfors. (Interaction strategies in

Helsinki]). In K. L. Berge and U.-B Kotsinas (eds) *Storstadsspråk och storstadskultur i Norden* (Meddelanden från Institutionen för nordiska språk vid Stockholms universitet 34). (pp. 200–12). Stockholm: Stockholms Universitet.

Saari, M. (1995) Synpunkter på svenskt språkbruk i Sverige och Finland. (Views on the usage of Swedish in Sweden and Finland) *Folkmålsstudier* 36, 75–108.

Schegloff, E. A. (1979) Identification and recognition in telephone conversation openings. In G. Psathas (ed.) *Everyday Language: Studies in Ethnomethodology* (pp. 23–78). New York: Irvington.

Schegloff, E. A. (1980) Preliminaries to preliminaries: 'Can I ask you a question?'. *Sociological Inquiry* 50 (3/4), 104–52.

Schegloff, E. A. (1986) The Routine as achievement. *Human Studies* 9 (2/3), 111–51.

Schegloff, E. A. (1988) Pre-sequences and indirection: Applying speech act theory to ordinary conversation. *Journal of Pragmatics* 12 (1), 55–62.

Schegloff, E. A. and Sacks, H. (1973) Opening up closings. *Semiotica* 8 (4), 289–327.

Sell, R. D. (1992) Literary texts and diachronic aspects of politeness. In R. J. Watts, S. Ide and K. Ehlich (eds) *Politeness in Language: Studies in its History, Theory and Practice.* (Trends in Linguistics. Studies and Monographs 59), (pp. 109–29). Berlin, New York: Mouton de Gruyter.

Sifianou, M. (1995) Do we need to be silent to be extremely polite? Silence and FTAs. *International Journal of Applied Linguistics* 5 (1), 95–110.

Tulviste, T. (1995) Mothers' regulation of their two-year-olds' behavior in two settings. In K. Junefelt (ed.) *Activity Theory. Proceedings of the XIVth Scandinavian Conference of Linguistics and the VIIIth Conference of Nordic and General Linguistics, 16–21 August 1993* (pp. 127–37). (Gothenburg Papers in Theoretical Linguistics 73). Gothenburg: Gothenburg University Press.

Tulviste, T. (1998) How much talk is expected from Estonian children. *Trames* 2 (1), 120–29.

Vellerind, R. (2000) Lähendav viisakus müügivestluste strateegiana. *Keel ja Kirjandus* 48 (10), 703–15.

Wierzbicka, A. (1985) Different cultures, different languages, different speech acts. Polish vs. English. *Journal of Pragmatics* 9 (2), 145–58.

Chapter 15

Politeness in Poland: From 'Titlemania' to Grammaticalised Honorifics

ROMUALD HUSZCZA

Among the Slavonic languages, Polish arguably has developed the most complex and original formal categories of politeness, going well beyond lexis. However, they have been neglected in the description of Polish grammar as in Slavonic linguistics in general, mostly due to the influence of Latin as the ideal model of a universal grammatical system. The Polish school grammar, deeply rooted in this tradition, and supported by the Port Royal grammatical doctrine, totally ignored politeness phenomena, and only touched on them under stylistic varieties of spoken Polish.

If we compare Polish with languages which have highly developed grammatical and lexical politeness, such as Japanese, Korean, or Vietnamese, modern Polish looks poor and simple. Nevertheless, it possesses a regular grammatical category of honorifics within certain verbal forms and within personal pronouns on two basic levels, namely the familiar (T) and the polite (V). The number of possible levels of honorifics in Polish in general will be discussed later in this chapter. The most important difference between, for example, Japanese and Polish is that in the former the distinction between the polite and the intimate verbal forms

kak-u (I, you, he, we, they etc. write)	*versus*	*kak-imas-u* (I, you, he, we, they etc. write)
-HON		+HON
i-u (say)	*versus*	*i-imas-u* (say)
-HON		+HON
mi-ru (see)	*versus*	*mi-mas-u* (see) etc.
-HON		+HON

largely covers all verbal forms and it is not possible to address anyone directly without encoding an honorific value. In Polish, the honorific value distinction overlaps the grammatical category of person and appears mostly in the second-person, with some pragmatically limited uses in the third-person.

Historically speaking, the honorific verbal forms in Polish developed from the pronominal use of personal nouns, namely *pan* (Mr, sir, gentleman) and its feminine and plural counterparts, i.e. *pani* (madam, lady), *panowie* (gentlemen), *panie* (ladies) and *państwo*, the latter originally referring to a married couple and later changing to refer to mixed gender groups, namely 'ladies and gentlemen'. This is a rare case where a separate mixed gender subcategory develops to refer to a pair of persons of different sexes or a group of people including at least one representative of each sex. All these personal nouns started to be used pronominally with second-person verbal forms by the 19th century (*pan jesteś* [you, sir, are…] or *pan byłeś* [(you, sir were…]) and later the constituent verbs were replaced by third-person forms (*pan jest* [you, sir, are…] or *pan był* [you, sir, were…]).

In present-day Polish we have, as a result, four, functionally and formally different, homophonic lexemes:

(1) *pan* a personal noun, meaning 'a man, a gentleman'; also used as an honorific lexical equivalent of *człowiek* (a man)
cf. *Do pokoju wszedł jakiś człowiek.* *versus* *Do pokoju wszedł jakiś pan.*
(a man came into the room) (a gentleman came into the room),

(2) *pan* an honorific title or even semi-prefix of analytic character, added to other personal nouns as a politeness marker: cf. *pan dyrektor, pan doktor, pan inżynier, pan kierowca, pan woźny, pan organista*, all honorific equivalents of their single counterparts *dyrektor, doktor, inżynier, kierowca, woźny, organista* (director, physician doctor, engineer, driver, school-keeper, parish organist),

(3) *pan* honorific second-person pronoun 'you',

(4) *pan* honorific third-person pronoun 'he', used in the presence of the person spoken about.

Each of these lexemes has its own properties that allow us to distinguish personal pronouns from nouns and titular semi-prefixes. The noun *pan* can be omitted or replaced by the anaphoric pronoun *on* (he), neutral as to its honorific value. The noun *pan* is used in conjunction with the demonstrative pronoun *ten pan* (this gentleman) or with attributive adjectives *miły pan* (nice gentleman), while the pronoun *pan* cannot appear in such constructions (the only acceptable construction uses predicative adjectives *Pan jest miły* (You are nice)). In nominal uses of *pan* and its morphemic derivatives in the third-person declarative, the noun can be omitted through ellipsis. However, the pronoun *pan* and its derivatives, either in second or third-person, cannot be omitted and must be repeated until completion of the utterance.

Widziałem ***go*** *przez chwilę.* Nominal use of *pan*
cf. *Przyszedł jakiś* ***pan****. Postał chwilę a poten spojrzał, na zegarek.*
(*A man* came in. *He* was standing for a while and then looked at his watch. I saw *him* for a moment.)

Pronominal use of *pan*
O, już ***pan*** *przyszedł? Dlaczego spogląda* ***pan*** *na zegarek?*
Tak dawno ***pana*** *tu nie było. W zeszłym roku widziałem* ***pana*** *tylko przez chwilę.* (Oh, you have come! Why you look at watch? You have not been here for so long. Last year I saw you only for a moment).

Even more important is the way in which the syntactic and morphemic rules allow the second and third-person to be differentiated. The second-person forms can appear in both regular and reversed order, namely *pan ma* and *ma pan* (you have), while the third-person forms cannot be reversed, i.e. *pan ma* (he has). The second-person pronoun *pan* has, in addition to the genitive, an adjectival form *pański* while the third-person pronoun *pan* can only be used in the genitive: *pana*. The personal pronoun *pan* has an analytic form of the vocative: *proszę pana!*, while its titular counterpart has a synthetic form, i.e. *panie (doktorze, inżynierze, kierowco, etc.)*. In the spoken Polish of less educated people one also hears the synthetic vocative form of *panie*, together with a second-person verbal form, cf. *Panie, masz pan papierosa?* (Do you have a cigarette?) which is at present perceived as strongly non-standard and even impolite but formerly, as already mentioned, it was a spoken honorific form, only slightly informal in tone.

All the *pan* lexemes quoted earlier have inflectional forms in the masculine and the plural.

Thus, the possible equivalents of the English *you* in second-person verbal phrases in Polish are:

(1) *(ty) piszesz* (you write) –HON +SG	*versus*	*pan pisze* (you write, sir) +MASC +HON+2P+SG. *pani pisze* (you write, madam) +FEM +HON +2P+SG
(2) *(wy) piszecie* (you write) –HON+PL	*versus*	*panowie piszą* (you write, gentlemen) +MASC +HON+2P+PL *panie piszą* (you write, ladies) +FEM +HON+2P+PL *państwo piszą* (you write, Ladies and gentlemen, Sir and Madam, etc.) +MIX GEN+HON+2P+PL

(3) *(ty) mówisz* (you say) *versus* *pan mówi* (you say, sir)
–HON+SG +MASC+HON+2P+SG
pani mówi (you say, madam)
+FEM+HON+2P+SG

(4) *(wy) mówicie* (you say) *versus* *panowie mówią* (you say, gentlemen)
–HON+PL +MASC+HON+2P +PL
panie mówią (you say, ladies)
+FEM+HON+2P +PL
państwo mówią (you say, Ladies and gentlemen, etc.)
+MIX GEN+HON+2P +PL

The set of honorific forms on the right can also be used to refer to a third-person participating in the act of communication not as an addressee but as a hearer spoken about, since the otherwise neutral third-person pronouns:

on (he) (+SG +MASC)
ona (she) (+SG +FEM)
oni (they) (+PL +MASC)
one (they) (+PL +FEM)

are communicatively unsuitable for direct interpersonal use due to their strictly familiar semantic value.

We should mention one further aspect of these plural honorifics connected strictly with the interpretation of the grammatical category of person and its markers. As we can see, honorific pronouns in standard Polish require verbal forms homophonic with those of the third-person, which here must be treated as the second-person even though historically they all belonged to the third-person paradigm. Therefore, the so-called third-person form addressative use must be included entirely in the second-person verbal paradigm. There are at least two reasons for this.

First, the honorific pronouns *pan, pani, panowie, panie, państwo* are inseparable from the verb and are in fact analytic second-person inflectional forms. Second, in modern standard Polish there are other, parallel, plural honorifics consisting of second-person verbal forms connected with *państwo, panie, panowie*. Therefore, apart from uses such as:

państwo mają you have, ladies and gentlemen, sir and madam, etc.
+MIX GEN+HON+2P+PL

panowie mają you have, gentlemen

	+MASC+HON+2P+PL
panie mają	you have, ladies +FEM+HON+2P+PL

we have also more familiar but still polite forms such as:

państwo macie	you have, ladies and gentlemen, sir and madam, etc. +MIX GEN+HON+2P+PL
panowie macie	you have, gentlemen +MASC+HON+2P+PL
panie macie	you have, ladies +FEM+HON+2P+PL

Unlike the non-standard 2.sg. uses, such as *pan jesteś, pan masz,* the use of 2.pl. verbs combined with honorific pronouns belongs to modern standard spoken Polish and connotes a degree of intimacy and informality. Thus, the set of forms described earlier must be enlarged to include three additional 2.pl.forms:

panowie piszecie	you write, gentlemen +MASC+HON+2P +PL
panie piszecie	you write, ladies +FEM+HON+2P+PL
państwo piszecie	you write, ladies and gentlemen, sir and madam, etc. +MIX GEN+HON+2P+PL

These forms are more colloquial and are used frequently in everyday speech. Thus, in the honorific 2.pl. paradigm, we have two slightly different V forms: more formal (V^1) and less formal (V^2).

When we compare Polish politeness with other European and non-European languages, we have to be aware that, on the one hand, it developed in a socially and culturally different environment while, on the other, it has been influenced in many ways from outside due to historical contacts with neighbouring languages, near and far. Thus, there are basic sociolinguistic differences between Polish and these other languages in the semantic content of the honorifics and the pragmatic models of linguistically manifested polite behaviour. Nevertheless, the relationship between the social environment and the shape and scope of the linguistic category in question cannot be explained merely as a case of direct influence.

Students of the Confucian tradition and its role in the development of honorifics in East Asian languages know that the language of the country where this tradition originates has the poorest system of honorifics in East Asia. Even if there are certain parallelisms between modern Chinese and Japanese or Vietnamese in the pronominal use of family terms or professional titles, Japanese now has the largest number of honorific levels in the world. This does not mean that the traditional Confucian hierarchy of social rank has disappeared in China. However, any natural language is itself an autonomous system and usually develops more independently of its direct social environment than might be expected. All the semiotic values present in a civilisation are not necessarily internalised into the grammatical system of its language. Thus, we cannot say that the Japanese system of honorifics is more Confucian than the Chinese even if it is more complex in terms of linguistic structure.

The same point arises in the Polish context: the role of the nobility and gentry and their culture are unquestionably a historic source of modern Polish politeness, with the present-day honorific pronoun *pan* being etymologically derived from the old word for 'lord'; however, it can hardly be seen as its direct reflection in today's language.

In dealing with pragmatic and grammatical aspects of politeness, the former can be clearly observed within address theory. Let us start with nominal forms in the vocative used phatically. These normally tend to be seen as markers of the social status of the speaker, listener or referent of the utterance. In Polish, however, the verbal category of honorifics is at the core of politeness with no direct link to social categories. It is true that the appropriate use of the grammatical honorific forms requires from the speaker a keen judgement as to the relative social status of self, the listener and, in certain situations, the person spoken about. Nevertheless, the category of honorifics is based on a notion of social rank (or status) in a pragmatic rather than a purely sociological sense.

The speaker decides what rank, higher or lower, to confer on the person spoken to or about. The inventory of ranks is not a closed one that can be labelled in clear-cut terms: it is a set of pragmatic oppositions of the higher–lower type. The very act of rank-conferment can be seen as a pragmatic gesture of rank elevation (or lowering) through linguistic distinction between levels of formality and deference.

Here, we should mention the largely universal phenomenon of pragmatic modesty directed towards the speaker (see Bencze, this volume). In linguistic etiquette, in general, we find certain important pragmatic rules. The most characteristic concerns the relationship between the speaker and the hearer who is not the addressee and is shown in the frequent symbolic lowering of the rank of the former and elevating of the rank of the latter. For example, in the speech of traditionally educated Polish waiters, shopkeepers, shop-assistants and customer-service personnel, there is an honorific use of nominal diminutives when referring to items provided or about to be provided to the customer. Thus, the social roles of the customers and the service personnel are encoded in honorific quasi-diminutive forms like

Książeczka już zapłacona (The book [you have kindly bought] is already paid for.)
Dzisiejsza gazetka dla pana! (Today's paper for you, sir!)
Już podaję kapelusik i płaszczyk (Here you have your hat and coat)
Taksóweczka zaraz będzie (Your taxi is coming soon.)
Już podaję zupkę (Just in a moment I will bring your soup.)
Ma być winko czy wódeczka? (You ordered wine or vodka?)
Mamy tylko pojedynczy pokoik (All we have is only single room.)
Życzy pan sobie mydełko? (Would you have a soap?)

These are opposed to neutral non-diminutive forms like *książka* (a book), *gazeta* (a newspaper), *kapelusz* (a hat), *taksówka* (a taxi), *zupa* (soup), *wódka* (vodka), *wino* (wine), *płaszcz* (coat), *mydło* (soap), *pokój* (room).

This behaviour also includes linguistic gestures of politeness such as rejections of compliments (cf. Polish *ależ nie!*, *bynajmniej!* [not at all]), of thanks (cf. Polish *Nie ma za co* [lit.'there is nothing to be thanked for'] as a reaction to *Dziękuję* [thank you]) and as indirect modesty (first person in form), positive appraisal of the opportunity to meet the addressee, talk or be introduced to them, etc. (cf. *Miałem zaszczyt już pana/panią spotkać* [I have already had the honour of meeting you, sir/madam], *To dla mnie zaszczyt/duża przyjemność* [It's an honour/ great pleasure for me], etc.).

Equally universal is positive appraisal of addressees, elevating their social or situational rank. One characteristic gesture is to ascribe the pragmatic role of grantor to the addressee and the role of beneficiary to the speaker. Thus, the speaker pragmatically acts as beneficiary of the addressee's will, generosity, acceptance, tolerance.

Pozwolę sobie zauważyć , że… (lit. I should let myself notice, that..., i.e. let me say, that…)

Za łaskawym pozwoleniem or *Za pozwoleniem, proszę mi (łaskawie) pozwolić, abym* (please kindly let me… [say or do something])

Mam nadzieję, iż zgodzą się państwo (na tę niewielką zamianę.) (I hope that you, ladies and gentlemen, will accept this small change)

The pragmatic role of beneficiary of the volition of the addressee is also a sort of politeness gesture, shown by the verb *zechcieć* (lit. to want, to wish) in imperative or formally interrogative requests:

Zechce pan/pani przyjść trochę, później. (Please, come later [sir, madam])
Może zechce pan/pani przyjść trochę, później. (Would you like to come later [sir, madam])
Czy zechciałby pan/zechciałaby pani przyjść trochę później? (Maybe, you would like to come later [sir, madam])
Czy nie zechciałby pan/nie zechciałaby pani przyjść trochę później? (Wouldn't you come later [sir, madam]?)

The verb *przyjść* (to come) can be replaced by its polite lexical equivalent, namely *pofatygować się,*, which (in its basic lexical form *fatygować się* [to trouble, to bother (oneself]), is a general verb used to positively appraise somebody's efforts and to ascribe to an addressee or someone spoken about the pragmatic role of donor or grantor, complimenting them on the trouble they have taken.

Czy nie zechciałby pan pofatygować się do nas osobiście? (Would you kindly bother yourself to come here in person?)

There are a number of phatic expressions and grammatical forms which are either central or peripheral to Polish politeness. Let us first distinguish forms of address and personal pronouns and then characterise their honorific level and sociopragmatic properties. Polish forms of address consist of vocative uses of personal nouns and proper names used as phatic signals to begin an utterance or inserted as a sort of interjection within it.

There are several categories of these, differing in their degree of honorific-marking:

(1) Extremely formal and solemn openings of official speeches, addresses, toasts etc., cf. *Ekscelencjo Panie Prezydencie* (*Panie Premierze; Księże Biskupie*) (Your Excellency the President [Prime Minister; Bishop]), *Eminencjo Księże Kardynale* (*Księże Prymasie*) (Your Eminence the Most Reverend Cardinal [Primate]), *Magnificencjo* – used to university rectors, *Wysoki Sejmie, Wysoki Senacie, Wysoka Izbo* – to the parliament when in session, *Wysoki Sądzie* – to a court in session, *Wasza Cesarska (Królewska) Mość* (Your Imperial [Royal] Majesty). In such address forms, certain complimentary or rank-elevating adjectives such as *Szanowny Panie Prezydencie* (lit. Most Esteemed President), *Czcigodny (Przewielebny) Księże Biskupie* (Reverend Bishop), *Wysoka Rado* (lit. High Council) appear. They are, however, in most cases omitted in the pronominal use of these titles, and replaced in written style by attributive personal pronouns: *Wasza Ekscelencja miał* (Your Excellency had +MASC), *Jego Ekscelencja miał* (His Excellency had +MASC.), *Jego Magnificencja miał* – to rectors, never used with second person attributive pronouns, etc.

(2) Professional titles with the titular honorific *pan* added before the noun, cf. *panie dyrektorze, panie profesorze, panie ambasadorze, panie kierowco* (masc.), *pani doktor, pani profesor, pani minister* (fem.),
(3) Vocative forms of honorific pronouns, cf. *Proszę pana!* (Sir!), *Proszę pani!* (Madame!), *Prosze panów!* (Gentlemen!), *Proszę pań!* (Ladies!), *Proszę państwa!* (Ladies and gentlemen!) (to a pair or group as discussed earlier, *Proszę księdza!* (Father!) (to priests)
(4) Vocative honorific forms of proper names, used mostly with first names, since last names used in this form sound impolite in Polish and are a marker of power or deference toward the addressee by failing to mention or even by denying their professional position, cf. *panie Jakubie, pani Barbaro* (Jacob!, Barbara!), as opposed to the extremely rare *panie Jankowski!* (Mr Jankowski!). These forms are frequently made more familiar by the use of diminutives, cf. *panie Janie* (*panie Janku, panie Jasiu, Jaśku*, (John!, Johnny!), *pani Basiu* (*pani Basieńko*, etc.) in contrast to vocative surnames without a title such as *Jankowski!*, e.g. as used by teachers with familiar vocative first names to pupils as a demonstration of power.

The nominal vocatives quoted earlier are included in the lexical category of politeness, as are certain lexical pairs of nouns and verbs:

rank-elevating lexeme	*versus*	neutral lexeme
(pana) godność (Your) last name	*versus*	*(moje) nazwisko* (my) last name
spocząć to (kindly) sit down	*versus*	*usiąść* to sit down
(pańska) małżonka Your wife	*versus*	*(moja) żona* my wife
(pani) małżonek Your husband	*versus*	*(mój) mąż* my husband

In modern use, honorific distinction of individual words in this way is very rare and has been replaced by stylistic (familiar *versus* official style) or grammatical markers.

The most important feature of Polish honorific pronouns and pronominal nouns is that the use of names in this function is not accepted in modern standard speech. The V pronouns (Brown & Gilman, 1960) form practically an open set of forms (including quasi-pronouns or pronominal uses of personal nouns). They include titular *pan* or *pani* combined with a professional, social or situational title and are used in both the second and third-persons.

O której pan/pani doktor tu przyjdzie?
What time will you come here?
(a second-person formal pronoun for physicians)

Czy pan/pani mecenas już jest?
Has he/she come?
(a third-person formal pronoun for lawyers)

Czy pan/pani redaktor o tym nie wie?
Don't you know that?
(a second-person formal pronoun for journalists, editors, TV presenters, etc.)

Among the ordinary honorific pronouns, there are separate forms used to speak to a priest, namely *ksiądz* (father), to a nun or nurse (*siostra*). While it is quite acceptable to replace *siostra* with *pani* in the case of nurses, it is not acceptable when talking to nuns or to use *ksiądz* with *pan* when talking to a priest.

As a core element of Polish politeness, we can now systematise honorific levels within personal pronouns:

The intimate level (T)
ty – HON +2P+SG
wy – HON +2P+PL

These are, however, marked as neutral when used reciprocally between children, relatives, students, soldiers and young people.

Recently the use of T has expanded but radical abuses of these forms in Polish TV programmes which imitate their American counterparts (quiz-games etc.), are commonly criticized by TV viewers, e.g. when a presenter addresses older participants with *ty*. In the same genre broadcast in Japan the analogous 'familiarisation' of honorific pronouns has proved impossible and the V forms are commonly used there.

The honorific level (V^1)
pan + HON +2P +SG
pani + HON +2P +SG
państwo + HON +2P +MIX GEN +PL
panie + HON +2P +FEM +PL
panowie + HON +2P +MASC +PL

and their extended particular equivalents such as *ksiądz* (father, lit. priest), *brat* (friar), *ojciec* (father), *siostra* (sister – to nuns or to nurses) with non-reciprocal titular pronouns used within the family by the older generation of Poles to address adult relatives of higher rank:

babcia (grandmother) used by grandchildren
ciocia (auntie) used by nephews and nieces
wujek (uncle) used by nephews and nieces
mama (mum)
tata, tatuś (dad) used by children.

In the 1950s, the communist authorities tried to introduce 'less bourgeois and more democratic' pronominal forms. Among the party cadres and members, use of the plural form *wy* in conjunction with 2.pl. verbs was obligatory together with the vocative and titular uses of *towarzysz* (comrade), cf. *Wy, towarzyszu, macie* (You, comrade, have). However, for non-party members, another pronoun, namely *obywatel* (citizen), was introduced for both functions. From the inflectional point of view, it was inconvenient to use *wy* with *obywatel* in the vocative (*Wy, obywatelu, macie* 'You, citizen, have') and it was replaced by the inflectional form clearly after the pronominal *pan* (*obywatel ma* (you have +MASC.), *obywatelka ma* (you have +FEM)). Used non-reciprocally by those in power – since among common Poles it was avoided as alien – this form quickly became marked as a pronoun of power in the political sense, albeit not in the sociocultural sense. The position of *pan* was, thus, strengthened and even a parallel form appeared, based on *pan*, e.g. *towarzysz ma* (you, comrade, have) in conjunction with the originally 3.sg. verbs or both 2.pl. and 3.pl. forms to *towarzysz* (comrade, within the party environment):

Towarzysze mają (you, comrades, have)
Towarzysze macie (you, comrades, have)

At the beginning of the 1990s, these officially promoted forms disappeared from use.

The higher honorific level (V^2)

This level includes the aforementioned 'compound' pronouns consisting of titular or prefixal *pan* in conjunction with professional titles:

Pan minister – Minister
Pan premier – Prime Minister
Pan dyrektor – Director
Pan kierowca – driver

Pan doktor – doctor
Pan redaktor – editor, journalist
Pan mecenas – lawyer (as opposed to common name of the profession *adwokat*)

All these forms are perceived as exceptionally formal, official (to the addressee) or self-abasing (for the speaker) and are peripheral to Polish politeness today. One aspect of their use, felt by Polish speakers to be inconvenient, is the distinction between masculine and feminine in titular *pan, pani,* combined with the originally masculine professional title which is inflected with Ø to mark it for feminine.

Pani doktor ma (You have)
Pani doktor miała (You had)
Czekam na panią doktor (I am waiting for you, etc).

From an interpersonal perspective, we can see that Polish honorifics enjoy a degree of interactivity that accounts primarily for their grammaticalisation. The strongest degree of interactivity is in the second-person because there is direct interaction between speaker and addressee. Both the subject of the verbal form in such constructions and the referent in other forms marked for second-person, such as personal pronouns used outside the predicate (i.e. in objective or attributive uses), are explicitly indicated as addressee. This may explain why the second-person honorific forms are central to this category. Honorific pragmatics in Polish is consequently a pragmatics of persons.

HIGHER DEGREE OF INTERACTIVITY

2P SG

-HON	+HON
(ty) masz	*pan ma* *pani ma*

2P PL

-HON	+HON
(wy) macie	*panie mają* *panowie mają* *państwo mają*
Implicit person	Explicit person
(I)	YOU have
The speaker →	The addressee

LOWER DEGREE OF INTERACTIVITY

3P SG

-HON	+HON
(on) ma	*pan ma* +MASC
(ona) ma	*pani ma* +FEM

3P PL

-HON	+HON
(one) mają	*panie mają* +FEM
(oni) mają	*panowie mają* +MASC
(oni) mają	*państwo mają* +MIX GEN

Implicit person		Explicit person
(I)	→	HE, SHE, THEY the hearer(s) spoken about

This figure shows particular communicative situations which determine the choice of honorific either to the addressee or about a hearer present at the time of utterance. The high degree of interactivity here stems from the fact that the speaker can look the addressee in the face and observe any immediate reaction, as is also the case with the hearer spoken about when present.

Pragmatically speaking, all these elements, regardless of whether they are pronouns or pronominal uses of nouns, are usually accompanied by pointing gestures such as looking at somebody's face, directing eyes or face (second person pronouns), pointing at somebody, turning one's head towards somebody (third person pronouns) and so on. This is reflected in the well-known logico-linguistic distinction between anaphoric and deictic pronouns. However, it concerns third person pronouns only since the first and second person pronouns are used solely for deictic purposes. The very use of the first person pronoun serves as an indicating gesture. Second person pronouns are also always used together with addressing gestures, such as looking the addressee in the face, calling a partner by name, title and so on. In this respect, when speakers address their utterances to an individual addressee within a group of hearers, their choice of honorific form can also be interpreted as an indicating gesture of this kind.

In the speech acts of commanding and requesting, the most commonly used structures are imperatives, similar in Polish to the second person, and which, as we have seen, are highly interactive. The imperative mood is pragmatically close in meaning to directive utterances, since the speaker uses it to show stronger or weaker power of influence. In present-day speech, we can distinguish at least four honorific levels in requesting and commanding:

Familiar level

+SG	+PL	
(ty) pisz!	*(wy) piszcie!*	write!

Honorific marking at this level corresponds to T. Therefore, imperatives of this kind used to non-familiar addressees sound extremely impolite and may appear to display anger or a form of verbal aggression in situations of conflict. The distinction between a command and a request is here effected by means of intonation contour, the command having a short and falling contour while the request is prolonged and slightly rising. In the traditional school grammar this was, strictly speaking, the only inflectional form of the imperative included in the verbal paradigm.

Apart from these uses, there are also honorific second person imperatives consisting of the preposition *niech* (let), a V^1 or V^2 honorific pronoun and a verb in honorific second-person (i.e. old third-person).

Honorific level A (relatively polite)

+SG	+PL
niech pan pisze! +MASC	*niech panowie piszą!* +MASC
	please, write!
niech pani pisze! +FEM	*niech panie piszą!* +FEM

In traditional grammar, this was regarded as a third-person imperative, contrary to both pragmatic and grammatical reality. The proper third-person imperative can only be used with personal nouns or names but its imperative function is indirect in utterances where the referent cannot be the addressee, cf. *Niech pan dyrektor (pan dyrektor Kowalski) do mnie zatelefonuje* (Please, tell the director (Kowalski) to call me) and the interactive command or request refers to the fact of telling and not of calling.

Honorific level B

+SG/PL	
proszę pisać!	please, write!

This form is felt to be a slightly more polite use of the imperative and consists of the preposition *proszę*, which was originally a 1.sg. form of the verb *prosić* (I ask) but in modern speech it is an entirely grammaticalised imperative marker of analytic character.

Honorific level C

+SG +MASC
pan będzie łaskaw / uprzejmy pisać! (please, write!)

+SG +FEM
pani będzie łaskawa / uprzejma pisać! (please, write!)
+PL +MASC
panowie będą łaskawi / uprzejmi pisać! (please, write!)

+PL +FEM
panie będę łaskawe / uprzejme pisać! (please, write!)

+PL +MIX GEN
państwo będą łaskawi / uprzejmi pisać! (please, write!)

This level is perceived as very polite and on occasion ceremonial, due to the self-abasement of the speaker and rank elevation of the addressee in the use of adjectives such as *łaskaw* (gracious) and *uprzejmy* (kind). The formal future analytic form *...będzie / będę ... pisać* (will write) is here accompanied by an imperative intonation and therefore cannot be interpreted as a declarative. Similar intonation is used in spoken commands which omit *niech*:

niech pan pisze	→	*pan pisze*	write, please +SG +MASC
niech pani zobaczy	→	*pani zobaczy*	look, please +SG +FEM
niech państwo mówią	→	*państwo mówią*	speak, please +PL +MIX GEN

In spoken Polish these forms are frequently heard along with the plural verbal imperative of the second-person added to honorific pronouns:

Siadajcie państwo (Sit down, ladies and gentlemen)
Siadajcie panie (Sit down, ladies)
Siadajcie panowie (Sit down, gentlemen)

Just like the declaratives, these imperatives, in conjunction with honorific personal pronouns, are analytic inflectional forms and their pronominal constituents cannot be omitted.

In modern Polish, there are some clear traces of a systemic conflict between grammatical person and pragmatic person and between grammatical and natural gender leading to violations of grammatical and pragmatic rules. It is pragmatics, however, that plays the decisive role in the gradual systemic resolution of this conflict. This is why the grammatically neutral gender is pragmatically absent in interpersonal communication and never used except in some declaratives (cf. *dziecko – ono miało* child neut. pron. had). This is also why the original meaning of *państwo*, semantically dominated somehow by the masculine (in its subordinate verb also), changed to mixed gender in both pronominal and titular uses, cf. *państwo studenci, państwo profesorowie, państwo dyrektorzy* used for addressing students, professors, directors of both sexes.

In general, then, politeness in Polish is a strongly titular category: the opposition between the sexes is clearly apparent in gender distinctions and the expansion of mixed gender forms seeks a sort of gender equality. For example, the verbal form in *państwo mieli*, namely *mieli*, contrary to current interpretation, must also be interpreted as a mixed gender marking, i.e. +pl.+mix gen and not as +masc. +human +pl. Traditional Polish 'titlemania' is thus gradually decreasing and Polish is moving towards a more transparent, grammaticalised system of honorifics.

References

Brown, R. and Gilman, A. (1960) The pronouns of power and solidarity. In T. A. Sebeok, (ed.) *Style in Language* (pp. 253–76). Cambridge, MA.: MIT Press.

Huszcza, R. (1980) O gramatyce grzeczności. *Pamiętnik Literacki* LXXI, 1. Wrocław: Ossolineum.

Huszcza, R. (1996) *Honoryfiktywność. Gramatyka. Pragmatyka. Typologia.* Warsaw: Wydawnictwo Akademickie Dialog.

Łaziński, M. (2000) *Pan ksiądz* i inni panowie. Wtórna funkcja lekceżaca jednostki *pan*. In *Poradnik językowy*. Wydawnictwa Uniwersytetu Warsaw: Warszawskiego.

Marcjanik, M. (1997) *Polska grzeczność językowa*. Kielce: Wyższa Szkoa Pedagogiczna im. Jana Kochanowskiego.

Stone, G. (1987) Polish. In B. Comrie (ed.) *The World's Major Languages* (pp. 348–66). London: Croom Helm.

Chapter 16

Politeness in Hungary: Uncertainty in a Changing Society

LÓRÁNT BENCZE

Introduction

In analysing politeness, this study attempts to incorporate not only (socio)linguistic and pragmatic aspects but also a rhetorical perspective, i.e. it is a part of a sociopragmatic approach examining how the individual tries to be effective in a given situation within the frame of historical and social change and how this effort influences stylistic choices in language and behaviour (Leech, 1980). In this analysis we outline the social context and analyse some naturally-occurring data in Hungarian. The extracts we use are followed first by a 'morpheme for morpheme' English translation (marked with an asterisk) for non-native speakers of Hungarian and then by an English equivalent.

At the turn of the 21st century, society in the Hungarian Republic seems split equally and strikingly into two groups and the division is not by generation. One group can be labelled 'the traditional cultural paradigm' and the other 'the recent cultural paradigm' (cf. Bencze *et al.*, 1999). The split is reflected in every aspect and in every manifestation of society, from language use to moral behaviour, from the way people dress to their membership of political parties and, last but not least, from politeness to impoliteness. Members of one group cannot understand members of the other group almost as if they did not speak the same mother tongue. The communication of the 'traditional paradigm' group is, in a sense, a discernment-oriented, closed communication. That of the 'new paradigm' group is a kind of volition-oriented, open one. There are little or no shared values between the two groups. They do not have a shared knowledge of philosophical ideas or a shared system of social rules and cultural maxims (Eelen, 2001:131). Consequently the intension and the extension of international technical terms, for example, can be totally different in contemporary Hungarian to what is the case in contemporary English or German. In contemporary Hungarian, 'liberal' can denote 'extreme left-wing communist' or 'anarchist', 'socialist' can denote 'liberal capitalist', 'national' can denote 'extreme nationalist'. I happened to be present when a husband (a Protestant university professor) mortally offended his wife (a Catholic artist) saying 'You are a liberal'. The wife burst into tears and later wanted to get a divorce. The pragmatic force of the sentence 'You are a liberal' had probably been 'You are lying, deceptive, impudent', etc.

There are two sets of social norms and this is *ab ovo* confusing. Communication loses its very essence if it becomes useless non-communication because information is not interpreted properly or mediated at all. Consequently, it is extremely difficult for foreigners to get their bearings in Hungary's contemporary society, politics and media. Misunderstandings are dangerously frequent both in the western and Hungarian media. By 'dangerously frequent', I mean that communication between these two paradigms does not appear to be a dialogue but rather two monologues. It deviates almost entirely from Gricean maxims, and conversational implicatures often cannot be followed by participants. The twin concepts of politeness and impoliteness are defined totally differently by the two groups in question. For the traditional paradigm group, politeness is a system of moral and societal norms. For the new paradigm group, politeness is instrumental (see later and Eelen, 2001: 10). This results in interaction where there is friction and which is characterised by a maximisation of 'the potential conflict and confrontation inherent in all human interchange' (Lakoff, 1990: 34, cited by Eelen, 2001: 2). A typical example can be seen in the early 1990s in the Hungarian Parliament during a left-wing opposition speech. A member of the right shouted:

Hordót a szónok<u>nak</u>!
| \ | \
* Barrel the speaker <u>to</u>!
A soapbox to the speaker!

The pragmatic meaning of the shout was that the speaker was a demagogue.

After some weeks, some left-wing members of the Parliament protested that the utterance was anti-Semitic for they had 'actually' heard:

Hordót a zsidónak!
A soapbox to the Jew!

The two expressions ('to the speaker', 'to the Jew') happen to sound similar in Hungarian.

This social divide is also reflected in several expressions and uncertainties of politeness, in similar misunderstandings and misinterpretations which are governed by the presuppositions and prejudices of a social paradigm and not by phonetic or other facts. People are generally inclined to hear what they want to hear and not to hear what is really uttered. On several occasions, Latin texts at a particular college were printed with mistakes. It was teachers who could not read Latin who found the mistakes not the teachers of Latin. People are generally inclined to see what they want to see and not what can really be seen. I shall now consider a number of uncertainties and confusions in politeness caused by the parallel existence of two paradigms. First of all, let us consider address.

Comrade *versus* Mr/Sir

The Hungarian word for 'comrade' is *elvtárs* and is a compound: *elv* (principle, policy, maxim) + *társ* (companion, fellow, partner). This was the obligatory form of address during communism. It followed the last name or sometimes the position or the profession of the addressee:

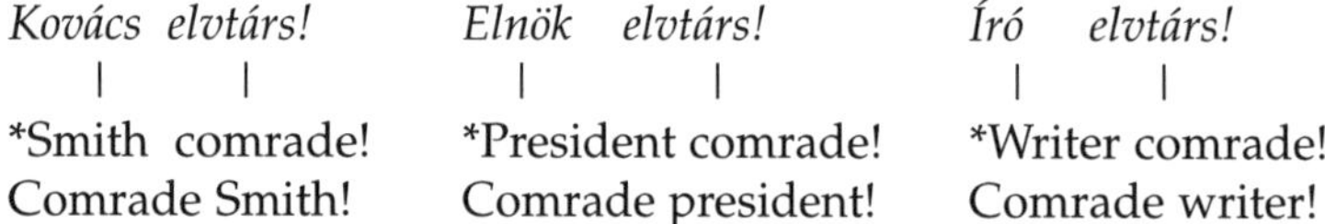

Kovács elvtárs!	*Elnök elvtárs!*	*Író elvtárs!*
| |	| |	| |
*Smith comrade!	*President comrade!	*Writer comrade!
Comrade Smith!	Comrade president!	Comrade writer!

'Comrade' replaced the former 'Mr, sir, gentleman'. The Hungarian word *úr* means 'Mister, gentleman, sir, lord, master, husband' (in old Hungarian it only meant 'king'). It was looked upon as a sign of decadent bourgeois society, of feudalism and of capitalism. It is ironic that after the 1970s when the Communist dictatorship was gradually weakening and artisans like plumbers, electricians, etc. were allowed to work privately again, they were called *úr* (Mr, sir):

Kovács úr
| |
*Smith Mr
Mr Smith

but all other people remained 'comrades'. Along with artisans, medical doctors also remained *úr* (*doktor úr* – * doctor Mr, *Herr Doktor*). The reason for this was probably that people, even communists, were anxious about their health and it was wiser to honour doctors with the old title than to call them 'comrades'. In the first half of the 20th century the use of *úr* without mention of rank was derogatory. It became neutral and started to mean 'Mr' (*Herr*) at the same time as its afore-mentioned revival in the 1970s.

Since the democratic transformation of the 1990s, most communist clerks have kept their office. They had no memory of how, in traditional

Hungarian culture before communism, the word *úr* (Mr, sir, gentleman, lord) had been used. So they simply replaced *elvtárs* (comrade) with *úr* (Mr, sir, gentleman). This led to a curious new mixture of two language uses which irritates people of the traditional cultural paradigm and is a part of the new paradigm.

Old paradigm:

Kovács (József) elnök úr
| | |
*Smith (József) president Mister
President (Joseph) Smith

Tisztelt Elnök Úr!
| | |
* Honoured President Mister!
Dear President

Tisztelt Professor Úr!
| | |
* Honoured Professor Mister!
Dear Sir

Communist paradigm:

Kovács (József) elvtárs, oktatási miniszter
| | | |
* Smith (Joseph) comrade, educational minister
Comrade Smith, Minister of Education

Tisztelt Kovács Elvtárs!
| | |
* Honoured Smith Comrade!
Dear Comrade Smith

New paradigm:

Kovács József úr, oktatási miniszter
| | | |
* Smith Joseph mister, educational minister
Mister Joseph Smith, Minister of Education

Tisztelt Kovács Úr!
| | |
*Honoured Smith Mister!
Dear Mister Smith

The address forms used by the new paradigm are considered rather rude by people of the old paradigm.

Formal and Informal Address as Strategic Choices

There once was a university professor who was in conflict with the government, mainly with one minister in particular. This conflict led to increasing communication between them. The communication led to the sharing of ideas and, after some time, to the mutual recognition that they were both on the same side. One day the professor was informed that the minister had been made president of his party. At a reception, the professor asked the minister who would be his replacement. The minister answered, 'Bill'. The fact that he called Mr William Brandy, the minister elect, by his nickname was a sign that the professor was no longer an opponent or an outsider but belonged to the inner circle of the government. Within a week, the professor was invited to have a desk in the Cabinet of the new minister.

This is one example of formal and informal speech events in which nicknames and official titles can be used according to situation and strategic aims; here senior clerks were speaking at meetings of this ministry. (The afore-mentioned professor collected the corpus for this chapter. Names have obviously been changed to preserve anonymity.) The chairman of the meetings was always a deputy Under-Secretary. The address expressed the following points:

(1) the distance or proximity of a clerk to the boss and to other clerks,
(2) momentary conflict of opinions,
(3) anticipated results of approaching national elections and
(4) manipulative politeness.

We shall see that address can be set in a system of coordinates of 'solidarity and hierarchy'.

Distance and Proximity

When the (deputy) Head of Department wanted to express proximity to the deputy Under-Secretary, he or she called him by his first name, *János* (John). The deputy Under-Secretary, however, called the deputy Head of Department by her nickname; e.g. *Bözsi* (Betty), and not by her first name *Erzsébet* (Elisabeth). In this situation, the difference signifies both a friendly relationship and dominance, i.e. it stresses an asymmetric relationship as well as acting as a face-saving action.

Once another deputy Under-Secretary turned up at a meeting. The deputy Head of Department called him *Józsi bácsi* (Uncle Joe) in his absence, yet at the same time, she called her boss, the deputy Under-Secretary, who was present, 'William'. *Józsi bácsi* (Uncle Joe) was responsible for finance at the Ministry. Consequently, he had more power as deputy Under-Secretary than other deputy Under-Secretaries. The use of his nickname was also a face-saving action on the part of the deputy Head of Department. It emphasised the fact not only that the deputy Head of Department was on good terms with the powerful deputy Under-Secretary but it also informed her boss, the deputy Under-Secretary, and her colleagues, that she had more power in her position than they might expect.

A permanent Under-Secretary in the new democracy of the Hungarian Republic is not really 'permanent' because he or she is replaced when a new government is elected. This means that a permanent Under-Secretary is not simply responsible for administration but has political power. On one particular occasion, the permanent Under-Secretary entered a meeting unexpectedly. He was addressed by the (deputy) Heads of Departments as *államtitkár úr* (state-secretary mister – Mr Under-Secretary) but, at the same time, the deputy Under-Secretary was addressed as *Vilmos* (William). This difference expressed both polite subjugation to the permanent Under-Secretary and, at the same time, informed the permanent Under-Secretary that 'We are on good terms with our boss'; 'We are a good team'; 'You do not belong to our team'. When the permanent Under-Secretary left the room, he was called by his first and last name(s) only: *Barna Róbert Sándor* (Robert Alexander Brown). Referring to somebody by first and last name is somewhat ironic and is a distancing strategy. This is especially true of one who is in power. At other times this permanent Under-Secretary and his clerks were referred to as *the Barna Róbert Sándorék* (the Robert Alexander Browns). This expressed distancing in that they were looked upon as 'another family'.

On one occasion, four top members of the Cabinet met and discussed the fact that the Minister, *William Brandy,* was isolated within the Ministry. The discussion gradually grew into a hot debate and someone shouted: 'Is there any senior clerk at the Ministry who supports [*the] Brandy?' The use of the last name with the definite article signifies that the speaker is on good terms with the Minister and also that the Minister is somebody who has a high position of authority and is not present. In certain situations, the definite article used with the last name can express hostility but it always includes the features 'authority' and 'not present'.

Senior clerks who previously had been university professors and who had kept their chairs continued to be addressed as they had been previously, not as

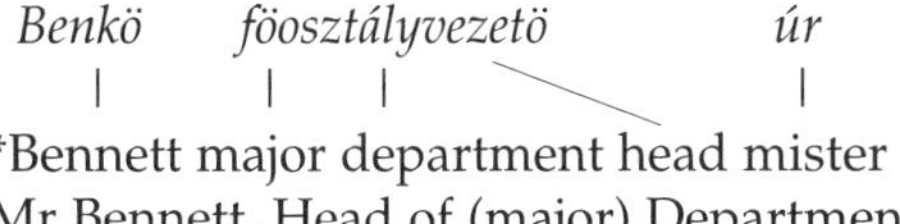
Benkö főosztályvezetö úr
*Bennett major department head mister
Mr Bennett, Head of (major) Department

but as

Benkö professzor úr
| | |
*Bennett professor mister
Professor Bennett

Heads of Departments who were also university professors never addressed the deputy Under-Secretary as *Vilmos* (William), but always as *államtitkár úr* (*state-secretary mister – Mr Under-Secretary). This signified that they belonged to the 'old paradigm'.

Momentary Conflict of Opinions

The alternation of nickname and title in address can also express momentary conflict. Whenever the opinion of a deputy Head of Department contradicted the opinion of the deputy Under-Secretary, the deputy Under-Secretary was addressed as *államtitkár úr* (*under-secretary mister – Mr Under-Secretary). Whenever a deputy Head of Department supported the opinion of the deputy Under-Secretary, he addressed the Under-Secretary as *Vilmos* (William). When a (deputy) Head of Department wanted to express good will towards the deputy Under-Secretary and inform him how to avoid a trap he also addressed him as *Vilmos* (William).

Anticipated Results of Approaching National Elections

The approaching national elections resulted not only in a different choice of nickname and title in address but also in a difference in atmosphere. Atmosphere depended on the latest public opinion poll. Clerks who had anti-government feelings addressed the deputy Under-Secretary more frequently as *államtitkár úr* (*state-secretary mister – Mr Under-Secretary) and not as *Vilmos* (William) if the polls forecast the government might lose the elections.

Manipulative Politeness

It is quite common in Hungarian for someone to 'promote' someone else deliberately if they want a favour (for rank elevation in Polish, see Hucsza, this volume). If someone wants to avoid being arrested by a policeman they 'promote' the policeman. They address a 'sergeant' as 'captain' etc. This readjustment of the conversational contract must be delicate; i.e. a manipulative 'promotion' of this kind is usually only to one or two ranks above the real rank. To address a sergeant as 'general' would be ironic, yet the less well-educated the addressee is, the higher they may be addressed without irony being perceived.

I found that if a deputy Under-Secretary were addressed simply as 'Under-Secretary' in a written request, it was not a disadvantage for the petitioner if the petitioner were a student, a primary school teacher or a 'commoner'. Yet it offended the deputy Under-Secretary if the petitioner were a Dean of Faculty or a University Chancellor because 'they ought to have known the proper title'.

At meetings or in informal conversation, 'promotion' was very frequent. Yet the title 'Under-Secretary' instead of 'deputy Under-Secretary' was sometimes used because it was easier and shorter to say and therefore manipulation was not the intent.

A manipulative use of Leech's (1980) modesty maxim can be found in certain uses of Present Conditional Tense:

Hát *itt* *volnék!*
| | |
*Well, here would be I! 1.sg. suffix
Well, I am here!

The Gricean conversational implicatures are: 'Isn't it nice that I am here! Though I am sure that I am an important person, I do not want to emphasise this because I am a modest person'.

Te versus *Ön* and *Maga* (*T versus V – Du versus Sie*)

In its origin, Hungarian culture was an ancient, probably 'Asian' and Old–Turkish culture, and its style of politeness followed the deference strategy. Under European influence of more than a 1000 years, fragments of distancing strategies were superimposed onto the former deference strategy. Since the end of the 20th century, American influence has been growing and fragments of the strategy of camaraderie have spread throughout Hungarian society (cf. Lakoff, 1990: 35). This, once again, is expressed in address. Confusion and uncertainty are the result of the combination of the three strategies. In Hungarian interaction, silence and long pauses characterise the 'Asian' non-verbal strategy. The communicating partners sit and renew talking with the address form: *(te)kegyelmed, kegyed, kend,* (* thou grace thine, i.e. your worship). *Kend* and *kelmed* are abbreviations of *(te)kegyelmed. Kend* was often used to address inferiors. (All three words are archaic and no longer used in everyday conversation.) In the strategy of distance, superiors sit and inferiors stand. They address each other as *ön* or *maga* and putting one or both hands into one's pocket is considered very impolite. There are hardly any pauses. Interrupting is impolite. If superiors address inferiors as *te* (T), it is paternalist or rude. In the strategy of camaraderie, people address each other as *te* (T) and putting one or both hands into one's pockets is common and neutral. There are no pauses. Conversationalists often interrupt each other and even speak at the same time.

There are two distant and formal modes of address in Hungarian, which are – to a certain extent – similar to French *vous* and German *Sie*: *ön* and *maga*. There is one informal and intimate mode of address (*tu, du*): *te*. The *te* form is more ancient than the *ön* and *maga,* yet the latter belong to today's traditional paradigm and *te* belongs to today's new paradigm. Perhaps this is the reason why the *te* form spread more quickly since the democratic transformation of the 1990s than before. Let us take the example of a Christian professor who was 50 years old when he was appointed associate professor in the last year of communism (in 1989). A student of about 20 years old entered his room in 1990 and addressed him as *te* (T). Otherwise, the student behaved politely in gesture and sentence style. The associate professor was surprised and did not know if he still looked young or was a subject of democratic transformation. Yet the *te* form was equally likely to be the influence of American Hungarians.

In the traditional cultural paradigm, an older man must first address a younger one as *te*, and only after that is a younger man allowed to address the older one as *te*. A man is not allowed to address a woman as *te* until the woman has addressed him as *te*. *Te* between a man and a woman is more intimate than it is between men. In the newer cultural paradigm, *te* tends to be the standard and is becoming increasingly neutral.

Ön (*you* in the sense of *vous, Sie*) has gradually disappeared from the new paradigm, but has survived, to a certain extent, in the traditional paradigm. One reason for this may be that the *Ön* form has been an artificial form, which was created as such at the beginning of the 19th century, having been a reflexive pronoun earlier. Another reflexive pronoun *maga* (him/herself) is used instead of *Ön* mainly by uneducated people of the traditional paradigm:

In the traditional educated paradigm:

Ön *tette* *ezt?*

*You do+ suffixes of past tense and of he/she/it this +accusative suffix?
Was it you who did that?

In the traditional but uneducated paradigm:

Maga *tette* *ezt?*

| |

*Himself/herself did **he/she** this + accusative suffix?

Was it you who did that?

The T (second-person singular) pronoun is informal and intimate in the traditional paradigm but is standard in the newer paradigm and can even be derogatory in certain cases. If a shop assistant says to a foreign customer who they realise does not understand Hungarian,

Ezt *vedd* *meg!*

| | |

*This (accusative) buy + suffixes of 2 sg. and of imperative suffix of perfect action

Take (T) this!

the T form is an expression of disdain and of xenophobia on the part of the shop assistant. If a mother says the same to her daughter or friends do to each other, etc., it is the expression of their close relationship. If someone says the same and adds *kérlek* (I ask you – also in T form), it signifies that they belong to the traditional cultural paradigm:

Ezt vedd meg, kérlek!
Will you take this, please!

If young people are targeted by an international firm, usually the T form is used in advertisements:

Jól *jársz* *vele!*
| | | |
* Well walk T with it!
You will be better off with it!

People of the traditional cultural paradigm are irritated by such advertisements because they find them impolite. They prefer the elliptical *ön* (you) form:

Jól *jár Ø* *vele!*
| | | |
* Well walk Ø with it!
Ø = *ön* – you, (he, she, it)
You will be better off with it!

In Hungarian, personal pronouns are normally not used because the verb encodes person and number (singular, plural):

Ott leszek.

*There fut. substantive verb + 1.sg. suffix
I will be there.
If a personal pronoun is used, it expresses stress (or is archaic):

ö ott leszö.

*He/she there fut. substantive + 3.sg. elliptic suffix
It is him/her who will be there (not me or others).

The use of the 1.sg. pronoun *én – I* expresses self-conceit. There is a spreading use of *magam* (myself) with the adjective *jó* (good) instead of *én – I* as an expression of (pseudo) modesty: *jómagam* (*good myself). Leech's (1980) sympathy maxim prevails in it.

If there are women and men in a group, then there is uncertainty over using T or V forms. Nowadays both forms are uttered one after the other. There is uncertainty about which form should be uttered first. Mainly the T form comes second:

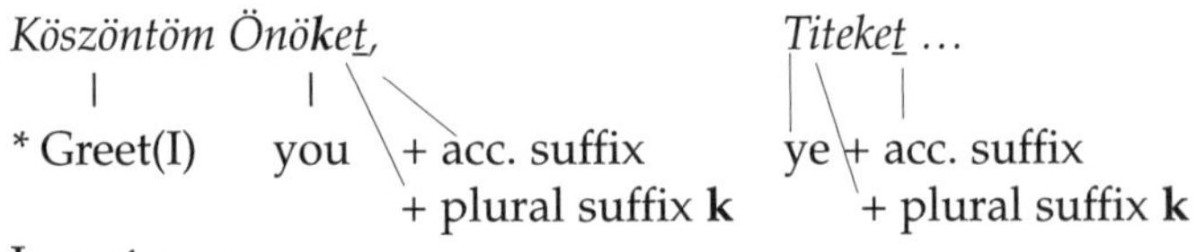

I greet you

The same happens in a request in a different conjugation:

Légyenek szívesek… *Legyetek szívessek*

3.pl. + plural suffix *k* 2.pl. + plural suffix *k*
Be you (V) kind (*hearty)… Be you (T) kind (*hearty) …
Will you (V) please … Will you (T) please …

When the deputy Under-Secretary would demand something from a member or members of his staff, he usually used the following request form:

Légy szíves …	Will you please (T form to one person)
Legyetek szívesek …	Will you please (T form to several persons)
Legyen szíves …	Will you please (non -T */ön/* form to one person)
Legyenek szívesek …	Will you please (non -T/*ön/* form to several persons)

If the deputy Under-Secretary was annoyed or was in a hurry, he would use the Future Tense or, if even more annoyed, the Present Tense:

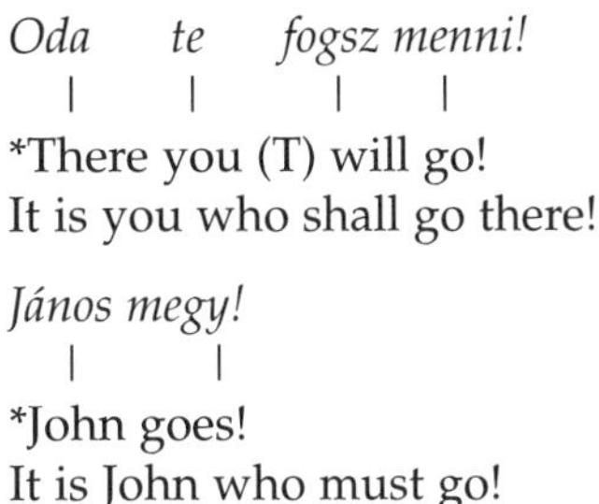

Oda te fogsz menni!
*There you (T) will go!
It is you who shall go there!

János megy!
*John goes!
It is John who must go!

If the task was unpleasant both for the deputy Under-Secretary and for his staff, he would use verbs in the imperative with an adverbial function of *már* (already) but his intonation would be requesting and even pleasing:

Menjetek már el oda!
* Go (T) already away there!
Will you/go there please!

If the deputy Under-Secretary was very angry with his staff, he used a polite request form in the T form and started his utterance with an informal address:

Gyerekek, nagyon kérlek titeket, ezt ne tegyétek a jövőben!
*Children, very ask (I) you (T) this no do (T) the future (in)!,
Dear colleagues, will you not do that in the future!

If a member of the staff or the deputy Under-Secretary made a mistake, and apologised for it, they never used the standard elliptic version *Bocsánat!* (*Pardon – I am sorry) or full version:

Bocsánatot kérek!
*Pardon ask (I)!
I am sorry!

They used the increasingly common elliptical form:

Elnézést!
*Indulgence! + acc. suffix
I am sorry!

To interrupt someone else, the full version of the previous expressions would be used:

Bocsánatot kérek, de ...!	*Elnézést kérek, de ...!*
| | |	| | |
*Pardon ask(I), but ...!	*Indulgence ask(I), but ...!
Sorry, but ...	Sorry, but ...

Globalisation - Emancipation - Gender

There is no gender in Hungarian morphology. That is why a native Russian translator of Hungarian novels, whose Hungarian was excellent, once said: 'When I translate a Hungarian novel, at page 100 I do not know who has entered and who has left the room.' Hungarian expresses male and female differently from Indo-European languages. The title of a book for teenagers 'He and she' can be translated as '*the boy and the girl – a boy and a girl'.

Masses of Hungarians of the new cultural paradigm are fond of imitating American and Western European customs and words, and they speak bad English. People of the new paradigm work in international firms and translate letters, speeches and advertisements. They always try to 'translate' gender. In addition, even well-educated Hungarians who have lived in the West for a long time try to introduce gender into Hungarian. (This tendency started in the 19th century.) For example, Hungarian has the same word for 'brother and sister', *testvér.* It is a compound of *test+vér,* i.e. body + blood. Yet Hungarian has separate words for 'younger brother' *(öcs),* 'elder brother' *(bátya* or *fivér),* 'younger sister' *(húg),* 'elder sister' *(nővér).* Priests address Christian communities as *Kedves Testvéreim!* (Dear brothers and sisters!). Thus when the Pope addressed Hungarians on his visit to Budapest as 'Dear brothers and sisters', it ought to have been translated as *Kedves Testvéreim!* Yet it was translated by a scrupulous theologian of good will as *Kedves fivéreim és növéreim* (Dear elder brothers and elder sisters!). This translation was ridiculous or, at least, enigmatic to the older cultural paradigm and acceptable to the new one, although most Catholics belong to the older cultural paradigm.

Politeness, then, in Hungary is clearly in a state of flux with competition between forms from both main paradigms, the traditional and the modern.

References

Bencze, L. Göbel, O., Osen, H., Reich, R., Rostás, R., Schenber, D., and Szabó, P. (1999) *Final Activity Report on Project JUNPO4869 to the Swiss National Foundation for Scientific Research.* Geneva: Swiss National Foundation for Scientific Research.

Eelen, G. (2001) *A Critique of Politeness Theories.* Manchester: St Jerome .

Lakoff, R. (1990) *Talking Power: The Politics of Language in our Lives.* Glasgow: Harper-Collins.

Leech, G. (1980) *Explorations in Semantics and Pragmatics.* Amsterdam: Benjamins.

Chapter 17

Politeness in the Czech Republic: Distance, Levels of Expression, Management and Intercultural Contact

JIŘÍ NEKVAPIL AND J.V. NEUSTUPNÝ

Introduction

In 1990, Bruce Fraser attempted to capture the principal approaches to politeness in recent literature, naming four principal views:

(1) the social norm view (traditional),
(2) the conversational maxim view (Lakoff, 1973; Leech, 1983),
(3) the face-saving view (Brown & Levinson, 1987) and
(4) the conversational contract view (Fraser, 1990).

The question which immediately comes to mind is where to place Brown and Gilman who, in 1960, without using the term politeness, developed a system of considerable sophistication, dealing with an important subsection of politeness in language. The point they considered was the structure of politeness within the grammatical systems of European languages. In particular, Brown and Gilman offered two key terms which subsequently were to prove useful in dealing with politeness in many languages: power and solidarity. This approach is worthy of being listed as a category additional to the four given by Fraser.

The framework applied in this chapter basically belongs to the same category as Brown and Gilman. We believe that the definition of politeness cannot ignore power and solidarity but that the range must be broadened. In an early article which used the concept of politeness as it is known now and applied it to a wide range of phenomena, Neustupný (1968) spoke of various types of social distance including power and solidarity but not limited to them. We can see that 'social equilibrium' or 'face' are important elements of distance which reach the peak of their importance in the contemporary period and that, for the study of politeness, reference to approaches (2) and (3) in Fraser's (1990) typology is indispensable. However, the central theme of politeness is how sociocultural distance between interactants is reflected in communication and how it is shaped by it. Hence, the first step of this process, which takes place within Hymes' (1972) model at the level of situation, cannot be ignored. This is the step at which sociocultural distance is identified. How are participants in speech acts socially categorized (Lepper, 2000) with regard to distance vis-à-vis others? Various types of sociocultural distance, such as Brown and Gilman's (1960) 'power' and 'solidarity', contribute to communicative styles of politeness. We propose to address this issue and how it relates to Czech society in the next section.

A further issue in the generation of politeness (see Neustupný, [1978: 214] for the whole sequence) is the question of the extent to which distance is conveyed through grammatical, or other, means, including so-called 'politeness strategies'. This is a question pertinent to most European languages which possess honorific distinctions in grammar and Czech is amongst them. A brief survey, necessarily limited in scope by research conducted to date, will be presented in the third section.

Another central issue will be that of honorific avoidance and the management of honorifics in general. The devices we employ to generate communication do not always work satisfactorily and it is necessary to apply a set of 'management' strategies to adjust the process. This is true of communication, in general, and also of politeness as one of its (central) components. What are the problems encountered in the generation of politeness in the case of Czech and how are these problems addressed? The fourth section will identify some of these issues.

Finally, we propose to consider the ways in which politeness becomes a problem in intercultural contact. With this in mind, we shall ask whether a particular politeness strategy is characteristic of Czech. Of course, the expression 'characteristic' will not mean 'solely occurring in Czech'. Within Europe we should not expect separate styles of politeness for each ethnic community but rather for areas that comprise the same or similar style, working either on a purely geographical basis (*Sprachbund/Sprechbund*) or on the basis of other possible groupings (genetic, interferential, grammatical or developmental, see Neustupný, [1978: 101]).

Sociocultural and Communicative Distance

The question of politeness is inseparable from the question of distance between participants in non-communicative interaction. Two prominent relationships of this kind are Brown and Gilman's power and solidarity (Brown & Gilman, 1960). However, there are other kinds of sociocultural distance, such as gender, age and physical or attitudinal distance. Communicative equality, particularly important in most strategies of what is called 'positive politeness' (Brown & Levinson, 1987), is a subclass of the power dimension.

For most of the second half of the 20th century, Czech history was dominated by the Communist Party. However, the party did not create extensive visible hierarchies (analogous to those of medieval nobility), influencing status or other components of distance. Indeed, it removed a number of existing occupational and other hierarchies.

Egalitarianism was further strengthened by two principal constraints on power evident over this period: the absence of the forces of a market economy and a chronic lack of labour. Because of the former, it was difficult for widely different permanent or semi-permanent statuses to be established. The lack of labour effectively limited the power of superiors. However, no factor appeared to foster 'solidarity' to a significant degree. The atmosphere was not necessarily one of general brotherhood or sisterhood. There was, in theory, equality between the sexes and most women were employed but this often meant that outside work was added to their household duties, which continued unchanged. The old were not miserable but neither did they command any special economic or social power.

After the Velvet Revolution at the end of 1989 things started changing (see also Damborský, 1993). Obviously, relationships which had existed for more than 40-years could not be altered overnight and the change is still incomplete. However, economic competition certainly resulted in a new power relationship between service personnel and customers: the introduction of market mechanisms means that services can be obtained from a variety of outlets and this provides customers with power that did not exist before.

A lack of reciprocity in linguistic usage may be only a matter of communicative style but there are indications that, in contemporary Czech, it frequently correlates with power. This lack of reciprocity seems to be more widespread than an account based on simple introspection might indicate. One of our subjects (in his late sixties, working in a research institute) reports about his friend Y and some other cases of non-reciprocal usage:

Example 1

Y v (místo pracoviště) *všem mladším dámám tyká a ony mu vykají. Nepovažují to za urážku. Viníkovi dopravní nehody (nebo jinému viníkovi) poškozený tyká a on si to zpravidla nechá líbit, i když je mnohem starší.*
[My colleague] Y in [the place of employment] uses T towards all younger ladies and they use V to him. They do not consider it insulting. In the case of a traffic accident the injured party uses T to the person responsible for the accident, and he does not normally object, even if he is much older.

Further empirical studies are needed for the Czech situation. From what we have said, there is both a possibility of

(A) relatively strong egalitarianism and
(B) a relatively strong assertion of differential social distance.

Needless to say, these two positions can co-occur.
In the case of (A), we need to explore at least two factors:

(1) the particular social situation between the end of the war and the Velvet Revolution of 1989, and
(2) the rural origins of Czech society in the nineteenth century.

However, when (B) is the case, the following factors would have to be considered:

(1) Since the return of the country to a market economy and a democratic political system, there has been the feeling that differential power, connected with the free market situation, is beneficial and that the release of power relations may be harmful.
(2) Owing to the role of the socially traditionalist Communist Party and, indirectly, of the influence of the Soviet Union, the process of post-modernisation of Czech society, the early stages of which could be felt in the late 1950s, has been delayed.
(3) The conservative character of Austro-Hungary, with which Czech society was interconnected until 1918, left its mark, not only on the language systems (Newerkla, 2001) of the component ethnic groups but also on their sociocultural structure (see Ehlers, 1999/2000).

However, we should also accept the possibility that either egalitarianism or social distance in the communication of politeness may be a matter of communicative style. A (communicative) style of politeness may become fossilised and remain unchanged, at least for some time. It is both questionable to assume that styles of politeness grow purely within a communicative space where power (and other social) relationships are absent and to assume that there is a one-to-one direct relationship between sociocultural input and the communicative style of politeness.

At What Level is Communicative Distance Expressed?

Politeness meanings are conveyed in a number of ways such as through grammatical competence (linguistic competence in the narrow sense of the word) or through non-grammatical communicative competence. Let us examine some of these forms of expression in the communicative style of Czech.

Grammatical means

Czech is one of the European languages in which the pronominal system and the verbal system (which are connected through congruence) are used to express politeness. The semantic features [+superior] and [+non-intimate] are conveyed by the second-person plural *vy* (V). In the 19th century, Czech was using, in addition to *vy*, forms corresponding to the German *er* and *sie* but by the end of that century they had already been ousted by *vy*: although they are not used any more, they are easily interpretable by native speakers when they appear in 19th-century literature (see Rulfová, 1984). As noted by Berger (1995), Czech differs from neighbouring languages, including Slovak, in requiring with the polite *vy* a singular past participle (when the referent is singular), while other languages (apart from Upper Sorbian) require the plural, whether the referent is singular or plural.

In a recent article, Jurman (2001) reports on a questionnaire he administered to university students and company employees, asking about their pronominal preferences. As the author himself notes, this method, though highly unreliable for drawing conclusions about actual usage, can be used for building up further hypotheses to test. In Jurman's data, *ty* seems to be gaining ground from *vy* among young speakers. In the case of university students speaking to their colleagues, reciprocal *ty* had already become the only pronoun in use by the beginning of the 1950s (see also Vachek, 1987: 281). Should we believe the trend discernible in Jurman's study, the practice has further extended and possibly now includes all first-time encounters between all young speakers, irrespective of gender. This can be confirmed in corpora that contain samples of everyday conversation (Zeman, 1999: 40).

In Jurman's data, reciprocity of pronominal address seems to be categorical, except in the case of children who are addressed by *ty* and return *vy* to non-solidary adults (confirmed again by Zeman, [1999: 48]). It is in the middle school that teachers first start to use *vy* to their pupils but not in a systematic fashion. In this case the formula first name + *vy* is sometimes used to communicate adult status concurrently with solidarity. Unlike Patočka (2000), who considers this practice recent, we had already registered it in the early 1970s.

We should not expect each individual case of the application of a *vy* form to refer to the degree of social distance. As argued by Neustupný (1986) in the case of Japanese honorifics, usage is often automised and does not communicate anything about social relationships, except when made overt. A train conductor, for instance, exchanges *vy* with passengers and, in everyday discourse, this usage does not convey any particular meaning except, for example, when, for some reason, the strategy is violated and the relationship must be reasserted. This, of course, applies to all politeness strategies: in each case we must ask whether and under what conditions the strategy is used overtly in discourse.

However, the communicative style of Czech grammatical politeness allows the intrusion of status distance relations into the address system. At the same time, social relations which rely more on equality within generational groups also assert themselves.

Address system

Berger (forthcoming) correctly notes that, in Czech, unlike German, titles such as *pane kolego/paní kolegyně* (German *Herr Kollege, Frau Kollegin* 'colleague') are non-reciprocal. They can only be used from [+superior] speakers downwards. However, the use of this address form may not be one-sidedly motivated by an active attempt to assert power. As one of our commentators mentions (Example 2), the usage may result from concerns other than those of social status.

Example 2

Já si jména studentů nepamatuju a tak jim říkám pane kolego nebo paní kolegyně
I don't remember names of my students, so I call them *pane kolego* or *paní kolegyně*

The *kolega/kolegyně* address is limited by domain; nonetheless, the use of titles has considerable functional significance in Czech. Titles stand out in comparison with German (as used in Germany), where they are used less frequently (Ehlers & Knéřová, 1997). There is no doubt they form an important component of the communicative style of politeness in Czech. Partly their relationship to sociocultural input is overt. For instance, in a factory the social status of an *inženýr* (graduate of a technical university) is high. The social status of medical doctors is consistently high, though not as high as in many English-speaking countries. However, in the case of some titles, their meaning in terms of status is, to a large extent, covert. They are automised address forms within the network in question and no longer communicate differences in status.

Standard and Common Czech

Goffman (1956) distinguished between deference (to a particular individual) and demeanour (communicating that the speaker is a person of certain qualities). In Neustupný (1978: 199), deference is interpreted as an expression of distance between individuals, while demeanour is considered to be the communication of distance between social groups: demeanour means that interactants maintain a certain behaviour in order to communicate the higher status of their own social group or because they want to adhere to a high prestige norm. In many communities the Standard or Official language has been reported to be such a prestige norm (Spanish in Paraguay, see Rubin, [1962]; Standard Japanese in Japan, Kokuritsu Kokugo Kenkyujo [1957]).

In Czech, the dichotomy between Standard and what is called Common Czech can be used in this way. The difference between these two varieties has sometimes been described as diglossia, with the Standard being the High and the Common Language (*obecná čeština*) the Low variety (for the current situation, see, e.g., Nekvapil, [2000]). Other factors of use may be present and demeanour politeness is one of them. The President of what was then Czechoslovakia, Václav Havel, who, on assuming office in 1989, spoke a variety with a high percentage of Common Czech forms (as befitted his position as an anti-establishment intellectual), soon learned to deliver his speeches in the Standard. Interestingly, service personnel and representatives of institutions are expected to speak the Standard even if their clients continue to speak Common Czech. Čmejrková (1996: 193) has suggested that the use of Common Czech relates to Brown and Levinson's positive politeness while the Standard is utilized for negative politeness.

The absence of a 'cultured' style of pronunciation

In English, French or German, there is an (exaggeratedly) 'cultured' style of pronunciation. This seems to be rare in Czech, although our judgement cannot at present be based on measurable scales. If true, the fact might be connected with the rural background of much of the Czech intelligentsia well into the 20th century, the paucity of Czech 'salons' (Kraus, 1999, van Leeuwen-Turnovcová, 2002) and effective constraints on social gatherings and public speaking both under German occupation and subsequently in the period from 1948 to 1989.

Weak constraints on 'bald on record'

Various other hypotheses deserve testing. One of them is the possibility that speakers differentiate relatively strongly between informal networks, in which minimum distance is communicated, and more formal networks. Thus, within families, little or no hedging may occur. Example 3 demonstrates this:

Example 3

Tak se to nedělá (One doesn't do it this way) (cf. *Myslím, že tak se to nedělá* [I think, one doesn't do it this way])
but representative data are lacking.

In public situations the expression of indignation and criticism of first-encounter participants occurs. For example,

Example 4

*Pani, nestujte tady ve dveřích (*Lady, don't block the door [on a tram]).

This stands out in situations of contact with cultures in which such comments appear to be more strongly constrained, but in fact such speech is socially constrained in Czech as well.

However, Czech conversation contains a variety of pre-sequences, the role of which is to protect the face of the interlocutor (Heritage, 1984: 268, 279; Yule, 1996: 67). A detailed analysis of Czech and American pre-requests in shopping situations revealed considerable structural as well as functional similarities (Nekvapil, 1997).

Requests

Obenbergerová (1992) compares Czech and English requests in order to establish a scale of politeness. She starts with a scale provided in Leech's (1983) *Principles of Pragmatics*, adapts it and compares it with Czech. While, on the English scale, the top request is 'Could you bring it tomorrow?', the most polite request in Czech on her scale is *Nemohl byste to přinést zítra?* (Couldn't you bring it tomorrow?) She concludes that 'the frequent occurrence of polite negative requests in Czech shows certain communicative pessimism' (p.93). Other differences between requesting in the two languages are mentioned and are useful for further hypothesis-building, although it seems that the research is not based on a sample of discourse data.

Ticket control

In this section, we shall examine certain speech events related to travelling on trains. Owing to the size of the corpus, the collection of which commenced in April 2001, we shall only concentrate on a single speech event type, the 'ticket control' as represented by the following example:

Example 5

A (= male, passenger, approx. 45 years), C (= male, conductor, approx. 50 years)

C: *dobrý den, kontrola jízdenek* (good morning, ticket control)
A: ((hands over his ticket))
C: ((returns the ticket)) *děkuji* (thank you)

The first observation we can make on the basis of this and other similar events is that the only verbally active participant on Czech trains is the conductor. In other communicative exchanges it is expected that *děkuji* (thank you) will be replicated by *prosím* (you are welcome) but this is not the case here. The role of the conductor is to check the ticket of each passenger and this requires issuing a request. In the previous situation, the request is issued by simply naming the activity involved (*kontrola jízdenek* [ticket control]). The fact that this is a request may be made clear by the optional element *prosím*, meaning 'please'. A higher level of politeness of conductors only became manifest after the Velvet Revolution and reflects the new relationship between service personnel and customers. A more exalted expression, unthinkable under the communist regime, appears in Example 6:

Example 6

C: *dobrý den dámy a pánové, (.) přistoupili* (good morning, ladies and gentlemen who have joined...) [Here only new passengers are asked for their tickets]

Czech politeness as a communicative style requires that a greeting ('Good morning', etc.) be used to open all these encounters. We do not claim that this style is solely Czech: being motivated by functional pressure, it is probably shared by a number of other European languages. Note that the opening greeting does not only convey politeness but also solicits the attention of passengers.

The Management of Politeness

Language is not used only to generate communicative acts. It also becomes the object of 'behaviour toward language' (Fishman's [1971] term). This results in the need for at least two kinds of linguistics: (1) generative linguistics and (2) management linguistics (see Neustupný, 1978, and 1983; also Jernudd & Neustupný, 1987). The process of management commences with attention to language ('noting') after which 'evaluation' takes place; next an 'adjustment plan' may be formulated and, finally, the plan may be 'implemented'. It is important to realise that management is not merely the implementation of an adjustment plan: the management process can be closed after each stage. For example, politeness may just be noted, without any evaluation attached to it, or it may be noted and evaluated but no adjustment planned, or adjustment plans can remain unimplemented.

There is no doubt that politeness is managed extensively in Czech discourse. In his comments on his own and others' speech, our subject quoted in Example 1 notes (he knows how people speak, including himself), evaluates (students *should* be addressed by *vy*), plans adjustment (he will give up calling his friend's daughter by her first name) and implements (addresses young adults by *vy*, to avoid a problem). Indeed, management of politeness is omnipresent. One of its frequent forms is politeness avoidance, studied in detail in Japanese (Miyazaki, 1991; Neustupný, 1983). In Czech, too, politeness avoidance plays an important role. For example, native speakers who meet acquaintances but do not remember whether they were on a *vy* or *ty* relationship can converse for some time avoiding grammatical patterns that require honorific distinctions. For example, in the Czech utterance:

Example 7

Bylo by dobré tam dojít, předat dokumenty a přinést další
(It would be good to go there [=if you went there], to hand [=if you handed] over the documents and to bring [=if you brought] more of them) (Quoted from Patočka 2000: 79)

infinitives are employed to avoid the choice of either a *ty* or a *vy* form of the verb.

In forms of address before 1989, *soudruhu!* (comrade!) was avoided, although in some situations the rules of the Communist Party explicitly required its use. Since the address *pane!* (Sir!) was ideologically tinted in the opposite direction, avoidance was widely practised by using *prosím vás*! (please, would you mind).

An interesting form appears in our train data:

Example 8

Conductor: *dobré/ý ráno, kontrola jízdenek ... děkuji/u ...* (Good morning, ticket control...thank you)

In these utterances, the ticket-collector, avoiding either a Standard or a Common language form, uses pronunciation that is half way between the two varieties (*dobré* versus *dobrý, děkuji* versus *děkuju*) belonging to different levels of demeanour. Since the difference is frequently located in an ending, it is relatively easy to render its pronunciation indistinct.

Hoffmannová (1994) provides a different example of politeness management by listeners in describing the decoding of two TV interviews by viewers. In the first interview, the viewers note the interviewee's ways of expressing politeness through the use of a subdued tone, absence of harsh evaluation of others, an optimistic and tactful approach. They evaluate the use of these strategies positively. The second interview uses less polite strategies, being more outspoken, emphatic, critical and even pushy and in Hoffmannová's data, these strategies were evaluated negatively.

Hoffmannová also noted corrections in TV interviews from Common to Standard Czech. After the interviewer sets the language at the Standard level, the interviewee follows and even hypercorrects his language (Hoffmannová, 1994:198). There are similar examples in our data.

The problem of the assertion of speaker's interests and their implementation through the use of power is one of the problems of management. Other speakers note that there are different interests and degrees of power, evaluating this fact negatively and assuming negative attitudes or attempts to adjust the relationship. In Example 1, our subject claimed the young ladies did not mind being addressed with *ty*. In fact, many speakers detest the 'abuse of power' of seniors and superiors who address them with *ty* or fail to use indirectness or other politeness strategies.

Politeness in Situations of Intercultural Contact

Contrastive studies

Individual comments on contrastive treatment appeared in the previous sections. Works providing comparative data are Berger (1995, forthcoming), Nekula (1994), Nekvapil (1997), Obenbergerová (1992), and Ueda Fidler (2000).

Ehlers and Knéřová (1997) have provided a useful study which can serve as a starting point for the further examination of grammatical politeness in intercultural contact. Their research, conducted in the Czech Republic and Germany by questionnaire, is useful for building hypotheses about the employment of address forms. The two researchers suggest, among other things, that

(1) titles are used significantly more often in Czech than in the German of Germany;
(2) the polite pronoun (*vy*, *Sie*) is used more in Czech than in German;
(3) on the whole, this trend is particularly valid for older speakers; and
(4) in Czech there is a trend to use *ty* with persons of the speaker's own generation.

We are not told who the Czech and German subjects in this study were. Neither do we know what beliefs about language were at play within the sample of respondents. Informality, particularly the place of the *du–Sie* distinction, has been discussed in Germany and the resulting beliefs may, to some extent, have encouraged the German subjects to play down the use of the titles and *Sie*. However, the return of Czech society to a free market economy has meant that old power relations within economic and social life have been reintroduced and this may well have led to the feeling of Czech speakers that titles used in address are legitimate – even beyond the limits of their actual use (see also Knéřová, 1995). Moreover, we should not forget that the Czechs lived for many centuries in close contact with Austrian German, which (as Ehlers & Knéřová remark) is characterised by frequent use of titles in address.

If there really is a difference, we should consider its sociocultural source but should not rush to quick conclusions. The difference between (non-Austrian) German and Czech is possibly a difference in communicative style: maybe among [-intimate] addressees one distinguishes between *pan doktor+N* (Mr doctor N), *pan+N* (Mr N), etc., in the same way as one distinguishes between different forms of the past tense. In this case no connection could be claimed with any sociocultural categorisation. However, there is the possibility of change in progress; as Ehlers and Knéřová suggest, we may be witnessing a process that reflects a change in sociocultural distance (such as that caused by post-modernisation). If there is such a change, it may only be an internal adaptation within communicative style; nevertheless, we must ask whether it can be attributed to sociocultural pressure. Such an examination can only be performed through an analysis of problems in discourse, followed by some introspective procedure, such as a follow-up interview.

The study of communication in contact situations

However, the important question for politeness in Europe is not 'comparison' but what actually happens in situations of contact. How are problems interpreted and how do they affect human relations in actual interaction? This is the basic question for sociolinguistic studies of politeness. In general, we can assume that much management takes place, with politeness norms being volatile, each speaker's native strategies being unwittingly used as norms, with many deviations being unnoticed and many adjustments unimplemented.

Skwarska (2001) notes that Czechs (like Poles) often use *ty* to foreigners in contact situations, especially to Vietnamese and Chinese. Since they interact with members of these ethnic groups mostly in transactional situations, the Vietnamese or Chinese being vendors and the Czechs customers, this might be explained as an expression of the Czech speakers' feeling of superiority. However, a similar observation was made by one of the present authors in the 1960s in situations where there was no clear distribution of power. The more likely explanation seemed to be pidginisation. In the meantime, it has been confirmed for other languages that large-scale pidginisation of politeness does occur in intercultural contact situations. The only way to proceed in the future is through the study of the whole process of management in such encounters, accompanied by follow-up interviews.

The situation is certainly different in the case of foreigners (so-called Western foreigners) who complain that Czechs refuse to communicate with them in Czech (cf. Crown, 1996). Although the power relationship is often to the advantage of the foreigners, the suggestion has been made that the refusal is intended to signal distance. Here again, the phenomenon is known in other cultural areas.

The lack of success of complimenting strategies, transferred from (American) English to Czech, has been reported by Tamah Sherman in an unpublished paper entitled 'An Analysis of Czech *versus* American English Responses to Compliments'. The author concludes that 'the key element of many Czech compliment responses is that they include some sort of reference to the negative – whether this be a complaint, a negative facial expression, an indication of doubt, or an outright rejection'. Whatever the case may be, it seems plausible to claim that problems in interaction exist.

Conclusions

We know today that politeness is one of the central components of communication. Europe cannot interact without politeness.

Different European societies probably shape sociocultural distance in different ways. On the basis of sociocultural distance, various communicative styles of politeness are established. However, the relationship between sociocultural facts and facts of politeness is neither direct nor simple. We have attempted to point to certain features of the style of politeness in contemporary Czech but it is too early to attempt to present an overall picture of the system. The relationship between politeness and power needs to be clarified but without rushing to premature conclusions.

Our chapter has also argued that the issue is not limited to the generation of politeness. Speakers and hearers note politeness in discourse, evaluate it, plan adjustment and implement their plans. In other words, the management of politeness is a matter of considerable importance. To understand the process involved, study of the management of politeness in intercultural contact discourse is urgently needed.

References

Berger, T. (1995) Versuch einer historischen Typologie ausgewählter slavischer Anredesysteme. In D. Weiss (ed.) *Slavistische Linguistik 1994* (pp. 15–64). München: Otto Sagner.

Berger, T. (forthcoming) Die Anrede mit *Kollege* im Tschechischen, Polnischen und Deutschen. In L. Udolph and V. Lehmann (eds) *Festschrift für Karl Gutschmidt*.

Brown, R. and Gilman, A. (1960) The pronouns of power and solidarity. In T. Sebeok (ed.) *Style in Language* (pp. 253–76). Cambridge, MA: MIT Press.

Brown, P. and Levinson, S. C. (1987) *Politeness*. Cambridge: Cambridge University Press.

Crown, D. (1996) Mluví se v České republice ještě česky? (Is Czech still spoken in the Czech Republic?) *Čeština doma a ve světě* IV, 150–55.

Čmejrková, S. (1996) Spisovnost a nespisovnost v současné rozhlasové a televizní publicistice (The standard and the non-standard in present-day radio and TV broadcasting). In R. Šrámek (ed.) *Spisovnost a nespisovnost dnes* (pp. 191–94). Brno: Masarykova univerzita v Brně.

Damborský, J. (1993) Změny v sociální modalitě (Changes in social modality). *Slovanské studie/Studia Slavica 1* (*Sborník prací filozofické fakulty Ostravské univerzity 140*), 11–16.

Ehlers, K.-H. (1999/2000) Anrede und Gruß im Deutschen und Tschechischen. Trainingsmodul. In *Trainingsmaterialien 'Internationales Teambuilding'*. Hof: Berufliche Fortbildungszentren der Bayerischen Wirtschaft (bfz) gGmbH, Internationaler Bereich (CD-ROM + video).

Ehlers, K.-H. and Knéřová, M. (1997) Tschechisch förmlich, unverschämt deutsch? Arbeitsbericht zu einer kontrastiven Untersuchung des Anredeverhaltens. In S. Höhne and M. Nekula (eds) *Sprache, Wirtschaft, Kultur. Deutsche und Tschechen in Interaktion* (pp. 189–214). München: Iudicium.

Fishman, J. A. (1971) The sociology of language. In J.A. Fishman (ed.) *Advances in the Sociology of Language* (pp. 217–404). The Hague: Mouton.

Fraser, B. (1990) Perspectives on politeness. *Journal of Pragmatics* 14, 219–36.

Goffman, E. (1956) The nature of deference and demeanor. *American Anthropologist* 58, 473–502. (Reprinted in *Interaction Ritual*. Harmondsworth: Penguin Books 1967, 47–95).

Heritage, J. (1984) *Garfinkel and Ethnomethodology*. Cambridge: Polity Press.

Hoffmannová, J. (1994) Projevy taktu (a beztaktnosti) v televizních rozhovorech (Manifestations of tact/tactlessness in TV interviews). *Slovo a slovesnost* 55, 194–201.

Hymes, D. (1972) Models of interaction of language and social life. In J.J. Gumperz and D. Hymes (eds) *Directions in Sociolinguistics* (pp. 35–71). New York: Holt, Rinehart and Wilson.

Jernudd, B. H. and Neustupný, J. V. (1987) Language planning: for whom? In Laforge, L. (ed.) *Proceedings of the International Colloquium on Language Planning* (pp. 69–84). Québec: Les Presses de l'Université Laval.

Jurman, A. (2001) Pronominální oslovení (tykání a vykání) v současné češtině [On pronominal address forms in contemporary Czech]. *Slovo a slovesnost* 62, 185–199.

Knéřová, M. (1995) Ke způsobům oslovování v mluvených projevech (Address forms in spoken discourse). *Naše řeč* 78, 36–44.

Kokuritsu Kokugo Kenkyujo (1957) *Keigo to keigo ishiki* (Honorofics and the Awareness of Honorifics). Tokyo: National Language Research Institute. (English summary of results in S. E. Martin, Speech levels in Japan and Korea. In D. Hymes (ed.) *Language in Culture and Society*. New York: Harper and Row, 407–15).

Kraus, J. (1999) Hledání české salonní mluvy (In search of Czech salon speech). *Salony v české kultuře 19. století* (pp. 88–91). Praha: KLP.

Lakoff, R. (1973) The logic of politeness; or minding your p's and q's. In *Papers from the Ninth Regional Meeting of the Chicago Linguistic Society* (pp. 292–305). Chicago: Department of Linguistics, Univesity of Chicago.

Leech, G. (1983) *Principles of Pragmatics*, London: Longman.

Lepper, G. (2000) *Categories in Text and Talk*. London: Sage.

Miyazaki, S. (1991) Nihongo kyooiku to keigo (Japanese language teaching and honorifics). *Sekai no nihongo kyooiku* 1, 91–103.

Nekula, Marek (1994) *Mal* und seine funktionalen Äquivalente im Tschechischen. Ein Beitrag zur Aspektualität. *Germanistica Pragensia* 12, 99–108.

Nekvapil, J. (1997) Some remarks on item orderings in Czech conversation: The issue of pre-sequences. In B. Palek (ed.) *Proceedings of LP's 1996. Typology: Prototypes, Item Orderings and Universals* (pp. 444–50). Prague: Charles University Press.

Nekvapil, J. (2000) Language management in a changing society: Sociolinguistic remarks from the Czech Republic. In B. Panzer (ed.) *Die sprachliche Situation in der Slavia zehn Jahre nach der Wende* (pp. 165–77). Frankfurt am Main: Peter Lang.

Neustupný, J.V. (1968) Politeness patterns in the system of communication. *Proceedings of Seventh International Congress of Anthropological and Ethnological Sciences* (Vol. III) (pp. 412–418). Tokyo: Science Council of Japan.

Neustupný, J.V. (1978) *Post-Structural Approaches to Language*. Tokyo: University of Tokyo Press.

Neustupný, J.V. (1983) Towards a paradigm for language planning. *Language Planning Newsletter* 9(4), 1–4.

Neustupný, J.V. (1986) Language and society: The case of Japanese honorifics. In J. A. Fishman (ed.) *The Fergusonian Impact* (pp. 59–71). Berlin: Mouton de Gruyter.

Newerkla, S.M. (2001) Sprachliche Konvergenzprozesse in Mitteleuropa. In I. Pospíšil (ed.) *The Crossroads of Cultures: Central Europe* (pp. 211–36). Brno: Masarykova univerzita.

Obenbergerová, D. (1992) Politeness of English and Czech requests. *Linguistica Pragensia* 2, 93–100.

Patočka, O. (2000) *O tykání a vykání* (On T and V Forms of Address). Praha: Grada.
Rubin, J. (1962) Bilingualism in Paraguay. *Anthropological Linguistics* 4(1), 10–28.
Rulfová, M. (1984) Zur Problematik der sprachlichen Etikette im Tschechischen. In J. Kořenský and J. Hoffmannová (eds) *Text and the Pragmatic Aspects of Language* (Linguistica X) (pp. 79–100). Praha: Ústav pro jazyk český.
Skwarska, K. (2001) Tykání a jeho zdvořilejší protějšek v češtine a polštině (T forms of address and their more polite counterpart in Czech and Polish). In I. Vaňková (ed.), *Obraz světa v jazyce* (pp. 137–145). Praha: Univerzita Karlova, Filozofická fakulta.
Ueda Fidler, M. (2000) Positive existentiality and politeness: A contrastive study of Czech, Russian, and Japanese. In J. Dingley and L. Ferder (eds) *In the Realm of Slavic Philology* (pp. 69–86). Bloomington: Indiana.
Vachek, J. (1987) Some remarks on personal pronouns in the addressing function. In J. Chloupek and J. Nekvapil (eds) *Reader in Czech Sociolinguistics* (pp. 274–86). Amsterdam/Philadelphia: Benjamins.
van Leeuwen-Turnovcová (2002) Diglosní situace z hlediska genderu. *Sociologický časopis/Czech Sociological Review* 38, 457–82.
Yule, G. (1996) *Pragmatics*. Oxford: Oxford University Press.
Zeman, J. (ed.) (1999) *Strukturace města ve verbální komunikaci: poznámky z výzkumu Hradce Králové* (Producing the structure of a town in conversations: Remarks on the research on Hradec Králové). (Zvláštní příloha devátého ročníku časopisu *Češtinář*). Hradec Králové: Gaudeamus.

Chapter 18

Politeness in Greece: The Politeness of Involvement

MARIA SIFIANOU AND ELENI ANTONOPOULOU

Introduction

Writing on politeness is a difficult task not because of scarcity of sources but rather because of the plethora of the available publications. Yet, even today, one would still agree with Ide (1989a: 97) that the more we learn about politeness the more we realise how little we, in fact, know about such exceedingly diverse and complex phenomena. Brown and Levinson's (1978/1987) theory of politeness was neither the first nor the only one, yet, admittedly, it has provided the most comprehensive and influential account of politeness phenomena so far. Thus, its contribution to the explosion of both intracultural and intercultural research is significant. However, as any theory so extensively used, Brown and Levinson's model has received both extensive support, especially in earlier publications, and a lot of criticism (see, e.g., Watts *et al.*, 1992; Kasper, 1997; Bayraktaroğlu and Sifianou, 2001). For instance, its universal applicability and, in particular, the notion of 'face' have been criticized as a Western European construct inapplicable to East Asian contexts (see e.g., Matsumoto, 1988; Ide, 1989b; Gu, 1990; Nwoye, 1989; Mao, 1994). Although such crtiticisms have subsequently been refuted (see, e.g., Kasper, 1997; Fukushima, 2000), Tracy (1990) argues that the theory is incapable of explaining the complexity of facework even within the society in which it was created. More recently, Eelen (2001) has criticised all current theoretical models of politeness as grounded on wrong premises, thus missing insights into the structure of social reality. Along similar lines, Watts (2003) views utterances as social acts and (im)politeness as part of the discursive social practice. Mills (2003) emphasises the need for a community-based, discourse-level, processual model of interaction to account for both gender and politeness and their relationship. However, despite valid or invalid criticisms, Brown and Levinson's theory has served and still remains a significant springboard for research on politeness phenomena.

Based on this dominant model, extensive research into politeness in Greek has been produced, even though in most cases the issue of politeness has not been the major aim of the research. Most studies have shown that Greece is basically a society with a positive politeness orientation and, in this sense, they provide support for Brown and Levinson's theory. Such findings should not be taken to mean that negative politeness has no place in Greek society but rather that, in interactions between people who know each other well and/or are of equal status, positive politeness strategies are preferred. Interestingly, there are cases (e.g. some TV panel discussions) where, although these variables may not hold, the conversational behaviour adopted mirrors the premium placed on positive politeness (see Tzanne, 2001: 303). This positive politeness orientation has not been refuted by any subsequent research. However, in most cases, emphasis has been attached to the need for contextual considerations and activity types, as these may reallocate the status of speech acts and the power (a)symmetry between interlocutors (see, e.g., Pavlidou, 2001: 130–31; Petrits, 1990).

The importance of contextual considerations is obvious. Yet this entails extensive and in-depth research of various activity types (and sub-types) in order to gain a clearer view of what happens in intracultural communication and to facilitate intercultural comparisons.

This chapter will focus on general aspects of the relevant research and point to directions for further investigation, considering also implications for Brown and Levinson's theory. We will start with speech acts, in particular directives and expressives, foregrounding their link to the notion of face threat and then proceed to discuss activity types.

Speech Acts

Understandably, early research influenced by Brown and Levinson's theory and the predominant trend at the time focused on isolated acts (e.g. requests) and later considered speech acts in context as well as various activity types. The most extensive research in the area of speech acts is the CCSARP project (Blum-Kulka *et al.*, 1989; Blum-Kulka & Olshtain, 1984) comparing and contrasting requests and apologies in eight languages. Its influence, along with the fact that requests are very frequent in daily interactions and closely linked to the expression of polite concerns, has contributed to the publication of a significant number of studies on requests.

A basic concept in Brown and Levinson's theory is that of the 'face-threatening act' (FTA) and they provide a classification of acts according to what aspect of the speaker's or addressee's face is threatened. Though useful, this classification obscures the fact that acts are multidirectional (see

Sifianou, 1997; Symeon, 2000). For example, although directives (e.g. requests) have been viewed as prime examples of acts that threaten the addressee's negative aspect of face, the possibility of simultaneous enhancement of their positive aspect of face has been underplayed. Asking for help or for a favour may also indicate closeness and solidarity (see Fukushima, 2000; Meier, 1995) and can be face-enhancing, since one must value somebody's views to ask for their comments (e.g. among colleagues).

Similarly, expressives like compliments and expressions of admiration have been considered acts primarily threatening the addressees' negative face in that speakers indicate that they would like something which belongs to the addressee. In the same vein, other expressives such as thanks and apologies are assumed to damage the speaker's face. However, viewing such acts as primarily face-threatening obscures their equally primary positive politeness function of enhancing one's interlocutor's face, especially since most such acts are *post event* (see Leech, 1977: 14), that is they are reactions to other acts which could be the source of threat, as in the case of apologies. Research on Greek has shown that an act should be seen in relation to the preceding act, since both acts will have repercussions not only on the conversational partner but also on the speaker.

On the basis of this research, the suggestion made here is that all acts can range on a continuum with face threat occupying one end and face enhancement the other. If one is to decide with any accuracy the degree of face threat and/or face enhancement of an act, one has to consider it in its sequential and wider socio-cultural environment. In the following sections requests in Greek will be discussed followed by a number of expressives.

Requests

Requests can be performed with a variety of constructions. Greek grammars distinguish three moods: (1) indicative, (2) subjunctive and (3) imperative and all three can be used in requesting constructions depending on the context of use. Being morphologically rich and thus functionally flexible, imperatives are frequently used for everyday requests in Greek (cf. [Leech, 1983: 119] for English, where imperatives are considered the least polite constructions when compared to declaratives and interrogatives). Subjunctive interrogatives are also used for requests, unlike affirmatives, since the former make it easier for the addressee, at least conventionally, to provide a negative response: for example, *Να πάρω το μολύβι σου;* (May I have your pencil?). Pavlidou (1991) focuses on subjunctive interrogatives and finds that they occur in formal and informal contexts when cooperation is high. She, therefore, suggests that cooperation should be granted a central position in politeness research.

In addition to imperatives and subjunctives, a common everyday conventionalised means of requesting is the present indicative interrogative, as in *Μου δίνεις το μολύβι σου;* (Do [can] you give me your pencil?) A plausible explanation for this use is that the present indicative expresses certainty, immediacy and present reality whereas modals and the subjunctive express uncertainty and distance to either the past or the future, thus enabling speakers to distance themselves from acts viewed as encoding imposing behaviour. It, therefore, seems that the Greek language offers a possibility for expressing involvement and immediacy through such requesting constructions. The absence of a descriptive verbial for common everyday requests should also be noted here as it may reflect the automaticity with which they are performed (see Verschueren, 1981: 135).[1]

When considering requests, one should not ignore their modification. Of the most common mitigating devices used with requests in Greek (with the exception of the very formal and elaborate ones) is the use of diminutives, which are considered next.

Diminutives

Diminutives (see also Terkourafi, this volume) are formed by adding special suffixes (e.g. *-άκι, -ίτσα, -ούλα, -ούτσικος*) to nouns and adjectives (e.g. *γάτα* [cat] / *γατ-ούλα* [cat.dim] *πικρός* [bitter] / *πικρ-ούτσικος* [bitter.dim]). Multiple suffixation is also possible (e.g. *γάτα* [cat] / *γατ-ούλα* [cat.dim]), *γατ-ουλ-ίτσα* [cat.dim+dim]). Although their prototypical function is to indicate smallness, they are used extensively to indicate affection, endearment and informality. Such uses are more frequent than speakers may realise, as indicated by relevant research (Daltas, 1985; Sifianou, 1992). For instance, in restaurants it is not uncommon to hear people asking for or offering *λεμονάκι* (lemon.dim), *κρασάκι* (wine.dim) *πατατούλες* (potatoes.dim) etc. Speakers are free to decide whether to use diminutives or not and use them only in relatively informal contexts. Learned words and abstract concepts cannot be diminutivised. For example, **Η τρυφεροτητούλα σου με συγκίνησε* (*Your tenderness.dim has moved me) is unacceptable. In other words, it appears that the system of diminutives has been developed in Greek for the purposes of expressing informal, positive politeness.

In conclusion, requests have been attributed features like *pre-event* and *anti-a* (Held, 1989: 181; House & Kasper, 1981: 159; Leech, 1977: 16) while thanks have been attributed features like *post-event, pro-a* and *anti-s*. Similarly congratulations are *post-event* and *pro-a*.[2] Although the validity of features like *pro-a* and *anti-s* can be challenged, this kind of semantic analysis clearly shows that speech acts cannot be treated in isolation. The actual event which triggers or is triggered by them must have a crucial bearing on the *pro-a* or *anti-s* variables. In other words, it must be related to the face threat or face enhancement they encode. So let us now turn to acts which are *post-event*, a large proportion of which fall into the domain of Searle's expressives.

Thanks and apologies

The expression of apologies in Greek is explored by Symeon (2000). She finds that apologies are rather infrequently used in Greek (as compared to English) (see also Hirschon, 2001: 29) and that the devices preferred in Greek are oriented towards the positive aspect of face (cf. Hickey 1991). She also considers thanking and argues for the multidirectionality of both these acts and the importance of considering their *post-event* nature. Koutsoulelou (2001) considers expressions of gratitude in Greek book and PhD prefaces and argues that such acts reflect positive politeness concerns and are face-boosting for both speaker and addressee rather than threatening the speaker's negative aspect of face because he or she accepts a debt (Brown & Levinson, 1987: 67). Research in this area shows that one cannot decide on the weight of debt of an act without considering the specific act that triggered it and the situational and sociocultural context in which both acts occur. In a Greek context, distance among closely related people and family members is assumed to be minimal (sometimes even non-existent). Therefore, expressions of thanks are considered redundant, perhaps even offensive in some cases. Similarly, 'imposing' or 'offensive' acts do not necessitate apologies.

Approbation

Makri-Tsilipakou (2001) considers a set of related expressives, namely approbation expressed with *συγχαρητήρια* (congratulations) and *μπράβο* (bravo). She explores them in natural contexts and argues that their affiliative role in interpersonal communication is reflected in the pattern of their social distribution. She explains their use and even 'abuse' as ultimately motivated by the positive politeness cultural drive for maximising praise. Similarly, Sifianou (2001) has shown that compliments constitute prime examples of the positive politeness orientation of Greek society. Both these studies are based on extended sequences and show the importance of both sequential and sociocultural context. Since discourse is sequentially organised, any utterance is linked to the preceding and subsequent discourse which contributes to its meaning and force. For instance, the following exchange occurred between a secretary and a patient at a doctor's surgery:

Example 1

S: *Έτος γεννήσεως;* (Year of birth?)
C: *Τριάντα οκτώ.* (Thirty-eight.)
S: *Όχι την ηλικία, το έτος γεννήσεως σας ζήτησα.* (Not your age, the year of birth I asked you for.)
C: *Κι εγώ το έτος γεννήσεως σας είπα.* (And I told you the year of birth.)
S: *Δεν το πιστεύω, φαίνεστε τόσο νέα!* (I can't believe it, you look so young!)
C: *Α, σας ευχαριστώ πολύ, μου το λένε συχνά αυτό.* (Ah, thank you very much, they frequently tell me so.)

The secretary's third turn is a very clear example of a non-formulaic compliment which occurred at a moment it was not socially expected. However, the patient's response *Α, σας ευχαριστώ πολύ* (Ah, thank you very much) legitimises it as a compliment. This example clearly illustrates that complimenting, like most verbal activity, is a joint process between two interlocutors who interactively contribute meaning to each other's utterances. The hearer is thus not a powerless automaton (see Eelen, 2001: 211) but somebody who actively contributes meaning to the speaker's utterances and responds accordingly. In addition, this example also illustrates the significance of the situational and wider socio-cultural context (cf. Holmes and Stubbe, 2003). Telling a woman (though not a nun) that they look young is a compliment in Greece, as in most Western cultures, but not in all others. In Japan, where maturity is assumed to come with age, telling somebody they look young may entail implications and/or inferences of immaturity. Considerations such as these have led scholars to turn their attention to specific social activity types, a concept introduced by Levinson (1979). A sample of this research is discussed here.

Activity Types

Announcements on board

Although her aim was to discuss translation issues, Marmaridou (1987) was one of the first to consider politeness phenomena in context, namely that of Greek and English announcements to passengers on board Olympic Airways aircraft (the Greek national air carrier). As she notes, since the setting is identical and the two languages are used because some people understand one and others understand the other, one could reasonably expect equivalent linguistic patterns. Interestingly enough this is not always the case as the following examples illustrate:

Example 2a

Ladies and gentlemen you are kindly requested to remain seated while cabin attendants take a passenger count. Thank you.

Example 2b

Κυρίες και κύριοι για να μη γίνουν λάθη και καθυστερήσει η αναχώρησή μας τώρα που το πλήρωμα ασχολείται με την καταμέτρηση παρακαλούμε να μείνετε στις θέσεις σας. Ευχαριστώ.
(Ladies and gentlemen so that no mistakes take place and delay our departure now that the crew are occupied with the count we request you to remain in your seats. Thank you).

A number of differences can be noted here. First, the underlined, subordinate clause offering explicit justification in the Greek text is absent from the English. It seems that performing a request of this sort in Greek without overt justification would violate the basic positive politeness strategy that the speaker and the addressee are co-operators, realised also in the use of 'our' in 'our departure'. However, in English such explicit information could be perceived as face-threatening on the addressees holding them responsible for any delay. Second, the active voice denoting immediacy is frequently used in the Greek texts examined while the passive voice of distance is more extensively used in the English ones (dotted underlining). Such differences are also evident in the following example which further illustrates that the Greek data are more direct and addressee-oriented, whereas the English data are more indirect and setting-oriented (underlined).

Example 3a

If you wish additional drinks, you are requested to order them as the carts pass by you.

Example 3b

Αν θέλετε περισσότερα ποτά από ένα, σας παρακαλούμε για τη δική σας εξυπηρέτηση να τα ζητήσετε συγχρόνως, όταν περάσουμε από κοντά σας.
(If you want more drinks than one we request you for your own convenience to ask for them at the same time when we come by you.)

The propositional content of both acts is identical but realised in ways which are deemed more effective in each language. As Marmaridou (1987: 733) suggests, personalising the message appears to have positive effects in Greek while the same effect is achieved in English by distancing the individuals concerned from the act. Thus clearly the type of social activity has to be considered along with the linguistic environment of the utterance before we can decide on the extent of the threat encoded in an act.

Telephone conversation openings and closings

Extensive research (Bakakou-Orfanou, 1988–89; Pavlidou, 1994; Sifianou, 1989; 2002) has considered both initial and final (Pavlidou, 1997) verbal telephone call behaviour among familiars and has shown these to reflect sociocultural dispositions. Greek callers tend to avoid overt self-identification probably because it sounds too formal and distancing. Similarly, answerers seem to assume that the caller will recognise them from clues such as pitch, intonation and characteristic answering phrases. This assumption could be related to linguistic optimism (see Brown & Levinson, 1987: 126). Failure to recognise somebody's voice is like forgetting his or her name (p. 39). Pavlidou (1994) comparing Greek and German has shown that Greeks prefer more initial enquiries ('howareyous') than Germans. Greeks have also been found to use more initial enquiries than greetings (Sifianou, 2002), which do not seem to be as obligatory as in other societies (Hopper, 1992: 61).

Besides such features relating to verbal telephone behaviour and reflecting the positive politeness orientation of Greek society, there are other features worth considering which relate to telephone usage in general, i.e. when and why one should use the telephone. Greeks rarely assume that their call will disturb anyone, as long as they stick to culturally acceptable hours for telephone calls but rather that it will indicate concern and interest, so there is no need to apologise for the intrusion. The more-or-less obligatory contact simply to exchange news or chat among friends seems to have replaced the unexpected visits people exchanged in the past. Thus, the primary function of the telephone in Greece seems to be enhancement of opportunities to talk more with friends, which explains the informality in the language used (no recitation of number, no identification, no apologies, etc.). In other words, the telephone does not seem to be reserved only for transactional purposes but to be frequently used for purely interactional ones.

Service encounters

Service encounters constitute another social activity type, that has been explored by Antonopoulou (2001) who is primarily concerned with gendered linguistic behaviour. At first sight, her data (400 exchanges in a small newsagent's) appear to indicate that men are less polite than women since they use fewer social acts like greetings, expressions of gratitude and leave-takings. However, closer inspection reveals a more complex picture. Like any activity type, this one is structured (see Levinson, 1979: 369) and it is the construction of this activity which appears to differ between men and women. Thus, while such activities are perceived as mainly transactional by men and do not, therefore, necessitate civilities, they are viewed as tripartite events by women, who include interactional introductory and closing sub-parts. Solidarity is shown to be conveyed through extensive use of playful language equally employed by both genders. In the service encounters examined, the preferred norm is positive politeness, regardless of variations in social distance, familiarity and gender characteristics of the speakers. Both men and women use solidarity-building devices, such as diminutives, informal terms of address and inclusive forms (i.e. first plural and ethic dative) on the morphosyntactic level and jokes on the discoursal level, even in cases where there is hardly any acquaintance between interlocutors.

Panel discussions

Another activity type that has received some attention recently is that of panel discussions. Tzanne (2001) examined five such all-male discussions with the aim of identifying the functions of presenter-initiated simultaneous speech. In addition to relationally neutral simultaneities (acts relating to presenters' rights and obligations to manage the flow or topic of conversation), there are cases involving politeness strategies that attend to either the positive or the negative face of the guests. Surprising is the finding that presenters may use strategies that enhance the participants' positive face even at the expense of their negative face. More specifically, presenters do not hesitate to project their talk into the middle of a guest's talk (thus threatening their negative face) in order to express their agreement with and approval of the point being made by the guest. All these create an atmosphere of closeness and solidarity through collaboratively produced joking and offering of reassurance and encouragement, for instance. Her findings provide further support of views which attribute a positive politeness orientation to Greek society, since, as she argues, they are not explainable on the basis of the specifics of the particular type of the encounter but mainly as a cultural trait characteristic of Greek people.

Georgakopoulou and Patrona (2000) also consider panel discussions and focus on acts of disagreement. In contrast to the previous explanation, they argue for contextual explanations rather than attributions to a general ethos of the Greek people. Such contradictory findings illustrate the need for more extensive research where additional factors such as topic of interaction (see Tzanne, 2001: 303) and roles and personalities of interlocutors should be considered. More generally, such findings indicate that the data analysed are restricted and probably reflect local discourse practices. If generalisations are to be drawn concerning even a single activity type, a great number and variety of these have to be explored.

Classroom interaction

Based on recorded data from high school classes in Greece, Pavlidou (2001) analyses classroom interaction and shows that students and teachers use differential patterns of politeness in class: while students invest more in negative politeness, teachers seem to pay greater attention to the students' positive face wants. However, on the whole, the classroom interactions considered are characterised by minimal politeness investments, especially on the students' part, explainable in terms of participants' roles and other institutional features of this type of activity.

Concluding Remarks

Research on politeness issues in Greek has been proliferating over recent years and this brief state-of-the-art chapter does not make any claims to exhaustive presentation. It is only indicative of the variety of research directions and can serve as the springboard for expansion and new research sites. Summarising the contribution of this research to politeness theory, the following issues suggest themselves.

It has been shown that while it is understandable why initially there was consideration of speech acts in isolation, the importance of context in interpretation is beyond doubt. To ignore this essential aspect of language use can yield results which would only partially account for the meaning and force of utterances. In addition, it has been shown that consideration of activity types provides a more secure framework for decisions about the degree of face threat encoded in specific acts and the extent to which an act is face-threatening and/or face-enhancing. For instance, requests in service encounters are not face-threatening and compliments and expressions of approbation are shown to be face-enhancing rather than face-threatening. However, one needs to explore considerable numbers of exemplar activity types to be able to draw local, let alone global, generalisations.

Despite extensive research into politeness phenomena in Greek, there are still areas in need of exploration. Ide's remark, mentioned earlier, to the effect that the more we learn about politeness phenomena the more we realise how little we still know seems to be verified. Exploration of a variety of speech acts in their contexts of use as well as extensive and in-depth study of many different activity types will provide the necessary insights for more secure and possibly general conclusions. Technological advance has created new domains of interaction governed by different rules which are worth exploring. In this line, Georgakopoulou (1997), examining e-mail discourse, argues that the positive politeness strategies attested in her data are explainable in terms of the contextualisation of the data.

One area which seems to have received no attention so far is the historical development of politeness norms and practices in Greece, 'an almost inalienable condition' for understanding the phenomenon of politeness, according to Ehlich (1992: 106). Historicity is related to issues of social structure, class and power (see Watts, 2003). Greece is a rather special case because of two contrasting ideologies: *Romiosyni* (relating to Byzantine and Turkish influence) and *Ellinismos* (relating to Classical and European influence) which have shaped Greek consciousness. The result has been a tension in social life which must have bearings on issues relating to politeness since Greeks frequently express ambivalence about their cultural affiliations both including and excluding themselves from Europe (Herzfeld, 1987).

In addition to looking into historical dimensions, the effect of globalisation and the advances in technology have bearings on the production and perception of language in general and the expression of politeness in particular. On the one hand, the English which dominates the Internet is reduced in stylistic range as it becomes more colloquial and multimodal and, on the other, interference from other languages will lead to serious changes as to what is polite and what is not. The term 'netiquette' already points in that direction.

Acknowledgements

This paper is part of a longer project funded by the University of Athens (Special research Account 70/4/5535 and 70/4/5754).

Notes

1. In formal contexts, the term 'request' could be rendered as *παράκληση* and in less formal (though not informal) ones as *αίτημα* or *αίτηση*. This may reflect specific conceptualisations that native speakers have of the social meanings and functions of their linguistic actions (Verschueren, 1981).

2. Leech (1997: 15) rightly points out that these variables should be seen as continuous rather than dichotomous.

References

Antonopoulou, E. (2001) Brief service encounters: Gender and politeness. In A. Bayraktaroğlu and M. Sifianou (eds) *Linguistic Politeness across Boundaries: The Case of Greek and Turkish* (pp. 241–69). Amsterdam/Philadelphia: John Benjamins.

Bakakou-Orfanou, E. (1988-1989) Τηλεφωνική επικοινωνία: Εκφωνηματική ποικιλία της παράκλησης για σύνδεση με το καλούμενο πρόσωπο (Telephone interaction: Variation in switchboard requests). *Glossologia* 7–8, 35–50.

Bayraktaroğlu, A. and Sifianou, M. (eds) (2001) *Linguistic Politeness across Boundaries: The Case of Greek and Turkish*. Amsterdam/Philadelphia: John Benjamins.

Blum-Kulka, S., House, J. and Kasper, G. (eds) (1989) *Cross-cultural Pragmatics: Requests and Apologies*. Norwood, NJ: Ablex.

Blum-Kulka, S. and Olshtain, E. (1984) Requests and apologies: A cross-cultural study of speech act realization patterns (CCSARP). *Applied Linguistics* 5 (3), 196–213.

Brown, P. and Levinson, S. (1978) Universals in language usage: Politeness phenomena. In E. Goody (ed.) *Questions and Politeness: Strategies in Social Interaction* (pp. 56–289). Cambridge: Cambridge University Press.

Brown, P. and Levinson, S. (1987) *Politeness: Some Universals in Language Usage*. Cambridge: Cambridge University Press.

Daltas, P. (1985) Some patterns of variability in the use of diminutive and augmentative suffixes in spoken Modern Greek Koine (MGK). *Glossologia* 4, 63–88.

Eelen, G. (2001) *A Critique of Politeness Theories*. Manchester: St Jerome.

Ehlich, K. (1992) On the historicity of politeness. In R. J. Watts, S. Ide and K. Ehlich (eds) *Politeness in Language: Studies in Its History, Theory and Practice* (pp. 71–107). Berlin/New York: Mouton de Gruyter.

Fukushima, S. (2000) *Requests and Culture*. Bern: Peter Lang.

Georgakopoulou, A. (1997) Self-presentation and interactional alliances in e-mail discourse: The style- and code-switches of Greek messages. *International Journal of Applied Linguistics* 7 (2), 141–64.

Georgakopoulou, A. and Patrona, M. (2000) Disagreements in television discussions: How small can small screen disagreements be? *Pragmatics* 10 (3), 323–38.

Gu, Y. (1990) Politeness phenomena in Modern Chinese. *Journal of Pragmatics* 14, 237–57.

Held, G. (1989) On the role of maximization in verbal politeness. *Multilingua* 8 (2/3), 167–206.

Herzfeld, M. (1987) *Anthropology through the Looking-glass*. Cambridge: Cambridge University Press.

Hickey, L. (1991) Surprise, surprise but do so politely. *Journal of Pragmatics* 15, 367–72.

Hirschon, R. (2001) Freedom, solidarity and obligation: The socio-cultural context of Greek politeness. In A. Bayraktaroğlu and M. Sifianou (eds) *Linguistic Politeness across Boundaries: The Case of Greek and Turkish* (pp. 17–42). Amsterdam/Philadelphia: John Benjamins.

Holmes, J. and Stubbe, M. (2003) *Power and Politeness in the Workplace*. London and New York: Longman.

Hopper, R. (1992) *Telephone Conversation*. Bloomington, IN: Indiana University Press.

House, J. and Kasper, G. (1981) Politeness markers in English and German. In F. Coulmas (ed.) *Conversational Routine* (pp. 157–85). The Hague: Mouton de Gruyter.

Ide, S. (1989a) Preface. *Multilingua* 8 (2/3), 97–9.

Ide, S. (1989b) Formal forms and discernment: Neglected aspects of linguistic politeness. *Multilingua* 8 (2), 223–48.

Kasper, G. (1997) Linguistic etiquette. In F. Coulmas (ed.) *The Handbook of Sociolinguistics* (pp. 374–85). Oxford: Blackwell.

Koutsoulelou, S. (2001) Οργάνωση και λειτουργία των ευχαριστιών στον γραπτό λόγο (Structure and function of thanks in written discourse). *Glossologia* 13, 47–74.

Leech, G. N. (1977) *Language and Tact*. (LAUT Paper 46). Trier: University of Trier.

Leech, G. N. (1983) *Principles of Pragmatics*. London: Longman.

Levinson, S. (1979) Activity types and language. *Linguistics* 17, 365–99.

Makri-Tsilipakou, M. (2001) Congratulations and bravo! In A. Bayraktaroğlu and M. Sifianou (eds) *Linguistic Politeness across Boundaries: The Case of Greek and Turkish* (pp. 137–78). Amsterdam/Philadelphia: John Benjamins.

Mao, L. R. (1994) Beyond politeness theory: 'Face' revisited and renewed. *Journal of Pragmatics* 21, 451–86.

Marmaridou, A. S. A. (1987) Semantic and pragmatic parameters of meaning: On the interface between contrastive text analysis and the production of translated texts. *Journal of Pragmatics* 11, 721–36.

Matsumoto, Y. (1988) Reexamination of the universality of face: Politeness phenomena in Japanese. *Journal of Pragmatics* 12, 403–26.

Meier, A.J. (1995) Passages of politeness. *Journal of Pragmatics* 24, 381–92.

Mills, S. (2003) *Gender and Politeness*. Cambridge: Cambridge University Press.

Nwoye, O. (1989) Linguistic politeness in Igbo. *Multilingua* 8 (2/3), 259–75.

Pavlidou, T. (1991) Cooperation and the choice of linguistic means: Some evidence from the use of the subjunctive in Modern Greek. *Journal of Pragmatics* 15, 11–42.

Pavlidou, T. (1994) Contrasting German-Greek politeness and the consequences. *Journal of Pragmatics* 21, 487–511.

Pavlidou, T. (1997) The last five turns: Preliminary remarks on closings in Greek and German telephone calls. *International Journal of the Sociology of Language* 126, 145–62.

Pavlidou, T. (2001) Politeness in the classroom? Evidence from a Greek high school. In A. Bayraktaroğlu and M. Sifianou (eds) *Linguistic Politeness across Boundaries: The Case of Greek and Turkish* (pp. 105–36). Amsterdam/Philadelphia: John Benjamins.

Petrits, A. (1990) Addressing in Modern Greek: Evidence from a case study in the Athens central market. *Sociolinguistics* 19, 125–44.

Sifianou, M. (1989) On the telephone again! Differences in telephone behaviour: England versus Greece. *Language in Society* 18, 527–44.

Sifianou, M. (1992) The use of diminutives in expressing politeness: Modern Greek versus English. *Journal of Pragmatics* 17, 155–73.

Sifianou, M. (1997) Silence and politeness. In A. Jaworski (ed.) *'Silence': Interdisciplinary Perspectives* (pp. 63–84). Berlin/New York: Mouton de Gruyter.

Sifianou, M. (2001) 'Oh! How appropriate!': Compliments and politeness. In A. Bayraktaroğlu and M. Sifianou (eds) *Linguistic Politeness across Boundaries: The Case of Greek and Turkish* (pp. 391–430). Amsterdam/Philadelphia: John Benjamins.

Sifianou, M. (2002) On the telephone again! Telephone conversation openings in Greek. In K.K. Luke and S. Pavlidou (eds) *Telephone Calls: Unity and Diversity of Conversational Structure across Languages and Cultures* (pp. 49–85). Amsterdam/Philadelphia: John Benjamins.

Symeon, D. (2000), Apologies in Greek and English. PhD thesis, University of Athens.

Tracy, K. (1990) The many faces of facework. In H. Giles and W.P. Robinson (eds) *Handbook of Language and Social Psychology* (pp. 209–26). Chichester: John Wiley and Sons.

Tzanne, A. (2001) 'What you're saying sounds very nice and I'm delighted to hear it!': Some considerations on the functions of presenter-initiated simultaneous speech in Greek panel discussions. In A. Bayraktaroğlu and M. Sifianou (eds) *Linguistic Politeness across Boundaries: The Case of Greek and Turkish* (pp. 271–306). Amsterdam/Philadelphia: John Benjamins.

Verschueren, J. (1981) The semantics of forgotten routines. In F. Coulmas (ed.) *Conversational Routine* (pp. 133–53). The Hague: Mouton de Gruyter.

Watts, R. (2003) *Politeness.* Cambridge: Cambridge University Press.

Watts, R. J., Ide, S. and Ehlich, K. (eds) (1992) *Politeness in Language: Studies in its History, Theory and Practice.* Berlin/New York: Mouton de Gruyter.

Chapter 19

Politeness in Cyprus: A Coffee or a Small Coffee?

MARINA TERKOURAFI

Introduction

In studying politeness in Cypriot Greek (henceforth CG), the scholar already familiar with politeness practices in Greece cannot help being struck by native Cypriot Greek speakers' remarks on the extensive use of derivational diminutives (e.g., *neraci*, [small-water], *kafeδaci*, [small-coffee]) and of the polite plural in Standard Modern Greek (henceforth SMG). Both derivational diminution and the polite plural are conventionally used in SMG to convey politeness (Bakakou-Orfanou, 1989; Sifianou, 1992a), achieving this effect by somehow making the speaker's utterance more indirect. Could it be, then, that conversational exchanges in CG are generally relatively direct? Is it possible to be direct and still be polite? (See Sifianou, this volume.) If politeness is an important reason for deviating from the rational efficiency in conversation captured in Grice's (1975/1989) Cooperative Principle, as often assumed (e.g. Brown & Levinson, 1978/1987; Lakoff, 1973; Leech, 1983), then how might politeness as directness be accounted for theoretically?

The study of politeness in CG gives us the opportunity to explore the close interplay between social (extra-linguistic) and structural (linguistic) factors shaping the linguistic idiosyncrasies of different communities, which may well share the same basic linguistic system. To do this, a shift of focus is required. Both derivational diminutives and the polite plural are used in CG and in SMG to express politeness. CG speakers' related remarks, then, reflect differences in the extent to which politeness is achieved through these devices in the two communities, rather than differences in the possibility itself of being polite by using these devices. Consequently, this chapter will focus not on how one *can* be polite in CG (i.e. describing the full range of linguistic means available in CG for conveying politeness) but on how one is *customarily* polite therein (i.e. identifying those linguistic means which CG speakers regularly use when being polite).

We begin with a brief overview of the linguistic situation in Cyprus today, then describe our processes of data collection and analysis. Politeness as directness is examined with the help of three case-studies on requests, the polite plural and diminution. When the linguistic means chosen in each case are considered against Brown and Levinson's (1987: 76ff.) variables of Distance, Power and Ranking of an imposition, it emerges that the indirectness of speakers' utterances does not increase proportionately to the sum of the values of these variables. Rather, immediately perceivable features of the situation appear to guide the selection of lexically specific expressions that are conventionalised in relation to the context of use, where conventionalisation is defined as a correlate of the (statistical) frequency with which an expression is used in one's experience in a particular context.

The search for a theoretically adequate explanation of this finding leads us away from viewing 'being polite' as applying a universal principle such as $W_X=D(S,H)+P(H,S)+R_X$ (Brown & Levinson, 1987: 76). If extra-linguistic features of the situation (sex, age, social class and relationship between interlocutors, the setting of the exchange, etc.) motivated the assessment of D, P and R_X, the sum of which then guided the selection of a politeness super-strategy from Brown and Levinson's (1987: 60) proposed hierarchy, then speakers' choices in context should be arbitrarily distributed across the various sub-strategies potentially realising each super-strategy (Brown & Levinson, 1987: 94ff.). However, contrary to this prediction, in the CG data, speakers' choices in a particular situation cluster around particular combinations of linguistic features, prompting us to view the emerging linguistic expressions as formulae (Coulmas, 1981, 1994). While rationally motivated when viewed against the backdrop of the language and the community at hand, politeness formulae are, in the end, just that: an aspect of speakers' conventional knowledge of what expressions to use in which situations, not creative unique applications of a universal principle by an individual rationality, bound by the consideration of ends and means *in vacuo*.

Issues in Data Collection

We define CG broadly as the variety of Greek spoken today in the major urban centres of the Republic of Cyprus – Lefkosia, Lemesos, Larnaka and Pafos. Greek is spoken as a first language by just over 620,000 Greek Cypriots living on the island[1] and is one of the two official languages of the Republic of Cyprus. While the second official language, Turkish, will not be covered in this chapter, the reader should remain aware that it is spoken as a first language by approximately 175,000 Turkish Cypriots living in the northern part of the island.[2]

Contemporary urban CG speech draws primarily on three sources: the Cypriot *koiné*, which has inherited almost all of the features of the variety of Mesaoria,[3] SMG and English. The prevailing situation of diglossia (Terkourafi, 2001: 75–77) means that Greek is used by speakers in its standard or in its local form distinctively (Le Page & Tabouret-Keller, 1985: 182): an emphasis on one's social or professional competence will elicit grammatical and lexical conformity with SMG – within the limits of one's previous experience of this variety – while foregrounding one's sincerity and friendliness will prompt the use of the Cypriot *koiné* (Papapavlou, 1998). Typically, the former type of situation will emerge in the presence of Mainland Greeks and on radio/TV, while the latter concerns interaction with family and colleagues. Naturally, this crude distinction does not reflect the multiple intermediate shades of speakers' intentions, which may be expressed by various combinations of standard and local forms.

The examples analysed here are drawn from approximately 115 hours of spontaneous conversation between native Cypriot Greek speakers of both sexes and various ages, recorded during spring 1997 and autumn 1998 in all four major towns, and in a variety of settings: at home/informal social gatherings, at work and at formal discussions/on radio/TV. Subjects were approached informally and in person by myself, along the lines of Milroy's (1980: 43ff.) 'friend of a friend' sampling procedure. According to the strategy of participant observation (Milroy, 1987: 60ff.), speakers were recorded in groups rather than individually and the asymmetrical relationship between researcher and informant was systematically undermined by my participation in ongoing group activities and willingness to answer questions. Information about the project was provided as requested. This helped ensure spontaneous interaction between informants while minimally interfering with their usual routines, by stressing that it was such interaction that was of interest.

Compared with evoking a situation through interview or questionnaire, this process has the advantage of ensuring greater authenticity of the data obtained, since

> 'the members of the group themselves exercise social constraint on one another's language. It would be quite unacceptable for someone in the group to put on an act during the recording and use a form of language which was not normally used in that speech community or among the individual speakers.' (Nordberg, 1980: 7 quoted in Milroy, 1987: 63)

Analysis

Politeness as directness: Requests

Performative acts (see Récanati, 1987: 160) were divided into two generic classes, offers and requests, based on a general dimension of *desirability* of the act predicated of the speaker or of the addressee in the utterance of a sentence (Sperber & Wilson, 1995: 250–1). This methodological decision avoids theoretical objections to the adequacy of proposed classifications of speech acts (Vanparys, 1996: 26). Moreover, it is empirically supported by evidence suggesting that speech-act theoretical descriptions play no actual part in comprehension (Geis, 1995: 31). The desirability of an act can be inferred from the propositional content of the utterance in conjunction with features of the situational context, even if the illocutionary force of the utterance cannot be further clarified. Once realisations of requests were identified in this way, they were semi-phonologically transcribed and analysed for a number of variables, linguistic and extra-linguistic.

Among the linguistic devices available in Modern Greek for performing requests (Sifianou, 1992a: 125ff.), our analysis considers: the presence/absence of a main-clause verb predicating an act *A* of the speaker or of the addressee, the type of main-clause verb, the subjective modality expressed by it[4], and the combination of number/person for which it is marked. Extra-linguistic features considered include the interlocutors' sex, age and social class, the relationship between them, the setting of the exchange, and whether the request occurs for the first time or is repeated. These provide the input for assessing the situation-specific values of *D*, *P* and R_x in the data collected, a move necessary to ensure a consistent way of assessing the values of these variables across members of a community. For, if this requirement is relaxed, the theory becomes unfalsifiable and it also becomes hard to explain how interlocutors may agree on their assessment of the FTA-specific values of *D*, *P* and R_x (and, hence, perceive each other to be polite), if not wholly by coincidence. To investigate the relationship between particular values of *D*, *P* and R_x and the degree/type of indirectness[5] of speakers' utterances, frequencies of co-occurrence of values of the extra-linguistic variables with values of the linguistic variables were established.

Realisations of requests at home/informal social gatherings and at work cluster around two main formulae: Action Verb[6]-Imperative-2sg. (1,2,3,4,5,6), and Action Verb-Subjunctive-2sg. (7,8,9,10,11).[7]

Example 1: [Speaker: female, over 51, middle-class; Addressee: female, 18–30, middle-class; Relationship: family; Setting: at home]
fer'to γala re aleksia (Hey Alex, get the milk.)

Example 2: [Speaker: male, 31-50, middle-class; Addressee: male, 31-50, middle-class; Relationship: friends; Setting: informal social gathering]
e fonakse tis koru na men eγraγi (Call the lass so it won't be recording.)

Example 3: [Speaker: male, 31-50, middle-class; Addressee: male, 31-50, middle-class; Relationship: colleagues; Setting: at work]
xoris' ta se θco set tʃe na ta valumen to·ra e ... kame ta khomplit (Divide them into two sets and let's put them now er ... make them complete.)

Example 4: [Speaker: male, 31-50, middle-class; Addressee: female, 18–30, middle-class; Relationship: employer to employee; Setting: at work]
tipose:, tipose enan tʃe fkale tʃ' ena khopi (Print, print one and make a copy too.)

Example 5: [Speaker: male, 18–31, working-class. Addressee: male, 31-50, middle-class; Relationship: employee to employer; Setting: at work]
kosta ela na ipoγrapsis eδo δame (Kosta come sign here, here.)

Example 6: [Speaker: female, 31-50, middle-class; Addressee: male, 31-50, middle-class; Relationship: service-provider to long-standing customer; Setting: at work]
pien:e pano en' o kostas. (Go upstairs, Kostas is there.)

Example 7: [Speaker 1: male, over 51, working-class; Speaker 2: female, over 51, working-class; Relationship: family, Setting: at home]
S1: *inda psarin eferes?* (What fish have you brought?)
S2: *γophan.* (Whitebait.)
S1: *e na pa na tin tianisis.* (Well, do go and fry it.)

Example 8: [Speaker: female, over 51, middle-class; Addressee: female, over 51, middle-class; Relationship: friends; Setting: informal social gathering]
θelma mu na fais tin, kolokotin su tʃe na pamen ap' eci (Thelma dear, do eat up your pastry so we can go to the other room.)

Example 9: [Speaker: male, 31-50, middle-class; Addressee: female, 31-50, middle-class; Relationship: employer to employee: Setting: at work]
avrion to proin avrion to proin na: mu pis, (Tomorrow morning tomorrow morning you let me know.)

Example 10: [Speaker: female, 18–30, middle-class; Addressee: male, 31-50, middle-class; Relationship: employee to employer; Setting: at work]
mixali? na 'rtis na δis kati? (Michael? Come and see something?)

Example 11: [Speaker 1: female, 31-50, middle-class; Speaker 2: female, 18–30, working-class; Relationship: service-provider (S1) and long-standing customer (S2)]
S1: *na metrisis ta mora, na δis ta xromata* (You count the kids, see the colours.)
((4 turns))
S2: *na: mu pis ce na δo ja times ...* (You tell me and I'll see about the prices.)

These formulae remain unaffected by changes in the sum of the social distance and relative power between interlocutors. As the examples show, they are equally used between family members and friends (1, 2, 7, 8), between colleagues, employers addressing employees and *vice versa* (3, 4, 5, 9, 10) and in commercial transactions (6, 11).

However, in first-time requests by customers addressing salespersons with whom they are not familiar, two further formulae predominate: *exo*, 'I-have'-indicative with rising intonation-2pl. (12) is preferred by middle-class speakers and is almost absent from the speech of working-class speakers, where it is replaced by *exo*-indicative with rising intonation-3sg. (13).

Example 12: [Speaker: male, 31-50, middle-class; Addressee: female, 18–30, working-class; Relationship: new customer to service-provider; Setting: at work]
eçete: phinats? (Do you have-2pl. {some} peanuts?)

Example 13: [Speaker: female, 31-50, working-class; Addressee: male, 31-50, working-class; Relationship: new customer to service-provider; Setting: at work]
eʎi mikres pu na min exun sçeδia pano? aspro (Are there any small plain ones? In white.)

These findings appear perplexing if the two expressions are equivalently indirect, as Brown and Levinson predict. In their hierarchy of strategies, both fall under negative politeness: they realise strategy 1, 'be conventionally indirect', by seeking to confirm whether the preparatory condition regarding the existence of goods requested holds (Brown & Levinson, 1987: 137), and strategy 7, 'impersonalise S and H' (p. 190ff.). Middle- and working-class speakers' consistently different solutions to the task of impersonalising the addressee suggest that, when first requesting something from an unfamiliar service-provider, speakers are also performing an act of identity (Le Page & Tabouret-Keller, 1985: 182), something which would appear redundant when the addressee is familiar. Crucially, the relevant notion of familiarity cannot be equated with Brown and Levinson's (1987: 76) variable of social Distance, defined as 'a general dimension of similarity/difference', of which frequency of interaction is only one aspect.

To the extent that non-literal use of the 2pl. in CG marks instances of standardising speech (see the next section), it is constrained by both having access to the standard code and the extent to which speakers find identifying themselves with 'the group of standard speakers' desirable in the situation. Middle-class speakers have greater access to SMG than working-class speakers: they have more opportunities to interact with Mainland Greeks, either in Greece, where they travel regularly, or in Cyprus, where Mainland Greeks often hold short-term contracts in white-collar jobs. Being socially stratified as a result, non-literal use of the 2pl. constitutes an outward manifestation of middle-class identity, to be used when asserting this identity is judged desirable, such as when requesting something for the first time from an unfamiliar service-provider. However, this motivation is constrained by the desire to accommodate one's speech to that of one's addressee. Consequently, middle-class speakers tend to use *exo*-indicative with rising intonation-2pl. more with middle-class addressees than with working-class ones. This analysis finds support in the phonetic realisations of the two variants, which largely conform to the phonological rules of SMG and CG respectively: in the data, *exo*-indicative with rising intonation-2pl. is realised as *eçete*, i.e. with suspension of a Cypriot-specific rule of softening of /x/ to [ʃ] (Newton, 1972: 51), five out of six times (83.34%), while *exo*-indicative with rising intonation-3sg. is realised as *eʃi*, i.e. applying softening of /x/ to [ʃ], six out of eight times (75%).

In requests performed in formal settings, most frequent are two further combinations, *θelo*,'I-want'-indicative-1sg. (14) and *θelo*-conditional-1sg. (15).

Example 14: [Speaker: male, 31-50, middle-class; Addressee: female, 31-50, middle-class; Relationship: interviewer to interviewee; Setting: Radio broadcast ('Gyro sto mikrofono', RIK1)]
θelo na apandisumen is ton akroatin pu ton afisamen (.) eh (I'd like {us} to answer the listener that we left (.) er)

Example 15: [Speaker: female, 31-50, middle-class; Addressee: male, 31-50, middle-class; Relationship: interviewee to interviewer; Setting: TV broadcast ('Sto mati tou kyklona', Sigma TV)]
θa iθela na prosθeso kati eδo omos. (I would like to add something here though.)

The first thing to note about these formulae is their attachment to formal settings. While the *θelo*-variants constitute indirect requests by affirming the sincerity condition, in the same way as the *exo*-variants with rising intonation-2pl./3sg. constitute indirect requests by questioning the preparatory condition concerning the existence of the goods sought (Brown & Levinsons, 1987: 137), these four formulae are not interchangeable. The relevant constraint appears to be interactionally rather than semantically motivated: affirming the sincerity condition functions equally well as a request as questioning the availability of goods sought (compare English 'Do you have NP?' with 'I'd like NP'). Yet the *exo*-variants predominate in first requests by customers addressing unfamiliar service-providers, while the *θelo*-variants take over in formal settings.

Focusing on the latter, *θelo*-indicative-1sg. is only marginally favoured by interviewers and by men, compared to *θelo*-conditional-1sg., which is clearly favoured by interviewees and by women. If we assess the relative salience of the two variants on several dimensions (articulatory and perceptual distance, phonemicity, lexicalisation, representation in lay dialect writing, areal distribution, and usage in code-alternation; cf. Auer *et al.*, [1998]), *θelo*-conditional-1sg. turns out to be objectively and subjectively more salient than *θelo*-indicative-1sg. According to Auer et al. (1998:163), [d]ialect features which are perceived by the speakers as 'salient' are taken up and given up more easily and faster than those which are perceived as 'less salient'. Considering that *θelo*-conditional-1sg. is virtually exclusive to formal settings, it is arguably not only associated with these settings, but a salient feature of 'media-speak' in CG. This would explain its more frequent adoption by speakers wishing to demonstrate their familiarity with 'media-speak' and the corresponding settings. Not appearing on radio/TV as regularly as their hosts, interviewees are one such group. Women are another: they appear on radio/TV less frequently than men, making up just over a quarter of interviewers recorded and only a fifth of interviewees. By opting for *θelo*-conditional-1sg. women and interviewees perform an act of identity: to identify themselves with the group of 'media-speakers' (as represented by interviewers and by men) they select a variant characteristic of this group's speech.

Politeness as directness: The 'polite' plural

When speaking to a single addressee, Cypriot Greeks fluctuate between the singular and the plural, often switching between the two a number of times.

Example 16: [Speaker: male, 31-50, middle-class. Addressee: female, over 51, middle-class; Relationship: interviewer to interviewee; Setting: TV broadcast ('Sto mati tou kyklona', Sigma TV)]
ciria vasiliu kliste mas aftin ti sizitisi. ti θa leγate (Mrs Vasiliou, close-2pl. this discussion for us. What do you think-2pl.?)
((one turn))
na se δiakopso? ixa δjavasi akrivos afto pu lete ... parakalo olokliroste (May I interrupt {you-2sg}? I had read exactly what you are saying-2pl. ...Please do conclude-2pl.)

Judging by the frequency of such fluctuation, it would appear that non-literal use of the 2pl. is felt by Cypriot Greeks to belong to the SMG code and, therefore, occurs when this code is called for, i.e. in formal settings and when the addressee is (classified as) a Mainland Greek. Thus, it may be interpreted as an instance of code-switching (McCormick, 1994: 581). Three observations support this view. First, when used non-literally, the 2pl. can only combine with the SMG future particle *θa,* and not with its CG equivalent *en:a* (17, 18). Furthermore, combinations of the 2pl./sg. with FN/title+LN respectively diverge from SMG usage (Bakakou-Orfanou, 1989: 175; Sifianou, 1992a: 64) (18, 19), and so do replies in the 1pl. (20). Explaining non-literal use of the 2pl. in the examples below as code-switching accounts for such divergences from SMG usage: speakers may perform less than optimally in a code for which they do not have native-speaker intuitions.

Example 17: [Speaker: female, 18–30; middle-class; Addressee: Mainland Greek; Relationship: acquaintances; Setting: at work]
θa pjite kati? na sas cerasume? (Will you have-2pl. something to drink? May we offer you-2pl. {something}?)

Example 18: [Speaker: female, 31-50, middle-class; Addressee: male, 31-50, middle-class; Relationship: speaker to member of the audience; Setting: formal discussion]
cirie panajo- ciriako θa mu epitrepsete, aplos θelo na mas to anaptiksete afto (Mr Panayo-Kyriakos, you will allow-2pl. me, I would just like you-2pl. to expand on this for us)

Example 19: [Speaker: male, 31-50, middle-class; Addressee: male, 31-50, middle-class; Relationship: interviewer to interviewee: Setting: TV broadcast ('Eks aformis', TV Pafos)]
s'efxaristo cirie fetha (Thank you-2sg. Mr Fetas.)

Example 20: [Speaker 1: female, over 51, middle-class; Speaker 2: male,

over 51, middle-class; Relationship: new colleagues; Setting: at work]
S1: *sas cerasumen kati?* (May we offer you-2pl. something?)
S2: *imasten endaksi* (We're fine.)

Non-literal use of the 2pl. in these examples is assessed as polite in the context of the formality of the setting or of the Mainland Greek identity of the addressee. Indeed, in a different context, informants commented on this usage as 'stand-offish' or 'inappropriate' (Terkourafi, 1997: 38–9). Further examples, however, suggest that at least some speakers consider this usage to be polite independently of context. These include examples recorded in a secretarial office, an insurance company, a legal firm and a number of shops fewer than half of which were 'upmarket', and occurred irrespective of the recipient's sex, age or social class. Speakers were all female and under 50 and unfamiliar with their interlocutors (21).

Example 21: [Speaker: female, 18–30, middle-class; Addressee: male, over 51, working-class; Relationship: service-provider to new customer; Setting: at work]
na mu pite ton ariθmon tis asfalias sas? ton ariθmon pu eçete (mazi) sas? (Can you tell-2pl. me the number of your-2pl. insurance? The number you-2pl. have with you-2pl.?)

Contrary to instances of code-switching, such as (16), where the verb is marked for 2pl. but the pronoun for 2sg., young working women's usage of V forms is consistent throughout their utterances and across turns. In line with findings regarding phonological change in the United States (Labov, 1994: 156), one may, therefore, surmise that young working (not necessarily working-class) women are leading a change pertaining to the non-literal use of the 2pl. in CG. In generalising its use to informal settings and non-Mainland addressees, young working women are dissociating this from the SMG code, and introducing it into the CG code as a conventional (rather than incidental, i.e. dependent on context) politeness marker.

Politeness as directness: Diminution

Babiniotis (1969:19) distinguishes three types of morphological/functional diminution in SMG: derivational via suffixation or via compounding and periphrastic diminution. Of these, only derivational diminution via suffixation is relevant to CG. While non-dialectal suffixes do occur,[8] the majority of diminutive suffixes used in CG are dialectal, with *-u(δ)i(n)/-u(δ)a* (plural: *-uθca/-uδes*) topping the list.

A straightforward frequency-count confirms the intuition that diminution is used emotively less frequently in CG than in SMG (Terkourafi, 1997:

14). Interestingly, nearly half of the literal occurrences but only a third of the non-literal ones in CG involve the suffix *–aci*, the SMG diminutive suffix *par excellence.* If this is actually associated in CG with literal diminution, it would explain why non-literal diminutives such as *kafeδaci* (=coffee-dim.) and *neraci* (=water-dim.) are not only not used by Cypriot Greeks but may even incur negative judgements.

In general, diminution in CG is primarily used by women to younger addressees and then to express positive feelings in familiar settings. In line with previous research linking the use of diminutives to the presence of young children (Jurafsky, 1996: 562–4; Sifianou, 1992b: 158), women's more extensive use of diminutives may be attributed at least partly to the presence of children, to whom many of these referred. By implication, the relative ages of speaker and addressee appear relevant to the selection of diminution as a communicative strategy in CG, with younger addressees receiving more non-literal diminutives than addressees of the same age or older.

An even stronger correlation exists between the use of diminutives and the topic of conversation. Discussions about politics, sports, financial or professional matters in the data show no diminutives, which are primarily found in task-oriented verbal exchanges. They are used to perform requests (22), offers (23), promises (24), compliments (25), refusals and acceptances of offers or thanks (26), and as downtoners of self-praise (27). However, unlike SMG, they do not occur when stating an opinion or trying to convince one's addressee or as downtoners of negative judgements and angry replies.[9]

Example 22: [Speaker: female, 18–30, middle-class: Addressee: female, 18–30, middle-class; Relationship: friends; Setting: at home]
pu 'n' tes <u>*sponduδes*</u> *moro mu? fer mu tes.* (Where are the <u>nails</u>-dim., darling? Bring them to me.)

Example 23: [Speaker: female, over 51, middle-class; Addressee: female, 18–30, middle-class; Relationship: family; Setting: at home]
vale <u>*patatuδes*</u> <u>*salatuδa*</u>. (Help yourself to <u>potatoes</u>-dim. {and} <u>salad</u>-dim.)

Example 24: [Speaker: female, 31-50, working-class: Addressee: female, 18–30, middle-class; Relationship: service-provider to new customer; Setting: at home]
avrion en:a pjumen ce to <u>*tʃaui*</u> *mas.* (Tomorrow we shall drink our <u>tea</u>-dim. too.)

Example 25: [Speaker: female, 18–30, middle-class; Addressee: male, 18–30 middle-class; Relationship: friends; Setting: at home] *inda orea bluzua!* (What a nice shirt-dim.!)

Example 26: [Speaker: female, 18–30, middle-class; Addressee: male, 18–30, middle-class; Relationship: friends; Setting: informal social gathering]
en:a pjo enan potirui. ate, enan potirui. (I'll have a glass-dim. {of wine}. OK, {just} one glass-dim.)

Example 27: [Speaker: female, 18–30, middle-class; Addressee: female, 18–30, middle-class; Relationship: friends; Setting: at home]
xriso mu, θelis na δis kati? ela na δis (.) leftuθca! (Chrissie, would you like to see something? Come see (.) Money-dim.!)

Not only is diminutive usage in CG relatively restrictive as regards its possible functions, it is also restricted with respect to the settings where it may occur. Though recorded instances of hypercorrection testify to Cypriot Greeks' awareness of the wide distribution of diminutives in SMG (where they are routinely heard in shops and restaurants, at doctors' surgeries, in taxis, at the airport, on the radio/television and between strangers in the street), diminutives are now primarily used only at home and at informal social gatherings.

The range of meanings which diminutives may express in CG, which include affection (28), sympathy (29), hedging (30) and approximation (31), but crucially exclude contempt, is not unrelated to these findings.

Example 28: [Speaker: female, 31-50, working-class; Addressee: female, 18–30, middle-class; Relationship: friends; Setting: at home; Referent of 'he': young boy]
arescen tu na mbi pu ka stin karkolu. (He liked to go under the bed-dim.)

Example 29: [Speaker: female, over 51, middle class; Addressee: female, 18–30, middle-class; Relationship: family; Setting: at home]
mana mu to alikuδin ti epaθe. (Poor Alice-dim. what happened to her.)

Example 30: [Speaker: male, 18–30, middle-class; Addressee: female, 18–30, middle-class; Relationship: friends; Setting: informal social gathering]
eʃi kreas enan kom:atui? (Is there a piece-dim. of meat?)

Example 31: [Speaker: female, 31-50, working-class; Addressee: female, 31-50, middle-class; Relationship: service-provider to long-standing customer; Setting: at work]
afto, cita, afton erçete olon kato (.) etsi (.) etsi, loksuδin δame tʃe δame pefti. (Look, this comes straight down (.) like this (.) like this, sort of diagonal here and here it falls.)

The absence of a 'negative' sense may well contribute to CG diminutives' strong connotations of affection. Diminutive usage in CG thus illustrates how the social and structural factors mutually reinforce one another. The dialectal origin of the most common diminutive suffixes excludes their use in more formal settings, or with unfamiliar addressees, promoting instead their use with in-group members towards whom one may want to express strong feelings of affection. At the same time, their affectionate connotations mean that they are inappropriate to express irony or contempt, making them more likely to occur with addressees to whom one wishes to express affection, namely, members of the in-group.

Conclusion

Direct expressions are the most frequent in a number of contexts in CG. Nevertheless (or rather, because of that), they are not perceived as impolite, but as socially appropriate in many contexts. Consequently, politeness becomes more a matter of conventionally knowing which expressions are expected in which situations than an online inference from the semantic representation of the utterance. The appropriateness of a linguistic means to achieve a desired end is hence more usefully construed as a qualitative notion, which may be explicated as appropriateness relevant to what is usual or expected in a certain situation within a community. A 'societal' aspect of rationality, different from that adopted by Brown and Levinson (1987: 64–5), can be seen to be in operation here, and to constrain individual speakers' choices:

> It is actually society itself that 'speaks' through the interactants when they try to influence each other .... The classical approach which bases itself upon the rational action performed by the single individual fails inasmuch as it does not take into account the degree to which this rationality itself is societal, hence supra-individual. (Mey, 1993: 263)

In this chapter, I have tried to show how we may begin to incorporate this societal aspect into our politeness theorising by drawing a three-way distinction which interposes between the 'formal' meaning potential of an expression as part of a system and the 'actual' meaning of that expression on an occasion of use, a level of socio-historically constrained preferred interpretations. The quantitative study of politeness emerges as a necessary precursor to this qualitative interpretation.

Notes

1. Source: *Population Census 2001*. Statistical Service of the Republic of Cyprus.
2. 1993 estimates. Source: http://www.trncwashdc.org/.
3. Mesaoria is the central plain area around the capital, Lefkosia. The elevation of this variety into the status of *koiné* is an instance of 'elevation of a dialect to a position of *primus inter pares*' (Jones, 1998: 289)
4 Term taken from Lyons (1995: 328ff).
5. Terkourafi (2001: 90–4) discusses some difficulties with applying this notion, quantitatively construed, to empirical data, and proposes a shift of focus to a qualitative understanding of indirectness, whereby priority is given to the form of words used. If nothing else, related problems caution against using this term unquestioningly, and prompt greater scrutiny of the actual expressions used, above and beyond *a priori* generalisations about their purported indirectness.
6. In an attempt to reflect both semantic and lexical considerations influencing indirectness, main-clause verbs whose propositional content expresses the (non-verbal) act to be performed are subsumed under this label. Common examples in the data are *δino*, 'I-give', *pjano*, 'I-pass, I-take, I-buy', *pino*, 'I-drink'.
7. Expressions discussed in the text are underlined in the examples, and in the glosses following them. Transcription conventions: FN = first name; LN = last name; 1sg. / 2sg. / 3sg. = first/second/third person singular; 1pl./2pl.= first/second person plural; dim.= diminutive; : = elongated sounds; (.) = brief pause; , = flat intonation; . = falling intonation; ? = rising intonation; ! = animated speech; ... = talk omitted from the data segment; {}=material inserted/omitted to make translation more comprehensible.
8. In descending order of frequency, these are *-aci*, *-itsa*, *-ula*.
9. The address term *peδaci mu* (=my child-dim.), frequent in SMG with disagreements and rebukes, is not used in a comparable way in CG.

References

Auer, P., Barden, B. and Grosskopf, B. (1998) Subjective and objective parameters determining 'salience' in long-term dialect accommodation. *Journal of Sociolinguistics* 2, 163–187.

Babiniotis, G. (1969) *Ο διά συνθέσεως εις τήν 'Ελληνικήν (Derivational Diminution via Compounding in Greek)*. Athens: Saripolos Library.

Bakakou-Orfanou, C. (1989) *Χρήσεις τον πληθυντικού τον προσώπον στη Νέα Ελληνική (Uses of the plural of person in Modern Greek)*. PhD dissertation, University of Athens

Brown, P. and Levinson, S. (1978) Universals in language usage: Politeness phenomena. In E. Goody (ed.) *Questions and Politeness: Strategies in Social Interaction* (pp. 56–289). Cambridge: Cambridge University Press.

Brown, P. and Levinson, S. (1987) *Politeness: Some Universals in Language Usage*. Cambridge: Cambridge University Press.

Coulmas, F. (1981) Introduction: Conversational routine. In F. Coulmas (ed.) *Conversational Routine: Explorations in Standardised Communication Situations and*

Prepatterned Speech (pp. 1-17). The Hague: Mouton.

Coulmas, F. (1994) Formulaic language. In N. Asher (ed.) *Encyclopedia of Language and Linguistics* (Vol. III) (pp. 1292–1293). Oxford: Permagon Press.

Geis, M. (1995) *Speech Acts and Conversational Interaction.* Cambridge: Cambridge University Press.

Grice, H. P. (1989) Logic and conversation. In H.P. Grice (1989) *Studies in the Way of Words* (pp. 22–40). Cambridge, MA: Harvard University Press.

Jones, M. (1998) *Language Obsolescence and Revitalisation: Linguistic Change in Two Sociolinguistically Contrasting Welsh Communities.* Oxford: Clarendon Press.

Jurafsky, D. (1996) Universal tendencies in the semantics of the diminutive. *Language* 72, 533–78.

Labov, W. (1994) *Principles of Linguistic Change. Vol. I: Internal Factors.* Oxford: Blackwell.

Lakoff, R. (1973) The logic of politeness; or minding your p's and q's. *Papers from the Ninth Regional Meeting of the Chicago Linguistic Society* (pp. 292–305). Chicago: Chicago Linguistic Society.

Leech, G. (1983) *Principles of Pragmatics.* London: Longman.

Le Page, R. and Tabouret-Keller, A. (1985) *Acts of Identity: Creole-based Approaches to Language and Ethnicity*. Cambridge: Cambridge University Press.

Lyons, J. (1995) *Linguistic Semantics*. Cambridge: Cambridge University Press.

McCormick, K. M. (1994) Code-switching and mixing. In R. Asher (ed.) *Encyclopedia of Language and Linguistics*, Vol. II (pp. 581-587). Oxford: Pergamon Press.

Mey, J. (1993) *Pragmatics: An Introduction*. Oxford: Blackwell

Milroy, L. (1980) *Language and Social Networks.* Oxford: Blackwell

Milroy, L. (1987) *Observing and Analysing Natural Language*. Oxford: Blackwell

Newton, B. (1972) *Cypriot Greek: Its Phonology and Inflections*. The Hague: Mouton.

Papapavlou, A. (1998) Attitudes toward the Greek Cypriot dialect: Sociocultural implications. *International Journal of the Sociolinguistics of Language* 184, 15–28.

Récanati, F. (1987) *Meaning and Force*. Cambridge: Cambridge University Press.

Sifianou, M. (1992a) *Politeness Phenomena in England and Greece: A Cross-cultural Perspective.* Oxford: Clarendon Press.

Sifianou, M. (1992b) The use of diminutives in expressing politeness: Modern Greek *versus* English. *Journal of Pragmatics* 17, 155–73.

Sperber, D. and Wilson, D. (1995/1986) *Relevance: Communication and Cognition.* Oxford: Blackwell.

Terkourafi, M. (1997) The discourse functions of diminutives in the speech of Cypriot Greeks and Mainland Greeks. MPhil dissertation, University of Cambridge.

Terkourafi, M (2001) Politeness in Cypriot Greek: A frame-based approach. PhD dissertation, University of Cambridge.

Vanparys, J. (1996) *Categories and Complements of Illocutionary Verbs in a Cognitive Perspective.* Frankfurt: Peter Lang.

Chapter 20

Politeness in Italy: The Art of Self-Representation in Requests

GUDRUN HELD

Introduction

Italy has provided both the common terminology of politeness phenomena for much of the rest of Europe (*cortesia, pulitezza*) and many of the formulae and rituals used for its verbal expression. Indeed, it is largely responsible for those language attitudes that show everybody's good manners and consideration for others, while still reflecting in many ways the once constricting tensions between social hierarchy, social status and individual desire. It is also true that politeness theory, within contemporary pragmatics, has been acknowledged by Italian linguists, although they have not fully joined in the boom which politeness studies have enjoyed in other countries. Although Goffman's work was immediately translated into Italian (Goffman, 1971; Lakoff, 1978) and Brown and Levinson's (1987) pioneering model has obviously not only been recognised (Benincà, 1977; Mullini, 1982; Stati, 1983; etc.) but has even been applied recently to language education for intercultural purposes (de Benedetti & Gatti, 1999), yet, with the exception of some papers on address forms (Bates & Benigni, 1975, Bates & Benigni, 1977) and routine formulae (Elwert, 1984; Pierini, 1983), little systematic work has been done on Italian politeness. Radtke's diachronic study (1994) and Held's synchronic study (1995) compare Italian politeness forms with those of French, limiting their results to contrastive pragmatic conclusions.

Perhaps it is the centuries-old *questione della lingua* which has prevented Italian linguists from treating problems of universal and anthropological interest more fully. The context of the Italian language is marked by the historical discrepancies between orality and literacy, between a geopolitically-dissociated spoken reality and the unrealisable ideal of written language unity with all its social implications. Perhaps as a result, academic treatment of politeness is still weak, limited to some sporadic data of a historical and experimental nature (see Held, 1995) and impressions drawn indirectly from sources such as books on etiquette from earlier times.

Doing politeness in Italy must, therefore, be considered as a complex field to be taken into account only in awareness of the permanent tension between past and present, between theory and practice, between anthropological universality and cultural specificity. To study the questions involved in this field, linguistic pragmatics must include historical and comparative dimensions.

I intend to give a brief outline of this complex phenomenon, with a theoretical introduction to some of the most common cultural implications Italian politeness raises and setting out some examples of how politeness has been verbally realised throughout history. I limit my view to the politeness-sensitive act of requesting which, due to its high conflict potential in threatening others' territory, leads to different kinds of redressive action and thus is one of the main areas where the Grice–Goffman paradigm can confirm its primarily face-saving standpoint. Requests have become a universal melting pot for a large inventory of types of indirectness and formulae, varying according to social relations and degrees of imposition and are easily comparable both intra- and interculturally.

Historical Outline: Foundation and Ideology of Italian Politeness

Doing politeness in Italy can be seen as an explicit expression of *italianità*, the point where ancient tradition, courteous civilisation and urban rationality meet, representing a general ideal in the European education of manners. Long before the Renaissance or the development of the first standards of civilisation propagated by the behaviour *tractates* of Castiglione, della Casa and Guazzo, the territory of Italy gave birth to the ideal of *urbanitas* which, with French courtesy, spread in the growing democratic city-communities as a high cultural attitude where self-representation was paramount. At the same time, scholars and well-situated citizens became conscious of the *volgare illustre,* institutions were established to teach good verbal manners and efficient rhetorical behaviour, and to make language socially worthy, smooth and adequate for economic purposes. As a result, disciplines such as the *ars dictandi* and the *ars arengandi* developed, distributing – based on ancient traditions – models of discourse, charters and epistles among the citizens. Among these, Guido Faba's translation of model Latin epistles into the vulgar language of Bologna reflects a range of polite and efficient language use in typical *petitio*-situations of former urban life, providing good testimony for reconstructing politeness in historical Italy (see my first example).

In the Italian Renaissance, the common ideal of human civilisation emerged. Embodied by Castiglione's *cortegiano,* it spread throughout

Europe, where it became, supported in particular, by the enormous reception it enjoyed in absolutist France, the standard of good, harmonious, social behaviour (Burke, 1988). Being an amalgamation of Cicero's value concept with courteous ideals and humanistic implications (Loos, 1980), the *cortegiano* represents the absolute perfection of that social individual who discreetly incorporates those necessary key concepts of *grazia, sprezzatura, disinvoltura, affettazione, sociabilità* and *prudenza* (see Montandon, 1993, Saccone, 1992) which are significant in Italian culture, generating the widespread ethno-stereotypes which identify the Italian way of interacting with people as open-minded, person-centred, pleasant and friendly. In relation to practical instructions for good manners given by della Casa in his Galateo – note the passage from the proper to the generic notion labelling generally all kinds of manner books – and Guazzo's instructions for efficient conversation (see Held, 1994), the Renaissance provides the fundamental basis of an attitude of politeness, built on the intentional conglomeration of education, spirit, tact and a sense of good communication. At the same time, the Renaissance is responsible for typical Western interactional behaviour, which modern pragmaticists know today to be aimed at cooperation and diplomatic avoidance of conflict.

Under the influence of both Spanish ceremonious formality and the affected gallantry of French etiquette, Italy was – due to an increasing cult of politeness and determined by social hierarchy and strict rank-orientated rules – turning the theatrical need for self-representation into exaggerated forms of self-stylisation. Goldoni's comedies are striking examples of this, reflecting the wide range of rank-bound, formalised, politeness behaviour (see my second example). Burke's ethnographic studies in 1987 (one of the few initiatives in the social history of communication), illustrate what he calls 'demonstrative consumption' (p. 111f.), an attitude which characterises people's interaction in the 'refeudalisation' period of the 17th and 18th centuries as the typical *fare bella figura*: continuous awareness of one's appearances and image.

Thus, Goffman's concept of face can be historically compounded by the culture-specific content that reflects the still-living social semiotics associated with appearances, attitude, theatre culture and simulation art. If we consider former everyday interaction, namely points of contact such as greetings, allocutions, wishes or leave-taking, or some common face-threatening acts such as requesting, advising, refusing or criticising, we find a dense inventory of various politeness forms, reflecting social power structures or ingeniously handling different implications of the master–servant constellations. Especially in their greetings, Goldoni, writing in the eighteenth century, presents figures who use a wide range of verbal and non-verbal submission strategies in order to simulate social equality and rhetorically create an intentional climate of harmony (see Held, 1999): *bacio le mani; (Vi sono) (vostro) schiavo* > *ciao* (de Boer, 1999); *servo umilissimo, servitor vostro, servitor umilissimo a lor signori; serva divota; per obbedirla; obligatissimo; la riverisco divotamente, faccio umilissima reverenza a lor siori; a buon reverirla; sono a' vostri comandi; per servirla; siete padrone; mi raccommando* etc.

One also observes testimonies of the development of a 'social grammar', the main parts of which are represented by the tripartite address system (TU – VOI – ELLA/LEI < *Sua maestà*) and the famous title mania (*Signore/Don; Signoria, Vostra Merced, Eccellenza, Cavaliere* and/or the epithets *illustrissimo, gentilissimo, chiarissimo, onorevole* etc.). At the core of this consideration lies what is now called 'social politeness' (Arndt & Janney, 1992) where all forms are exposed to continuous overstatement and semantic reshaping (Haferland & Paul, 1996): abuse or total desemantisation (e.g. *ciao, mi raccomando*) are natural consequences of this socially–determined field, as well as borrowing into other languages and further semantic change (cf. the old Austrian greeting *Gschamster Diener*, the Portuguese thanking *muito obrigado*, the French *s'il vous plaît* etc.)

Using Eelen's (2001) framework (following Ehlich, 1992), we can say that in the 17th and 18th centuries, in line with the growing culture of social distinction at all European courts, Italy developed a strictly regimented 'first-order politeness' where speakers had to use a fixed inventory of forms according to their social provenance and situational intentions. The manner of using the constrictive inventory – what we call 'social tact' and what can be considered as the social lubricant in any interpersonal communication – is a matter of pure Italian ability: combining *garbo* and *virtuosità*, Italians are absolute artists of the effective verbal *compiacimento*, the character of which constitutes a great deal of the proverbial *dolce vita* and associated forms of happiness and warmth (see Barzini, 1964; Kainz, 1965).

Thus, the unique nature of Italian politeness consists of a specific interpersonal sensibility created by the heightened desire for self-representation and self-assertion which, according to the principle of reciprocity, naturally requires high esteem and awareness of others, creating – at least from an exterior point of view – an inimitable climate of human communication throughout all classes, regions and channels, regardless of the controversial linguistic divide between the masses and academia. Verbal politeness is, therefore, motivated both by the stereotyped conception of Mediterranean immediacy and by sociocultural facts throughout history. Consequently, ethno-stereotypes typically label Italians as hot-tempered, curious, eloquent and even 'verbose', and their language as a typical conversation or dialogue language (Spitzer, 1922). It is not surprising that Italy is one of the greatest consumers of new media such as mobile phones, e-mails, chat-lines and internet connections, thus supplying the traditional need for personal communication with new and differentiated forms and attitudes.

The Act of Requesting in Different Periods: Examples of Italian Politeness

I will now attempt to depict the historical development of verbal politeness in Italy. In treating requests, I deal with an easily identifiable field of face-threatening acts, limiting my discussion to three examples which, representing different periods, vary in context, discourse conception, degree of literacy/orality and authenticity, thus ensuring varying perspectives on earlier and current social practices.

My first example is from an epistolary model suggested by Guido Faba in 1240 in the vernacular appendix of his manual of rhetoric. It is embedded in a corpus of models for discourse-making and letter-writing in the tradition of the *ars dictandi,* in its popular form devised to achieve efficient public communication in the everyday life of early urban citizens. One of the main tasks of this philologically important text was to teach people, in their own language, how to behave verbally in accordance with the given social power structure and with personal objectives, and how to manage interaction efficiently, maintaining a continuous balance between self-denigration and other-appreciation. Politeness in the 13th century must be seen within the constraints of an ancient Christian value system that required a permanent, well-directed interchange of submission strategies, on the one hand, and of honorifics, on the other.

In requesting, complex verbal procedures had to be enacted in order to gain the other's acceptance and *a priori* a positive reaction. The metaphorical exchange between the topoi of modesty and compliments increased according to social hierarchy, thus strictly regimenting the language forms used from low to high status. My example can be interpreted as a typical *petitio* utterance, or verbal 'knee-bending', which an inferior was expected to make when begging a favour of a superior.

> *Supplica la mia parvitade a la vostra segnoria devota mente, ke vui per Deo e per lo vostro honore, segunda la vostra força, ch'è sufficiente in questa parte, vuglae dare overa ke possa avere officio in Comuno.* (III formula from *Gemma purpurea,* quoted from Monaci, 1955: 58)

In my opinion, politeness here consists of structural complexity, on the one hand, (the performative act of requesting embedded in a series of compliment strategies, thus achieving the proliptic 'verbosity' considered in the Middle Ages to be deferential, not only because this was the required way to emphasise the urgency of the demand but also because of the increased time spent and the cost of affectation). On the other hand, the example is full of those redressive forms identified by the Grice–Goffman paradigm as weakeners and understaters intended to defuse the illocutionary force and thus not violate the other's private sphere – in this case that of a potential superior in the city community. Operating on the lexical, morphological and syntactic levels, they constitute a system in modern pragmatics because of their modalising functions according to social constraints, recognised by Leech (1983) as the *politeness principle*. From the speaker's point of view, we find classical self-humbling forms such as *la mia parvidade* and various lexical or morphological submission gestures such as *supplicare, devota mente, per Deo, vuglae*. We also find signs of deference to the addressee (*per lo vostro honore*), compliment and appreciation strategies (*la vostra segnoria, è sufficiente*) and of freedom of decision expressed by hedging deictic devices such as conditionals, the interchange of modal verbs or conditional restrictions: *segunda la vostra força, vuglae dare overa che possa* – all parts of complex, fine-meshed face-work, typical of this early social power system and its social constraints on language use. This 750–year-old epistolary model thus contains a variety of procedures which Brown and Levinson (1987) might describe as positive and negative politeness, intended to achieve smooth face-saving communication. Changes since then can be observed more on the formal and textual level than on the modal or conceptual level. In Faba's Bologna urban life, politeness was likely to be an expensive, value-laden, composition of power-oriented formulae and socially dependent formalities intended – in terms of Leech's model of the cost–benefit scale – to maximise the recipient's favour (see Beetz [1990] for German and Dumonceaux, [1975] for French). Procedures grow in accordance with the social rank of the interactants making communication a permanent metaphor for the balancing of social power relations in order to be recognised and successfully answered, especially in lower social positions.

My second example reflects requesting behaviour in the social context of a whole period. I refer to three comedies by Carlo Goldoni where requesting is an important and variable dramatic act which, according to various social constraints, is mostly performed in a cult-like way, using a wide inventory of fixed phrases and routine formulae. Speaking in the 18th century was like a role-play on the stage of life, where all participants know their part and do their best to maintain a balance between social obligation and personal interest. In an attempt to define their own position, to be taken seriously, speakers' utterances are constantly strengthened and intensified, thus undergoing a continuous semantic loss which has to be countered by further hyperbolisation: the cult of form loses itself in a vicious circle, finally ending in empty ceremonial behaviour.

Nevertheless, a sense of situational appropriateness remains, with most of the formulae being intentionally varied according to circumstance and, more particularly, to the social importance of the act conveyed. The following examples are categorised according to the interpersonal relationship involved and they show such variable use:

Example A: Requests by a superior to servants

Fulgenzio: *Eugenia carissima, voi mi avete da* ***accordare una grazia.***
Eugenia: *Non* ***siete voi padrone*** *di comandarmi?*
F: *Me* ***l'avete da far con buon animo.***
E: *Se non desidero che* ***compiacervi****!*
F: *Mi* ***avete a*** *permettere, ch'io possa ricondurre mia cognata alla propria casa.* (Goldoni, 1759)

Eugenio: *Ditemi, vi* ***dà l'animo di*** *darmi un caffè, ma buono?* ***Via, da bravo.*** (Goldoni, 1750)

Pandolfo: *Sono qui per* ***servirla****.*
Leandro: *Volete* ***farci il piacere*** *di prestarci i vostri stanzini per desinare?*
P: *Son padroni, ma vede, anch'io … pago la pigione.*
L: *Si sa, pagheremo l'incomodo.* (Goldoni, 1750)

Example B: Requests between equals (mostly with a sense of irony)

Vittoria: *Signor Don Marzio,* ***la riverisco.***
Don Marzio: *Oh signora mascheretta,* ***vi sono schiavo.***
V: *A sorte,* ***avreste voi*** *veduto mio marito?*
DM: *Si signora, l'ho veduto.*
V: *Mi* ***sapreste dire*** *dove presentemente egli sia?*
DM: *Lo so benissimo.*
V: *La* ***supplico dirmelo per cortesia****.*

V: *Vi* ***prego dirmi*** *che cosa ha impegnato. Può essere che io non lo sappia.*
DM: *Andate, che avete un bel marito.*
V: *Mi volete dire che cosa ha impegnato?*
DM: *Son galantuomo, non vi voglio dir nulla.* (Goldoni, 1750)

Conte: *Fate preparare nella mia camera per tre.* ***Vi degnerete di***

	favorirmi?
Ortensia:	*Riceveremo le vostre finezze.* (Goldoni, 1753)

Example C: Requests by an inferior to a superior:

Placida:	*Quel giovine,* ***ditemi in grazia*** *chi vi è lassù in quei camerini?* *... Caro galantuomo,* ***fatemi un piacere****, conducetemi su da questi signori che voglio loro fare una burla.* (Goldoni, 1750)
Mirandolina (al cavaliere):	
	La supplico almeno degnarsi *vedere se è di suo genio.* (Goldoni, 1753)
M:	***Se le piacesse*** *qualche intingoletto, qualche salsetta,* ***favorisca di dirlo a me.*** (Goldoni, 1753)
Fabrizio:	*Intanto* ***le supplico, illustrissime signore, favorirmi*** *il loro riverito nome per la consegna.* (Goldoni, 1753)
M:	*Signore mie,* ***favoriscano in grazia.*** *Siamo sole, nessuno ci sente.* (Goldoni, 1753)
M al cavaliere:	***Degnateci per un momento*** *della vostra amabile conversazione.* (Goldoni, 1753)
C:	*Apritemi.*
M:	***Favorisca andare nella camera sua****, e mi aspetti, che or ora sono da lei.*
C:	*Perché non volete aprirmi?*
M:	*Arrivano de' forestieri.* ***Mi faccia questa grazia****, vada, che or ora sono da lei.*
C:	*Vado, se non venite, povera voi.* (Goldoni 1753)
M:	***Le supplico per atto di grazia****, a provvedersi d'un'altra locanda.* (Goldoni, 1753)

Goldoni's plays show that speech attitude varies according to social origin. For reasons of deference and humility, the servants' inventory of politeness forms seems more extensive and thus more likely to be modally differentiated (see the imperative forms *avete da versus* the conditionals *avreste, sapreste* or the increasing performatives *pregare, supplicare*). In considering the semantic meaning of particular formulae, not only are key terms of Italian politeness such as *grazia, piacere* (somewhat less frequent), *favore* > *favorire, carità, cortesia* revealed but they turn out to be frozen compliment procedures intended deferentially to extenuate the desired act and thus to appreciate and anticipate the honour of the other. Most of the deference-oriented requesting formulae focus on the concept of *grazia* (*accordare, fare una grazia, pregare di una grazia, per grazia, per atto di grazia, in grazia*) inherently reflecting all social components of the act of begging (cf. Held, 1995: 132f.). We also find forms that verbalise social positions or social directions of speaking: the verbs *favorire* and, in particular, *degnare* emphasise attitudes of condescension, *siete padrone, per servirla* being common responses by inferiors, while superiors more self-consciously use *Son galantuomo.*

Although limited mainly to the performative act, the examples show some typical supportive means: flattering appellatives (*Signor don Marzio, illustrissime signore*), intentionally differentiated allocutionary pronouns (*ella* versus *voi*), modalisations and compliments such as *vostra amabile conversazione, il riverito nome,* as well as situation-appropriate grounders (*Può essere che io non lo sappia, ... che voglio fare una burla* etc.). In the gallant 18th century, verbal politeness was a regimented code of social behaviour skilfully manipulated by its users to demonstrate their social ability, enhance their image in society and achieve their social objectives.

My third example focuses on present-day Italian politeness behaviour. It originates from an experimental analysis carried out in the 1980s by means of a questionnaire (Held, 1995) where, amongst other tasks, Italian students had to produce, as spontaneously as possible, requests they considered appropriate to a given situation. The situations were intentionally differentiated according to specific parameters intended to increase the social weightiness of the request, allowing the investigation to evaluate the theoretical correlation between politeness strategies and the imposition involved in the speech act, thus revealing the range of structural and formal modalities used in face-threatening demands in different cultures.

Here I have chosen one situation likely to stimulate various verbal procedures to counteract embarrassment and high virtual transgression and, therefore, – within its methodological limits – thus allowing us to observe the actual politeness attitudes of young people. The situation is described in the following statement which alludes to face-wants and self-consciousness:

> The new tenant in the apartment above yours seems to walk all the time wearing clogs because there is a continuous clattering on the ceiling, which makes you nervous and irritated. One evening you can't stand it any more and, at the limits of your patience, you decide to go upstairs and complain. Furious and embarrassed as you ring the doorbell, which is opened by a surprisingly distinguished elderly woman – what do you

say?

One informant wrote:

Signora, buona sera, mi scusi tanto. Sono X e abito al piano di sotto. Mi dispiace disturbarla a quest'ora ma vorrei pregarla di una vera cortesia. Be' vede, non si secchi, ma da un po' di tempo si sente un rumore tremendo giù da noi ... come se qualcuno camminasse continuamente con degli zoccoli o qualcosa. Guardi, non so s'è lei ... comunque, ecco, capisco ch'è colpa del soffitto leggero, ma sa, io la sera devo lavorare e così non riesco proprio a concentrarmi. In più c'è mia madre ch'è anziana e la sera vuole dormire presto. Allora gentilmente volevo chiederle se potrebbe evitare di usare quelle scarpe – abbia pazienza, sono sicura che lei non si rende conto, ma le giuro che questo continuo sbattere è veramente fastidioso. Se vuole, signora, le posso offrire io in alternativa un bel paio di ciabatte di stoffa che tra l'altro sono anche più calde e più comode.

(Good evening, Madam, please forgive me. I'm X from downstairs. I'm sorry to disturb you at this hour but I would like to ask you a special favour. You see, don't worry, but for some little time now I have been hearing a tremendous noise upstairs, as if somebody were continually walking in clogs or something like that. You see, I don't know...Anyway, I'm sure this is the fault of the thin walls but, you see, I have to work in the evenings and I can't concentrate with this going on. Besides, my mother is old and likes to go to bed early. So I wanted to ask you in a friendly way if you could possibly avoid using these shoes – be patient with us, I'm sure you do not realise it, but I swear to you that this constant knocking is most annoying. If you wish, Madam, I can offer you as an alternative a lovely pair of slippers which happen to be warmer and more comfortable.)

The utterance quoted proves Held's (1995) premiss, showing politeness as a complex of means used in everyday interaction simultaneously on the levels of action and textual structure and on the levels of forms and verbal markedness. We can describe the example as follows.

In its discursive dimension, the utterance is based on a transparent, three-dimensional structural scheme. We see the 'pre-phases', intended to establish contact, define the relationship (*Signora, buona sera, sono X*), and give a first, largely conventionalised, evaluation of the forthcoming face-threatening act and its possible consequences. We find the typical adversative structure of an excuse followed by the directly performed announcement of the purpose (*mi dispiace disturbarla ... ma vorrei pregarla di...*), a sure step in the conscious and rather ritualised balancing procedure of the respective costs and benefits, taking for granted possibly positive eventual reactions from the interlocutor. Further, we observe a doubly split head-act of requesting marked by different degrees of direction (*allora gentilmente volevo chiederle se ... potrebbe evitare di...*). Finally, the utterance shows several supportive acts which, in my opinion, are likely to be most responsible for any politeness effect caused by verbal attitude: grounders referring to the situational conditions justifying the necessity, urgency and reasonableness of the request, even if they are only excuses or pretexts (*si sente un rumore ...come se qualcuno camminasse ...io la sera devo lavorare ... in più c'è mia madre ch'è anziana e...*); disarmers, mostly in routinised forms, attempts to prevent a priori the interlocutor's negative reaction or disapproval (*non si secchi ... non so s'è lei ... capisco ch'è colpa del soffitto...sono sicura che lei non si rende conto..*). In the case of high imposition, one also finds offers of compensation: *le posso offrire io in alternativa…*

The example demonstrates a well-constructed, clearly–planned, argumentative utterance, comparable to a divertive pattern: the progression to the face-threatening communicative aim is reached by several partial regressions which immediately but, little by little, repair any potential face-damage.

In its formal dimension, within this structural framework, politeness is achieved by a wide range of modality markers, from the necessary mitigators or minimisers (playing down any conflictive impact of the illocutionary force) to the less-expected emphasisers or maximisers (intended to strengthen personal involvement and credibility of somewhat too 'chilling' statements). As minimisers, we find negative politeness strategies such as interrogatives, deictic distance devices, the polite subjunctive and the polite past tense (*vorrei pregarla, volevo chiedere se potrebbe ...*, see Held, [1993]), relativising adverbs or locutions (*per cortesia, per favore, gentilmente, se vuole, s'è possibile, eventualmente*) and a preference for general terms in the head-acts; epistemological qualifiers e.g. *credo che qualcuno caminasse, non so s'è lei...*, indeterminacy markers (*se qualcuno caminasse, o qualcosa, quelle scarpe ...*), 'belittlement' strategies (*da un po' di tempo*), litotes and restriction strategies (*qualche volta*) or hedges in the supportive acts.

The opposite function of strengthening, also frequent in the supportives, is conveyed by the reinforcement of truth and certainty (*sono sicura che..., le giuro che ..., una vera cortesia, è veramente fastidioso...*), by overstatements (*non riesco proprio a concentrarmi ..., devo lavorare...*), overmarkings of the time element (*come se qualcuno caminasse continuamente, questo continuo sbattere*) and other hyperbolic means (*si sente un rumore tremendo*). Finally, we find a striking application of so-called 'relation signals' (Goffman): different types of lexical units that explicitly refer to the ongoing interpersonal relationship (*be' vede, guardi*) or that manage and connect discourse structure in order to keep up a common base of knowledge (*ecco, allora, comunque, così*). Conversational routines such as *abbi pazienza* have left their formerly exhortative function and now simply underline the theoretical concept of 'recipient design' as necessary deference to the other.

This example demonstrates the feeling which young people still have for situation-appropriate speech attitude, showing well-developed competence in linguistic nuance, resulting from the usage of a passive repertoire of social forms and from an active sense of personal delicacy, acquired in the complex, culturally-bound, socialisation process. The findings represent many of those forms Brown and Levinson (1987) identified as positive and negative politeness strategies used in order to be as polite as possible, given one's own purposes. As this ability of language can be called an art form, significantly defined as 'a gymnastic of expression' (Dhoquois, 1991), we disagree with the Italian proverb which states: *Cortesia di bocca assai vale e poco costa* (Politeness from the mouth is high in value and low in cost). On the contrary, politeness today in Italy – as in many other western cultures – seems to imply a high verbal cost shown by a conscious balancing of different kinds of minimisation and maximisation procedures within a precise structural behaviour framework. Being verbally polite requires high effort informed by social competence and psychological pressure in order to maintain harmonious, efficient interaction.

Concluding Remarks

In attempting to study Italian politeness, I have kept in mind historical pragmatics, a new research field which, based on the ethnography of communication, should function similarly to Interlanguage Pragmatics, in order to compare stages or phases of speaking and their cultural framework (see Wierzbicka, 1991). Within this promising but still largely absent perspective, we can say that, generally, according to the basic linguistic situation expressed by the theoretically still unresolved *questione della lingua,* there is – at least on the level of evaluation and prestige – a striking difference between written and spoken Italian politeness. The former is still trapped in formalities and formal routines unconsciously reflecting centuries-old scales and social hierarchies and their regulative impact (institutionalised text genres, public instructions, demands and prohibitions, official letters, administration texts etc.). The latter represents a mobile, innovative area which, in line with global trends towards orality, dominates subjective disformalisation and personal individualism, the logical consequence of which is rightly defined by Radtke (1995:186) as a 'nuova cortesia familiare (...) orientata verso un'apertura al substandard linguistico'.

Corpus literature

Faba, G., Parlamenti ed epistole, Nr. 3 from: *Gemma Purpurea. Doctrina ad inveniendas incipiendas et formandas materias*. Bologna 1240. In E. Monaci (1955) Crestomazia italiana die primi secoli (p. 58) Roma/Napoli: Società Editrice Dante Alighieri.

Goldoni, C., *La bottega del café* (1750), *La locandiera* (1753), *Gl'innamorati* (1759). In C. Goldoni (1981), *Commedie*. Milano: Garzanti.

References

Arndt, H. and Janney, R. (1992) Intracultural tact versus intercultural tact. In R.J. Watts, S. Ide and K. Ehlich (eds) *Politeness in Language: Studies in Its History, Theory and Practice* (pp. 21–43). Berlin/New York: Mouton de Gruyter.

Barzini, L. (1964) *Die Italiener*. Frankfurt: Scheffer.

Bates, E. and Benigni, L. (1975) Rules for address in Italy: A sociological survey. *Language in Society* 4, 271–88.

Bates, E. and Benigni, L. (1977) Interazione sociale e linguaggio: analisi pragmatica dei pronomi allocutivi italiani. In R. Simone and G. Ruggiero (eds) *Aspetti sociolinguistici dell'Italia contemporanea* (pp. 141–65). Roma: Bulzoni.

Beetz, M. (1990) *Frühmoderne Höflichkeit. Komplimentierkunst und Gesellschaftsrituale im altdeutschen Sprachraum*. Stuttgart: Metzler.

Benincà, P., Cinque, G., Fava, E., Leonardi, P. and Piva, P (1977) 101 modi per richiedere. In R. Simone and G. Ruggiero (eds) *Aspetti sociolinguistici dell'Italia contemporanea* (pp. 501–33). Roma: Bulzoni.

Brown, P. and Levinson, S. (1987) *Politeness: Some Universals in Language Usage*. Cambridge: Cambridge University Press.

Burke, P. (1987) *Städtische Kultur in Italien zwischen Hochrenaissance und Barock*. Berlin: Wagenbach.

Burke, P. (1988) *Die Renaissance in Italien. Sozialgeschichte einer Kultur zwischen Tradition und Erfindung*. München: Deutscher Taschenbuch.

De Benedetti, A. and Gatti, F. (1999) *Routine e rituali nella comunicazione*. Torino: Paravia.

De Boer, M.G. (1999) Riflessioni intorno a un saluto: la storia di 'ciao'. *Lingua e Stile* 34(3), 431–48.

Dhoquois, R. (1991) *La politesse. Vertu des apparences*. Paris: Ed. Autrement.

Dumonceaux, P. (1975) *Langue et sensibilité au XVIIe siècle*. Genève: Droz.

Eelen, g. (2001) *A Critique of Politeness Theories*. Manchester: St Jerome

Ehlich, K. (1992) On the historicity of politeness. In R. J. Watts, S. Ide and K. Ehlich (eds) *Politeness in Language. Studies in Its History, Theory and Practice* (pp. 7–107). Berlin: Mouton de Gruyer.

Elwert, T. (1984) Höflichkeitsformeln im Italienischen. In G. Holtus and E. Radtke (eds) *Umgangssprache in der Iberoromania* (pp. 405–413). Tübingen: Narr.

Goffman, E. (1971) *Modelli di interazione*. Bologna: Il Mulino. (Translation of *Interaction Ritual*. New York, 1967.)

Haferland, H. and Paul, I. (1996) Eine Theorie der Höflichkeit. In H. Haferland and L. Paul (eds) *Höflichkeit Osnabrücker Beiträge zur Sprachtheorie 52* (pp. 7–69).

Held, G. (1993) *'Volevo chiederti una cosa'* oder *'vorrei chiederti una cosa'*? Zur morpho-pragmatischen Distinktion in höflichen Interaktionseinheiten. *Italienische Studien* 14, 5–33.

Held, G. (1994) Höflichkeitsstrategien in der Alltagsinteraktion (mit einem Bittbeispiel aus dem Italienischen). In G. Held (ed.) *Verbale Interaktion* (pp. 101–24). Hamburg: Kovac.

Held, G. (1995) *Verbale Höflichkeit. Studien zur linguistischen Theorienbildung und Untersuchung zum Sprachverhalten französischer und italienischer Jugendlicher in Bitt- und Dankessituationen.* Tübingen: Narr.

Held, G. (1999) Submission strategies as an expression of the ideology of politeness: Reflection on the verbalisation of social power relations. *Pragmatics* 9, 21–37.

Kainz, F. (1965) *Psychologie der Sprache. Vol.5: Psychologie der Einzelsprachen.* Stuttgart: Enke.

Lakoff, R.(1978) La logica della cortesia ovvero bada come parli. In M. Sbisà (ed.) *Gli atti linguistici* (pp. 220–39). Milano: Feltrinelli.

Leech, G. N. (1983) *Principles of Pragmatics*. London: Longman.

Loos, E. (1980) *Literatur und Formung eines Menschenideals. Das 'Libro del Cortegiano' von Baldassare Castiglione*. Wiesbaden: Steiner.

Montandon, A. (1995) *Dictionnaire raisonné de la politesse et du savoir-vivre.* Paris: Seuil.

Mullini, R. (1982) Il rinvio della sfida e le regole del salotto in 'A woman of no importance' di O. Wilde. In G. Aston (ed.) *Interazione, dialogo, convenzioni* (pp. 223–34). Bologna: CLUEB.

Pierini, P. (1983) Struttura e uso di alcune formule di cortesia. In F. Orletti (ed.) *Comunicare nella vita quotidiana* (pp.105–17). Bologna: Il Mulino.

Radtke, E. (1994) *Gesprochenes Französisch und Sprachgeschichte. Zur Rekonstruktion der Gesprächskonstitution in Dialogen französischer Sprachlehrbücher*. Tübingen: Niemeyer.

Radtke, E. (1995) Segnali di cortesia nell'italiano parlato. *Romanistik in Geschichte und Gegenwart* 2(2), 163–88.

Saccone, E. (1992) *Le buone e le cattive maniere. Letterature e Galateo nel Cinquecento.* Bologna: Il Mulino.

Spitzer, L. (1922) *Italienische Umgangssprache*. Bonn/Leipzig: Schröder.

Stati, S. (1983) Tre dimensioni pragmatiche delle repliche oppure come si reagisce agli imperativi. *Grazer Linguistische Studien* 20, 153–69.

Wierzbicka, A. (1991) *Cross-cultural Pragmatics: The Semantics of Human Interaction.* Berlin: Mouton de Gruyter.

Chapter 21

Politeness in Portugal: How to Address Others

MARIA HELENA ARAÚJO CARREIRA

Individuals in interaction with others, whatever social or cultural group they belong to, pay a greater or lesser degree of attention to the needs and desires of these others. This attention, which Pottier (1992) describes as highly polysemiological, varies according to cultural, social and individual factors.

If we merely consider linguistic manifestations of politeness, we cannot but note their importance in discourse, in verbal interaction in particular, but also in the language system itself. Language systems have within them the means to convey politeness. In Weinrich's (1986: 11) view politeness should not be sought outside of verbal behaviour which would be a sterile, commonsensical exercise of a merely informative nature; rather, politeness should be located within the very inner core of language.

It is indeed within the inner core of language and discourse that we should locate linguistic realisations of politeness. Within this view, human language behaviour is not merely cognitive in nature; we must also take into consideration its social and affective or emotional dimensions, which are of supreme importance in verbal communication.

Depending on the language, there are different linguistic resources available for conveying politeness although similar solutions may be found from one language to another. This is the case, for example, with greetings, compliments, thanks, apologies and mitigators of remarks considered too abrupt, or even offensive, different ways of expressing deference towards one's interlocutor, lexical euphemisms, phatic discourse markers, and also a variety of ways of conveying modality, to mention but a few of these resources.

Politeness appears at the level of discourse where the illocutionary force of the utterance (by the speaker) is or is not identified (by the hearer).

The idea of appropriateness to the context is central to any study of linguistic politeness. A linguistic form or phrase divorced from its context of utterance cannot in itself be considered to be polite or impolite: it is speakers and hearers who, through their utterances and verbal interaction, confer on them such significance.

Of course, rules vary according to individuals, social groups within a particular culture and *a fortiori* from one culture to another but, as studies based on Brown and Levinson's (1978, 1987) model show, there are universal principles which govern politeness. Essentially there is the notion of 'positive face' and 'negative face' (Goffman, 1973, 1974). 'Positive politeness' (for example, praise or compliments) seeks to enhance the Hearer's face; what is called 'negative' politeness, which is compensatory (as seen, for example, in apologies), seeks to repair acts likely to threaten the Hearer's 'face' or 'territory'.

In this chapter, our aim is to study how politeness is realised culturally and linguistically in European Portuguese. Studies of politeness in other cultures will enable us to study its realisation in Portuguese and to look at the particularly rich linguistic resources available in this language. We will concentrate, in particular, on interactional openings and closures, on the address system and on resources available for indirectness and mitigation.

Individuals, just like social groups and cultures, have their own particular 'styles'; consequently, 'positive' and 'negative' politeness are realised in different ways and using different resources, the richness of which also varies (Haverkate, 1994, Kerbrat-Orecchioni, 1991; *Les Langues Modernes*, 2000). However, according to Brown and Levinson (1987: 134) 'negative politeness is more important in Western societies and consequently is more developed linguistically'.

Cross-cultural politeness studies reveal the parameters at work at different levels (from macro- to micro-analysis). We identify a number of these presented by their authors as opposites which we situate as the extreme values of a continuum.

On tact *versus* frankness, Béal's (1993: 105) work on conversational strategies in French and English in Australia shows how the 'frankness of the French becomes "abruptness" to Australians' and how 'Australian tact is seen as hypocritical by the French'.

On consensus *versus* conflict (see Kerbrat-Orecchioni, 1994: 82–8), studies of Japanese society have shown the importance of values such as empathy, a desire for harmony and an aversion to conflict. This kind of society, with a 'consensus ethos', is diametrically opposed to societies with a 'confrontational ethos' (e.g. Israeli society).

On exchanges focused on content *versus* those focused on relationships (Kerbrat-Orecchioni, 1994: 84), the Germans are said to attach greater importance to 'establishing the truth of the matter', while Anglo-Saxons are more concerned with the personal relationships than with the content (for German, see House, this volume).

On gregarious relationships *versus* the safeguarding of individuality, the comparison drawn by Sifianou (1992) between the Greek and English systems shows that Greek relationships within the group are considered more important while, in English, safeguarding one's individuality is highlighted. This distinction is closely related to that of 'positive' and 'negative politeness'.

Bearing in mind these types of distinction, found in comparative macro-studies of linguistic politeness across different societies, if we wish to locate Portuguese politeness along these axes, we could say that gregarious relationships, consensus and tact are favoured over confrontation, frankness or the protection of an individual's territory. Cooperative strategies are consequently of great importance in verbal interaction in Portuguese. Specific speech acts (greetings, closing conversations, thanking, congratulating, requesting, expressing disagreement etc.), choice of theme and rhematic development are conveyed by linguistic structures and politeness strategies which the conversational maxims of Grice (1975/9), based on the cognitive structure of conversation, would find it difficult to account for. Leech's (1983) politeness principle, however, with its tact, generosity, approval, modesty and sympathy maxims, which relate to the psycho-social dimension of verbal interaction, here comes into force. The importance the Portuguese pay to relationships with others (whether within the family, amongst friends or neighbours etc.) gives rise to many communication rituals which express solidarity and sharing at an affective level. Thus, when attention is paid to the Hearer's territory, the Speaker often engages in self-abasement and other forms of modesty. From a cross-cultural perspective, the German Romance linguist Kröll (1980–86:71) draws our attention to the large number of politeness formulae in spoken Portuguese (see also Ribeiro Pedro, 1993). He notes that in a country like Portugal, where conviviality (*a convivência*) is considered so important, it is hardly surprising that this imposes linguistic constraints on speakers.

If we look at the initial moves in openings and closures of conversations, there are a great number of formulas commonly used. For example, *Português Fundamental* and *Nível Limial,* which present only the most frequently recurring forms, provide 19 openings and 11 closures:

(1) three can be used for both functions: *bom dia, boa tarde, boa noite;*
(2) 16 are specific to openings: *olá, como estás/está/estão?; estás/está bom/boa?; estão bons/boas?; passaste/passou bem?; como tens/tem/têm passado?; viva; então; bem obrigado/a (e o/a senhor/a); vou indo, vou andando; menos mal; tudo bem/óptimo (e tu?); mais ou menos (e você?); vai-se andando; vai-se indo;*
(3) eight are specific to closures: *até já; até logo; até amanhã; adeus; (tive) muito prazer em vê-lo/a; (tive) muito gosto; ciao; adeuzinho.*

We should also bear in mind other formulas, not mentioned in these reference books because they occur less frequently, because they are less representative or because they were not yet so when *Português Fundamental* (1984, 1987a, 1987b) and *Nível Limiar* (Malaca Casteleiro *et al.* 1988) were published (for example, the greeting *tudo bem contigo/consigo?*). These formulas combine with a variety of sequences which make up the opening or closure, giving rise to complex sequences where greetings are combined with one or more of the following elements:

- expression of positive feelings towards the other (e.g. *Que bom ver-te! Estás óptimo/a! Que bem te fica o azul!*); and
- requests for information about (i) health, (ii) work or (iii) other activities of Hearer, (iv) family, friends and relatives e.g. (i) *Como está?; Como vai essa saúde?*; (ii) *O trabalho está a correr bem?);* (iii) *Como correu a viagem?;* (iv) *A familia está bem?/Estão todos bem?.*

These elements, typical of opening sequences, obviously vary, enabling speakers to regulate the relationship they are creating by their very interaction.

When we look at brief exchanges, verbal interaction may be reduced merely to opening and closing elements. However, openings frequently become more complex and more lengthy and provide the core of the conversation: thematic implications of the initial elements are expanded upon to various degrees of complexity.

Closure is rarely carried out merely by a simple leave-taking formula (e.g. *adeus/até logo/bom dia/ boa tarde/ boa noite…)*. The moment of closure is frequently postponed by speakers and hearers:

- expressing how happy they are to have met (e.g. *gostei tanto de te ver; tive muito prazer em o encontrar; foi um prazer*);
- giving an excuse for being unable to continue the conversation (e.g. *tenho de ir andando, estão à minha espera/está a chegar a hora do comboio*);
- apologising (e.g. *desculpe; peço desculpa; queira desculpar*);
- giving or sending good wishes to the hearer and his or her friends and relations (e.g. *que tudo corra bem; felicidades; boa viagem*);
- sending greetings to the family or friends of the hearer (e.g. *cumprimentos à família; dê um abraço meu ao João; beijinhos à Ana*); and
- offering help (e.g. *se precisares de alguma coisa, diz!; fico ao dispor*);

and, at the moment of final closure, they may even pick up the conversation again by reviving a previous topic (e.g. *E a reunião de ontem correu bem?* [Did yesterday's meeting go well?]*; Ah, é verdade, os tratamentos da tua mãe estão a dar bom resultado?* [Oh, by the way, is your mother's treatment going well?]). Closure may in this way be protracted even by re-commencing the interaction: interactants exchange hugs, shake hands, reinitiate the conversation and then take leave again. The time for separation is thus deferred so that the verbal interaction can close within a climate of warmth, solidarity and mutual affection.

Obviously, to succeed at this kind of interaction, it is essential for the interlocutors to have communicative and conversational competence. They need to come to a judgement about relationships and all other pragmatic variables (to whom, about whom, where, about what, how, with what purpose are the speakers talking?). From a politeness perspective, too much or no linguistic politeness may be perceived as impolite. Weinrich (1986: 27) draws our attention to the unwelcome effects of 'exaggerated politeness'. Whether the verbal interaction merely comprises openings and closures or something more, it is easy to understand the importance for the interpersonal relationship of the different moves as they develop, providing face-work or *figuração* (Fonseca, 1992: 298; 2001: 147). That is why it is essential to match selected linguistic forms to the context of interaction.

As this matching is often difficult to achieve at an interpersonal level and in social relationships within a given culture, it is not surprising that it can give rise to cross-cultural misunderstandings. That is why a sequence of opening and closing moves which appear polite to a Portuguese speaker may appear as 'exaggerated politeness' to foreigners whose culture does not value (at least to the same degree) 'positive politeness', that is the relationship dimension of verbal interaction. Likewise, when Portuguese people are in contact with foreign cultures and languages which attach less importance to gregarious relationships, the enhancement of the face of the interlocutor or a harmonious interpersonal relationship, they perceive as lacking in politeness or even as downright rude certain verbal behaviours (or their absence), which, within that culture, may be perfectly appropriate in terms of politeness. More insidiously, cross-cultural misunderstandings arise when utterances produced in one language are given the illocutionary force and interpersonal meaning they would have in another culture (see Hickey [2000] who shows how acts of politeness in an English text are not perceived as such in a Spanish translation by Spanish readers).

Opening and closing sequences, as constitutive elements of verbal interaction, are an ideal arena in which to study politeness cross-culturally. A comparative glance at some of the psychosocial behaviour of different cultures allows us to take a relativistic view of politeness. For example, the French expression *filer à l'anglaise* is found in Portuguese as *despedir-se à francesa* (like the English phrase 'to take French leave'), that is to evade something, to leave without saying goodbye, to fail to close an interaction appropriately. This behaviour is perceived as impolite within the politeness rules governing the Portuguese system. As we have seen, closure of verbal interaction in Portuguese serves to soften the separation, to attenuate the breaking of the interaction, to enhance the positive face of oneself and others, and to stress the quality of the interpersonal relationship.

The mitigating effect of what might be perceived as being too abrupt can also be found in apologies and requests for permission. They may precede:

- a change of topic (e.g. ***desculpe****, mas lembrei-me agora que o João chega amanhã*);
- brief leave-taking (e.g. ***com licença****, volto já*);
- hanging up at the end of a telephone call (e.g. *com licença*);
- entering a private space or one considered to be such (*com licença*);
- certain actions thought to be disagreeable to the hearer, such as tearing paper (*com licença/desculpe*), opening or closing a door between speaker and hearer or closing a car door, particularly if it is on the hearer's side (*com licença).*

Although this list is far from exhaustive, it shows the type of situation which elicits politeness routines in Portuguese. Leech's (1983) tact maxim is clearly exemplified.

The maxims of tact and modesty (Leech, 1983) find in the system of address forms in Portuguese an inexhaustible range of resources for regulating verbal interaction. This is a complex system with a large number of forms which allow fine nuancing in differentiating between referring to self and others.

If we take as our reference point the classic study by Brown and Gilman (1960) of pronouns of address, we cannot but conclude that this model does not fully describe the Portuguese system. The basic opposition established by these authors between 'pronouns of power' and 'pronouns of solidarity' is reduced to two paradigmatic forms, T/V, which, according to them, account for the forms of address used by most languages in the world (for Spanish, see Hickey, this volume). However, if we examine closely the address forms in Portuguese, we can see that this model does not apply, a conclusion reached also by Oliveira Medeiros in her doctoral thesis (1985; see also 1993). The complexity of the Portuguese system derives mainly from the fact that there are innumerable nominal other-address forms which are used delocutively, with the verb in the third-person, or without any pronoun or noun at all (null pronoun), in which case the form of address is encoded in the morphology of the verb.

If we take the example of *tu/vous* in French, which fits within Brown and Gilman's model, and look for possible equivalents in general use in

Portuguese, we immediately see the variety of ways in which V can be expressed: Portuguese offers a whole range of forms, the use of which may vary slightly from one social or geographical group to another. If we chart the main nuances which emerge in referring to the hearer along the axis of familiarity/distance and try to compare the two languages, we find several differences in degree and reference.

Thus, *tu* in French only partially equates to *tu* in Portuguese because even though its use is becoming more common in Portuguese, it is not used in any case as much as in French. For example, unlike French the Portuguese *tu* is not used with older members of the family or at work with colleagues with whom one is not on familiar terms. Therefore, *tu* in French corresponds to certain V forms in Portuguese which express familiarity. This is the case for many uses of *você* (Hammermüller, 1993a) and for certain nominal forms of other-address (followed, like *você*, by the verb in the third-person singular).

Nominal forms of other-address (followed by the verb in the third-person) in European Portuguese allow differentiation along the axis of familiarity/distance similar to that of oriental languages which encode honorifics morphologically (a feature which does not exist in Portuguese). This differentiation is commonly expressed in French by the vocative, by the choice of first or last name, accompanied or not by the honorific *Monsieur* or *Madame.*

Let us consider some common examples of forms of address and use of V in Portuguese, ranging from + familiar to – familiar, along with their equivalents in French. It should be said that the noun form followed by a third-person used to an addressee does exist in French (e.g. *Ana sait ce qui se passe?* [Ana knows what is happening?] but its use is much less common than in Portuguese.

- *Você* + third-person verb
  Você sabe o que se passa?
  (Fr. *Est-ce que tu sais/vous savez ce qui se passe?*)

- First name + third-person verb
  A Ana sabe o que se passa?
  (Fr. *Ana, est-ce que vous savez ce qui se passe?*)
- [Masculine addressee] Last name + third-person verb
  O Soares sabe o que se passa?
  (Fr. *Soares, est-ce que vous savez ce qui se passe?*)

- [Masculine addressee] *O senhor* + first name (+ last name) + third-person verb

O senhor Carlos/Soares/Carlos Soares tem horas, por favor?
(Fr. *Monsieur…, est-ce que vous avez l'heure, s'il vous plaît?*)

- [Feminine addressee] *A senhora/A dona/A senhora dona* + first name + third-person verb
  A senhora Maria/A dona Maria/A senhora dona Maria tem horas, por favor?
  (Fr. *Madame…, est-ce que vous avez l'heure, s'il vous plaît?*)
- *O senhor/A senhora* + third-person verb
- *O senhor* + professional title (+ last name) + third-person verb
  Common professional titles: *dr.* (*doutor*), *engenheiro*, *arquitecto*
- *A senhora* + professional title (+ first name [first name + last name]) + third-person verb
  Common professional titles: *dra* (*doutora*), *engenheira*, *arquitecta*
- *O senhor* + function + title (+ first name) + last name + third-person verb
- *A senhora* + function + title (+ first name/[first name + last name]) + third-person verb
- *V. Ex^{a}* (*Vossa excelência*) + third-person verb
  (in official ceremonial greetings)

The importance given to delocutive forms used for addressee reference is quite striking. Portuguese provides a prime example of the codification of indirectness (negative politeness) both within the structure of the language itself and in the rules for its use.

Let us mention that, in Brazil, *você* is gradually replacing *tu* (see, e.g., Camargo Biderman, 1972–73). It is used more widely than in Portugal, covering intimacy and familiarity as well as an intermediate area between familiarity and deference. The polite form of address in Brazil is simply *o(s) senhor(es)/a(s) senhora(s)*. This variety of Portuguese fits in with Brown and Gilman's T/V model.

The absence or dropping of a nominal or pronominal other-address form with the verb in the third-person (in European Portuguese) provides a kind of zero degree of politeness and allows speakers to avoid making what could be a delicate choice.

The variety of address forms in European Portuguese which are in common everyday use allows differentiation along hierarchical lines (notably according to age, kinship, profession) and along the axis of familiarity/distance. The interpersonal relationship is played out along both axes: the vertical hierarchical and the horizontal axes of relative distance. Consequently, the geometry of verbal interaction is variable and conveyed by the means used to refer to oneself and others (see Araújo Carreira, 1997, 2001). The use of an inappropriate form by which to address one's interlocutor must have implications for the expression of politeness.

The differentiation which Portuguese offers in terms of forms of address is a perfect example of Weinrich's (1986: 16) rule governing verbal politeness: 'When two expressions are available for a given situation, one of which is clearly delimited and the other more fuzzy, it is always the fuzzier form which will be considered as the more polite.'

If we take as an example of the use of V (to one's addressee), in a dative construction, then the cline of politeness – in relation with the situation of utterance – is as follows:

Este livro é para	*si*	(this book is for you)
	o Senhor António	(this book is for you Mr António)
	o Senhor Sousa	(this book is for you Mr Sousa)
	o senhor	(this book is for you, sir)

Para si, which is a truly deictic construction, is a 'clearly delimited' term, whereas *para o senhor* is a 'fuzzier' form, as the deictic function of this form of other-address is elided by its referential meaning (see Hammermüller, 1993b); it acts to attenuate the directness of the reference.

Pluralisation is another resource for attenuating self- and other-reference. Thus, *nós* (we) may replace *eu* (I) in speech, that is, a delocutive plural can take the place of a singular (this is very common in scientific articles). (For a nice example of the pluralisation of *eu* in Portuguese in an utterance where criticism is mitigated by pluralisation see Said Ali (1951: 76).

Mitigation strategies suggest fuzziness and indeterminacy. In this connection, Weinrich (1986: 17) recalls the anthropologist Plessner (1981), according to whom indirectness 'is the defining feature of man compared with animal'.

Politeness is frequently conveyed through indeterminacy and indirectness. From the point of view of theme management, the fact that Portuguese enables the speaker to avoid expressing the subject or the complement(s) of an utterance is frequently exploited to make reference 'fuzzier' and to avoid negative effects on the smooth running of the interaction. Reference is thus 'filtered' by politeness which, as Leech (1983) has convincingly argued, is a fundamental element of all verbal interaction (the 'politeness principle').

The study of linguistic politeness in Portugal, then, illustrated here by some examples of how it is realised both linguistically and culturally, allows us to stress the importance of the psycho-social dimension of verbal interaction, as well as the shared and specific ways in which it is conveyed.

References

Araújo Carreira, M.A. (1997) *Modalisation linguistique en situation d'interlocution: proxémique verbale et modalités en portugais.* Louvain, Paris: Peeters (Col. Bibliothèque de l'Information Grammaticale 37).

Araújo Carreira, M.A. (2001) *Semântica e Discurso. Estudos de Linguística portuguesa e comparativa (Português/Francês).* Porto: Porto Editora (Col. Linguística 13).

Béal, C. (1993) Les stratégies conversationnelles en français et en anglais. *Langue Française*, 98, 79–106.

Brown, P. and Levinson, S. (1978) Universals in language usage: Politeness phenomena. In E. Goody (ed.) *Questions and Politeness: Strategies in Social Interaction* (pp. 56–289). Cambridge: Cambridge University Press.

Brown, P. and Levinson, S. (1987) *Politeness: Some Universals in Language Usage.* Cambridge: Cambridge University Press.

Brown, R. and Gilman, A. (1960) The pronouns of power and solidarity. In T.A. Sebeok (ed.) *Style in language* (pp. 253–76). Cambridge, MA: MIT Press.

Camargo Biderman, M.T. (1972–73) Formas de tratamento e estruturas sociais. *ALFA 18/19*, 339–81.

Fonseca, J. (1992) As articulações discurso-metadiscurso e a sua exploração na didáctica do português como língua estrangeira. In J. Fonseca (ed.) *Linguística e Texto / Discurso. Teoria, descrição, aplicação* (pp. 293–313). Lisboa: Instituto de Cultura e Língua Portuguesa.

Fonseca, J. (2001) *Língua e discurso* (Col. Linguística 14). Porto: Porto Editora .

Goffman, E. (1973) *La mise en scène de la vie quotidienne. Vol. 1. La présentation de soi. Vol. 2. Les relations en public.* Paris: Minuit.

Goffman, E. (1974) *Les rites d'interaction.* Paris: Minuit.

Grice, H. P. (1979) Logic and conversation. In P. Cole (ed.) *Syntax and Semantics (Vol. 3, Syntax and Semantics).* New York: Academic Press.

Hammermüller, G. (1993a) *Die Anrede im Portugiesischen. Eine sociolinguistische Untersuchung zu Anredekonventionen des gegenwärtigen europäischen Portugiesisch.* Chemnitz: Nov Never.

Hammermüller, G. (1993b) Ist die portugiesische Anredeform 'o senhor' ein Nomen, ein Pronomen oder gar ein Pro-pronomen? In A. Schönberger and M. Scotti-Rosin (eds) *Einzelfragen der portugiesische sprachwissenschaft. Acten des 2. gemeinsamen Kolloquiums der deutschsprachiger Lusitanistik und Katalanistik (Berlin, 10–12 sept. 1992). Band 2. Lusitanistischer Teil* (pp. 34–43). Frankfurt am Main: TFM / Domus Editoria Europea.

Haverkate, H (1994) *La cortesía verbal: estudio pragmalingüístico.* Madrid: Gredos.

Hickey, L. (2000) Politeness in translation between English and Spanish. *Target 12* (2), 229–240.

Kerbrat-Orecchioni, C. (1991) La politesse dans les interactions verbales. In *Dialoganalyse III Actes du Congrès de Bologna 1990* (Vol. I) (pp. 39–59). Tübingen: Max Niemeyer.

Kröll, H. (1980–86) Contribuições para o estudo da linguagem falada em português. *Revista Portuguesa de Filologia* (Coimbra) XVIII, 71–96.

Les Langues Modernes. Dossier: La politesse (2000). Février–mars–avril, N° 1. Paris: Association des Professeurs de Langues Vivantes

Leech, G. N. (1983) *Principles of Pragmatics*. London / NewYork: Longman.

Malaca Casteleiro, J., Meira, A. and Pascoal, J. (1988) *Nível Limiar*. Lisboa: ICALP, Ministério da Educação (Conselho da Europa).

Oliveira Medeiros, S.M. (1985) A model of address forms in negotiation: A socio-linguistic study of continental Portuguese. Dissertation, University of Texas.

Oliveira Medeiros, S.M. (1993) Um modelo psico-sociolinguístico de formas de tratamento. *Actas do VIII° Encontro da Associação Portuguesa de Linguística* (Lisboa, Universidade Nova, Faculdade de Ciências Sociais e Humanas, 1–3 de Outubro de 1992) (pp. 330–42). Lisboa: Associação Portuguesa de Linguística.

Pottier, B. (1992) *Sémantique générale*. Paris: PUF.

Português Fundamental (1984). Vol. 1. Vocabulário e Gramática: Tomo 1. Vocabulário. Lisboa: Instituto Nacional de Investigação Científica, Centro de Linguística da Universidade de Lisboa.

Português Fundamental (1987a) Bacelar do Nascimento. In M.F. Garcia, M.L. Marques and M.L. Segura da Cruz (eds) *Português Fundamental: Vol. 2. Métodos e Documentos: Tomo I. Inquérito de frequência.* Lisboa: Instituto Nacional de Investigação Científica, Centro de Linguística da Universidade de Lisboa.

Português Fundamental (1987b). Bacelar do Nascimento. In M.F. Garcia, P. Rivenc and M.L. Segura da Cruz (eds) *Português Fundamental: Vol. 2. Métodos e Documentos: Tomo II. Inquérito de disponibilidade.* Lisboa: Instituto Nacional de Investigação Científica, Centro de Linguística da Universidade de Lisboa.

Ribeiro Pedro, E. (1993) À volta dos diminutivos – uma análise contrastiva entre o português e o inglês. *Actas do VIII° Encontro da Associação Portuguesa de Linguística* (Lisboa, Universidade Nova, Faculdade de Ciências Sociais e Humanas, 1–3 de Outubro de 1992) (pp. 402–17). Lisboa: Associação Portuguesa de Linguística.

Said Ali, M. (1951) *Meios de expressão e alterações semânticas* (2nd edn). Rio de Janeiro: Fundação Getúlio Vargas. (First edition 1930)

Sifianou, M. (1992) The use of diminutives in expressing politeness: Modern Greek *versus* English. *Journal of Pragmatics* 17 (2), 155–73.

Weinrich, H. (1986) *Lügt man im Deutschen, wenn man höflich ist?* Wien, Zürich, Mannheim: Bibliographisches Institut.

Chapter 22

Politeness in Spain: Thanks But No 'Thanks'

LEO HICKEY

The Spanish language has no single term corresponding to 'politeness'. The range of behaviour encompassed by the English term can be analysed into various concepts including *cortesía*, courtesy, *educación*, good behaviour, *buenos modales*, good manners, *formalidad*, correct behaviour, *simpatía*, friendliness, and qualities like *fino*, refined. Brown and Levinson's (1987: 129–30) claim 'When we think of politeness in Western cultures, it is negative-politeness behaviour that springs to mind' may be applicable to Spanish culture but with the stress on 'thinking' not 'doing'. Spaniards admire people who say 'please', 'thanks, 'sorry' and 'excuse me' and, indeed, their practice is moving towards this model but negative-politeness practices such as leaving others alone to live in peace and quiet find little favour with them.

By a happy symmetry, however, just as Spaniards seldom leave others alone to live quietly, neither do they like being left alone themselves: the average Spaniard's image of hell is close to others' 'peace and quiet'. Happily, too, millions of tourists who visit Spain each year perceive Spaniards as friendly, outgoing, likeable, jolly people and thoughts of 'politeness' get lost in these warmly admired qualities. Of the three dimensions into which the great politeness expert Victoria Escandell Vidal (1998a: 46) divides politeness (civil/social correctness, kindness/friendliness, tact/diplomacy), the second is the most visible in Spanish practice.

In reviewing Spanish contributions to politeness theory, Silvia Iglesias Recuero (2001: 245–298) highlights investigations of turn-taking in conversation, participant-reference and speech acts.

On turn-taking, Ana María Cestero, among others, has studied turn-taking strategies, length of turns, friendly and unfriendly interruptions and overlapping. Though using a Spanish corpus, Cestero follows non-Spanish models in postulating:

> The appropriate point for speakers to switch is when the speaker concludes her message…all other switches are inappropriate…Improper

> switching is characterised by an 'interruption', meaning an action to impede the beginning, continuation or conclusion of a message...switches via an interruption are unjustified' (Cestero, 1994: 87–94).

Observation of Spanish conversations, however, in all but very formal meetings between strangers, suggests that Spaniards talk over each other (a) without necessarily 'interrupting' the speaker, (b) without any intention of impeding the beginning, middle or end of a message, but rather (c) most often simply to express an opinion forcefully, showing enthusiasm, passion and positive involvement in the conversation, factors rated more highly than silently awaiting one's 'turn'.

Another great authority on the subject, Henk Haverkate (1988: 385–409), reflects Spanish practice more closely when he explains that Spanish speakers are 'very tolerant' with regard to the maxim 'Don't interrupt'. Hernández Flores (1999: 39) accurately observes that, in colloquial conversation, 'the desire to be unimpeded (negative face) is not a requirement for the smooth running of the interaction ... controversy is appreciated because it shows engagement with the conversation'. Following Bravo's (1998) work, she describes two features of Spanish face as the need for autonomy – manifested in the desire to be perceived as original and sociable -, and affiliation – seen in *confianza*, the closeness which allows people to speak and act freely and openly with one another, showing the individual as integrated into the group (see also Hornero, 2000; Testa, 1988).

Associated with the desire for *confianza*, closeness to others, is the perception of strangers and even absent acquaintances as having few rights. This tendency is noticeable everywhere: e.g. people are unaware of others in the street and move aside only grudgingly to avoid head-on collisions; telephone conversations may take the form: 'Yes? Is Pepe there? No. O.K.'; it would be exceptional to tell friends who are to meet one at the station one's expected time of arrival – that is for them to find out; public officials (like their Ecuadorian counterparts described in Placencia, [2001]) utter scarcely a syllable more than essential to despatch those unfortunate citizens who approach them, although the *ventanilla* – the little window in the partition which keeps the public at arm's length, situated at the level of the victims' navel, obliging them to bow low in order to be seen and heard – has almost disappeared. It may also explain why individuals use first-person singular or ethic datives to represent their employer, as in *No tengo* (I haven't any) or *Cuídeme eso* (Take care of that for me), uttered to a customer by a junior employee in a company employing thousands.

Conversation is the most cherished Spanish social activity: it proceeds incessantly, seldom inhibited by extraneous factors like television or other conversations going on simultaneously. Silence is not so much embarrassing as a stimulus to more talk: it would be interesting to investigate the average number of milliseconds of silence that elapse before one interlocutor asks another whether they are ill or depressed.

The enormous subject of participant-reference ('I', 'you'), treated by other contributors to this volume, is complicated in Spain (for the Portuguese system see Araújo Carreira, this volume) by the historical evolution of the forms of address (generally away from formal, towards informal, alternatives) from 1931, when the Second Republic favoured 'brotherly' informality, through the 1936–39 Civil War and a 35 year dictatorship (which also promoted the 'comradely' alternatives), through a long post-1975 transition period (witnessing a fairly radical move, or perhaps return, from the informal to the formal alternatives). While the choice of how to address others is presumably based on objective and observable factors in each situation, mainly the interactants' age (see Escandell Vidal, 1998b:17), their social status, personal relationships, physical surroundings and even the weather and time of day (sunshine or night-time probably favouring informality), yet these parameters are impossible to summarise accurately.

Briefly, there is a choice of informal/formal ways of saying 'you': *tú/vosotros* take the second-person of the verb, singular and plural, respectively, *usted/ustedes* take the third-person, singular and plural. The second-person is used among relatives, friends, colleagues, young people and others of equal 'status', whether acquainted or not, while the third-person prevails in formal situations or among strangers of, say, 50 upwards who do not envisage having any personal relationship with one another. The usage is not necessarily reciprocal: older persons may use *tú* to youngsters, who in turn use *usted*. There is little or no embarrassment about changing forms (usually from third to second-person): either participant can simply propose a change or ask the other which they prefer. If unsure, a speaker may use a first-person plural to encompass herself and the hearer, thus avoiding the formal/informal dichotomy and also allowing self-implication in the other's affairs, as in *¿Cómo estamos?* (How are we?). In violent rows, speakers may repeatedly apologise for using *tú* (*y perdona que te tutee*) and then go on insulting one another ever more vehemently using the same 'comradely' form. The usage, which is therefore scarcely comparable with other European patterns, varies considerably throughout Latin America.

Before treating speech acts, I must state baldly that Brown and Levinson's division of politeness into positive and negative applies directly to Spanish society which, on a positive-negative cline, is very close to the positive end (for a similar conclusion relating to Greece, see Sifianou, this volume). This has been agreed since 1991 by virtually all investigators (see e.g. Ballesteros, 2001; Hickey, 1991; Portolés & Vázquez, 2000). Positive politeness, however, is not a homogeneous phenomenon and I must continue to outline the specific forms it takes in Spain.

These include lavish compliments and expressions of praise and appreciation. *¡Qué x eres!* (How x you are!) is a common construction, with virtually any positive-sounding adjective occupying the x slot: good, intelligent, punctual, clever... Such compliments or reassurances as *Te aprecio mucho, Mi mujer te admira, Mis hijos te quieren mucho* ('I appreciate you very much', 'My wife admires you', 'My children like you'), often accompanied by physical contact, seldom count as flattery or insincerity but as cornerstones of friendship and solidarity. Spanish speakers thus expend much time and energy stressing that everything their hearers possess, do, are, say, think and believe is admirable. They do this either directly ('Your Spanish is perfect', said to first-year foreign students practising the dozen words they know) or indirectly ('Our friend Mariano speaks of your brilliant exploits', 'I met that extraordinary person your brother'). It also takes forms like waiting for friends to turn up, e.g., to dine or go out together – obliging others also to wait, of course – much longer after the agreed time than would be acceptable in negative-politeness societies.

Spaniards are relatively tolerant of, or not over-sensitive to, intrusions into their privacy, their space, physical rights or their lives generally. Pushing past others in public places or accidental invasions of others' territory would not necessarily be followed by anything like 'sorry'. Likewise, requests for small favours (such as a cigarette or to be told the time) addressed to friends or strangers in the street would seldom include anything corresponding to 'please' or 'thanks'. Keeping friends waiting might be accompanied, at most, by a perfunctory apology.

We must always keep in mind several intersecting variables in Spanish politeness, such as age, social class, educational level, geographical area (Southerners being more positive-polite and effusive, Northerners more negative-polite and deferential), the degree of solidarity/friendship/intimacy/*confianza*, the formality of the situation and perhaps the language being used (Castilian, Catalan, Galician, Basque etc.). Here I can only give a broad overview as if depicting a homogeneous society. Politeness theory being a descriptive, not a prescriptive, approach to social phenomena, my aim is to describe what happens in real situations, not what might happen according to some ideal norms.

In dealing with speech acts (see Placencia & Bravo, 2002), I will refer to the four varieties of illocutionary function postulated by Leech specifically with politeness in mind (1983: 104–130), namely: (1) the competitive, (2) convivial, (3) collaborative and (4) conflictive functions.

The Competitive Function

The competitive function (where the social goal of having a smooth, pleasant, exchange may conflict with the illocutionary goal of achieving the speakers' objectives) is realised in ordering, requesting, demanding etc. The numerous studies of linguistic mechanisms for performing these speech acts agree that Spanish has various forms of indirectness, but uses them differently and less frequently than other languages. Iglesias (2001: 274–75) writes: '...the imperative in Spanish is not inherently impolite... It is possible that...the direct formulation of requests is considered to be a positive feature in an interaction'. In commanding or requesting, Spaniards (see Márquez Reiter, [2000:171] for the practice in Uruguay) use indirect forms sparingly ('Could you close the door?', 'It's cold in here'), preferring direct alternatives ('Close the door'), sometimes with a compensator, as in 'Close the door, woman' (*Cierra la puerta, mujer*) or 'Shut up, man' (*Cállate, hombre*), where the 'man/woman' tag compensates for the directness by showing sympathy for the addressee (see Portolés & Vázquez, 2000).

However, sometimes interrogatives may replace imperatives: *¿Me podrías llevar a la estación?'/ ¿Me puedes llevar a la estación?/¿Me llevas a la estación?*, ('Could you take me to the station?'/ 'Can you take me to the station?'/ 'Are you taking me to the station?'), with the last form presupposing no previous agreement or request while the first, and most indirect, is the least likely to be used among friends (see Sifianou, this volume). Similarly, speakers may presuppose that a favour has already been granted, as in: 'I'm counting on you to give a lecture tomorrow', this presupposition being the first intimation the hearer has received of any request and not simply a way of confirming something previously agreed.

The Convivial Function

The convivial function, where the social and illocutionary goals coincide, is performed in offering, inviting, greeting, thanking, promising etc. Speech acts are not functionally univocal: for example, a friendly offer or invitation may be interpreted by the receiver as a threat or imposition. Offers and invitations may be formulated as imperatives ('Take it', 'Come to dinner') or the host may simply drive a friend home for dinner without saying a single word about dinner or the invitee's view on the matter. Greetings and congratulations tend to be more effusive than in negative-politeness societies but, for example, the multiple kisses exchanged by persons of either sex on being introduced in some African countries are reflected by only two in Spain and then only between women or persons of the opposite sex; men embrace but only if closely acquainted and after long absences. Here social class, age and the formality of the occasion are crucial: the 'higher' the class, the older the participants or the more formal the situation, the more likely it is that participants will merely shake hands on being introduced and on special occasions thereafter.

Promises, apparently, do not exist in all societies. In Tonga, a locutionary act which looks like a western-type promise is 'not regarded as creating an obligation' but is rather 'an expression of solidarity and concern' (Korn & Korn, 1983). Whether utterances like 'We'll go riding tomorrow' do or do not create an obligation in other societies, in Spain – a society in which promises certainly exist – such utterances would also probably constitute expressions of 'solidarity and concern' and it would be indelicate to remind someone six months later of their failure to fulfil such a 'promise'.

The Collaborative Function

Leech's collaborative function ignores social goals, concentrating on illocutionary goals, in acts such as asserting, reporting, announcing or instructing, to which 'politeness is largely irrelevant' (Leech, 1983:105). These acts may be performed with varying degrees of certainty, as in: 'It will rain', 'I think it will rain', 'I wonder if it will rain' etc. Everyday observation suggests that, in asserting or affirming, Spaniards tend to invest much of their credibility in committing themselves strongly to what they believe, sometimes using personal or metalinguistic implicators such as 'I'm telling you' (*Te lo digo yo*), 'Believe me' (*Créeme*), 'Have no doubt about it' (*No lo dudes*).

The Conflictive Function

On the Conflictive function, where the social and the illocutionary goals conflict, as in threatening, accusing, cursing or reprimanding, Leech (1983: 105) claims that 'politeness is out of the question, because conflictive illocutions are, by their very nature, designed to cause offence'. In everyday Spanish conversation, however, 'conflict' may constitute a form of social interaction, somewhat like playing dominoes, and expressions of conflicting opinions tend to be quite strong. Grounded on the general principle that Spaniards value self-commitment and passionate involvement in the social exchange of views, they unequivocally judge others' statements: 'Don't talk rubbish' (*No diga chorradas*) (see Blas Arroyo, 2001) 'You're stupid' (*Eres tonto*), 'You're mad' (*Estás loco*), before expressing their own – opposing – views on the matter.

Spanish Positive Politeness in Practice

I now wish to report on a small-scale experiment, as an example and an exemplar of how Spanish positive politeness works in practice. Over a number of years, I observed and took notes immediately after each event of every act of present-giving which I witnessed or in which I participated, where the gift was either (a) totally unexpected (Examples 1, 3, 4, see later), (b) unearned but not wholly unexpected (Examples 2, 6, 7) or (c) not really a gift at all but something given at another's request (Example 5). The study, therefore, covers only a particular kind of present-giving (see the classification of thanks in Coulmas, [1981: 74]), ignoring other situations in which one person might thank another: for invitations, congratulations, favours etc. (see Haverkate, 1994: 149–80). I selected six of these authentic events on the criterion of their 'spread of differences', adding a seventh, No. 5, as a control, for the purposes of my experiment.

The object of the experiment was to see (a) whether Spaniards give thanks when they receive gifts and (b), if so, how. Naturally, each interaction involving the present-giving included talk of various kinds but I was interested only in those parts which might be construed as giving thanks and I report below here on those specific segments of each exchange.

With a female colleague, I re-enacted the present-giving scenes in a 'focus group' composed of nine Spanish postgraduate students, five female and four male, aged between 22 and 26. I repeated the situations in two control groups consisting of (a) eight female and four male Spanish and (b) seven female and three male English, first -year university students all aged between 18 and 23. The participants were self-selected from larger groups of about 30 students who were simply invited to participate in 'an experiment on human behaviour'.

After briefly setting each scene and using the original words of each exchange in Spanish (with close idiomatic translations for the English group) and identical gifts (except for Example 3, which I could not replicate), making slight changes for the English control group (e.g. Irish whiskey became caipirinha and *zarzuela* became Egyptology), the groups were asked to comment on the 'behaviour of the persons involved in the following situations', with no hint that politeness – much less only the giving of thanks on the part of the recipient – was being tested. The discussions were openly recorded and I sat taking notes without intervening. The discussions (lasting between four and seven minutes each) went as summarised here, with even briefer summaries of the control groups' comments in square brackets.

Example 1

A customer of a bank in which Elena works brings her a box of chocolates on the day after he has withdrawn a large sum of money in cash, for which she had to work for several hours.

Bank clerk: *¿Pero qué es esto?* (But what's this?).
Grateful customer: *Eso no es nada* (It's nothing).

Comments included: it was nice of the customer to express his gratitude (*agradecimiento*, mentioned three times), after all it was part of her job and there was no reason for him to do this but it showed his gratefulness, *un detalle* (a nice or thoughtful gesture, a token). Note: the recipient's utterance evokes no comment. [Spanish control: He didn't have to do this: Elena was only doing her job. Elena's reaction is quite normal. English control: 'What's this?' means 'What's this for?']

Example 2

The President of a Law Society is given a bottle of Irish whiskey by a colleague from another Law Society who has come to give a lecture at the former's invitation. They have never met before.

Visitor: I don't know if you like Irish whiskey. We were in Ireland last week and I noticed the spelling of 'whiskey' with an 'e'.
Host: Well (*Hombre*), I don't know. Is it different from Scotch? I think I've seen the label but I've never tried it before.

Comments included: This is a *detalle* (twice), it creates a good impression (twice), it makes for good relations, a typical thing to do when you visit someone. Note: the recipient's reaction evokes no comment. [Spanish control: I would have said *Hombre, cómo te has molestado,* ('You shouldn't have gone to that trouble'). English control: He's obviously impressed by the bottle].

Example 3

The Secretary of a Law Society has worked hard organising a visiting lecture and the visitor presents her with an attractive ornamental object. They have spoken by telephone but have never met before.

Visitor: I have given you a lot of work in organising this. Well, now I'm here, let's see how the lecture goes.
Secretary: It's lovely! I love it! I don't know what to say. Anyway, the President is waiting for you in his office, follow me.

Comments included: This is a *detalle* to show gratitude (twice), it doesn't matter what the present is, it's a way of saying *gracias, gracias* (thanks,

thanks), it is a normal thing to do (all agree), the visitor may have felt obliged to bring something, maybe he brought it so as not to *quedar mal* (show himself up, lose face). Note: the recipient's words evoke no comment. [Spanish control: They never say *gracias*, this is typically Spanish, I've spent some time to England and the English always say 'thanks', the English are more *formales* ('correct' in their behaviour), 'I love it' is a way of giving thanks. English control: The secretary's reaction is over the top.]

Example 4

A lady brings her neighbour, an electrician, a pair of wire-strippers back from her holiday.

Neighbour: Look what I've brought you. I don't know how it works but I think it's a new model, German or something.

Electrician: *Huy*, yes, in German it's called a striptease or stripwire, I don't know. How much did it cost you? Wait, I'll put it in the van and I'll be back in a minute. Thanks, eh.

Comments included: The question about how much it cost is strange: does he think she wants him to pay for it? Neighbours don't give one another presents. Maybe she brought it as a souvenir. Note: there is no comment on the recipient's reaction. [Spanish control: The electrician's reaction equals 'thanks'. English control: The electrician is not impressed, his words don't make sense.]

Example 5

A person who taught at University X many years ago telephones a colleague asking her to send him a fairly expensive scarf with the University logo and name. She does so. Three months later, when they meet, she asks him whether it arrived safely.

Former lecturer: Yes, it did. I just wanted a souvenir of the University.

Comments included: This man is *un mal educado increíble* (incredibly bad-mannered); he should have thanked her (*dar las gracias*) – one participant says she had not noticed that point. Apart from the cost of the scarf, he should have shown signs of life, he should have given thanks. All the comments refer to the recipient's attitude as *mala educación*. [Spanish control: He should have said that the scarf had arrived. English control: Didn't even say thanks, he should have replied to say thanks, doesn't offer to pay for the scarf.]

Example 6

A University lecturer visits an old friend living in a distant town.

Knowing that the host likes *zarzuela* (Spanish light opera), the guest brings her an expensive edition of a book on *zarzuela*.

Host: Ah, *El mundo de la zarzuela*. So it's out at last. I saw it advertised but I hadn't seen it yet. It is an important work and I'm sure it's well written.

Comments included: She gives thanks, she appreciates the present, but she should have said *gracias,* anyway she has given thanks; no, I don't know, that depends on the degree of friendship between them, the expression is what matters, it's implicit. Anyway, she has thanked him. *Note*: only the recipient's reaction evokes comments. [Spanish control: All these people (referring to this and the preceding situations) give thanks implicitly but close friends do not give thanks. English control: Like the last one, doesn't say thanks. 'I've just realised that none of these people have said thanks', the first girl in the bank was caught out, taken unawares, but the others... whether you should say thanks depends on the context.]

Example 7:

A lawyer from Madrid visits his friend, also a lawyer, in Alicante and takes him a bottle of Scotch.

Visitor: You know I appreciate you very much (*te aprecio mucho*). I've brought you this, I don't know if you'll like it [probably referring to the particular brand]. I never touch whisky so I don't know what it's like.

Host: Oh, that's great (*Vaya, qué estupendo*). Would you like to come to a concert with us? We were just about to set out. There'll be no problem with tickets.

Comments included: He shows his gratitude, no he doesn't, he feels under an obligation, 'That's great' says nothing, it was too abrupt, he should first have given thanks, should have said *gracias*, 'thanks'. 'If someone brought me a present I'd forget the concert', he hasn't given thanks, that's no way to say *gracias*, 'thanks', if he had shown he appreciated something it would show that he was grateful. [Spanish control: Worse than the last one, doesn't give thanks, very curt. English control: This is a brush-off, as if putting the bottle to one side, but at least he offers to take the friend out; 'you can come' is a kind of thanks, the first thing you'd say is thanks, I would say thanks, you'd think these people would say thanks.]

An analysis of the discussion, in which I will not include gender-related differences, suggests the following:

(a) Giving thanks in Spain (for comparable practices in Greece see

Hirschon, [2001]) is expected in situations in which a person gives a present or does a favour, including inviting someone to visit or to give a lecture but doing one's job, even if onerous and beneficial to another, does not require thanks.

(b) Giving thanks is an action which may or may not be performed formulaically e.g. with ready-made devices, like the word *gracias* or similar: only in Example 4 is *gracias* used and this elicits no comment.

(c) Any expression of appreciation of the object presented counts as giving thanks provided it is reasonably explicit and sincere: the bank clerk in Example 1, the President of the Law Society in Example 2, the Secretary in Example 3, the electrician in Example 4 and the host in Example 6 have all given thanks adequately but the lawyer in Example 7 has not and, this being so, the group requires him to utter the word *gracias*, 'thanks', which I, therefore, suggest is the 'unmarked' or 'default' way of thanking.

(d) Silence does not count as giving thanks: the reactions to the ex-university lecturer in Example 5 were all negative.

If we return to Escandell Vidal's (1998a) tripartite classification of politeness into civil/socially correct, kind/friendly and tactful/diplomatic, we can now say that thanking in Spain fulfils, and is required to fulfil, a 'civil/socially correct' function – in addition to the kind/friendly function mentioned earlier. Escandell Vidal (1998a: 48) writes: 'if I do you a favour, I would probably expect that you expressed gratitude!'. This may be true but it seems that expressing gratitude is not necessarily doing or saying anything that sounds like 'thanks'. As Haverkate explains (1993:150), a person who fails to give thanks 'will be considered as...an impolite speaker'. This is confirmed here but the issue is what constitutes 'giving thanks'. Haverkate (p 160) goes on:

> giving thanks is a speech act which serves specifically to redress the balance in the cost–benefit relation between speaker and hearer, which means that the thanking formulas compensate symbolically for the cost invested by the hearer for the benefit of the speaker... not to redress the cost–benefit balance by not thanking the other ...is considered as a form of impolite behaviour.

Following Searle, Norrick (1978) writes: 'The social function of thanking is generally the acknowledgement of one's having benefited from the actions of another person...expressive illocutionary acts [of which thanking is one] are associated with the speaker's presupposition of the truth of the proposition expressed', that is the speaker presupposes that the hearer has done something for the speaker's benefit. Held (1999: 30) goes further, saying:

> the receiver of a gift [,] is manoeuvred into a particular kind of dependency ... The consequence is a feeling of guilt. The speaker therefore attempts to level out the degree of guilt verbally with forms of self-denigration and somehow to 'deal' with her/his personal insecurity or discomfort in accordance with the circumstance.

Could it be, then, that at least one Spanish way of thanking, discussed earlier, counts as giving thanks but without admitting, even implicitly, that any debt has been incurred or that any balance needs to be redressed, without acknowledging or presupposing that the hearer has done anything for the speaker's benefit? Brown and Levinson (1987: 67) claim that, in thanking, 'S accepts a debt, humbles his own face': but this is precisely what does not happen in (at least this kind of) Spanish thanking.

Bernard de Clerck points out (personal communication, 2003) that, in certain situations, Dutch thanking formulas do not primarily convey gratitude, which is Searle's sincerity condition for thanking (Searle, 1969: 65–7), but rather mark positive politeness so that, if left unuttered, Dutch interlocutors would not be offended by the lack of gratefulness manifested but by the lack of politeness. With different situations in mind, Haverkate (1988: 392) writes:

> the act of thanking shows culture-specific properties because it is not performed in the same sort of communication situations everywhere. In Spain, for example, normative rules governing client-waiter interaction exclude the act of thanking by the client when the food is put in front of him or her by the waiter.

Likewise, neither shop-assistants, administrators, public transport officials nor their clients usually thank one another nor do members of one family. For example, when a shop-assistant sells something, normally neither the assistant nor the customer thanks the other. So when Coulmas (1981: 81) postulates that every language provides a stock of conventionalised means for giving thanks, he may be right – Spanish certainly does so – but its speakers do not always dip into that stock to fulfil it. Interestingly, unlike English, where the thanks formula and the name of the person thanked ('Thanks, Mary') form one prosodic unit with descending pitch, in Spanish they retain their bipartite composition with the two words (*Gracias María*) uttered on the same level with a break in between: they do not constitute one unit or formula.

Perhaps we may now tentatively conclude that positive politeness is manifested in Spanish non-formulaic, non-self-humbling, non-deferential thanking by showing interest in the object presented, while the effort made by the giver, which in negative-politeness societies might evoke expressions of gratitude, is ignored, just as Spanish politeness generally takes the positive form of effusiveness, personal enthusiasm, admiration and praise of others, rather than negative forms like avoiding intrusion or apologising for any imposition inadvertently caused. In other words, perhaps thanking without 'thanks' gives thanks, while the receiver of the gift is untroubled about the giver's trouble in giving it, thus getting the best of both worlds: the gift without the guilt.

References

Ballesteros Martín, F.J. (2001) La cortesía española frente a la cortesía inglesa. Estudio pragmalingüístico de las exhortaciones impositivas. *Estudios Ingleses de la Universidad Complutense* 9, 191–207.

Blas Arroyo, J. L. (2001) 'No diga chorradas…' La descortesía en el debate político cara a cara. Una aproximación pragma-variacionista. *Oralia* 4, 9–45.

Bravo, D. (1998) ¿Reírse juntos?: un estudio de las imágenes sociales de hablantes españoles, mexicanos y suecos'. *Diálogos Hispánicos* 22, 315–64.

Brown, P. and Levinson, S. (1987) *Politeness: Some Universals in Language Usage.* Cambridge: Cambridge University Press.

Cestero Mancera, A. M. (1994) Intercambio de turnos de habla en la conversación en lengua española. *Revista Española de Lingüística* 24, 1, 77–99.

Coulmas, F. (1981) 'Poison to your soul': Thanks and apologies contrastively viewed. In F. Coulmas (ed.) *Conversational Routine* (pp. 69–91). The Hague: Mouton.

Escandell Vidal, M. V. (1998a) Politeness: A relevant issue for relevance theory. *Revista Alicantina de Estudios Ingleses* 11, 45–57.

Escandell Vidal, M. V. (1998b) Cortesía y relevancia. *Diálogos Hispánicos* 22, 7–24.

Haverkate, H. (1988) Toward a typology of politeness strategies in communicative interaction. *Multilingua* 7(4), 385–409.

Haverkate, H. (1993), Acerca de los actos de habla expresivos y comisivos en español. *Diálogos Hispánicos* 12, 149–180.

Haverkate, H. (1994) *La cortesía verbal: Estudio pragmalingüístico.* Madrid: Gredos.

Held, G. (1999) Submission strategies as an expression of the ideology of politeness: Reflections on the verbalization of social power relations. *Journal of Pragmatics* 9, (1), 21–36.

Hernández Flores, N. (1999) Politeness ideology in Spanish colloquial conversations: The case of advice. *Journal of Pragmatics* 9, (1), 37–49.

Hickey, L. (1991) Comparatively polite people in Spain and Britain. *ACIS Journal* 4, (2), 2–6.

Hirschon, R. (2001) Freedom, solidarity and obligation: The sociocultural context of Greek politeness. In A. Bayraktaroğlu and M. Sifianou (eds) *Linguistic Politeness across Boundaries: The Case of Greek and Turkish* (pp. 17–42). Amsterdam/ Philadelphia: John Benjamins.

Hornero Corisco, A.M. (2000) Conversational style differences: The case of interruptions in cross-sex conversations. In M.P. Navarro Errasti, R. Lorés Sanz, A. Murillo Ornat and C. Buesa Gómez (eds) *Transcultural Communication: Pragmalinguistic Aspects* (pp. 227–34). Zaragoza: Anubar.

Iglesias Recuero, S. (2001) Los estudios de la cortesía en el mundo hispánico. Estado de la cuestión. *Oralia* 4, 245–98.

Korn, F. and Korn, S.R.D. (1983) Where people don't promise. *Ethics* 93 (3), 445–50.

Leech, G.N. (1983) *Principles of Pragmatics*. London: Longman.

Márquez Reiter, R. (2000) *Linguistic Politeness in Britain and Uruguay: A Contrastive Study of Requests and Apologies*.Amsterdam: John Benjamins.

Norrick , N.R.(1978) Expressive illocutionary acts. *Journal of Pragmatics* 2 (3), 277–91.

Placencia, M.E. (2001) Percepciones y manifestaciones de la (des)cortesía en la atención al público. El caso de una institución pública ecuatoriana. *Oralia* 4, 177–212.

Placencia, M.E. and Bravo, D. (eds) (2002) *Actos de habla y cortesía en español*. Munich: Lincom.

Portolés Lázaro, J. and Vázquez Orta, I. (2000) Mitigating or compensatory strategies in the expression of politeness in Spanish and English? 'Hombre'/'mujer' as politeness discourse markers revisited. In M.P. Navarro Errasti, R. Lorés Sanz, A. Murillo Ornat and C. Buesa Gómez (eds) *Transcultural Communication: Pragmalinguistic Aspects* (pp. 219–226). Zaragoza: Anubar.

Searle, J.R. (1969) *Speech Acts: An Essay in the Philosophy of Language*. Cambridge: Cambridge University Press.

Testa, R. (1988) Interruptive strategies in English and Italian conversation: Smooth *versus* contrastive linguistic preferences. *Multilingua* 7 (3), 285–312.

Index